YUGOSLAV
SOCIALISM

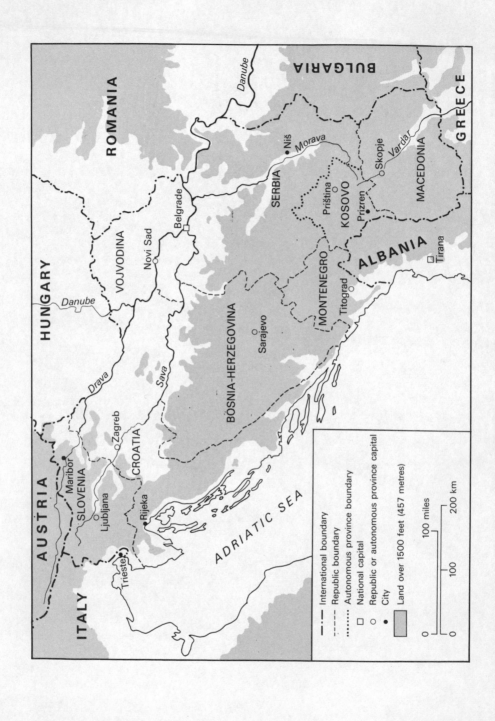

YUGOSLAV SOCIALISM

Theory and Practice

HAROLD LYDALL

CLARENDON PRESS · OXFORD
1984

Oxford University Press, Walton Street, Oxford OX2 6DP

London Glasgow New York Toronto
Delhi Bombay Calcutta Madras Karachi
Kuala Lumpur Singapore Hong Kong Tokyo
Nairobi Dar es Salaam Cape Town
Melbourne Auckland
and associated companies in
Beirut Berlin Ibadan Mexico City Nicosia

Oxford is a trade mark of Oxford University Press

Published in the United States
by Oxford University Press, New York

British Library Cataloguing in Publication data

Lydall, Harold
Yugoslav socialism.
1. Socialism—Yugoslavia
I. Title
335.5'09497   HX365.5.A6

ISBN 0-19-828481-0

Library of Congress Cataloging in Publication Data

Lydall, Harold.
Yugoslav socialism.
Bibliography: p.
Includes index.
1. Communism—Yugoslavia.   I. Title.
HX365.5.A6L92 1984   335.43'44   83-19453

ISBN 0-19-828481-0

Phototypeset at M/s Taj Services Limited
New Delhi India
and printed in Great Britain
by Billing & Sons Limited, Worcester

PREFACE

People sometimes ask me why I decided to make a special study of Yugoslavia. The general answer is that I have always had an interest in comparative economic systems. But a more specific answer would be that in the late 1970s I, like many other people, became increasingly concerned about current economic and social trends in Britain. Was there, I asked myself, some change in property rights which would close the gulf between 'them' and 'us', and bring about a release of national energy? The Soviet system was both economically inefficient and morally and politically bankrupt. Was there, perhaps, a viable alternative in 'workers' self-management', with a market economy, as practised in Yugoslavia?

I decided that it was not good enough to rely on the English-language literature on Yugoslavia, voluminous though it is. It was necessary to learn to read Serbo-Croat and to visit the country. Financial support for two visits was generously given by the Nuffield Foundation, which also supported other research costs. But most of the benefit from these visits is owed to the Yugoslav economists whom I met in Zagreb and Belgrade, and who gave freely of their time for my instruction. They should not, however, be held responsible for any opinions which I have expressed.

Useful additional help was given by the British Embassy in Belgrade and by the Consulate-General in Zagreb. I am especially indebted to Derek Špoljarić-Woodgate, Commercial Officer in the Zagreb Consulate, who has a wide knowledge of life and work in Croatia.

Research facilities in Oxford were kindly provided by Nuffield College and by the Institute of Economics and Statistics. A heavy programme of computing was carried out at the Institute, with the able assistance of Gillian Holliday. Use was also made of the library facilities of the Bodleian and St Antony's College, while Nikola Djurišić kindly passed on to me his copies of *Borba*.

Most of the draft typescript was read by Michael Kaser, of St Antony's College, Oxford, and by Professor Alberto Chilosi of the University of Pisa. Several central chapters were also read by Dr W. Brus, of Wolfson College, Oxford. To all of these I am most grateful. While many of their suggestions for improvement were accepted, they are not, of course, responsible for the final product.

The bulk of the typing was done by Mrs C. Dyett, of Deddington. She was a marvel of speed and efficiency. Additional help was kindly given by secretaries at Nuffield College and the Institute of Economics and Statistics.

As always, I owe an enormous debt to my wife.

Nuffield College   H. F. L.
Oxford
July 1983

CONTENTS

NOTATION

References to books and articles by named authors are given in the form: Rusinow (1977), usually followed by the relevant page numbers, e.g. Rusinow (1977, 243). A list of these references, with details of title and publisher, is given at the end of the book.

References to tables derived from the Yugoslav Yearbooks of Statistics (official title: *Statistički godišnjak Jugoslavie*) are in the form: YB81, 102 – 13, which means 1981 Yearbook, Table 102 – 13.

References to Yugoslav newspapers, e.g. *Borba* and *Vjesnik*, as well as to the weekly journal *Ekonomska politika*, show the date of publication and, in most cases, the relevant page numbers, e.g. *Ekonomska politika*, 7 December 1981, pp. 10–11. English-language Yugoslav journals, such as *Yugoslav Survey* and *Socialist Thought and Practice*, are referenced in the standard manner.

The following symbols are used in the text tables:

. .	not available
-	zero
0.0	positive but less than 0.05
( )	estimated

All dinar values are expressed in 'new' dinars (unless otherwise stated), each of which is equal to 100 'old' dinars.

CHAPTER 1

INTRODUCTION

It seems that increasing numbers of people—especially of young people—
are interested in alternative social and economic systems. In earlier times,
those who were disillusioned with one or more aspects of capitalism mainly
turned towards 'socialism', which was believed to be an ideal form of
society. But experience of various kinds of socialist regime, and especially
of communist regimes, has raised doubts about the socialist panacea.
There is now a clearer appreciation of the wide range of alternative forms
of socialism and of some of the practical difficulties of creating a social
system which combines such qualities as liberty, equality, fraternity,
democracy, efficiency, creativity, respect for human rights, and the rule of
law.

In the revulsion against the inhuman and tyrannical Soviet system,
increasingly imposed by military force on millions of non-Russian people,
there has been a movement to revive the concept of *alienation*. For those
who are anxious to keep their Marxist credentials it was a fortunate
accident that this concept was found to have been an integral part of
Marx's thinking when he was a young man. The concept is, in fact,
ill-defined. In Marx's view it described a situation in which people used
their labour to produce goods and services for exchange with others, a
situation characteristic of capitalism. It was capitalism, also, which was
held responsible for the division of labour within enterprises and the
division of roles between workers and managers. All of this was considered
to be destructive of the essential human personality and, by implication,
could be avoided under socialism. In practice, however, Marxist socialists
have tried, in Lenin's words, to organize everyone into 'a single office and
a single factory', the whole vast machine being directed by bureaucrats
from some remote centre. What they have created may be a form of
socialism, but it is also a kind of 'super-alienation'. Not surprisingly, the
works of the young Marx are not studied or quoted in communist
countries.

Those who wish to reduce (or eliminate?) alienation are confronted by a
series of dilemmas. If they wish above all to exclude the market, there is a
choice between the centrally planned command economy on the one hand,
which entails super-alienation, or the disintegration of the economy into
autarkic households (or, if feasible, communes). There is no guarantee

that self-sufficient households will be free of alienation, especially for the women and the younger members, but it is certain that such households can never produce a high material or intellectual way of life. Marx, at least, would not have agreed that a mass of self-sufficient peasant households could be described as socialism. If, however, it is decided that a good society requires a high material standard of life, which implies the need for specialization and much large-scale production, a choice must be made between the super-alienation of the command economy or the maintenance of the market. If the market is considered to be the lesser evil, the struggle against alienation must take the form of an improvement of social relations within enterprises.

Reduction of intra-enterprise alienation can take a variety of forms. It may mean only that workers are better informed about management policy, i.e. that they are kept 'in the picture'. This may be accompanied by a system of collective bonuses or profit-sharing. A further step is to establish a consultative committee, at which elected workers' representatives are informed about and discuss selected aspects of management policy. This arrangement may also be upgraded to one in which the workers' representatives sit on a policy-making board, but in a minority. From the managers' point of view, each of these proposals has some potential advantages in strengthening morale and creating a co-operative attitude among the workers. But they also have certain costs. Time must be spent in giving information and, if there are also committee meetings, both managers' and workers' representatives will be taken off their normal work. But the most serious costs arise if management decisions are increasingly biased away from efficient business operations and towards the 'feather-bedding' of the existing work-force. It may be argued that these dangers arise primarily from the subordinate position of the workers and their lack of a full sense of responsibility for the success or failure of the enterprise. A radical remedy would, therefore, be to go the whole way and hand over management completely to the workers. This is one line of reasoning which leads to the proposal that enterprises should become labour co-operatives, managed by their workers.[1]

The most usual conception of a labour co-operative is that the members of the co-operative are those, and only those, who work in the enterprise. Normally, this implies also that all who work are also members, and that all members have equal rights in electing the management bodies and in determining enterprise policy. But some co-operatives allow non-workers to be members, and some allow workers to be non-members. There are also many possible rules in relation to capital contributions by members, and the rights which accrue to such capital. Another important distinction is between a society in which the co-operative method of production is *permitted* and one in which it is *enforced*, either universally or in particular industries.

---

[1] The proposal may, of course, be made for more elementary 'class war' reasons, as a method of expropriating the capitalists and establishing workers' rule at the level of the enterprise. This is one of the mainsprings of anarchism, which is discussed further in Chapter 2.

Labour co-operatives established during the nineteenth century or in the first half of the twentieth century were mostly either small groups of skilled workers in such industries as building, printing, or shoe-making, or agricultural co-operatives formed voluntarily—as in India and in some other less developed countries—or compulsorily—as in the communist countries. They were never particularly successful and, except under communist forced-draft conditions, they usually stagnated and eventually disappeared. But in recent years in advanced capitalist countries there has been a growth of voluntary co-operatives using modern technical methods in dynamic industries. The outstanding example is the Mondragon group of co-operatives in the Basque region of Spain, but there are signs that similar developments could occur in other countries. Meanwhile in Yugoslavia, under a Marxist-Leninist party, nationalized enterprises have gradually been transferred to the nominal control of their workers, central command planning has been abolished and enterprises have been obliged, in principle, to work for the market.

If, as seems probable, interest in and the growth of labour co-operatives are not phenomena of passing significance, it is desirable to look more closely at the likely economic (and non-economic) effects of the establishment of an economy consisting wholly or predominantly of such co-operatives. Some valuable theoretical work has been done in this area by Ward, Domar, Vanek, Meade and others. But these theories have been constructed, for the most part, on the conventional assumption of perfect competition. On normal scientific grounds it is important to confront such theories with relevant facts of observation, with a view to their possible revision or improvement. Since the only predominantly labour-co-operative economy is that of Yugoslavia, it is natural to turn to Yugoslav experience to see what can be learnt about the working of such an economy. This is the essential purpose of the present book.

There have, of course, been a considerable number of previous studies of the Yugoslav system. But many of them have been written from an official or semi-official point of view and, for obvious reasons, these tend to be somewhat apologetic and bland. Valuable insights can be gained from various monographs, especially those by Western economists who have taken a special interest in one or other aspect of the Yugoslav system. But there have not been many, or perhaps any, full-length studies of the system which attempts a sympathetic but critical analysis of the inherent tendencies of a labour-managed economy of the Yugoslav type.

There are many difficulties in using Yugoslav experience as a basis for drawing general conclusions about the working of a labour-managed economy. Every country has its own peculiar history and institutions; but Yugoslavia is more unusual than most. It originated as an artificial creation of the Versailles Peace Treaty, bringing together Serbia, Montenegro, and substantial parts of Austria-Hungary. It is a land of many nationalities, several languages and three major religions. During the inter-war period it was never completely united, and it was shattered by the Axis invasion of 1941. In the fire of resistance to the occupiers the guerrilla movement came increasingly under the control of the Communist Party, which took complete power at the end of the war. As an apparently standard Marxist-Leninist Party, it planned to make Yugoslavia a copy of Stalinist Russia. But after three years there was a violent break with the Soviet Party and its satellites, and Yugoslavia started on an independent path. With some time-lag, the ideology was re-examined and in 1950 Tito announced the policy of 'the factories to the workers'. All nationalized enterprises—covering almost all of industry and services and part of agriculture—were gradually transferred to nominal workers' control, or 'self-management', and directed to work for the market. Self-management rights were increased in 1965 but considerably restricted again in 1971. Since 1974 Yugoslavia has been organized under a complex constitution, which theoretically gives workers complete economic and political power, but in practice ensures that power is held firmly in the hands of the Party. Nevertheless, enterprises still have a good deal of autonomy; they are supposed to work for the market; and the workers are supposed to have full responsibility for the success or failure of their enterprises. Yugoslavia is not a 'pure' example of a labour-managed economy; but it has enough of the characteristics of such an economy to make it possible to learn something about the inherent tendencies of such an economy.

In addition to the problems of isolating the effects of labour-management as such from the complex matrix of political, national, and cultural relations of Yugoslav society, the outside observer is confronted by a number of language barriers. Not only is there the normal barrier of a foreign language, but there are also the barriers of Marxist jargon and of a special Yugoslav 'self-management' jargon. Serbo-Croat can be translated into English, but the other two languages are more difficult and tortuous, and require a good deal of special explanation.

Part I of this book is concerned with two aspects of the theory of a labour-managed economy. In Chapter 2 we review three alternative concepts of socialism in order to classify the Yugoslav system according to its socialist characteristics. It will be found to be a peculiar mixture of a one-party Marxist regime (modified in practice, as will be shown in later chapters, by a considerable degree of federalization) with decentralized enterprises enjoying 'self-management'.

Chapter 3 is devoted to the economic theory of a labour-managed economy, which is assumed for this purpose to be a *laissez-faire* market economy. After a review of conventional theories based on the assumption of perfect competition, it is shown that this assumption is inappropriate for either Mondragon or Yugoslavia, or indeed for any conceivable modern industrial economy. This leads to a reformulation of the theory on a new set of assumptions which allow for imperfections in product markets, the capital market, and the transfer of technique. The resulting model yields predictions about the short-run response of co-operatives to changes in demand which are different from those of the conventional model. Long-run adjustment, as in the conventional model, depends crucially on the degree of freedom of entry, but on the new assumptions it does not generate a zero-profit equilibrium. Because of the assumed imperfections, co-operatives with more accumulated internal finance and private knowledge of technique enjoy higher long-term rents than more inexperienced or less successful co-operatives. This leads, also, to significant differences in personal incomes between co-operatives apparently producing the same product, and hence to a number of unfortunate economic effects. These include a bias towards capital-intensity, and a general immobility of resources, which tend to be locked into the co-operatives which already employ them or, in the case of capital, accumulate them. This also creates a serious obstacle to the spread of resources and techniques to less developed regions, which is an acute problem in the case of Yugoslavia. Finally, the model throws some light on the difficulty of controlling inflation in a labour-managed economy.

Part II is designed to provide an historical and institutional background to the analysis of Yugoslav economic performance. Chapter 4 contains a brief recapitulation of Yugoslav history from 1918 to 1950, in which year the first crucial decision was taken to move towards a self-management form of socialism. The evolution of that system, however, took a long time, with many changes in the rules and institutions. These are considered in some detail in Chapter 5. With the adoption of the 1974 Constitution this evolution was largely brought to an end. With only minor changes, the rules and institutions established in that constitution have been maintained up to the present time. Chapter 6 contains a description of the new system according to official documents and commentaries.

But the real operation of the system is something different, and Chapter 7 is an attempt to bring the system to life. The questions which it tries to answer include the following: Who really controls the policies of Yugoslav 'self-managed' enterprises? What are the respective roles of the workers, the managers, and the Party? What are the levers in the hands of the Party? Is the Party genuinely willing to allow the workers to manage? Do the workers, in fact, want to take responsibility for major enterprise decisions? Are they equipped to do so? What is the role of the banks, and who controls them? Are the workers able to control the financing and operation of the social services, as they are supposed to do? Why are there so many complaints about the excessive cost of social services? Does the political system give the workers effective control over their 'delegates'? Is democracy possible in the Yugoslav system of indirect elections? What is the role of the 'socio-political organizations', especially the Party, the trade unions, and the Socialist Alliance? Do they offer effective channels for worker or citizen influence on public affairs? How much freedom of public criticism is allowed? What are the limits on civil liberties? What have been the effects of increasing federalization of government and the Party? A number of crucial questions need also to be asked about the system of 'socialist self-management planning'. How can voluntary plans be made 'from the bottom up'? What means are available for reconciling decentralized plans? Are plans enforced? How much influence does Yugoslav planning have on the real development of the economy?

In Part III we move on to an appraisal of the economic results of the Yugoslav system. Chapter 8 is concerned with macroeconomic measures of performance, such as: the rates of growth of real gross domestic product and of real gross domestic product per head; the respective rates of growth of real gross material product in the social and private sectors; the growth of social sector employment and the stock of fixed capital; the growth of factor productivity, for each factor separately and in combination; similar data for the industrial sector; changes in the distribution of the labour force; the growth and composition of unemployment; changes in personal income and consumption; changes in prices; changes in the major components of the balance of payments and trends in merchandise trade; changes in levels of regional development and some of the factors responsible for such changes; the level of inter-regional assistance; some recent indicators of comparative regional levels of economic and social development; and, finally, a comparison of levels and rates of growth of gross domestic product between Yugoslavia and some other countries.

In Chapter 9 an attempt is made to measure changes in the distribution of income during the self-management period, and to compare the distribution of income in Yugoslavia with similar data for other countries.

In Chapter 10 we turn to the discussion of a central problem of any economic system—the efficiency of allocation of resources to different uses. For the reasons already mentioned, and for others which are peculiar to the Yugoslav political system, the allocation of resources is found to be a point of considerable weakness. Capital tends to be concentrated on existing enterprises or in plants established for reasons of politics or local prestige. There is a bias towards capital-intensive industries and towards the use of capital-intensive techniques in general, and this is one of the main factors responsible for high unemployment (and emigration) and the continued lag in the development of the poorer regions. Many of the economic and political weaknesses of the Yugoslav system are revealed in a study of housing policy.

Efficient allocation of resources is only one kind of economic efficiency. The other is organizational efficiency, or 'X-efficiency', which is discussed in Chapter 11. It is often claimed that self-managed enterprises will be more productive, with given resources, than 'alienated' capitalist or state socialist enterprises. But a crucial condition for attracting and maintaining 'social' motivation is an effective level of discipline to discourage exploitation of the self-management system by 'free riders'. Unfortunately, discipline in Yugoslav enterprises is very weak, and labour productivity is low. Self-management itself, and other institutional factors, reduce the amount of time and effort devoted to productive work in the social sector, and there is a huge amount of 'moonlighting'. The important question which arises is whether these defects are the result of self-management as such, or rather of the special conditions in which self-management operates in Yugoslavia.

Chapter 12 is concerned with the problem of controlling inflation in a self-managed economy. In the absence of external causes of inflation, such as increases in world prices or excessive aggregate domestic demand, a self-management system, which has no labour market and hence no collective labour contracts, is likely to be more stable than a modern capitalist economy, in which trade unions vie with one another to achieve large wage increases. But, once an inflationary process has started, the advantage of having no wage contracts turns into a disadvantage. There is no possibility of restricting increases in prices by holding down wage costs, either by reducing demand in the labour market or by an explicit incomes policy. In the absence of 'wage drag', devaluation tends to be reflected very rapidly in a rise of domestic prices, thus weakening the favourable effects of devaluation on the balance of payments. The only remaining remedy for inflation and a balance of payments deficit is deflation of demand, which may bring results only slowly and painfully.

In the final chapter attention is turned to the private sector, which is still large in Yugoslavia, especially in agriculture. The problems discussed are not inherent in a self-management system but arise from the special political conditions existing in Yugoslavia, which is ruled by a Marxist party fundamentally hostile to private enterprise. The bias against private enterprise has done, and is doing, great damage to the Yugoslav economy and standard of living of the people. The facts are beginning to be more widely recognized, but it is difficult, or perhaps impossible, for a communist regime to change its attitude on this question. This reinforces the conclusion, which is relevant also to the question of organizational efficiency, that compulsory self-management is not good for economic performance. But if self-management is to be voluntary, and competition is to be allowed between self-managed, private, and state enterprises, efficient self-management may be incompatible with a one-party Marxist regime. We shall have to ask ourselves whether this is not the central problem of the Yugoslav system.

PART I

Theory

CHAPTER 2

ALTERNATIVE CONCEPTS OF SOCIALISM

The main reason which prompts people to become socialists is a desire for greater equality. But equality is a vague idea which can be, and is, interpreted in a variety of ways. Moreover, equality is not the only social value. Some socialists give at least equal weight to liberty; others are more concerned with achieving power. The divisions between socialists on these and other issues frequently become so acute that they lose sight of the original motive which brought almost all of them into political activity.

There are four main kinds of inequality to which socialists are opposed. First, there is national inequality, as when one nation occupies the land of another, depriving the latter of its independence and usually subjecting it to economic exploitation. Secondly, there is discrimination between people on grounds of sex, race, religion, caste, or the like. Thirdly, there is inequality of income or consumption. Fourthly, there is inequality in the sources of income, as when some people depend on labour income while others receive income from property. The first two types of inequality are opposed also by non-socialists, who often take the lead in struggles for national independence or non-discrimination on racial or other grounds. Most socialists support such struggles because they genuinely believe in national independence and non-discrimination; but some make use of these struggles only to further their ultimate plans to take over power and revolutionize society. The types of inequality which are of primary concern to socialists, however, are those of the third and fourth kinds.

So far there is broad agreement between socialists. But, as soon as they begin to consider how to achieve their aims, divisions appear. The first division is between those who prefer to move forward slowly and piecemeal, without precipitating a civil war, and those who declare that such a policy is a 'betrayal' of socialism (or the working class), and in any case is likely to fail. But this second group is further divided into those who want to use the revolution in order to establish a 'proletarian dictatorship' and those who want to eliminate all centralized state authority. These three groups are, respectively, the Social Democrats, the Marxists and the Anarchists; and in the subsequent discussion the main emphasis will be on clarifying the differences between them. We shall be concerned, first, with differences in aims, secondly, with differences in methods and, thirdly, with differences in results.

1. DIFFERENCES IN AIMS

All socialists start from the society in which they live; and all of them, even in the most undeveloped countries, have seen themselves as in some sense the 'heirs' of capitalism. But capitalism is not a frozen society. During its brief period of existence—industrial capitalism has existed for only two centuries—it has changed enormously. In the early days, when enterprises were small, technique was backward, and there was a vast reservoir of cheap and inefficient labour coming out of agriculture, capitalism acquired a reputation for ruthless slave-driving, exploitation, and inhuman conditions of work. It was this kind of experience in Britain up to the middle of the nineteenth century which made the socialists of that period despair that the workers would ever derive any benefits from capitalism. Marx and Engels, writing at this time, not only depicted the horrors of early British industrialism but also predicted that conditions would inevitably get worse. The natural inference was that socialists should concentrate on only one objective: to replace capitalism by a new form of society.

But no sooner had Marx and Engels arrived at this conclusion than the conditions of the British workers began to improve. The statistics of that period are not very reliable, but all the evidence points to a real rise in living standards between 1850 and 1870.[1] From the latter date onwards, as is now clear, real wages rose in all industrializing countries at an extraordinary pace. From 1870 to 1976, for example, real hourly wage earnings increased eightfold in the United Kingdom and twelvefold in France, Germany, and the United States.[2] This experience of rising living standards under capitalism was bound to have an effect on the attitudes of socialists who lived in these countries. It had little or no effect, however, on the attitudes of Lenin, who lived in a mainly pre-capitalist country and whose views about the probable effects of capitalist development in Russia were based on reading descriptions of British conditions in the middle of the nineteenth century.

Until about 1940, this enormous growth in wages was not achieved at the expense of profits. Since both sources of income rose roughly in step, there was an equal growth in national output per worker and in the scope for government intervention to transfer benefits from one section of the community to another. The first to recognize this opportunity were non-socialists, such as Bismarck and Lloyd George. Their schemes for social security were not so much schemes for redistribution from the permanently rich to the permanently poor as for compulsory insurance of the workers against periods of poverty in sickness, old age, or—later—unemployment.[3] The growth of the welfare state was already far advanced before any socialists were in government, although the stimulus to initiate

---

[1] See, for example, Pollard and Crossley (1968, 214–22).

[2] From 1870 to 1960: annual real wages from Phelps Brown (1973) and hours worked from Maddison (1979). Estimates for 1960–76 from data in ILO *Yearbooks of Labour Statistics*.

[3] The history of the growth of the welfare state is well summarized in Flora and Heidenheimer (1981), especially Chapter 2.

such reforms may have come from the threat that voters would move in that direction.

For socialists living in an industrialized country in the first half of the twentieth century there were always competing arguments about the proper aims of socialism. At one extreme were those who saw nothing but evil in capitalism and who confidently predicted that conditions would inevitably get worse. But conditions did not inevitably get worse. And many socialists recognized that, for all its blemishes, capitalism had brought great benefits to the workers. These Social Democrats, or 'revisionists' as the Marxists called them, set themselves the more modest aim of trying to improve conditions for the workers under capitalism. They would concentrate on the problems of poverty and unemployment, and hence on the general development of the social services and the welfare state, and government intervention to secure full employment. The latter aim apparently became feasible, and indeed rather easy to achieve, as a result of Keynes's *General Theory*.[4]

It is sometimes suggested that the only differences between Social Democrats and Marxists are in methods, not in ultimate aims. But this is a fallacy. It is true that some socialists who start by being 'reformists' become disillusioned with the progress made towards their objectives and turn towards more violent methods. But the convinced Marxist rejects all liberal ideas and 'bourgeois' morality. He no longer gives priority to traditional socialist aims, such as freedom, equality, and democracy, but subordinates everything to one goal: the capture of power. This attitude was already explicit in the *Communist Manifesto* of 1848. Replying to objectors who said 'There are, besides, eternal truths, such as Freedom, Justice, etc., that are common to all states of society', Marx and Engels wrote: 'But communism abolishes eternal truths, it abolishes all religion, and all morality . . .' (*Selected Works*, 52). Lenin merely elaborated this theme in 1920 when he said: 'We say that our morality is entirely subordinated to the interests of the proletariat's class struggle . . . We do not believe in an eternal morality, and we expose the falseness of all fables about morality.'[5] At an early stage in his conversion to Marxism Lenin had already agreed that 'in Marxism itself there is not a grain of ethics from beginning to end'.[6]

It is true that in his pre-communist phase Marx spoke out in favour of freedom of the press. In one of his early journalistic articles he wrote:

The freedom of the Press has quite a different basis from censorship, for it is the form of an idea, namely freedom, and is an actual good; censorship is a form of servitude, the weapon of a world view based on appearances against one based on the nature of things . . . Freedom lies so deeply in human nature that even the opponents of freedom help to bring it about by combating its reality . . . A

---

[4] A classic statement of the Social Democratic point of view is Crosland's (1956) book on *The Future of Socialism*.

[5] Quoted by Kolakowski (1978, II, 515–16) from Lenin's *Works*, vol. 31, pp. 291–4.

[6] Kolakowski (1978, II, 373) quoting from Lenin's *Works*, vol. 1, p. 421.

censored press is a thing without a backbone, a vampire of slavery, a civilized monstrosity, a scented freak of nature.[7]

But for Lenin, after the Revolution, it was different: 'the "so-called freedom of the Press" was a bourgeois deceit, like freedom of assembly and the right to form parties'.[8]

Naturally, some socialists saw clearly from the outset what was implied by the Marxist rejection of the basic principles of morality, freedom, democracy, and the like. The first of these was Proudhon, who argued that, since in the Communist system the individual would have no property,

the whole lawlessness of its use would be conferred upon the state, which would own the country's wealth and the bodies of its citizens as well. The lives, talents, and aspirations of human beings would, at a stroke, become state property, and the monopoly principle, the source of all social evil, would be intensified to the utmost. Communism, in short, had nothing to offer but the extremity of police despotism.[9]

But the most forceful socialist opponent of Marxism during the nineteenth century was Bakunin. With typical forthrightness, he declared his basic principles and aims:

I am a fanatical lover of freedom, viewing it as the only milieu in the midst of which the intelligence, dignity, and happiness of men can grow . . . I am a convinced partisan of *economic and social equality*, because I know that outside of this equality, freedom, justice, human dignity, morality, and the well-being of individuals as well as the flourishing of nations, are a lie.[10]

The Marxists were determined to create a dictatorship, a 'despotism of a governing minority'.

But, the Marxists say, this minority will consist of workers. Yes, indeed, of *ex-workers*, who, once they become rulers or representatives of the people, cease to be workers and begin to look down upon the toiling people. From that time on they represent not the people but themselves and their own claims to govern the people. Those who doubt this know precious little about human nature.[11]

And he concluded: 'No dictatorship can have any other aim but that of self-perpetuation, and it can beget only slavery in the people tolerating it.'[12]

Both Proudhon and Bakunin were anarchists; indeed, Proudhon is said to have invented the name. Proudhon proposed the establishment of a system of industrial and agricultural co-operatives, linked by free exchange; as a result, the state would wither away. Bakunin wanted to

---

[7] Kolakowski (1978, I, 121). The early Marx would have been dismayed to find the universal spread of such 'civilized monstrosities' in all the countries claiming to be his followers.

[8] Kolakowski (1978, II, 487).

[9] Kolakowski (1978, I, 208).

[10] Quoted from collection of Bakunin's writings edited by Maximoff (1953, 270–1).

[11] Ibid., p. 287.

[12] Ibid., p. 288.

smash the state decisively from the beginning, and to take all power into the hands of small autonomous groups of the population—the communes—within which there would be perfect freedom. Production would be organized, as suggested by Proudhon, in independent co-operative enterprises. Hostility to the power of the state went hand-in-hand, as was logical, with support for co-operatives, linked together by the market. The Marxists agreed with the anarchists on the need to smash the existing state, but they proposed to replace it by their own state—the dictatorship of the proletariat. They claimed that the dictatorship would be short-lived and would soon begin to 'wither away'. But the anarchists did not believe them.

Meanwhile, in the last decades of the nineteenth century the growing Continental socialist parties, although avowedly Marxist, were beginning to move away from Marxist dogma and to adopt a reformist position. Specifically, they began to reject the plans of both the Marxists and the anarchists to smash the existing state, preferring to make use of the existing state to extend democracy and to improve the conditions of the workers. They, and the British Labour Party which now came into existence, were, in other words, 'state socialists', but not in the Marxist sense; for, instead of creating a new dictatorial state to force socialism on the people, they were committed to the idea of using the democratic state for a gradual advance towards socialism.

Thus both Social Democrats and anarchists are usually firmly committed not only to the aim of equality but also to liberty, democracy, and human rights. Where Social Democrats differ from anarchists is in their assessment of the scope for real progress towards greater equality within a 'bourgeois democratic' system. Where they differ from more recent movements in support of industrial co-operatives, or 'workers' control', is in their assessment of the possibility of establishing genuine industrial democracy in large enterprises while also maintaining efficiency. But these are questions on which experience can eventually provide the answers. The differences between Social Democrats and anarchists on the one hand and Marxists on the other are much more profound. For these differences concern ultimate values. The true Marxist has no ultimate values. He has been convinced by the logic of 'scientific socialism' that history is on the side of the proletarian revolution, and that he can best satisfy his own resentments and ambitions by taking command over the wave of the future. The seizure of power becomes his only aim; and, when power has been won, its maintenance is then the aim. All other values must be subordinated to that.

The Yugoslav Communists, with whose activities this book is primarily concerned, do not fit neatly into the above classification. Originally, they were nearly pure Marxists. But the nature of their experiences during the partisan war transformed their slogans of national liberation and internal 'brotherhood and unity' into independent values with a life of their own. Eventually, as we shall see in Chapter 6, the Yugoslav Communists moved away from strict Marxism towards a kind of anarchism. Although they retained monopoly control of the state machine, with all the trappings of dictatorship, they made real changes in the organization of industry and local government. To their wartime values of national independence and brotherhood and unity they now added a new goal—'self-management'—which has also acquired a life of its own. It is now scarcely conceivable that the Yugoslav Communists can ever repudiate it. .

2. DIFFERENCES IN METHODS

In politics, aims and methods are never sharply separated, and in the previous section we have already touched on some of the differences between the methods of different groups of socialists. But there is more to be said on these differences, especially in respect of the methods used by the Marxists.

Social Democrats are prepared to work within a parliamentary system or, if such a system does not already exist, to work for its establishment. This means that they do not believe in trying to browbeat or terrorize the population into accepting their policies. It also means, of course, that they are prepared to allow other democratic parties to operate freely and to stand for election, and that they will accept the verdict of the polls. They believe in the rule of law; they are unwilling to use torture, or to agree to its use by others; they are upholders of civil rights. Social Democrats are not always so clear or united in their attitudes to the use of trade union power. Since they are usually allied with the unions, and in some countries even subject to union control, Social Democrats are tempted to go to the support of trade unions in all circumstances, even when the unions are trying to exert political influence contrary to the wishes of the electorate. It is in this area that Social Democrats are confronted by some of their most difficult choices.

In some circumstances, Marxists use methods which are superficially similar to those of the Social Democrats. They contest elections, participate in parliaments, and even at times in coalition governments. But, as the great Marxist teachers and leaders have always made clear, they do all this, not because they believe in parliamentary government, democracy, or the rule of law, but solely as a means of increasing their popularity and strengthening their position for the ultimate conquest of power. The preferred situation for Marxists is one of crisis and the breakdown of parliamentary government. Best of all, a war of independence or a civil war, when the communists can show their great capacity for organization and propaganda and lift themselves into the leadership. Once they have acquired such a position in an armed conflict they are virtually irremoveable, since they can use their position to inflame class relations, to encourage forcible expropriations, arbitrary arrests, and finally all-out terror against their opponents. By systematically incriminating the workers and the peasants, they undermine respect for impartial justice, truthful reporting, tolerance, and eventually all human values except those which serve their immediate interests.

The key element in twentieth-century Marxist method, and the source of all their successes, has been the Leninist system of organization. Marx and

Engels were propagators of Marxist ideas, and Marx played an important part in the Council of the First International. But neither Marx nor Engels ever set about the creation of a communist party of the type which is now familiar. They seem to have believed that the workers would spontaneously gravitate towards a revolutionary posture and the acceptance of Marxist ideas. It never occurred to them that they should form a select, strictly Marxist, party of dedicated revolutionaries, who would eventually take control of the whole movement. This concept of the 'revolutionary vanguard' was Lenin's decisive contribution to Marxism.

In 1902, Lenin set about the creation of a professional party of revolutionaries, ideologically united and organizationally disciplined, who would respond to their leaders' instructions in a critical situation as soldiers are trained to respond to their officers, with unquestioning obedience. Recruits to such a party were accepted only on probation; there was frequent 'criticism and self-criticism'; and regular purges. Lenin enjoyed purges: 'a party strengthens itself by purging itself', he often said. And, for the purpose which he had in mind, he was undoubtedly right.

Lenin directed his party to the task of penetrating, and eventually taking over the control of, all democratic organizations which might serve its interests: above all the trade unions. In later years communist parties the world over have practised this technique with remarkable results, even succeeding in acquiring influence within other political parties, as well as in religious and *ad hoc* 'front' organizations, such as peace movements, anti-apartheid movements, and the like.

When the party has won power, the standard prescription is to establish the 'dictatorship of the proletariat'. Initially, the workers, and even the peasants, are encouraged to take the law into their own hands. But, after a short period of revolutionary euphoria, order is established and power is firmly taken into the hands of the party. From that moment onwards, the dictatorship is clearly a dictatorship of the party in the name of the proletariat.

In the economic sphere, the purpose of the dictatorship is, in the words of the *Manifesto*, 'to wrest, by degrees, all capital from the bourgeoisie, to centralise all instruments of production in the hands of the State' (Marx and Engels, *Selected Works*, 52). In Lenin's words, seventy years later, this meant organizing 'the *whole* economy on the lines of the postal service', so that 'The whole of society will have become a single office and a single factory' (Lenin, *Selected Works*, 299 and 337). And this necessarily implies that the whole economy must be centrally planned.[13] The official Marxist

[13] Marx never said anything specific about the need for planning. But he was totally opposed to the market, which he regarded as an inevitable generator of capitalism. Engels came closest to explaining what they had in mind when he wrote, in *Socialism: Utopian and Scientific*, 'it is the masses of the proletariat again who will finally put an end to the anarchy in production', and 'the social anarchy of production gives place to a social regulation of production upon a definite plan'. (Marx and Engels, *Selected Works*, 417–18 and 423.) But there was never any recognition of the difficulties of efficiently planning a whole economy from a single centre, or of the probable effects of such centralized planning on incentives, initiative, quality of production, and the feelings of the workers.

view, therefore, except in Yugoslavia and perhaps more recently in Hungary, is that 'market socialism' is a contradiction in terms, indeed worse than that, a disguise for the revival of capitalism. Some concessions towards incentives can be made by a limited amount of profit-sharing. But there can be no question of allowing prices to be determined by supply and demand, or of enterprises being allowed to divert resources towards the production of more profitable products, or of obtaining their materials and components from the least costly or most reliable suppliers. This would lead to 'anarchy' in production and, more important, it would reduce the power of the central oligarchy.

Since anarchists wish to destroy all state structures, it is impossible for them to use the same methods as either the Social Democrats, on the one hand, or the Marxists, on the other. It makes no sense to try to build up a great parliamentary party if one intends to eliminate the national parliament; and it would clearly be abhorrent to anarchists to form themselves into a Leninist-style party aiming to establish its own dictatorship. Anarchists, therefore, have tended to rely on the trade unions to carry out the revolution, mainly by means of a general strike. The trade unions, in their view, have the capacity to destroy the existing state but not to create a new one. They will have a major role to play in the new co-operatives, but only in a decentralized manner. This is the syndicalist variant of anarchism, which took a slightly different form in Britain under the title of Guild Socialism.

The great weakness of anarchism has been its own internal conflict between a desire for revolution and a fear of creating a strong centrally-controlled party to carry out such a revolution. It is not surprising, therefore, that the only example of a country which has attempted to introduce many anarchist ideas—Yugoslavia—is one in which the revolution was originally carried out by a Leninist party. The central problem of Yugoslavia remains the reconciliation of a powerful one-party state with the degree of political and economic decentralization recommended by anarchism.

3. DIFFERENCES IN RESULTS

When in government, Social Democrats have mainly concentrated on (1) developing the welfare state, and redistribution of income and wealth through taxation, (2) Keynesian-type macroeconomic management, designed to steer a course between inflation and unemployment, and (3) at least in Britain, strengthening the powers of trade unions. Some Social Democratic parties are also committed to a policy of progressive nationalization of industry, but others have treated that as a subsidiary issue. The case in favour of nationalization has usually been based either on socialist arguments for redistributing property or on considerations of efficiency. But the support which is given to such proposals from the workers in these industries seems to derive mainly from a desire to protect their jobs and to improve their own conditions at the expense of the rest of the community.

Social Democrats have had some success in strengthening the welfare state and, by their electoral competition, they have encouraged other parties to move in the same direction. The expansion of welfare facilities during the 1960s in western Europe was, in fact, so rapid that the burden on the economy has now become excessive, especially since the deceleration of growth caused by the petroleum crisis.[14] In a sense, therefore, Social Democrats have been too successful in this part of their programme. As regards macroeconomic management, it is difficult to say whether Social Democratic governments have been more successful than others. During the 1950s and 1960s there was full employment without excessive inflation in almost all OECD countries, irrespective of whether they had Socialist or Conservative governments; and in the 1970s all these countries have suffered from high inflation, and almost all from growing unemployment, again without systematic relation to the type of government. In the 1980s Conservative governments seem to be prepared to tolerate more unemployment rather than more inflation, while Socialist parties promise to reduce the former without specifying what will happen to the latter. The crucial weakness of their position is that their followers in the unions are not prepared to accept a restraint on wage increases in return for a reduction in unemployment. And this is where the third major component of the Social Democratic programme—the strengthening of the powers and privileges of the unions—comes into conflict with their other objectives.

While Social Democrats have been only partially successful in achieving their aims, the ruling communist parties have been almost completely successful in achieving theirs. After taking power, they have suppressed all other parties, imposed total control over the press and other media, locked the frontiers, expanded the secret police, introduced universal surveillance of the population, destroyed the independence of the trade unions, persecuted religion, regimented the youth, eliminated freedom of thought, and forced all ideas into the strait-jacket of Marxism. In return for these sacrifices the population has seen a high rate of investment, steady economic growth, more or less full employment, and suppressed inflation. The system of central planning, however, is unwieldy, inefficient, and wasteful. It achieves results, but only at enormous cost. Wherever personal judgement and personal commitment are essential for success, as in agriculture and personal services, the central planning system is an obvious failure. The more enlightened government of Hungary has managed to improve things by allowing greater scope for market incentives; and it seems that the Chinese government is moving in the same direction. But the Russians are so entrenched in their doctrinaire position that it is difficult to see how they will ever dig themselves out.

The fundamental problem is that communist political dictatorship and central planning go hand in hand. A centrally planned system, which

[14] The situation in Yugoslavia in this respect is almost exactly as in western Europe. The government, the Party, and the press continually complain about the rise in the costs of social services and efforts have been made to restrict the amounts of social insurance contributions. In addition, services are limited and people are obliged to pay for some of them.

implies state ownership, requires the maintenance of a one-party state: it would be unthinkable for the communists to allow 'their' economy to pass into other hands. And a one-party state naturally gravitates towards central planning. Lenin many times warned that decentralization and free exchange would lead to the revival of capitalism. But, even more immediately, the party cannot tolerate any independent centres of decision-making, which would strengthen people's sense of independence and give them a taste for wider freedom. Any serious reduction in the degree of central planning would be a form of communist *laissez-faire*, which is contrary to the whole nature of communism.

Thus the communist system, while partially successful on the economic side, is unable to make any progress on the political side. The people have more food, houses, clothes, and cars, but they are still not allowed to express in public a single independent thought, let alone to bring together those who share a common opinion on any subject. The only area in which the system has failed to achieve total control is religion, which is a powerful force in Poland and survives elsewhere. It would not be surprising if the increasing internal contradictions—to use a Marxist phrase—between economic and political conditions in advanced communist countries led to a strengthening of religion. But there will also be, as seen in Czechoslovakia and Poland, increasing interest in the Yugoslav system of decentralized 'self-management'.

This brings us to the question of the results achieved by the third group of socialists—the anarchists. Anarchists themselves have never succeeded in creating an anarchist society, although individuals and groups who support such ideas have formed isolated colonies and co-operatives. The most successful movement of this sort has been the Mondragon group of industrial co-operatives in the Basque country of northern Spain. But the only complete society which has attempted to apply some of the ideas of anarchism has been Yugoslavia. The assessment of the results of this experiment is the main purpose of Chapters 6–14 of this book.

CHAPTER 3

ECONOMIC THEORY OF A LABOUR-MANAGED SYSTEM

1. INTRODUCTION

When, in 1950, the Yugoslav Communists set off along the road towards the establishment of a system of market-related industrial co-operatives, or a labour-managed system, they had no clear idea of how such a system would operate. They were not anarchists; indeed, they had been until only a year or two previously the hardest of Stalinist centralizers. It is doubtful whether any of them had read a word of Proudhon. All that some of them would have known about Proudhon was the abuse heaped on him by Marx in *The Poverty of Philosophy*. Even to this day Yugoslav official circles acknowledge no debt to Proudhon or other advocates of a co-operative system but prefer to maintain that they are faithful followers of Marx, Engels, and Lenin.

For many years after the introduction of a labour-management system in Yugoslavia no serious attempt was made to consider the economic implications of such a system. It was realized that decentralized labour-management of enterprises was incompatible with full central planning and entailed dependence on the equilibrating role of the market. It was assumed that the market system would operate as depicted by Marx in *Capital*. But, since Marx had offered two alternative descriptions—in volumes I and III respectively—it was not easy to know exactly what to expect. In any case, it was scarcely reasonable to assume that a labour-managed system would develop exactly in the same way as a private capitalist system. But there was no time to work out a new economic theory.

The first attempts to create a theory of a labour-managed system were made by Western economists. A pioneering article was published by Ward in 1958; which was followed in 1966 by Domar, with further comments by Sen (1966) and Robinson (1967). During the 1970s there was a rapid growth of interest in the subject, the most noteworthy contributions being those of Vanek (1970) and Meade (1972).[1] Apart from an early article by Horvat (1967), Yugoslav economists have not added any significant new ideas.[2] Some of the younger economists, however, are beginning to discuss

---

[1] See also Bonin (1983) and additional references cited there.
[2] Horvat (1982, 342–3) contains an English summary of his theory.

Western models of a labour-managed economy and to attempt to use them and improve them.

It is perhaps not surprising that the approach of Western economists to a labour-managed system has been to attempt to apply the same tools of analysis as those which are used in constructing models of a capitalist market system. The normal assumption is, therefore, that the labour-managed system operates in a perfectly competitive market, with a single going price for each good or factor service and no limitations on sales or purchases by individual persons or enterprises at that set of prices. This also implies that there is 'free entry' of new enterprises, which can be established without difficulty whenever an entrepreneur believes that he sees a market opportunity. The only change in assumptions is one which follows strictly from the substitution of labour-managed enterprises for private capitalist enterprises. In place of the assumption that the capitalist entrepreneur aims to maximize his total profit it is assumed that the members of co-operatives aim to maximize value added per member (net of interest payments). The rest of the exercise is to work out the implications of this change.

As a subsidiary exercise, some consideration is given to the situation where there is a monopoly, or 'monopolistic competition'. As before, this is followed through by changing only one assumption—the maximand of the firm. The impression is given, as in Western textbooks, that monopoly is an exception and that the conclusions drawn from the perfect competition model are still broadly valid.

Now the case for assuming perfect competition in developed capitalist economies was already disintegrating half a century ago, and in the past thirty years the general assumption of perfect competition has become quite obviously absurd. In the modern world, only the producers of some primary products are still in a position to ignore the state of demand for their own particular good or service. At least 80 per cent of all goods and services are sold in markets where the seller faces a limited demand for his product, which can be expanded only by incurring additional costs, such as an increase in selling expenses, or by a reduction in sales price. Moreover, in the markets for factor services, the supply of capital has never been perfectly elastic to the individual purchaser; and technology is not, as assumed in the perfect market model, a free good.

Despite the inappropriateness of the perfect competition model, we shall start by making a brief review of its results. Next, we shall consider some of the institutional features of two existing labour-managed systems. After that, we shall proceed to outline a theory of a labour-managed economy with the help of more realistic assumptions. Finally, we shall discuss some of the further implications of the theory. For simplicity of exposition we shall for the remainder of this chapter call a labour-managed enterprise a co-operative, and a labour-management system a co-operative system.

2. THE PERFECT COMPETITION MODEL

In a perfectly competitive capitalist system it is easy to show that in full long-term equilibrium all firms will be operating at minimum average cost, price will everywhere equal marginal cost, wages will equal the value of the marginal product of labour, and the rate of interest will equal the value of the marginal product of capital; pure profits will have been eliminated, everyone will be fully satisfied with the results of his own decisions about how much to work, what to consume, and so forth, and—apart from one exception—the economy will be at a Pareto optimum, i.e. in a situation where it is impossible to make any person better off without making someone else worse off. The exception arises from the existence of 'external' effects, i.e. effects of production or consumption decisions which are not traded on the market. In principle, some of these effects might be dealt with by special taxes and subsidies, but this becomes extremely complicated and could require such a large amount of government intervention as to cause more harm than good. Nevertheless, the model of a perfectly competitive capitalist system provides a standard against which to judge the results of monopoly, trade protection, and other 'distortions'.[3]

When applied to the short-run behaviour of a capitalist firm the perfect competition model predicts that the firm will seek to make marginal cost equal to the externally given price of its product. Since in the short run only fixed capital is assumed to be unchangeable, it will normally be possible for the firm to increase its output by hiring more labour and using more materials, but only at increasing marginal cost. The consequence is that the short-run supply curve of the firm will be positively sloped, and this will ensure that short-run supply and demand curves for the industry will intersect in a manner which makes the short-run equilibrium point a stable one. Moreover, the short-run supply response of the firms in an industry will be in the same direction as the long-run supply response of the industry as a whole.[4]

Almost all of the discussion about the behaviour of the co-operative firm has been concerned with the nature of its short-run responses to changes in prices or costs. For this purpose it is often assumed that the definition of the short run used in the capitalist model should be used also in the co-operative model. In the simplest case, the co-operative short-run model is based on the following assumptions: (1) perfect competition in all

---

[3] Important further questions arise as to whether a perfectly competitive capitalist system would ever in fact be in long-term equilibrium, how closely it is likely to approximate to it, and with what time-lags. There are no *a priori* answers to such questions and most economists simply take it as a matter of faith that the system would be fairly close to equilibrium most of the time. Paradoxically, both theory and historical experience suggest that the more perfect the level of competition the greater the degree of instability of the system, and that it is the growth of market imperfections which has helped to make modern capitalism more stable than its nineteenth-century counterpart.

[4] This does not, however, guarantee that the transition from one long-run equilibrium point to another will be smooth. Under strictly perfect competitive conditions the rise in short-run supply price in response to a rise in demand may attract an excessive number of new entrants, leading eventually to a fall in market price below its new long-run equilibrium level.

markets; (2) only fixed capital is unchangeable in the short run; (3) all labour is homogeneous; (4) labour input can be varied only by changing the number of workers employed (implicitly, for a fixed number of hours and with a fixed degree of intensity of work). The responses of the co-operative firm to changes in prices and costs can then be demonstrated with the help of diagrams similar to those used by Ward, Vanek, and Meade.

In Figure 3.1 the curve AB measures value added per worker at different levels of employment in a single-product firm, with given fixed capital and with given prices for its product and for its material inputs. The curve is assumed to rise at first as the number of workers increases towards the number most appropriate for the given equipment, and then to decline. The curve JK measures the cost per worker of the capital equipment of the firm. Since the total cost, in interest and depreciation, will not vary appreciably as the number of workers employed is increased, the curve is approximately a rectangular hyperbola. A co-operative which aims to maximize income per worker will choose to employ the number of workers (or members) at which the vertical distance between AB and JK is greatest, in this case to employ OL_1 workers who will each receive an income of EF. At the points E and F the slopes of the two curves AB and JK will then be identical.

Now consider the effect of an increase in the price of the product, with no change in the prices of material inputs or the cost of fixed capital.[5] The value added curve will shift upwards from AB to CD, while JK is unchanged. By the nature of the curves the new maximum income per worker, GH, will be at a level of employment lower than the previous

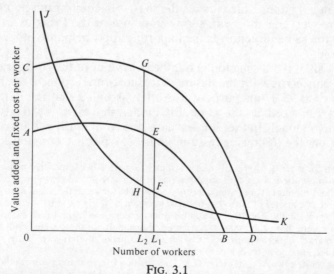

FIG. 3.1

[5] It is reasonable to assume also that in the short run there will be no substitution between labour and material inputs.

level, i.e. at OL_2. As before, the slopes of the curves CD and JK at points G and H will be identical.

These results may now be transferred to Figure 3.2, which relates income per worker directly to the number of workers employed. The curve MN plots the vertical differences between curves AB and JK at each level of employment in the previous figure, while $M'N'$ similarly plots the vertical differences between curves CD and JK. MN reaches a maximum at R such that RL_1 is equal to EF; and $M'N'$ reaches a maximum at T, where TL_2 is equal to GH. The dashed lines RS and TV plot marginal income (or product) per worker corresponding to the average income (or product) curves MN and $M'N'$.

The advantage of the second diagram is that it allows a direct comparison between the responses of a capitalist firm and an identical co-operative firm to a change in product price. When the price rises, MN shifts upwards to $M'N'$ and RS to TV. If the wage rate facing the capitalist firm was initially RL_1, the same as the income of the workers in the co-operative, and this is unchanged by the rise in the product price, the capitalist firm will increase employment from OL_1 to OL_3, where the new marginal product per worker is equal to the wage. But, as already shown, the co-operative firm will attempt to reduce employment from OL_1 to OL_2. The conclusion is that in the short run both output and employment will tend to be positively related to price in capitalist firms but, as far as practicable, negatively related in co-operative firms.

The precise effect of a change in product price on the level of employment (and hence output) in a co-operative will depend in part on its rules regarding membership. Consider the case where the rule is that all workers are members and all members are workers. For simplicity, also, at this stage we may assume that all workers are of equal skill, and that the total income of the co-operative is divided equally in each period among its

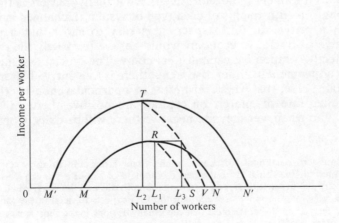

FIG. 3.2

members. This means that any newly employed worker automatically becomes a full member and is entitled to an equal share of the co-operative income. But what happens when the co-operative, or some of its members, suggest that the surviving members would be better off if some members were to be excluded? It seems probable that in a truly equal co-operative such a proposal would be rejected. Indeed, the rules might specify that no one could be excluded from membership against his will. In that case, the scope for reducing co-operative membership would be limited to natural wastage (retirements, deaths, invalidity, and voluntary quits). If in the short run there were no reduction in membership, both employment and output would therefore remain at the level existing before the increase in product price.

As pointed out by Domar (1966) this model is unsatisfactory, because it assumes that the input of labour per worker is fixed (either in hours or in intensity of work). Thus, even if the number of co-operative members cannot be changed in the short run, the amount of work performed can be varied; and, in general, it can be expected that it will vary positively with income per worker. The effect of this would be to make the short-run supply curve positively elastic, although not so elastic as it would be in a capitalist firm with instant possibilities of hiring and firing labour.[6] A co-operative would also show a greater positive response to product price changes if it produced more than one good and the price of one or more of its products rose in relation to the prices of others.

The focus of the above discussion has been on short-run adjustments to market conditions. But major short-run changes in relative prices are important only in the case of primary products, where the scope for short-run changes in supply are usually quite small for technical reasons.[7] Moreover, the nature of short-run adjustments to relative price changes is not of great significance from a welfare point of view, precisely because any losses of welfare which result from the inappropriateness of such adjustments are likely to be short-lived. What really matters is the nature of the long-run adjustments of each type of system to changes in long-run equilibrium prices. In this respect, it is easy to show that a perfectly competitive co-operative economy would behave in exactly the same way as a perfectly competitive capitalist economy. The crucial assumption for long-run adjustment in either case is that there is free entry. This means, in the capitalist case, that whenever profits in a particular industry (in excess of the ruling rate of interest on capital) are positive there will be new entrants, and whenever they are negative there will be exits. Consequent-

---

[6] Under modern conditions, of course, such instant hiring and firing is very far from realistic, especially the firing. Even the new recruitment of labour is a much slower process than a century ago because of greater differentiation of skills and the risks, created by firing restrictions, of taking on more workers than the firm expects to need in the longer term.

[7] For agricultural products, the most that can usually be done in the short run is to vary the speed and intensity of harvesting. Even under co-operative conditions it may well be possible to hire temporary workers for this purpose.

ly, in long-run equilibrium profits will be zero, and owners of capital will receive only the ruling rate of interest. Similarly, in a competitive co-operative economy, if net income per worker (after interest charges on capital) in one industry were to rise above, or fall below, net income per worker in other industries, there would be new entrants to, or exits from, the former industry (and vice versa for the other industries).[8] In long-run equilibrium, therefore, net income per worker will be the same in all industries and the interest rate on capital will be the same everywhere. Hence the welfare theorems of competitive capitalism will have the same degree of validity in a competitive co-operative system (and be subject to the same qualifications on account of external effects).

If the co-operative economy were identical with an alternative capitalist economy in respect of its technology and the supply conditions of labour and capital, equilibrium net income per worker in the co-operative economy would be the same as the wage in the capitalist economy, and the rate of interest would be the same in both. The distribution of personal incomes, however, would be different, because in the co-operative economy the ownership of capital (in the form of loans to co-operatives, either directly or through banks) would be more equally distributed than under capitalism, where large fortunes can sometimes be accumulated during the process of transition to long-run equilibrium.

It is often argued that the level of efficiency, in the sense of so-called X-efficiency, would be superior in a co-operative economy, because workers would be more willing to adjust to new conditions or to relax labour demarcation rules. On the other hand, co-operative entrepreneurship, management, and labour discipline may well be inferior. These are questions which need to be studied empirically.[9] Evidence from Yugoslavia on some of them will be given later in this book.

The whole of the above discussion is based on the assumption of perfect competition. Its relevance, therefore, depends on whether that assumption is at least approximately justified. In the next section we shall consider the competitive conditions likely to obtain in a co-operative economy.

2. CONDITIONS OF COMPETITION IN A CO-OPERATIVE ECONOMY

We have already given reasons why a modern capitalist economy cannot be described as a perfectly competitive system. In approaching the analysis of a co-operative economy it is not good enough simply to impose the assumption that the economy operates under perfectly competitive conditions. Before any model of such an economy is constructed, it is necessary to consider what kind of competitive conditions are likely to exist in it. In particular, it is necessary to consider whether, and in what way,

---

[8] In the real world, where firms are not limited to the sale of a single product, new entrants or exits may take the form of changes in the product ranges of existing co-operatives instead of the creation or elimination of entire enterprises.

[9] Professor Alberto Chilosi tells me that dockers' co-operatives in Italy show no willingness to adjust to new conditons.

competition in a co-operative economy is likely to differ from competition in a modern capitalist economy. For this purpose it is helpful to make a brief survey of the conditions obtaining in the two examples of industrial co-operative systems already in existence: the Mondragon group of co-operatives in the Basque region of northern Spain, and the Yugoslav system of labour-managed enterprises.[10]

The main distinguishing feature of the Mondragon co-operatives is that they are entirely voluntary organizations of individuals wishing to establish a co-operative.[11] As in any other commerical partnership, the members provide part of the capital of the business out of their own resources, and retain ownership rights in that capital. Additional funds can be obtained, within limits, from the movement's own savings bank—the *Caja Laboral Popular*—which collects savings deposits from the population of the region with the purpose of providing finance for the co-operatives. All workers employed by a co-operative are, with some small exceptions, members of that co-operative. They have equal rights to participate in assembly meetings and to elect the supervisory board of the enterprise which, in turn, appoints the management. All members are paid advances of wages, differentiated according to skills and responsibilities, and, in the case of manual workers, related to local trade union rates in private industry. At the end of each accounting period the surplus of revenue over costs—including wage advances, taxes, and depreciation—is divided up. Part of the surplus is used to pay interest on members' capital (at a minimum rate of 6 per cent per annum), and most of this can be drawn out in cash. The remainder is divided into a small part—only 10 per cent—which is paid out to members in proportion to their earnings, another part—at least 30 per cent—which is set aside for reserve and social funds, and a third part which is added to the capital accounts of members in proportion to their earnings. Capital accounts are revalued in line with inflation, but cannot normally be withdrawn by members until their retirement.

Apart from the special rules on the uses of the surplus and the limitation on withdrawal of capital the Mondragon co-operatives are very like capitalist partnerships. The difference is that they are inspired by an ideology and supported by local nationalism. This has also affected the supply of able managers, who have been willing to work for the co-operatives at lower rates of pay than they would receive in private firms.[12] The Mondragon group has created its own technical school and, more recently, its own polytechnic institute providing courses of university standard. It has also established an institute for research and development to give advice to individual co-operatives about new products and

---

[10] The Yugoslavs do not call their socialized enterprises co-operatives but 'organizations of associated labour'. This reflects a desire to distinguish between co-operatives, in which the members retain some individual ownership rights over their invested capital, and Yugoslav enterprises in which they have no such rights.

[11] The following description is based on the useful book by Thomas and Logan (1982).

[12] It is estimated that top managers in the largest co-operative, Ulgor, could obtain about twice as great an income in a similar private enterprise.

processes. The *Caja Laboral Popular* has a Management Services Division, employing at the end of 1978 more than a hundred engineers, economists, lawyers, and other experts, which advises new co-operatives on all aspects of their plans, and existing co-operatives on how to improve their performance. These organizations play a vital role in nursing new co-operatives into existence, providing them with a supply of skilled workers, technicians, and managers, finance, and detailed advice on product design, technology, and markets.

The Mondragon group has been highly successful. The first industrial co-operative was established in 1956. By 1979 there were 70 co-operatives with a total employment of over 15,000, all but 2,000 of whom were in industry. In the same year, the largest co-operative—Ulgor, manufacturing household durables—employed nearly 4,000 workers. During the 1960s and 1970s on the average nearly three new co-operatives were established each year, and only one—a fishermen's co-operative—had failed by the end of that period.

It is clear from this brief description that the Mondragon co-operatives are not operating in a perfectly competitive market. They need advice on product design and marketing strategy; they need help with the provision of loan finance; and they all plan to reinvest profits and to expand their scale of operations. Like new firms entering an ordinary (imperfect) capitalist market, they are obliged to start on a small scale, because of limited technical experience and limited funds; but they hope to expand both these limits as time passes, thus moving towards a more efficient and profitable scale of operation. Small capitalist new entrants are usually entirely on their own; they receive no special advice or assistance, and would usually prefer not to receive such assistance if it imposed obligations or burdens, especially the loss of their independence. The consequence is that many small capitalist new entrants are unsuccessful. But those that are successful become larger, stronger, and more profitable. The most successful of all grow into great enterprises yielding large profits to the initial investor and, if he wishes, allowing him eventually to sell the enterprise, or part of it, and make a substantial capital gain.[13] Thus, both the rewards and penalties of capitalist entrepreneurship are widely scattered around the average, and this is why only people who are risk-takers will be attracted into such activity. Those who start a co-operative in Mondragon, on the other hand, receive much more initial and continued support, which reduces—although it does not eliminate— the risks of the enterprise. In return for this support, the co-operative is obliged to accept rules which prevent its top decision-makers from

---

[13] The capital value of the enterprise is not the balance-sheet value of the equity but the value at which the enterprise can be sold to outside investors. An enterprise with a high profit rate, calculated in relation to its equity, or with specially good prospects, will sell for much more than its balance-sheet value. This ultimate capitalization of profits is the great prize awarded to the successful capitalist entrepreneur, and perhaps a major inducement to new entrants to take the risks of starting work on their own account.

receiving the full benefits of successful operation (or incurring the full costs of failure).

Let us now consider briefly the situation in Yugoslavia. Most of the Yugoslav co-operatives originated in nationalized enterprises, which were gradually transferred to labour-management. The workers in these co-operatives acquired management rights and, in theory, the right to allocate the net income of the enterprise either to themselves or to collective consumption or savings. At first, they were obliged to pay interest on the capital invested in the enterprise, but later this obligation was cancelled. The workers in these enterprises, therefore, received a windfall gain in the form of a right to use the inherited capital free of charge. But in the meantime the stock of capital had been augmented by reinvested income and by loans, originally from government funds but later predominantly from banks. Yugoslav co-operatives are supposed to be managed along similar lines to those in Mondragon. But, as will be shown in Chapter 7, there are many other (political) pressures on Yugoslav co-operatives besides the market environment in which they operate. Apart from this, a major difference is that Yugoslav workers do not make initial contributions to the equity of the co-operative, nor do they acquire full ownership rights in respect of reinvested co-operative income. Any additions to the 'own funds' of the co-operative officially belong to 'society' but, once the investment has been made, the co-operative has an obligation to maintain the capital intact. Nevertheless, these investments normally raise the productivity of the co-operative and improve the income prospects of its members. So long as a worker remains with the co-operative he enjoys some benefits from these savings, but he cannot withdraw them when he leaves, dies, or retires. New members pay no entrance fee (except unofficially in cases of corruption) and automatically receive the benefits of the past savings of existing and previous members.

Since Yugoslav co-operatives cover virtually all industry and services, and part of agriculture, the scope for forming new co-operatives is (relatively) more restricted than in Mondragon, which is only a small island in a sea of capitalism. But Yugoslavia has a large pool of unemployed as well as a similar number of workers temporarily employed abroad. In principle, therefore, there could be a rather rapid increase in the number of co-operatives to absorb these reserves of labour. In practice, however, Yugoslav policy in recent years has not encouraged the formation of new enterprises but has tended to concentrate on the expansion of existing enterprises. There are no facilities to provide management advisory services as in Mondragon and such new enterprises as are established are usually promoted by local government (communes) under the influence of various political as well as economic considerations. Loan finance is always in short supply in relation to current demands and its allocation is much influenced by political pressures. Although any group of workers is entitled to form a new co-operative, their chances of obtaining financial support would be remote unless their project had local political approval.

The large pool of unemployed, the imperfections in the capital market, the lack of free availability of technical knowledge, and the normal product market imperfections in non-primary industries sufficiently show that the Yugoslav co-operatives are not operating under conditions of perfect competition. There is some competitive pressure from imports and from the threat of entry through the diversification of existing enterprises. But the degree of competition is more imperfect than under capitalism and the concept of long-run competitive equilibrium is no more appropriate to Yugoslav conditions than it is to modern capitalism.

What both these examples show is that there is no more reason to assume that the model of perfect competition can be applied to a co-operative economy than to modern capitalism. For there are three deviations from perfect competition which are inherent in any conceivable modern market economy. The first is the fragmentation of the product market through variations in product design; the second is the imperfection of the capital market which arises from the risks inherent in making financial loans which can be converted by the borrowers into physical investments; and the third is the imperfect availability of technical knowledge, especially of practical knowledge of how to operate an enterprise efficiently. In the next section we shall describe a model of the behaviour of a co-operative economy under these imperfectly competitive conditions.

4. A MODEL OF A CO-OPERATIVE ECONOMY[14]

Although our ultimate objective is to predict the behaviour of co-operatives in a Yugoslav environment, we shall start by making a number of simplifying assumptions which are not in accordance with actual Yugoslav conditions. These assumptions will be changed later. The economy which we shall discuss has the following characteristics: (1) it is isolated from the outside world; (2) all enterprises must be co-operatives; (3) any group of workers can form a co-operative but, as in Mondragon, they must supply part of the initial capital out of their own resources; (4) interest is paid at a standard rate on members' capital, equal to the rate on outside loans; (5) members exercise full democratic control over the policy of the enterprise and the appointment of top management; (6) all members are workers and all workers are members; (7) except for disciplinary reasons, which are subject to approval by the members or their representatives, a member cannot be excluded from the co-operative without his consent; (8) each member is given a points rating (by agreement between the elected organs and the professional management) which determines his share of co-operative income; (9) advances of wages are paid in proportion to these points; (10) at the end of each accounting period the residual income, after allocations for costs, taxes, depreciation, interest charges, and wage advances, is divided, by the democratic decision of the members, into two parts: funds for reinvestment in the enterprise

[14] This model is similar in many respects to the model of a capitalist economy presented in Lydall (1979, Part II).

and a balance of income for distribution among the members; (11) when income is reinvested, the capital account of each member is increased by an amount equal to his share of the total, calculated on the basis of his points rating; when income is distributed, the amount paid to each member is determined on the same principle; (12) capital accounts are revalued each year in line with an index of the prices of capital goods; (13) except with the special permission of the co-operative, members' capital accounts can be withdrawn only on death or retirement.

The co-operatives operate in a market environment. They can freely buy materials and supplies at market prices and sell their own products at whatever prices they consider most advantageous to them. We shall be concerned mainly with the behaviour of co-operatives which face an imperfect, i.e. limited, market for their products; but some remarks will be made at appropriate points about the minority of enterprises which operate in a perfect product market. All co-operatives, irrespective of the nature of their product market, are confronted by an imperfect capital market. They can obtain bank loans, at a standard rate of interest, but only up to limits determined by the banks. These limits will depend on the degree of proved efficiency of the co-operative and the funds contributed by the members out of their own resources or reinvested income.

In general, for simplicity, we shall assume that each co-operative makes only one product. In order to produce that product, the co-operative requires not only labour and capital but some technical knowledge. For reasons which will soon become apparent, we shall draw a distinction between public technique and private technique. Public technique is information about production methods which is publicly available, for example, in textbooks and public technical training courses, and to some extent through inspection of the products of other enterprises. Public technique is the only kind of technique assumed to exist under conditions of perfect competition, where all potential producers of a product are assumed to have free access to the knowledge required to produce the product with the same degree of efficiency. But there is another important kind of technique, which is internal to the enterprise, and hence called private technique. This is a stock of knowledge about technical methods and systems of organization, as well as about marketing conditions and methods, which has been accumulated by the enterprise, or by its members, on the basis of practical experience of producing and selling its own product. Private technique, or 'know-how', normally increases inside the enterprise as time passes, thus permitting it to operate more efficiently—even with no change in public techniques—and, above all, to operate successfully on a larger scale. An improvement in its private technique is a necessary condition for the efficient operation of an enterprise on a larger scale, and this means that a completely new enterprise will not have the necessary private technique to operate efficiently at more than a small scale. It can expand the size of its operation efficiently only if it allows sufficient time to accumulate the necessary practical experience.

Private technique can be transferred to some extent from one enterprise to another, if the transferring enterprise is willing to train the management and workers of the receiving enterprise. But such a transfer of technology represents the transfer of an important asset and, under either capitalism or a co-operative system, the transferring enterprise will usually be unwilling to make the transfer unless it receives suitable compensation, and perhaps a guarantee that the technology will not be used in such a way as to damage its own market position. Over a period of time, private technology can usually be gradually transferred from one enterprise to another within a single economy by personal contact, movement of management and workers between enterprises, and so forth. In other words, part of private technology gradually becomes public technology for that economy. But, in the meantime, new forms of private technology are likely to have come into existence, so that enterprises continue to differ in their capacity to operate efficiently on a larger scale.

Long-run equilibrium

It is a normal characteristic of modern industrial enterprises that there are considerable economies of large-scale operation. Economies of scale vary with the product: they are usually smaller for personal services or for custom-built products, but they are usually very large for most manufactured products and for some services, such as railways or financial services. For some products, so far as we know, there is no end to the possibility of further economies of scale or, at the least, there is no evidence that costs ever begin to rise as output increases. From the point of view of cost it would be desirable that all enterprises should operate at a scale of production at which their costs were as low as technically possible or, if that would entail producing more than could be sold in the domestic market, at the largest scale which is consistent with these market constraints. In practice, however, this position is never achieved.

The reasons why enterprises—whether capitalist or co-operative—are not universally of optimum size, and indeed usually deviate very substantially from that size, are crucial to our understanding of how a market system operates. On the one hand, there is an incentive for every enterprise to move towards the optimum size; on the other, there are three constraints which prevent it from reaching that size as quickly as it would like. The first is that a new enterprise lacks the private technology which would permit it to operate efficiently on a large scale. The second is that it is unable to raise the necessary finance to operate on a large scale, because lenders are unwilling to take the risk of lending large sums of money to an inexperienced organization. And the third is that, when it first enters an imperfect market, a new enterprise will have difficulty in selling more than a limited quantity of its product.

Co-operatives, like capitalist firms, differ in their efficiency as well as in their size, partly because they have different levels of private technology and partly because of differences between people in their inherent abilities. For co-operatives of average efficiency producing a given product X we can draw a long-run average cost curve which shows what would be the average cost of production at different hypothetical levels of ouput of X. The position and shape of this curve depends on the level of public technology and on the assumed costs of material and factor inputs. It is also drawn on the assumption that a co-operative which wishes to operate at a particular scale of output has the necessary private technology to operate efficiently on that scale, and has access to sufficient finance at the market rate of interest. In a co-operative economy, unlike capitalism, the cost of labour cannot be measured by wages, since the workers receive residual incomes, equivalent to the sum of wages and profits under capitalism. In constructing the long-run average cost curve of a co-operative we shall calculate the cost of labour by imputing a rate of income per worker equal to that income per worker the expectation of which is just sufficient to induce a group of workers to establish a new co-operative. Hence, only in the case of a co-operative of new entrant size will the cost of labour included in the cost curve be exactly the amount received as income by the workers. In all other cases, the workers' actual incomes will be greater than this.

The cost curves in Figure 3.3, which are drawn on these assumptions, have three alternative shapes. The curve CC_1 is the traditional U-shaped cost curve; CC_2 is the cost curve of a product which exhibits economies of scale up to a certain point, and constant costs thereafter; and CC_3 is a cost curve for a product which is believed to enjoy indefinitely increasing economies of scale. Only the curve CC_1 is compatible with perfect competition, and then only if the optimum size of firm, OF, is small enough to permit the existence of a large number of firms in the same market. However, since we are not assuming perfect competition, we are not restricted to a cost curve of type CC_1. Any of the three types of curve is acceptable for our model.[15]

If the economy were perfectly competitive, and in equilibrium, all co-operatives making product X would be operating at point E. They would each produce exactly OF of X and their average cost of production would be EF. This would also be the long-run equilibrium price of X, at which the average income per worker, after paying interest on the capital employed in the co-operative, would be no more than the amount required to induce a group of workers to establish a new co-operative. In our model, however, because of the constraints imposed by limited markets, limited private technology, and limited access to capital, a new co-operative of average efficiency cannot be established at point E, but can only operate at first on a smaller scale, e.g. at point B. At this point the average long-run cost of X is BD and, for reasons which will be given below, BD will be the normal long-run equilibrium price of X. When this is so, a new

---

[15] As will be explained in Section 5 below, the long-run average cost curve of a co-operative may have a somewhat different shape from the long-run average cost curve of a capitalist firm, even when both enterprises use the same technology and pay the same rate of interest on loans, because at each level of output the co-operative will use more capital per worker. But there will still be a phase in which the co-operative enterprise will enjoy economies of scale.

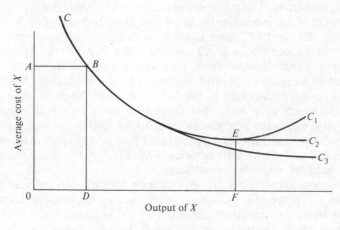

FIG. 3.3

co-operative making X, which, because of greater-than-average efficiency or greater-than-average luck, is able to produce at an average cost lower than BD, will enjoy a higher-than-average income per worker. This will permit such a co-operative, if it wishes, to reinvest part of its income and, because of the increase in its own funds and the evidence of its superior performance, it will be able to raise additional loan finance, and so to expand even further. Moreover, the experience of operating successfully at output OD will have increased the co-operative's stock of private technology, and so permit it to operate with equal efficiency on a larger scale. At the same time, the market for the co-operative's product X will probably have increased, partly spontaneously as a result of wider public knowledge of the product, and partly through the efforts of the co-operative to increase its sales.

From the shape of the cost curve it is clear that, with the price of X remaining at BD, average income per worker will increase as the scale of output of X increases, at least as far as point E. There is, therefore, a constant incentive for the co-operative to expand, and this will encourage the members to agree to the reinvestment of part of their income, especially since this will usually be a necessary condition for attracting additional outside finance. Moreover, as income per worker increases it becomes easier for the members to agree to reinvest part of their income, so that the proportion of co-operative income saved is likely to increase with the average level of income per worker, and hence in general with the size of the co-operative. Hence, larger co-operatives are likely to grow faster than smaller ones, and the dispersion of income per worker between different co-operatives is likely to widen over time.

Before we proceed further, it is necessary to justify the proposition that the equilibrium price of each product will tend to be in the region of the average cost of production of a co-operative of minimum size, i.e. of the size of a new entrant. The proposition can be established if it can be shown that (1) there is no incentive for a co-operative producing X to raise its price above BD, and (2) there is no incentive for such a co-operative to reduce its price more than a small amount below BD. On the first aspect, a co-operative which is concerned with the long-term protection of the incomes of its members will not take action which encourages the entry of competing co-operatives into its market. If it raises the price of product X above BD, which may be called the *entry price*, this will attract new entrants (who will make a product similar to X), and in the long run reduce the co-operative's market for its product. From a long-term point of view, therefore, BD is the competitive price of X, though X is a unique product currently sold by only one producer.

On the second aspect, it will only pay a co-operative to reduce the price of X below BD if the effect will be to increase average income per worker. There are some circumstances, which will be discussed later, in which a co-operative might derive a short-term benefit by making such a price reduction. But, if the co-operative's policies are determined predominantly by long-term considerations, it is very unlikely to derive any advantage from reducing its price below BD. The condition for deriving such an advantage would be that the downward slope of the demand curve for X would be flatter than the downward slope of the average cost of production of X. But this would imply that the demand for X is highly elastic, which is contrary to our initial assumption that all co-operatives are operating under conditions of imperfect competition.

Entry into the X market, or into the production of a product very similar to X, may be made not only by new co-operatives starting on a small scale. It is also possible that existing co-operatives, which are making another product, may be attracted into the X market. If they were to give up their old product and concentrate on X, this would be consistent with our present assumption that each co-operative produces only one product. More realistically, the newly entering co-operative may add product X to its existing product range. In that case, we have to allow for the existence of multi-product co-operatives. But this does not make any fundamental difference to the conditions under which the entry of existing co-operatives into the X market will occur. An existing co-operative of more than minimum size will, if it is of at least average efficiency, have lower average costs per unit of its existing product than a new entrant into its own market; and this implies that it will have a higher income per worker than such a new entrant co-operative. If, then, this existing co-operative is to be attracted into the X market, it must expect to be able to earn at least as great an income per worker as it would obtain by concentrating on the expansion of production of its own product. Since it is an established enterprise, it will possess the necessary private technology to operate on its present scale in its own market, and much of this technology will be useful to it if it decides to enter the X market. But it will not be able to aim at a scale of production of X, measured in terms of the resources employed, much greater than its existing scale. Hence, if the price of X is maintained at BD, an existing co-operative will be attracted to enter the X market only if the income per worker which it receives on its scale of production in its own market is less than the income per worker which it might expect to receive on a similar scale of production in the X market. In view of the difficulties of breaking into a new market and of mastering a new technology specific to X, it is rather unlikely that existing co-operatives will be attracted into the X market as long as the price is maintained at BD. If, however, there is such a threat, the co-operative producing X will be likely to reduce the price of X below BD. This is something which it may have already decided to do in any case in order to discourage the entry of new co-operatives. The general outcome is, therefore, that BD will be the maximum long-term competitive price of X but that the actual price maintained by a producer of X may be somewhat lower.

Short-run equilibrium

The conclusion from the above discussion is that, in an imperfect market, each co-operative will determine a maximum price for its product, which will be maintained irrespective of changes in the conditions of demand. This price will, of course, be adjusted if the entry price for the product changes. The entry price for a given product X depends on (1) the state of public technology for producing X, (2) the level of material input costs, (3) the rate of interest on capital, and (4) the level of expected income per worker which is sufficient to induce a group of workers to establish a new co-operative for the production of X. Thus a co-operative which produces X will tend to reduce the price of X when technology improves, when input prices or the rate of interest fall, or when the expected income of workers starting new co-operatives falls. In normal conditions, the level of technology gradually rises, the expected income of workers starting new co-operatives also gradually rises, and the rate of interest remains fairly stable. In such conditions, sharp changes in the price of X will occur only when there are sharp changes in the prices of its material inputs.

Although each co-operative will determine the maximum price for its product in this way, we need to consider in more detail how it is likely to respond to changes in the conditions of demand for its product. In Figure 3.4, the vertical distance OA measures the pre-determined maximum price of X, and D_1D_1 and D_2D_2 are alternative positions of the demand for X. The line CG represents the marginal cost of X to the co-operative in the short run. In the usual capitalist model the short run is defined as the situation in which fixed capital is unchangeable but other factors and material inputs can be varied. For a co-operative model, however, it is inappropriate to make a distinction between the period of adjustment of capital and the period of adjustment of labour, since a co-operative will not adjust its number of members instantaneously in response to changes in market conditions. Hence, for the co-operative short run we shall assume that both fixed capital and the number of workers are unchangeable. There remains, however, the possibility of changing the amount of work done per worker, by changing either the number of hours or the intensity of work. In

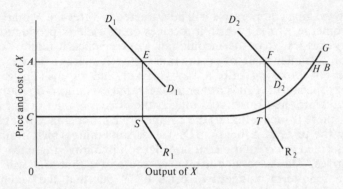

FIG. 3.4

the figure, the line CG measures the short-run marginal cost of X on these assumptions. It has an approximately horizontal section so long as the hours and intensity of work per worker are no greater than normal. The main component of marginal cost in this phase is the increase of material inputs as output increases. Beyond some point, however, with the given equipment and the given workforce, the marginal cost of output will begin to rise, a major cause of this rise being the increasing real costs to the workers of extending either their hours of work or their intensity of work.

When the demand for X is at D_1D_1 and OA is the maximum price of X, the marginal revenue curve will be $AESR_1$, which has a vertical section, ES, below the point at which D_1D_1 intersects the maximum price line, AB. Normally, we may expect this vertical section of the marginal revenue curve to intersect the marginal cost curve. In that case, the output which will yield the most acceptable income per worker will be given by AE, the amount which can be sold at the maximum price under existing demand conditions. Similarly, when the demand curve shifts to D_2D_2, the income-maximizing output will be AF. In no circumstances will output in the short run be greater than AH, given by the intersection of the maximum price line AB and the marginal cost curve CC. This is the point of 'maximum capacity'.[16]

In exceptional circumstances, the demand for X may be very elastic (but not infinitely elastic, since this would contradict the assumptions of the model). An example is given in Figure 3.5. As before, OA is the maximum price and CG is the marginal cost curve. The marginal revenue curve is $AESR$, and this intersects CG at F, giving an income-maximizing price of KL and a corresponding output of OL. In such circumstances, there could be a short-term advantage to the co-operative in cutting its price below the maximum. Whether this occurs often in practice is a matter for empirical

---

[16] For an enterprise operating under conditions of perfect competition in the product market the line AB represents the demand for its product, and the enterprise will always aim to produce AH. Whether it succeeds in doing so depends on the speed with which the price is changing and the speed with which the enterprise can adjust to such changes.

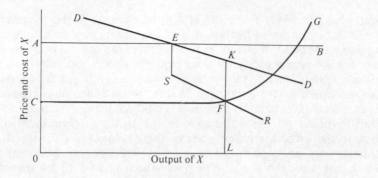

FIG. 3.5

study; but the general expectation, based on experience of imperfect markets, is that the product demand curve is unlikely to be sufficiently elastic to justify a reduction in price below the maximum.[17]

Apart from the exception just mentioned, we may expect co-operatives in an imperfect market to respond to changes in demand in a very simple manner. So long as technology, input prices, and so forth are constant, and with given fixed capital and a given work-force, a co-operative will supply its product at a fixed price—at or slightly below the entry price—and will produce the amount required to satisfy demand at that price, but not beyond the point of full capacity. Thus, when demand increases, output will expand (subject to the capacity limit), and when demand falls output will fall. This pattern of responses is precisely the same as the pattern of responses of a capitalist firm operating under similar conditions.[18] Hence the prediction of the perfect competition model that co-operative firms will respond in a perverse fashion to changes in demand are not supported by the present model. Moreover, the present model shows that the short-run responses of the co-operative will normally be the same, irrespective of whether its assumed maximand is total income, income per worker, sales (at a given price), or—as in Horvat's (1967) model—surplus over some predetermined level of income per worker.

5. SOME FURTHER IMPLICATIONS OF THE THEORY

In this section we shall draw attention to some further implications of our model for the functioning of a co-operative economy. In particular we shall

---

[17] It must also be remembered that firms do not know very much about the elasticity of demand for their products, and that experiments with price-cutting can be very damaging if it turns out that demand is not sufficiently elastic.

[18] Because the capitalist firm can change the number of workers in the short run, the horizontal section of its marginal cost curve will lie above the corresponding section of the co-operative's marginal cost curve, and it will begin to slope upwards only when it reaches a greater volume of output. This means that the short-run capacity point of the capitalist firm, for a given set of equipment, will be more extended than in a corresponding co-operative. It also means that the exceptional case illustrated in Figure 3.5 is more unlikely to occur under capitalist conditions.

consider what are likely to be the effects of changes in the assumptions
listed at the beginning of Section 4. An especially important change in
assumptions concerns the financial structure of the co-operative. In
constructing the model of Section 4 we assumed that co-operatives were of
the Mondragon type, i.e. that new members are obliged to contribute
towards the capital of the enterprise, that reinvested income is credited to
individual capital accounts, that interest is paid on these accounts, and that
the sums involved can be withdrawn on the death or retirement of the
member. In the Yugoslav system none of these rules applies. Instead, new
co-operatives are financed out of bank loans and other credits, reinvested
income disappears into a common pool which is said to be owned by
'society', and members do not own individual capital accounts. For
convenience, when considering the effects of operating a co-operative
system of this second type rather than of the first type, we shall say that we
assume Yugoslav-type co-operatives in place of Mondragon-type co-
operatives. But first we must deal with an important question, which arises
irrespective of the type of co-operative, namely, whether there is a
tendency for co-operatives to be more capital-intensive than corresponding
capitalist enterprises.

The degree of capital-intensity

Consider two parallel enterprises—a co-operative and a capitalist firm—
each of which produces the same product X in the same quantity, each of
which has the same choice of technology, and each of which pays the same
rate of interest on loans. We shall assume that the capitalist firm pays its
workers the same wage at all scales of output (as was assumed in
constructing the long-run average cost curves in Figure 3.3).[19] Thus, both
the rate of interest and the wage rate of labour are assumed to be given by
the market and to be unaffected by the firm's scale of production. The firm
will then choose for any given output of X that combination of labour and
capital which gives the lowest possible cost of production.

Except in the case of a new entrant, the workers in a co-operative of
average efficiency which pays the market rate of interest on its capital will
receive an income which is above the standard wage assumed to be paid by
the capitalist firm. If this level of income per worker is to be maintained, or
if possible increased, this must be treated by the co-operative as the cost of
labour which is relevant for its choice of the least cost combination of
labour and capital for the production of an extra unit of X in the long run.
Since the cost of labour in such a co-operative is above the standard wage
paid by a capitalist firm, while the rate of interest is the same, there will be

---

[19] In reality, under modern capitalist conditions the average wage per worker tends to
increase with the size of enterprise. In so far as this represents a genuine increase in wage
rates for labour of constant quality (and it probably does so to some extent) the tendency
discussed below of a co-operative to have a bias towards capital-intensive investment
decisions exists also in capitalist enterprises. But the tendency will not be so pronounced,
because the increase in wage rates with size of enterprise in capitalist firms is not so great as to
absorb the whole of the benefits of economies of scale.

a tendency for the co-operative to choose a more capital-intensive method of production than the capitalist firm. While this tendency will exist in a Mondragon-type co-operative, it will be even stronger in a Yugoslav-type co-operative. The reason is that Yugoslav co-operatives administer a substantial amount of interest-free capital, which was either inherited from the period of nationalization or ploughed back subsequently without incurring any debts to the members. The income produced by this capital increases the residual income of the co-operative, which can be divided among the members in proportion to their points rating, and thus serves to increase the cost of labour which is relevant for future investment decisions.[20]

Vanek (1970) has drawn attention to the possibility that a co-operative of the Yugoslav type, which possesses a large quantity of interest-free capital, might use its annual flow of depreciation allowances to install more and more capital-intensive plant and machinery, and at the same time reduce the number of persons employed. In the end, a small handful of surviving members of the co-operative could be using an enormous stock of capital equipment to give themselves high incomes and an easy life. The practical difficulties in the way of achieving this result seem to be considerable, since the workers' council of the co-operative would have to take an explicit decision to follow this policy and to pursue it over a long period, using recurrent depreciation allowances gradually to transform the enterprise's technology (and probably its product range) without damaging its existing income flow. Pressure from existing members, as well as from the local community, which would see the prospects for local employment being diminished, would probably be sufficient to present the adoption of such a policy. But the risk would be eliminated altogether if co-operatives were obliged to pay interest on all their capital, which is desirable anyway on grounds of equity.

Major effects of assuming Yugoslav-type co-operatives

There are two main effects of replacing Mondragon-type co-operatives by Yugoslav-type co-operatives. The first concerns the conditions of entry of new co-operatives. In the Mondragon case the members of the new co-operative must either save up the amount of their contribution before they start or agree to save the required amount out of their incomes during the first few years of membership. The amounts involved do not seem to have acted as a serious deterrent to the formation of new co-operatives in Mondragon, but similar rules might be more restrictive in a poorer country. However, the Yugoslav population already owns very large savings deposits, and there must be many workers in existing co-operatives, or among those who have been working abroad, who would be glad to have the opportunity to join a co-operative of the Mondragon type.

[20] There is much evidence in Yugoslavia of a tendency towards increasing capital-intensity in existing enterprises. While this is probably partly the result of the considerations mentioned here, Yugoslav policies in regard to self-finance and the level of the real interest rate also encourage the same tendency. These matters will be discussed further in Chapter 10.

The formation of new co-operatives in Yugoslavia depends essentially on political decisions, and in current conditions the formation of new co-operatives does not seem to be determined primarily by the desire to offer serious competition to existing co-operatives but rather to replace imports or to satisfy local political ambitions. Nevertheless, there is a continuing threat that existing co-operatives will extend their product range and move into the market of any co-operative which tries to set too high a price for its product; and in the background there is also the possibility of establishing new co-operatives under the same circumstances. In the short term, the main pressure on co-operative prices in Yugoslavia is the state of world prices, modified by tariffs, subsidies, import restrictions and the exchange rate for the dinar.

The second major effect of replacing Mondragon-type co-operatives by Yugoslav-type co-operatives in that the members will have less incentive to reinvest income in their own co-operative. In the Mondragon type of co-operative the member who agrees to reinvest income in his co-operative derives most of the benefit of the investment. Since he is in the privileged position of being able to obtain the rewards of the expected economies of scale resulting from further expansion, the expected rate of return on reinvestment will normally be larger than the rate of interest payable on savings deposits. He may still wish to retain some of his savings in liquid form, or for investment in housing, or for other purposes, but in general he will be well disposed towards reinvestment in the co–operative. In the Yugoslav case, on the other hand, while the worker who reinvests income in his co-operative derives the benefit of a higher expected income, this benefit continues only so long as he remains a member of the co-operative. At the end of that time the benefit accrues to the surviving members, some of whom may have made little or no contribution to the reinvestment fund. There will, therefore, be a tendency for younger members to be more favourably disposed to reinvestment than other members, especially since in Yugoslavia the worker's retirement pension is based on the amount paid out in income to him during his last few years of work, not on his share of total income generated, including the amount reinvested.[21]

The general effect of these arrangements is to give members of Yugoslav-type co-operatives less incentive to reinvest income than members of Mondragon-type co-operatives; and in so far as the total amount of investment finance depends on the volume of reinvested funds, Yugoslav-type co-operatives will have a slower rate of growth than Mondragon-type co-operatives. In practice, however, in Yugoslavia this braking factor has usually been more than offset, especially in recent years, by the fact that the rate of inflation has been in excess of the rate of interest on bank loans. When the real rate of interest is negative, there is a powerful incentive to borrow for investment and, when this is combined with the rule that the volume of investment loans which a co-operative can borrow

---

[21] The disincentive to reinvest in Yugoslav-type co-operatives has been much emphasized by Furubotn and Pejovich (e.g. 1970).

is related to the volume of its own reinvestment fund, co-operatives will have a strong incentive to reinvest part of their income.

In Yugoslavia, co-operatives are also under strong political pressure to maintain a high saving rate. This is mainly a reflection of an ideological belief that, so far as possible, the co-operatives should be self-financed and not dependent on outside loans. The actual pattern of savings, however, is also influenced by the desire to prevent the richer co-operatives from distributing too much of their income to their members, so as to restrict the range of differences in currently distributed income. The combination of pressure in favour of self-finance, cheap—but rationed—credit, and the rule that any technically separate section of an enterprise can be separated off into the control of its own workers creates some serious barriers to the mobility of capital between industries and regions. This is a matter which we shall explore further in Chapter 10.

Inter-co-operative inequality of income

Our model provides a simple explanation for the fact, which is well established in Yugoslavia, that income per worker can vary considerably across co-operatives. It is sometimes alleged that paid-out incomes for similar jobs in different enterprises in the same area can differ by as much as 4 to 1. If this is so, it would imply that income generated per worker can vary by more than this ratio. The explanation provided by our model centres mainly on the effects of economies of scale. Other factors which may also lead to differences in income per worker in different Yugoslav co-operatives include differences in the level of X-efficiency of managers and/or workers, differences in the availability of natural resources provided to enterprises at less than their true value, differences in the effects of price controls, and pure luck.[22]

In so far as inter-co-operative differences in income per worker are due to economies of scale they would not disappear if there were no self-finance. The cost curves drawn in Figure 3.3 include interest on all the capital required for each scale of production. Even so, larger co-operatives, on the average, generate higher incomes per worker than smaller co-operatives. These income differences cannot be eliminated by any feasible changes in the capital market, although they could be somewhat reduced if new entrants and other small enterprises were given more favourable treatment in the provision of credits—both in amount and in terms. The risk of going very far in this direction, however, is that many inefficient enterprises would be brought into existence and helped to survive.

One method by which inter-co-operative differences in disposable income per worker could be reduced would be to impose a progressive income tax on co-operatives, calculated on the basis of their income per worker. If the tax were carefully judged, it might have the desired effect of

---

[22] Some differences will also be due to previous reinvestments of income on which no interest is paid. But such differences are, in a sense, spurious, since they would disappear if interest were paid or imputed on such reinvestments.

reducing disposable income differences without significantly reducing the incentives for efficient operation.

The size of co-operative enterprises

Vanek (1970) has argued that co-operatives will tend to be smaller than capitalist enterprises, and that this will be good for competition. On the theoretical level, his conclusion about size is broadly consistent with our model, if the long-run average cost curve is either U-shaped or becomes horizontal at some point, as in curves CC_1 and CC_2 in Figure 3.3. For a capitalist firm may have a continuing incentive to increase in size beyond the point E in the figure, since it is unlikely to be able to redirect its energies and investible funds to enterprises which would yield a higher rate of return than it can obtain in the further expansion of the production of X. A co-operative, on the other hand, which expanded beyond point E could almost certainly reduce income per worker if its average cost curve were CC_1, and it would probably not increase income per worker if its cost curve were CC_2.[23]

At the other end of the scale, however, a co-operative economy would have fewer small enterprises than a capitalist economy, which always contains a very large number of firms employing (including the proprietor) between 1 and 10 persons. In Yugoslavia, where there seems to have been a bias against small co-operatives and in favour of larger enterprises, the degree of concentration of industry is very high. In 1981, for example, the largest 96 enterprises in industry and mining received 74.4 per cent of gross revenue in that sector, generated 62.6 per cent of gross value added, possessed 69.6 per cent of total capital, and employed 49.6 per cent of the total number of workers.[24]

Effects of fluctuations in aggregate demand

Vanek (1970) also claims that a co-operative economy will respond to fluctuations in aggregate demand mainly by changes in prices rather than by changes in output and employment. But this conclusion follows only if one assumes perfect competition. In our model, the normal short-run response of a co-operative enterprise to a change in the level of demand will be to adjust its output by increasing or reducing the consumption of material inputs and by using its labour force more or less intensively. The scope for increasing output is smaller than under capitalism, because a co-operative will be reluctant to take in new members if it believes that the increase in demand is only temporary; but, when demand declines, a co-operative operating in an imperfect market will be no more willing to reduce its price than a capitalist firm.

The security of tenure of co-operative workers is likely to have an

[23] The exact outcome depends on changes in the composition of costs as the scale of production increases. For example, if on curve CC_2 output per worker continued to increase beyond point E, even though cost per unit of output, including capital cost, was constant, there would still be some incentive for a co-operative to expand beyond point E.

[24] *Ekonomska politika*, 4 October 1982, special supplement, p. 43.

influence on their response to a decline in the demand for their enterprise's product (or products). Just as in Japan, where capitalist firms follow a policy of lifetime employment, all members of the enterprise are likely to make an effort to find new products to replace the loss of sales on existing products. The enterprise as a whole will be more resilient and more adaptable than in an economy where it is easy to get rid of workers.

PART II

Yugoslav History and Institutions

CHAPTER 4

THE HISTORICAL BACKGROUND

1. THE LAND

The state of Yugoslavia came into existence in 1918 under the name—at that time—of the Kingdom of the Serbs, Croats, and Slovenes. It was a creation of the Versailles peace settlement, bringing together the hitherto independent Kingdoms of Serbia and Montenegro with four parts of the former Austro-Hungarian Empire: Slovenia, Croatia, Vojvodina, and Bosnia and Herzegovina. Small areas previously under Bulgarian rule were added in the following year. Apart from the cession of Istria and part of Goricia by Italy after the Second World War, the present frontiers of Yugoslavia are those which were established in 1919.

The area included in the new state covers the greater part of the north-west of the Balkan peninsula. It is bounded by Italy, Austria, Hungary, Romania, Bulgaria, Greece, and Albania. Although Yugoslavia is quite a large country by European standards, endowed with varied natural resources, nearly half of its land surface is mountainous. The greatest continuous area of mountains is in the south-west, occupying most of Bosnia-Herzegovina and Montenegro, and extending inland from the Adriatic coast for a hundred miles or more. This is the military 'heartland', from which resistance to Turkish rule was maintained for several centuries, especially in Montenegro, which was never subjugated. It is also the area in which Tito's main forces of partisans survived and multiplied during the first three years of their National Liberation War. Since many of the mountain ranges in this area run parallel to the coast, access from the Adriatic to the lowland country of the north and east is difficult except along three or four traditional routes, of which the most important is that running from Rijeka to Zagreb. This remains, as it has been since Roman times, a major outlet from the north and central Balkans to the Mediterranean.

Although there are other considerable groups of mountains—in Slovenia, along the eastern border of Serbia, and in the extreme south-west, facing Albania—it is a reasonable approximation to say that the remainder of Yugoslavia is distributed along four great river valleys: the Sava (and part of the Drava), the Danube, the Morava, and the Vardar. The Sava rises in north-western Slovenia and flows eastward through Slovenia, part of Croatia, then along the boundary between

Croatia and Bosnia, and finally into Serbia, where it joins the Danube at Belgrade. To the north of the Sava, and flowing roughly parallel with it, the Drava traces over part of its course the boundary with Hungary. The Danube, which enters Yugoslavia from Hungary, flows through the plain of Vojvodina, past Belgrade, and so to the Iron Gate and beyond. The Morava is the major river of Serbia, flowing northwards from close to the present northern boundary of Macedonia for more than 200 miles and eventually joining the Danube to the east of Belgrade. In the south, the river Vardar flows southward through the heart of Macedonia and reaches the Aegean Sea near Thessaloniki in Greece.

Thus the 'spine' of Yugoslavia—the river valleys of the Sava, Danube, Morava, and Vardar—traces a wide arc running from north-west to south-east. It is along these river valleys that there have grown up the major road and railway routes, with important branches reaching out to Rijeka, Split, and Sarajevo on the southern (or inner) side of the arc, and to Maribor (and hence to Austria) and to the rich lands of the Vojvodina on the northern side. In these valleys also are situated almost all the major cities—Ljubljana, capital of Slovenia, Zagreb, capital of Croatia, Novi Sad, capital of Vojvodina, Belgrade, federal capital and capital of Serbia, Niš, a major industrial city, and Skopje, capital of Macedonia. The only republican capital cities not on this route are Sarajevo, in the heart of Bosnia, and Titograd in remote Montenegro. Priština, capital of the autonomous province of Kosovo, is situated not far to the west of the Morava, near a tributary of that river.

Somewhat isolated from the rest of the country is the coastal region of Dalmatia and Montenegro. Although important manufacturing industries have been established in northern and central Dalmatia, and to a lesser extent in Montenegro, the greatest natural advantage of this area is its exceptional beauty, which has encouraged the development of a consider- able tourist industry.

The natural resources of the mountainous areas of Bosnia-Herzegovina are mainly timber, pastures, minerals, and rivers suitable for hydroelectric power generation. The richest agricultural area in Yugoslavia is the plain of the Vojvodina, which forms part of the fertile Pannonian basin. But all of the lowland areas along the major river valleys have important agricultural potential, as well as being suitable for industry. Agricultural output ranges from grains and rootcrops to meat, fruit, wine, cotton, and tobacco, and the wide variation of climate and soil offers great scope for further development and diversification of Yugoslav agriculture.

2. THE PEOPLE

At the time of its creation the state of Yugoslavia had a population of about 12 million, of which, to judge by the Census of 1921 and later information, approximately 6 million were Serbs (including Montenegrins and Macedonians), 3 million Croats, 1 million Slovenes, and 2 million other national minorities. Amongst the latter were half a million Germans, nearly as many Hungarians and Albanians, and a significant number of Romanians, Slovaks, and Turks. There were also many thousands of Vlachs, Gypsies, Bulgars, Czechs, and Russians.

Most of the Germans and Hungarians were concentrated in the Vojvodina; most of the Albanians in south-eastern Serbia, mainly in Kosovo and along the Albanian border with Macedonia. Although most of the Serbs were living in Serbia and Montenegro (a Serbian-speaking area), there were large Serbian minorities in Croatia, amounting to about 15 per cent of the population, and in Bosnia-Herzegovina, where Serbian-speakers were the majority and Croatian-speakers a minority. The Croats also constituted a significant minority of the population of Vojvodina. In the inter-war period, Macedonians, who are concentrated in southern Yugoslavia in what is now the republic of Macedonia, were officially considered to be Serbs. The Muslims of Bosnia-Herzegovina, who are descended from Slavs converted to Islam under the Turks, were not treated then, as they are now, as a separate 'nation', but were divided between Serbs and Croats according to their language.

In the Balkan region, language and religion have historically been closely associated together. A Serb, for example, was both a speaker of Serbian (using the Cyrillic script in his writing) and a member of the Serbian Orthodox Church. Croats, on the other hand, who have a slightly different language with a script derived from Latin, have traditionally belonged to the Roman Catholic Church. Slovenes have their own distinct—although Slavic—language, and were firmly Catholic. It was natural, therefore, that most people identified themselves as Serbs, Croats, or Slovenes according to both their language and their religion. But this system does not work for the Bosnian Muslims, who are either Serb or Croat by language but Islamic by religion, nor for the Montenegrins, who speak Croatian but adhered to the Orthodox Church. Curiously enough, it is the Communists, although fundamentally hostile to all religions, who have decided that the Bosnian Muslims are a 'nation'. Similarly, with the intention of encouraging the growth of a distinct Macedonian national consciousness the Communists have emphasized the differences between the Macedonian and Serbian languages (and with Bulgarian on the other side) and have helped to establish a separate Macedonian Orthodox Church. The latter decision has been a source of considerable irritation to the Serbian Church.

Since in 1921 Macedonians were counted as Serbs, it could be claimed that at that time about three-quarters of the population of Yugoslavia were either Serbs or Croats. Moreover, with the addition of the Slovenes and a few Slovaks, over 80 per cent of the population were Slavs. Unfortunately, however, these figures give a quite misleading impression of the degree of potential unity in the new Kingdom.

The people were deeply divided in two major respects: by religion, and by level of economic and social development. And these differences, in conjunction with the intrinsically less important differences of language, combined to create wide differences of culture, attitude, and behaviour.

For nearly a thousand years the western Slavs had been Catholics, and for much of that time Slovenia, Croatia, and Vojvodina had been under Austro-Hungarian rule. As a result, these peoples were 'Western' in outlook and had received some of the benefits of Western technology. On the other side of the line—a line which corresponds closely with the original division between the Western and Eastern Roman Empires—the Southern Slav peoples were Orthodox by religion and economically and socially backward. Much of this backwardness, though perhaps not all, was a consequence of the long centuries of Turkish rule. In any case, the people of Serbia, although a proud and heroic people, were overwhelmingly small peasant cultivators, using primitive methods and largely illiterate. Although Serbia became semi-independent in the early nineteenth century, and fully independent in 1878, there had been little industrial development. Macedonia, which languished under Turkish rule until 1912, was in an even worse state; and Montenegro, although preserving its independence, was a land of soldier-shepherds.

Probably the most backward of all were the people of Bosnia-Herzegovina, isolated in their wild mountain valleys, and the Albanians of Kosovo, with a different language, a different religion, and a powerful fear of their Serbian masters.

Although the level of economic and social development of each of these areas has risen enormously since 1918, and especially since 1950, many of the differences of culture, attitude, and behaviour remain. *Relative* levels of economic development are almost unchanged, or in some cases have become even more unequal. Yugoslavia is still a country, as it was in 1918, which embraces some of the most modern with some of the most traditional ways of life, a combination within the same state of what is now called on the world stage the 'North' and the 'South'.

3. THE INTER-WAR PERIOD[1]

In view of the above-mentioned wide differences in history, culture, and level of economic development it is not surprising that the creation of the new state encountered great obstacles. Although the 'Yugoslav idea' had been circulating for half a century or more, especially in Croatia, neither the majority of the Serbs nor the majority of the Croats initially favoured this solution. For the Serbs, who already had their own Kingdom, with a tradition of Serbian nationhood and of struggle for survival reaching back to the time of the Empire of Tsar Dušan in the fourteenth century, and who had never been completely crushed by four centuries of Turkish rule, the first preference was the creation of a Greater Serbia. Victory over the central powers, and the resulting collapse of Austria-Hungary, would open the door to the annexation of the Serbian-speaking areas of Vojvodina, Bosnia-Herzegovina, and Croatia. Although the boundaries of Great Serbia would probably be drawn in such a way as to include some Croats

[1] In this section I have drawn heavily on the excellent book by Seton-Watson (1945), supplemented by Hoffman and Neal (1962).

and others, there was no desire to absorb the whole of Croatia or Slovenia. Not only were the western Slavs different in language, religion and so forth, but the Serbs were—justifiably—proud of the tremendous sacrifices which they had made on the Allied side during the war, and probably not too enthusiastic to have to adjust to living with people who, although more economically advanced, had loyally fought for Austria against their Slav brethren.

Amongst the Slovenes and Croats, on the other hand, there was initially quite strong support for the idea of creating a third—Slav—Kingdom within Austria-Hungary. It was only when it became clear that in the peace settlement Austria-Hungary would be completely broken into its component parts that the Slovenes and Croats recognized that their effective choice lay between independence and a merger with Serbia. Since it was thought that a small western Slav state would be economically and politically insecure, the balance of educated opinion eventually swung behind the 'Yugoslav' solution. Once the Slovenes and Croats came round to this view it was easier to persuade the Serbs to accept it also, although they did so reluctantly. Since their acceptance of the adhesion of the Slovenes and Croats was, in a sense, a concession, the Serbs were all the more inclined to assume that it was they who would have the real authority in the new state, which would be a kind of enlargement of the original conception of a Great Serbia. This was certainly the view of King Alexander.

Although the establishment of the new Kingdom of the Serbs, Croats, and Slovenes was at first greeted with general enthusiasm, supported by a wave of pan-Slav emotion, it was not long before the Croats, in particular, began to have second thoughts. As the largest non-Serb group, accustomed to life under the sophisticated rule of Austria-Hungary, they were dismayed to find that they had exchanged Austrian rule for rule by Serbs. The new state inherited the Serbian king, the Serbian capital, and the Serbian military and civilian bureaucracy. Moreover, in the 1921 elections for the Constituent Assembly all parties except the Communists were organized on national lines, and the Serbian parties, which were inevitably in the majority, were able to disregard the Croat Peasant Party's demand for a federal constitution.

After the elections to the new Parliament, the King invited Pašić, the leader of the Serbian Radical Party, to form a government. The Croat Peasant Party, led by Radić, swept the board in Croatia but was forced into opposition in the National Assembly. Thereafter the gulf between Serbs and Croats steadily widened. There was a temporary lull in 1925 when Radić, who had been imprisoned on his return from a visit to Moscow, was unexpectedly released to join a coalition government. But no progress was made in meeting Croat demands, and after a year Radić resigned. Two years later Radić and two other Croat members were shot and killed in the assembly by a Montenegrin member. 'The Croatian members left the Parliament, and deadlock was complete. Hatred grew on both sides' (Seton-Watson 1945, 224). The King, after trying unsuccessfully to find a compromise, finally decided early in 1929 to suspend the constitution and to declare a royal dictatorship.

Later in the same year the division of the country into thirty-three departments was replaced by a set of nine new administrative districts, cutting across the old boundaries. The state was now called Yugoslavia. The intention behind this change may have been good; but the Croats saw it as a method of undermining their own demand for federation. In the circumstances, the resort to the 'Yugoslav idea' seemed to be only a cover for Great Serbism.[2] As time passed, suspicions continued to grow, and the Croats became increasingly alienated from the Kingdom of Yugoslavia. The King's Serbian officials and police ruthlessly suppressed all opposition, whether it came from Croat nationalists, impoverished peasants suffering acutely from the effects of the Great Depression, the Communists, whose party had been illegal since 1921, or the middle-class students of Belgrade University.

In 1934 Alexander was assassinated by a Macedonian terrorist while on a visit to Marseilles. He was succeeded by his cousin Prince Paul, who acted as regent for Alexander's young son Peter. Meanwhile, as a result of the Nazi victory in Germany, pressure on Yugoslavia was beginning to build up in that quarter, as well as from Mussolini, who had his eyes on parts of Yugoslavia. Paul, who was strongly anti-communist, as Alexander had been before him, and who believed that he had a talent for foreign policy, began to move towards a rapprochement with the Nazis.

On the domestic front conditions continued to deteriorate. There were some temporarily hopeful signs when a section of the Serbs agreed to unite with the Croats in order to solve the 'Croat question'. Maček, the new leader of the Croat Peasant Party, was received with enthusiasm by a crowd of 50,000 people when he arrived in Belgrade in August 1938. Many of these were Serbian peasants who were as bitterly opposed to the Serbian gendarmes as were the Croats (Seton-Watson 1945, 236). At the elections in December the Government managed to win a majority but only, it was believed, by pressure and bribery. Alarmed by the Czech crisis, Paul now moved towards an agreement with the Croats. This, the so-called *Sporazum* (meaning agreement), which was finally concluded in August 1939, gave the Croats a *Banovina*, i.e. an area of regional autonomy, covering Croatia, Dalmatia, and some parts of Bosnia-Herzegovina. But it was now the turn of the Serbs to feel discontented, insisting that they also should have a Serbian *Banovina*. Anti-Croat feeling was whipped up in Serbia, and the Croats began to respond in kind.

At this point Yugoslavia's internal problems merged with the general European crisis. Following the German–Soviet pact, which gave Germany a free hand in western and southern Europe, Poland was overrun from both sides, and in the following year Hitler's armies occupied Norway, Denmark, Holland, Belgium, and France. In 1941 Hitler moved

---

[2] There was a similar response from Croats and others in 1962 when Tito temporarily espoused the cause of 'Yugoslavism'. He quickly retreated and the official doctrine has since remained that Yugoslavia is a state, not a nation.

into Romania and, when Mussolini encountered resistance to his designs on Greece, German armies poured into Bulgaria. The Germans now began to put increasing pressure on Yugoslavia to collaborate with them, and in March the Yugoslav government signed the Tripartite Pact. This act of national betrayal produced a popular revolt, led by the army; the government fell and Paul went into exile. As Seton-Watson remarks (1945, 408), this was 'the first slap in the face that Hitler had received. It showed him that there was one people at least in Europe that cared nothing for the benefits of his New Order, that could never be bribed into gilded slavery.' He could not forgive them. Ten days later the German airforce began bombing the open city of Belgrade, and German, Italian, and Bulgarian troops began to advance into the country. Within two weeks the Yugoslav armies had collapsed and the King and his government had fled. The State of Yugoslavia was temporarily at an end.

4. THE PARTISANS[3]

By decision of the Axis powers Yugoslavia was broken into pieces. Italy annexed southern Slovenia and part of Dalmatia, and 'administered' Montenegro. Kosovo and the western parts of Macedonia, largely inhabited by Albanians, were annexed to Albania, which was already under Italian occupation. Germany annexed northern Slovenia, and Hungary took part of the Vojvodina. Bulgaria, as reward for its participation, was given the rest of Macedonia and part of southern Serbia. A new 'independent' state of Croatia was created, embracing most of Croatia and Bosnia-Herzegovina. It was placed under the rule of Ante Pavelić, leader of a Croat fascist party known as the Ustashi. The rump of Serbia was maintained as a separate state under German administration, with General Nedić, after August, as its nominal premier.

The surrender of the Yugoslav army and the flight of the government created a sense of popular confusion and despair. Never before had the Serbian state been overrun in such an ignominious fashion. In Croatia, confusion was all the greater because the Croats now received from the hands of the Axis conquerors the separate state which many of them had been so long demanding. Similarly, many Macedonians were not averse to being united with Bulgaria, with whom they had historically been closely related; and most of the Albanians of southern Serbia were probably pleased to be annexed to Albania.[4]

But the Serbs have a long tradition of resistance to foreign oppressors and, within weeks of the surrender groups of Chetniks, or guerrilla bands, were being formed in central Serbia from ex-members of the Royal Army. Most of them accepted the leadership of Colonel Mihailović, previously of the general staff, and they began limited operations against the German

[3] In this section I have drawn on Seton-Watson (1950), Hoffman and Neal (1962), and other sources.
[4] The Yugoslav Communists had, in fact, previously advocated precisely this arrangement for the Albanians.

and Italian forces. But Mihailović was essentially a Serbian nationalist, where the word Serb is taken in its widest sense, to include Montenegrins and the Serbs of Bosnia-Herzegovina and Croatia. Although he was loyal to his Serbian King, Mihailović was not particularly well disposed towards Croats, Muslims, Albanians, or any of the other Yugoslav minorities. Moreover, he was anxious to preserve his own people from the terrible losses which they had suffered during the First World War. This caution was powerfully reinforced by the German announcement that for every German soldier killed by resisters, 100 hostages would be shot, a policy which was duly implemented in Kragujevac in October when about 7,000 inhabitants were massacred.

Within the boundaries of the new state of Croatia Pavelić's Ustashi were soon active in hounding all non-Croats, mainly Serbs, Jews, and Muslims, and either forcibly converting them to Catholicism or killing them. The Serbian Chetniks attempted to protect their own people, but frequently extended their operations to retaliate against all Croats and Muslims found in the area. As a consequence, Croatia became the scene of terrible fratricidal strife, in the course of which many hundreds of thousands of people were killed. Similarly, in Montenegro the Italians encouraged the Albanians to take revenge on the Montenegrin Serbs for centuries of discrimination.

When the war broke out, the Communist Party of Yugoslavia had a membership of about 8,000, of whom 3,000 were in prison. In addition, the Young Communist League, an auxiliary organization, had a membership of about 30,000 (Vusković, 1981). The Yugoslav Communists were fervent supporters of the Soviet Union, which was then collaborating with the Nazis. The Communist International had denounced the war between Germany and the Western democracies as an imperialist war in which the workers, especially in the West, should be encouraged to do everything possible to weaken the resistance of their own governments. The same doctrine was spread in Yugoslavia right up to the day of the German invasion. The Communists claim that they immediately began to prepare plans for resistance. But, in fact, they did nothing overtly until after the German invasion of the Soviet Union on June 22. As soon as this happened, the 'imperialist' war became a 'just patriotic' war for the defence of the Soviet Union, and the Yugoslav Communists, like others elsewhere, rallied to the support of the Soviet Union.

The German invasion of the Soviet Union had an electrifying effect in Serbia, where there were long memories of Russian support for Serbian independence, and where pan-Slav emotions were mixed, in many cases, with pro-Soviet attitudes, especially among the students and the poorer peasants. Moreover, Russian and Communist propaganda had convinced most people that the Red Army would rapidly throw back any invader, and that within a few months Nazi Germany would be defeated. As a result, many Serbian peasants spontaneously rose in revolt against the Germans. By September the Communists had established a headquarters in western Serbia for the control of their own resistance forces, which they now called partisans. Josip Broz, under the *nom de guerre* of Tito, was the Secretary-General of the Party. He and the other members of the Politburo, mainly younger men previously promoted by Tito and intensely loyal to him, became the General Staff of the new resistance movement.

In comparison with Mihailović, the Communists had one disadvantage and a number of advantages. The disadvantage, for the majority of the population, was that their ultimate aim was clearly to use the present emergency as a means of hoisting themselves into power and eventually to introduce a communist system. But against this they had enormous advantages. In the first place, they were activists, which appealed to the Serbian military tradition. Secondly, they were well organized. Thirdly, they were not only pro-Yugoslav, but were also unashamedly pro-Soviet, at a time when the two streams had suddenly flowed together. Finally, and perhaps most important of all, the Communists were not tied to any one national or religious group, but could clearly enunciate the goal of unity of all Yugoslavs, irrespective of nationality or religion, against the common enemy. So, while Mihailović's Chetniks held back from confrontations with the Germans in Serbia, and became increasingly entangled in the civil war raging in Croatia between Serbs, Croats, Muslims, and others, Tito and the partisans could stand forth as champions of all-Yugoslav 'brotherhood and unity' in the common struggle against the fascist invaders.

For a few months the main partisan headquarters was at Užice in western Serbia, on the edge of the mountain 'heartland', but there were other partisan groups operating in Montenegro and Slovenia, and sporadic resistance developed elsewhere. In November the Germans drove Tito and his partisan forces out of Užice into the Bosnian mountains, where they formed a new headquarters at Foča. But for the next two years they were almost continually on the move as the Germans, and to a less extent the Italians, launched offensives against them. Their forces steadily grew, with most recruits coming from peasants in the war zone itself, supplemented by an inflow of volunteers from towns and villages in the more populated areas of Serbia and Croatia.

The partisans never disguised the fact that they were under Communist control, and in Foča they created shock troops under the title of 'Proletarian Brigades', a decision which met with strong disapproval from the Russians, who were at that time doing their best to emphasize the purely patriotic aspects of their own war. This may, indeed, have been the beginning of the eventual rift between the Yugoslav and Soviet Communists. In the areas under their control the partisans established People's Liberation Committees, which were popular organizations supported by local sympathizers. A year later, at Bihać in north-west Bosnia, the Communists arranged a meeting of an Anti-Fascist Council for the National Liberation of Yugoslavia which included some non-Communist participants. But within a few months the partisans were driven out of Bihać and for almost the whole of 1943 they were on the run. At first they retreated into Montenegro, but later they carried out a desperate march back again toward the north-west in the course of which they came close to being destroyed. By heroic efforts and with enormous sacrifices they survived, and all this time their reputation was increasing, both inside Yugoslavia and in the outside world.

The partisans received a splendid windfall when Italy collapsed in September 1943. There were large Italian supplies of arms, ammunition, and equipment in Dalmatia, Montenegro, and western Bosnia; and the partisans managed to capture most of it. Recruits began to flow in more rapidly from the Croats in these areas, and even from some Serbian Chetniks. The partisans, who had by now been officially recognized by the Allies, established communications with the Allied forces in Italy and began to receive some supplies from them. In November they summoned the Anti-Fascist Council to a new meeting in Jajce and converted it, in effect, into a provisional government of Yugoslavia. Tito was made a Marshal, to the considerable annoyance of Stalin, who persisted, even after the war, in calling Tito by his old Comintern name of Walter.

During all this time Mihailović's Chetniks had continued to operate in all contested areas. But they had become increasingly hostile to the partisans. These attitudes led them at first into a neutral position between the partisans and the Axis authorities, and later into acts of collaboration with the occupying forces. Mihailović increasingly lost support among the population and eventually, under British pressure, he was abandoned by the Royal government in exile. Thereafter, his forces gradually melted away and the partisans achieved complete mastery of the Yugoslav resistance movement.

Meanwhile the Red Army was steadily pushing the Germans back, out of Russia itself and into eastern Europe. In the spring of 1944 partisan activity revived in western Serbia and when, in the autumn of that year, the Red Army approached Belgrade the partisans were already in control of the whole of western Serbia and could participate in the entry into Belgrade. By agreement with the Russians, Tito and his Council for National Liberation were given control of Belgrade. The Council was enlarged by the addition of some non-Communist members, who were either Communist sympathizers or were rendered impotent by their minority position. One or two non-Communist politicians were also included in the Committee for National Liberation, which was a provisional government. The war continued in the north and west of the country until May 1945, and during this time both the partisan armies and the Communist Party grew in size. Communist control over the areas which they occupied became virtually complete.

In November 1945 elections were held for the Constituent Assembly. A single list of candidates was nominated by the People's Front, a Communist-controlled 'front' which included a few representatives of the non-Communist parties. Candidates of other parties were harassed and restricted in every possible way. Many of their leaders and supporters were accused of collaboration and hence disfranchised. Eventually, the two non-Communist ministers, Šubašić and Grol, resigned from the government and called on their supporters to boycott the elections. With no opposition candidates in the field, and in view of the considerable popularity of Tito and the partisans, it is not surprising that the People's Front won an overwhelming victory, although the official figure of 96 per cent of the vote is suspect. From that moment onwards Yugoslavia bacame a one-party Communist state.

5. THE STALINIST PERIOD

The Party which took power in Yugoslavia was a strictly Marxist-Leninist Party. It believed in the dictatorship of the proletariat, to be operated by the Communist Party as the vanguard of the proletariat. No other parties would be tolerated; indeed, with one exception, no other organizations of any kind would be allowed to exist unless they were under the control of the Communist Party. The one exception was the Church, which could not easily be suppressed. But, so far as possible, the churches were emasculated and restricted. They were strictly prohibited from engaging in education or in expressing views about political or social questions.

All printing and publishing was quickly brought under Party control, and radio and other means of communication were used to push a single set of propaganda themes provided by the Party. An elaborate secret police system was created, giving the Party officials in charge of it, and largely staffing it, enormous power over the whole population, including the Party itself. The head of this police apparatus, Ranković, was also the member of the Politburo in charge of all appointments to positions of authority in the Party itself, in government, in industry, in the army, and in every social organization except the Church.

Since all of industry, trade, and services, except the smallest 'artisan' workshops, were rapidly nationalized, the state had total power over these sectors of the economy. Managers were appointed by Communist ministers and given detailed instructions on what to produce, with what materials, with whom to trade, and at what prices. This central planning system, which also included central decisions about investments, location of industry and foreign trade was, like the whole of the rest of the system, a strict copy of the Stalinist Soviet system.

Unlike the rest of the People's Democracies of Eastern Europe, which were brought under Communist dictatorship only by stages, Yugoslavia, under its genuinely popular People's Front government, plunged ahead into full-blown Stalinism from the moment of victory. The only temporary exception was that the peasants, although harassed and pushed around by the new government, were not forcibly collectivized until 1949. But this was always the Party's clear intention. It was held back by the magnitude of the task of bullying 70 per cent of the population into doing something which they detested; and by the fact that the overwhelming majority of the partisans, and at least half of the Party itself at that time, were either peasants or of recent peasant origin.

In foreign relations the Yugoslav government was the most ardent and loyal supporter of the Soviet Union, and often pushed itself forward at the

United Nations as a spokesman from the most extreme Communist views. There was even some talk in the Yugoslav Party about joining the Soviet Union. But this was only a temporary aberration. The Serbs, and especially the Montenegrins, who, because of their exceptional role in the partisan movement, held many leading positions in the Party and the army, have a strong tradition of independence. And the long and victorious partisan struggle had endowed the Party and the Yugoslav people as a whole with a sense of their national achievement. There was, therefore, never any serious possibility that they would agree to subordinate themselves to a foreign power, even to the great and, at that time, much respected Soviet Union.

It is, at first sight, a remarkable paradox that during the years 1945–8, when Stalin was undermining and finally bringing under his control all the other countries of Eastern Europe, the Yugoslavs, who had been the most faithful and consistent supporters of the Soviet Union, were moving in the opposite direction. The explanation is, of course, that while the other Communist governments of Eastern Europe were Soviet puppets, the Yugoslav Communists had fought their way to power and popularity by their own efforts. They were not beholden to Stalin. They regarded him as their great leader and teacher. But their first loyalty was to their own people, the source of their own authority.

Small signs of cracks in the Soviet–Yugoslav relationship soon began to appear. The Red Army, in temporary occupation of Belgrade, treated the Yugoslav population not as dear Slav cousins and comrades but as objects of looting and raping; and the Yugoslav Party leaders complained. Stalin never forgave them for that. Then the Russians failed to give Yugoslavia full support in its demand for the cession of Trieste from Italy. Next, the Russians proposed arrangements for certain joint-stock companies, in air transport and in river transport on the Danube, on highly inequitable financial terms. Finally, the Yugoslavs discovered that the Russians were recruiting Yugoslav citizens into their intelligence services, to operate on Yugoslav soil, and clearly with only one intention—to spy on the Yugoslav Party and government.

But it was not the Yugoslavs who took the initiative in bringing matters to a head. Indeed, even after their formal expulsion from the Cominform (the body which had been set up to act as a partial substitute for the Communist International) they were still shouting 'Long live the Soviet Union! Long live Stalin!' (Hoffman and Neal 1962, 141.) At some point Stalin decided that the Yugoslavs were behaving in an intolerable fashion, and must be taught a lesson. There was a whole catalogue of incidents leading up to the final break. But Stalin chose to confuse the Yugoslavs by constantly changing the suggestions which he made about their relations with their Balkan neighbours. At one moment he encouraged the idea of a Yugoslav–Bulgarian merger. At another he denounced this proposal. On one occasion the suggested to the Yugoslav leaders that they should annex Albania. Later, this suggestion was repudiated and used to incriminate them. Stalin was an outstandingly clever manipulator, cunning and ruthless. The Yugoslavs, although self-confident, were in his judgement mere country cousins. Because of their naïve belief in him, they came close to being ensnared. But their fundamental good sense and national loyalty always reasserted themselves.

The more that the Yugoslavs resisted Stalin's manoeuvres the more furious he became. In the spring of 1948 he began his final campaign to bring them to heel. His first step was to postpone negotiations for a renewal of the Soviet–Yugoslav trade agreement, which was the keystone of Yugoslav economic policy. Tito called a meeting of the Yugoslav Party's Central Committee, in the course of which he said that the issue was now Yugoslavia's independence. The Soviet's main supporter, Andrija Hebrang, was expelled from the Committee. The Rusians responded by withdrawing all military and civilian advisers. Tito now wrote on behalf of the Yugoslav Central Committee to the Soviet Central Committee saying, *inter alia*, 'we are deeply hurt by not being informed of the true reason for this decision by the government of the USSR', and asking for an explanation. This led to an increasingly acrimonious correspondence between the two Parties in the course of which the Russians wrote three long letters and the Yugoslavs several.[5]

In their first letter, the Russians accused the Yugoslavs of being anti-Soviet, and of having Trotskyist and Bukharinist tendencies. Their leaders were accused of making derogatory remarks in private, such as 'the CPSU is degenerate', or 'socialism in the Soviet Union has ceased to be revolutionary'. Individual leaders—Djilas, Vukmanović-Tempo, Kidrič and Ranković—were named as the authors of such remarks. The Yugoslav Party was accused of hiding itself behind the People's Front and of being undemocratic. Vladimir Velebit, a leading partisan commander and then Deputy Foreign Minister, was denounced as an 'English spy', and it was alleged that the Yugoslav government was fully aware of this fact.

In their reply, the Yugoslavs used a telling phrase: 'No matter how much each of us loves the land of Socialism, the USSR, he can, in no case, love his own country less.' The Yugoslavs explained that they had asked the Soviets to reduce the number of their military experts because the Soviets demanded that their experts should be paid four times as much as a Yugoslav minister. The alleged criticisms of the Soviet Union were repudiated. Djilas and the others were, and always had been, completely loyal to the Soviet Union. The Communist Party of Yugoslavia was not hiding behind the People's Front: 'the CPY has a completely assured leadership in the People's Front because the CPY is the nucleus of the People's Front'. The Soviets were accused of recruiting intelligence agents in Yugoslavia, including 'various leaders'. But the Yugoslavs claimed to be the Soviets' 'most faithful friend and ally'. 'Our only desire is to eliminate every doubt and disbelief in the purity of the comradely and brotherly feeling of loyalty of our CC of the CPY to the CPSU. . . .'

[5] Only three have been published. Details of this correspondence, given below, are taken from Bass and Marbury (1959).

The Soviet response to this moderate, almost cringing, letter, was vicious. Written in a peremptory, dictatorial style, the letter accused the Yugoslavs of lying and of deliberately creating difficulties. No such complaints as those made by the Yugoslavs had been made in other People's Democracies. As regards the pay of Soviet generals, the rates expected were the same as those paid in the Soviet Union. The Soviet ambassador, as a Communist and a representative of the Soviet Union, as well as other Soviet officials, had a perfect right to ask Yugoslav Party members and others for information about their Party and other matters. The Soviet government had bitterly resented a speech of Tito's of May 1945 in which he had implied that the Soviet Union had betrayed Yugoslavia's right to Trieste. The Yugoslav leaders, accused of 'unbounded arrogance', were said to 'feel that the depth of the sea reaches only up to their knees'. The other Communist Parties of Eastern Europe had done just as much as the Yugoslavs. (This was probably the most wounding and infuriating remark.) The Yugoslavs had contributed nothing new to partisan warfare, which was invented long ago by the Spaniards. The letter contained a new, and sinister, reference to Trotsky who, 'in his time . . . also rendered revolutionary services'. The Soviet Party refused to enter into direct negotiations about all these matters. Instead, it proposed to bring them up at the next meeting of the Cominform.

The Yugoslavs replied briefly. They referred to the 'discouraging impression created on us' by the Soviet's last letter. They refused to be arraigned in front of the Cominform, where they would be 'at such a disadvantage', since the other eight Parties had already publicly condemned them. But they concluded by promising to 'remain loyal to the Soviet Union; remain loyal to the doctrine of Marx, Engels, Lenin and Stalin'.

In their final letter the Soviet Party rejected the Yugoslav claim that they would be at a disadvantage at the meeting of the Cominform. Disingenuously, the Russians claimed that in that forum there would be a genuine democratic discussion between brotherly Parties. The Yugoslavs were accused of deviating from Marxism-Leninism and of extreme ignorance of Marxist principles. The promises made by the Yugoslav leaders were false and worthless. The Yugoslav Politburo, and Tito in particular, were guilty of 'anti-Soviet and anti-Russian policy'. If they refused to attend the Cominform meeting, that would be a tacit admission of guilt and a step towards 'betrayal of the united front of people's democracies and the USSR', leading to nationalism and hostility to the working class.

On 28 June 1949, the ominous anniversary of Vidovdan, the day on which the Serbs were decisively defeated by the Turks in 1389, the Cominform adopted a resolution which, in effect, expelled the Yugoslav Party from the world Communist movement. The Yugoslav Party leaders were accused of deviation from Marxism-Leninism, of being hostile to the Soviet Union and the Soviet Party, of borrowing from 'the arsenal of counter-revolutionary Trotskyism', of becoming nationalists, of ignoring the class struggle in agriculture, of disguising the role of the Party, of refusing to accept criticism, and of 'boundless ambition, arrogance and conceit'. The source of the trouble was alleged to be the fact that 'during the past five or six months' nationalist elements had taken over a dominant position in the leadership of the Yugoslav Party, and that this 'can only lead to Yugoslavia's degeneration into an ordinary bourgeois republic, to the loss of its independence and to its transformation into a colony of the imperialist countries'. The resolution concluded with an appeal to 'healthy elements' in the Party to 'compel their present leaders to recognize their mistakes openly and honestly and to rectify them' and, if necessary, 'to replace them and to advance a new internationalist leadership of the Party'.

The appeal to pro-Soviet members of the Yugoslav Party was unsuccessful. Two members of the Yugoslav Central Committee, Hebrang and Žujović, had previously been arrested; General Arso Jovanović, former chief of staff, was shot while trying to cross into Romania; and two other high officers, who had escaped, were later captured and imprisoned. According to Djilas (1980, 82–7) some 15,000 'Cominformists' (of whom 7,000 were army officers) were arrested and sent to the newly created concentration camp on the Adriatic island of Goli Otok. But the overwhelming majority of the Party supported their leaders, who now also became more popular with many non-Communists.

The Soviet bloc next attempted to bring Yugoslavia to its knees by enforcing an economic blockade. The ambitious Five-Year Plan depended crucially on trade with the Soviet Union and Eastern Europe, which took 50 per cent of Yugoslav exports in 1945 and provided nearly as large a proportion of its imports. Deliveries of goods from these countries began to slow down from the autumn of 1948, and by 1950 all trade between Yugoslavia and Eastern Europe had ceased. The effect on the Yugoslav economy was disastrous. The situation was made worse by the wanton attempt, launched in 1949, to collectivize the peasants, by a severe drought in 1950, and by mounting defence expenditures. By 1952 industrial production had fallen below its 1949 level, although fixed capital in industry had increased by more than a quarter. Aid from the West was not actively sought for some time, but Britain, France, and the United States all offered help, and by the end of 1950 the United States had begun a programme of assistance which grew in scale over subsequent years. As a result, the Yugoslavs began to moderate their previous extreme anti-Western attitudes.

Finally, it became clear to the Yugoslav leaders that there was no prospect of healing their rift with the Soviet Union except by accepting total subordination, which they refused. They were, therefore, confronted by the necessity of steering a new course. In the absence of support from the Communist countries, they would need to rely on (1) their own people, and (2) assistance from the West. For both these reasons, they were gradually forced to recognize the need to re-examine their fundamental strategy and ideology. Clearly, they could no longer continue to hold up the Soviet system as a model, when they were receiving from that direction nothing but foul abuse and deliberate efforts to sabotage their own economy. As intelligent and courageous men, they were led to search for the basic reasons for the evil face of Soviet Communism. While some were willing to place all the blame on Stalin, this was not a sound Marxist method of interpreting disagreeable phenomena. Nor was it a sufficient way of differentiating themselves from the Soviet bloc. If they were to strengthen the resolve of their own Party and sympathizers among the population, it was necessary to have a deeper, ideological, explanation of the rift.

From a theoretical re-examination of Marxism and a comparison of that theory with the practice of the Soviet Union the Yugoslav leaders came, by degrees, to the point of complete rejection, not only of Stalin personally but of Stalinism, which they defined as state, or bureaucratic, socialism. Later they were to call this '*etatisam*', or 'statism'. But for Marxists it is not enough to find fault with political phenomena, which are merely part of the superstructure. If a system is bad, it must be because there is something wrong at the economic base, in the 'relations of production'. So the Yugoslavs began to reconsider the system of nationalized industries and central planning which they had taken over from the Soviet Union. And this led them, perhaps instinctively rather than purely rationally, to the idea of decentralized socialism, or 'factories to the workers'. So began their long journey towards the creation of a 'self-management' system. The main stages in that journey will be described in the following chapter.

CHAPTER 5

THE EVOLUTION OF YUGOSLAV
SELF-MANAGEMENT

1. THE NATURE OF THE PROCESS

The Yugoslav system of enterprise self-management evolved over a period of twenty-five years, approximately from 1949 to 1974. The first steps were tentative and, although in introducing them some high-sounding principles and objectives were enunciated, there was not much immediate change in practice. Nevertheless, the Party had chosen a new path and, since the reasons for making that choice grew stronger over time, it continued along the new path without knowing precisely where it would lead. Important legal and institutional changes were made in almost every one of these twenty-five years, but there were three periods of especially active reform (during each of which Yugoslavia was given a new constitution). The first such period was from 1949 to 1953; the second from 1961 to 1965; and the third from 1971 to 1974. New constitutions were adopted in 1953, 1963, and 1974. After 1974 some important laws were introduced to specify in more detail the methods of applying the 1974 constitution, in particular the Law on Associated Labour of 1976, which was intended to be a complete codification of enterprise behaviour. There have also been minor subsequent changes in constitutional practice and, of course, many changes in current economic policy. So far, however, there has been no proposal for any fundamental new amendments to the 1974 system. But, given the Yugoslav propensity to experiment and to adjust to new situations, there is no guarantee that such changes will not occur in the future.

Before we look more closely at the history of this period, it will be useful to consider the main motives which drove the reformers forward and the obstacles which stood in their path. For it is only from an understanding of these underlying determinants of the process that one can make sense of the actual evolution of the reforms.

The first motive was to create a new ideology. The Communist Party, as the self-appointed vanguard of the proletariat and ruler of society, is obliged to have a conscious ideology, a theoretical justification for its role and programme. Otherwise, it might eventually relapse into being a mere servant of the people instead of its master.[1] When the Yugoslav

---

[1] One of Lenin's famous dicta was: 'Without a revolutionary theory there can be no revolutionary movement.'

Communists took power they were equipped with the orthodox Soviet interpretation of Marxist-Leninist theory, codified by Stalin. At first they saw their task as making a simple copy of Soviet practice, for which Soviet theory would be the perfect justification. None of the Yugoslav leaders had made any important contribution to Marxist theory. Indeed, if any of them had dared to do so before the war, they would have been purged; and any who were so unwise as to visit Moscow would have been 'liquidated', like many of their compatriots.[2] But in 1948 this comfortable world of orthodoxy was shattered. The Soviet Union, with Stalin at its head, and followed by the other member parties of the Cominform, turned savagely on the Yugoslav Party leaders and denounced them as anti-Marxists and anti-Soviet. Within a few more months they were being described as Trotskyists, spies, fascists, imperialist agents, and murderers.

The shock of this experience was so great that at first the Yugoslav leaders simply did not believe it. They said, and they probably believed, that it was all a great mistake. No one was more orthodox than they. But gradually it became clear that there was no mistake. Stalin intended to destroy them and to absorb Yugoslavia into his empire, along with the other satellite countries. Since the Yugoslavs were not prepared to submit, but were determined to maintain their independence against the Russians, just as they had done against the Germans, there opened up a yawning 'contradiction' between the acceptance of Soviet Marxist theory on the one hand and the rejection of Soviet domination on the other. Sooner or later it would become a matter of urgency to discover a theoretical explanation for Soviet behaviour and a theoretical justification for Yugoslav independence. Since the Yugoslav leaders had no intention of abandoning their right to call themselves Marxists, which was their only long-term justification for retaining power, the new theory would have to be a reinterpretation of Marxism-Leninism or, as their opponents would call it, a 'revision'.

To start with, the Yugoslavs concentrated on the immediate need to find a theoretical explanation for the Soviet policy of 'hegemony'. But, once theory's box was opened, it proved impossible to stop at that point. If Stalin was an imperialist, there must be some explanation for his rise to power in a Communist state. So the internal situation in the Soviet Union had to be examined. This suggested the existence of a 'bureaucratic deformation' of the socialist system.[3] But, to a Marxist, such a political phenomenon must have an economic explanation. It was along this path that the Yugoslavs eventually came to the concept of self-management, which they saw as the answer to the whole tangled problem. It was the absence of self-management, the existence of the great centralized power of the state over the economy, which accounted for the Soviet deviation

---

[2] Tito survived partly because the Yugoslav government kept him in prison for many years, thus preventing him from visiting Moscow for more than a short time during the period of the Stalinist purges, and partly because he was not a theoretician.

[3] This was, of course, the conclusion reached much earlier by Trotsky and his supporters.

from Marxism. The obvious implication was that Yugoslavia must reduce the power of the state and move towards self-management.

The second motive for reform, at least at the beginning, was the acute economic difficulties created by the Cominform blockade. In order to survive the period of austerity which this imposed, it was necessary to strengthen the morale of the people. The main instrument for morale-building was the appeal to patriotism and the old partisan spirit. But the regime could also win popularity by announcing measures to reduce central authority, to encourage local participation and to give greater management rights to the workers. At the same time the blockade forced the Yugoslavs to search for other trading partners, primarily in the West, but in any case with market-economy countries. Such trade is best promoted by independent enterprises which can deal directly with their foreign trade partners. From a political point of view, also, if Yugoslavia wanted to receive credits from the West to replace those cancelled by the Soviet bloc, it would be an advantage to show that the Yugoslav system was no longer the standard centrally-planned Soviet-type system.

The third motive for reform, which was probably only of minor importance at the beginning, but which steadily grew in influence as the years passed, was the suspicion felt by the non-Serb nations for any kind of centralized political and economic system. On this point there was a clear inner contradiction within the system. During the war the Party's greatest source of popularity was its slogan of 'brotherhood and unity'. In the Jajce declaration of 1943 the Anti-Fascist Council of National Liberation had firmly insisted on the need for a post-war federation in which no single nation would dominate; and the 1946 Constitution, honouring that promise, created a federation of six republics and two autonomous provinces (one of which, Kosovo, was for a few years called an autonomous region). The Constitution, moreover, explicitly gave the republics the nominal right to secede. Yet, at the same time, the government which now held power was committed to a system of central planning. All decisions about economic matters, ranging from general policies down to the location of new enterprises and the precise arrangements for the operation of existing enterprises, were taken in Belgrade. While this system may have been tolerable for the first few years of emergency reconstruction, it was obviously incompatible with genuine federalism. To many Yugoslavs, especially the non-Serbs, it must have seemed that Communist federalism boiled down to old-style Royal Serbian centralism in a new dress. Even if there had never been a quarrel with Stalin, it is unlikely that Yugoslavia could have maintained such an arrangement indefinitely.

While these were the main motives for the search for a new ideology and a new political and economic system, the Yugoslav leaders were obliged to overcome a number of difficulties before they could reach their objectives. In the first place, they started by being committed Stalinists, who not only themselves believed in Stalin but had recruited and instructed hundreds of thousands of young Party members in the same spirit. It was a terrible psychological experience for them to be forced to criticize Stalin and the Soviet Union. Indeed, in the case of Tito himself, it is doubtful whether he ever brought himself to the point of making a fundamental critique. Secondly, as already mentioned, the Yugoslav leaders were not expert Marxist theoreticians. Thirdly, there was, in any case, very little in the writings of Marx, Engels, and Lenin which dealt specifically with the organization of a socialist society. They had made a few *obiter dicta*, but none of them had written even a dozen pages which gave a coherent account of how the new socialist system would work in practice. The nearest which any of them came to this was Lenin's booklet on *State and Revolution*, written in great haste during the interlude between the February and October Revolutions. The most notable features of this work are, first, that it says scarcely anything very precise about the economic organization of a socialist system and, secondly, that virtually everything it prescribes for the political system was ignored by the Bolsheviks once they were in power.[4] This was the main text which the Yugoslav theoreticians used in their efforts to criticize Stalinism and to develop an alternative system of ideas and institutions in Yugoslavia.

There was one further problem, which was the greatest of them all. While the Yugoslav leaders needed an ideological justification for their resistance to Stalin, it was essential that any new ideology should not weaken their own position as the vanguard, and hence the unchallengeable rulers of Yugoslavia. Thus, while self-management could be used as a concept with which to criticize bureaucratic, or state, socialism, it must not be allowed to weaken the monopoly position of the Party.[5] This is, however, an impossible requirement. Either the workers are genuinely allowed to make their own decisions, which is the only logical interpretation of the concept of self-management, or they are constantly being monitored, 'led' or bullied by the Party into doing what the Party believes to be in their best interests; in which case 'self-management' is just another empty hypocritical phrase like 'Soviet democracy'. The history of the evolution of self-management in Yugoslavia cannot be understood

[4] On the economic organization of socialism Lenin suggested that the Communists would 'organise the *whole* economy on the lines of the postal service so that the technicians, foremen and accountants, as well as *all* officials, shall receive salaries no higher than "a workman's wage" ' (*State and Revolution*, Chapter III, Section 3). 'The whole of society will have become a single office and a single factory, with equality of labour and pay' (Chapter V, Section 4). He was prepared to accept Kautsky's suggestion that in every large enterprise the workers should elect a 'sort of parliament' to supervise the management (Chapter VI, Section 2), but he made no attempt to reconcile these two ideas. In practice, the Bolsheviks very quickly got rid of workers' councils and established complete central control over socialized enterprises. In *State and Revolution* there is a passing reference to planning, but nothing at all about the role of the market under socialism. The description of how political authority and administration would be organized under socialism—with rotation, recall, workman's wages, and so on, not only for the politicians but also for the bureaucrats—is the most astonishing piece of deception ever practised by a serious politician.

[5] It was on this issue that Djilas in 1953 'broke the rules', separated himself from the others, and was immediately repudiated and excluded from power.

correctly unless one looks behind each institutional change to discover what were its real effects on the locus of power.

2. THE FIRST STEPS: 1949–53

For nearly a year after the Cominform denunciation there was no overt sign that the Yugoslavs intended to start a real deviation from Stalinist ideology and practice. It is true that Djilas, in a speech at a meeting of the Central Committee in January 1949, accused the Soviet Party of revisionism, and forecast that the conflict between the two Parties would 'inevitably sharpen' (Johnson 1972, 79). But it was not until May, when Kardelj addressed the Skupština (parliament), that the first indications of the nature of the differences began to appear. Kardelj did not attack the Soviet Union directly; but, by pressing the argument that socialism requires not only a revolution but, as Lenin had emphasized in *State and Revolution*, the immediate beginning of the process of 'withering away' of the state, he implicitly launched a critique of Soviet practice. Kardelj was speaking in support of a law designed to give somewhat greater powers to the local people's committees, i.e. to local government. In passing, he also suggested that the directors of enterprises should consult 'with groups of the best workers on all questions of managing the enterprise' (Johnson 1972, 88). It may have been a lagged response to this suggestion which led the Politburo of the Party in December to order the establishment of workers' councils as advisory bodies in 215 large enterprises (Johnson 1972, 161). But the first real step forward towards self-management was not made until June 1950, when Tito proposed to the Skupština the Basic Law on the Management of State Economic Enterprises and Higher Economic Associations by the Work Collectives.

There is no published record of the discussions which led up to this momentous decision.[6] But a brief account has been given by Djilas in an interesting passage in one of his books. He wrote as follows (Djilas 1969, 157–8):

Soon after the outbreak of the quarrel with Stalin, in 1949, as far as I remember, I began to reread Marx's *Capital*, this time with much greater care, to see if I could find the answer to the riddle of why, to put it in simplistic terms, Stalinism was bad and Yugoslavia was good. I discovered many new ideas and, most interesting of all, ideas about a future society in which the immediate producers, through free association, would themselves make the decisions regarding production and distribution—would, in effect, run their own lives and their own future.

The country was in the stranglehold of the bureaucracy, and the party leaders were in the grip of rage and horror over the incorrigibly arbitrary nature of the party machine they had set up and that kept them in power. One day—it must have been in the spring of 1950—it occurred to me that we Yugoslav Communists were

[6] This is characteristic of Communist 'democratic centralism'. Important decisions are always taken in secret by a few people at the top. Sometimes they are discussed and voted on by the Party, or by its various committees. But in these discussions anyone who dared to criticize or oppose the leadership's proposals would be denounced as an enemy of the Party. Hence, either such votes are unanimous or the objectors are expelled.

now in a position to start creating Marx's free association of producers. The factories would be left in their hands, with the sole proviso that they should pay a tax for military and other state needs 'still remaining essential'.

He mentioned the idea to Kardelj and Kidrič, 'while we sat in a car parked in front of the villa where I lived'. He found that he was 'able all too easily to convince them of the indisputable harmony' between his ideas and Marx's teaching. But both thought that it would need another five or six years before such a plan could be implemented. Next day, however, Kidrič telephoned to say that he wanted to go ahead immediately. Discussions with the trade union leaders and others continued for some months and a Workers' Self-Management Bill to establish workers' councils was drafted. Tito was busy with other matters and often absent abroad. When, at a late stage, he was told about the Bill by Kardelj and Djilas, his first reaction was that 'our workers are not ready for that yet'. But Kardelj and Djilas pressed him.

The most important part of our case was that this would be the beginning of democracy, something that socialism had not yet achieved; further, it could be plainly seen by the world and the international workers' movement as a radical departure from Stalinism. Tito paced up and down, as though completely wrapped in his own thoughts. Suddenly he stopped and exclaimed: 'Factories belonging to the workers—something that has never yet been achieved!'

He immediately gave his approval.

Whether this is an accurate description of the birth of the idea of workers' management it is difficult to know. Kidrič died in 1953 and Kardelj, who lived until 1979, never published any memoirs. But it has about it the ring of truth, especially the sudden Djilas vision, the quick, almost casual, acceptance by the other two, and above all Tito's conversion, not on any theoretical grounds, not from a rereading of the Marxist texts, but on a pragmatic political basis. Here was a fine new slogan, a slogan that would differentiate the Yugoslavs from all other Communist countries, and one that would go down well with the Yugoslav people at a time when they were faced with deep economic difficulties.

It seems unlikely that, at that point, any of the four—Djilas, Kardelj, Kidrič and Tito—had thought out the wider economic implications of the new proposal. Their main preoccupation was to differentiate Yugoslavia from Stalinism in the political sphere, to claim that Yugoslavia was not a 'statist' system but a real workers' democracy. But it is possible that, even at this stage, nationalist centrifugal tendencies were already beginning to be felt. Devolution of power to the enterprises would inevitably weaken the power of Belgrade, although it would not necessarily increase the powers of the republics.

The immediate effects of the new law were small. Workers' councils were to be established in all socialized enterprises and, in theory, they had powers of management. But, since the state continued to appoint the directors and to specify each firm's inputs, outputs, wage levels, and investment expenditures, the councils' functions were merely advisory.

Decisions about hiring and firing of labour remained in the province of the director, although in the latter case there was provision for appeals (Rusinow 1977, 58–9). Nevertheless, the creation of elected workers' councils, even if their powers were largely nominal, prepared the way for a movement towards an entirely new economic system, a system of market socialism.

Officially, Yugoslav socialism goes under the title of 'self-management'. But, as will be shown later, although there are elements of workers' management in Yugoslav enterprises, it is impossible to maintain that the workers 'really' manage. Self-management has been, and still is to some extent, a popular slogan, an expression of hope and of ultimate aim; but the essence of the Yugoslav system is decentralization. Although the question of who really controls enterprise policy in Yugoslavia is difficult to answer precisely, the existence of a system of decentralized management clearly requires some sort of market economy. Under full central planning, enterprise managers have little scope for independent decisions, and scarcely any incentive to show initiative or to try to satisfy their customers. The great achievement of the Yugoslav system is that it has given managers both the opportunity and the incentive to show initiative and to respond to market stimuli, even if these opportunities and incentives are more limited than under capitalism.

One must assume that at some point in 1950 or 1951 the Yugoslav leaders began to recognize that their main objective was not self-management as such but a market system. Self-management was a means of legitimizing the market, of differentiating it from capitalism. Having set up workers' councils, the Party leaders' next moves were in the direction of dismantling centralized planning and forcing enterprises to face the market. At the end of 1950, Kidrič began to speak about 'socialist commodity production', i.e. a system of socialist ownership combined with a market (Johnson 1972, 165). In April 1951 the Federal Planning Commission was abolished, together with most federal and republican economic ministries and directorates-general, and at the end of the year a new Law on the Planned Management of the National Economy was passed. Under this law, central planning was replaced by indicative planning, with no compulsory powers (Rusinow 1977, 62–3). In spite of many subsequent legal changes, this has remained the position ever since.

Although enterprise managers were now obliged to direct their thoughts to the market, there were still government controls over prices, wages, imports, and investment expenditures. Moreover, the government levied heavy taxes on enterprise revenues through the so-called 'rate of accumulation and funds'. The rate was fixed for each enterprise as a proportion of its total wage and material costs with the aim of leaving it with a planned residual, or 'surplus' (Milenkovitch 1971, 85–6). To begin with, the workers' councils had no power to dispose of this surplus.

During 1951 and 1952 there were several efforts to free prices, and several devaluations. In the latter year it was decided to give the communes (the local governments) the right to appoint enterprise directors; and by a decree of December 1953 this right was transferred to a selection committee, two-thirds of whom were to be appointed by the commune and one-third by the workers' council (Rusinow 1977, 66). By the same decree, the previous form of taxation on enterprise revenue—'the rate of accumulation and funds'—was replaced by a 6 per cent interest charge on the value of fixed assets together with various taxes on turnover and income. Residual net income, or 'profit' as it was now called, was then divided between the local commune, which had the right to decide on its own share, and the workers' council of the enterprise, which could use the balance either for increases in wages and collective benefits, or for reinvestment. In fact, there was usually very little for the workers' council to allocate: in 1954 there was only 4.8 per cent of net profits, and this rose gradually to 9.2 per cent in 1957. But the principle of profit-sharing had been accepted (Rusinow 1977, 66). The interest charge on assets now became the main source of central finance for investment through the General Investment Fund. But instead of receiving direct allocations from the centre, enterprises were invited to submit bids for finance to the National Bank, which held 'investment auctions' (Horvat 1976, 210); and the allocations no longer took the form of grants but of investment credits, repayable with interest (Rusinow 1977, 64)[7]

In the meantime, the Sixth Congress of the Party in 1952 had decided that henceforward the Party was to disengage somewhat from direct power and to try to achieve its objectives by persuasion rather than by giving orders. Since, however, the Party remained the only permitted political party, and all important offices in the state and in industry were occupied by its members, what this really meant was that Party members in such positions were allowed more latitude to make their own decisions, without constantly receiving detailed instructions from Party committees and functionaries. In the case of enterprises this was obviously a necessary change, since it would be absurd to expect managers to respond to market signals if they were at the same time being given detailed orders by outside functionaries. The Party's decision to change its name to League of Communists of Yugoslavia was intended to be symbolic of this alteration in its role. But the change was largely cosmetic, and the League continued to enjoy all its previous monopoly powers.

The 1953 Constitution made no fundamental changes in the economic system, but it gave greater authority to the communes. In subsequent years the influence of the communes over the policies of local enterprises steadily increased and the reasons for this development deserve some consideration. As explained earlier, the Yugoslav Communists had powerful reasons for experimenting with a decentralized 'self-management' system. At the same time, they were determined to keep control exclusively in their own hands. How were they to reconcile these

---

[7] Investment auctions soon proved to be an unsatisfactory method of allocating funds. After experimenting with them during 1954, in the following year 'the bank fell back on the traditional banking practice of the individual evaluation of every credit request' (Horvat 1976, 210).

two objectives? If the central command organs were to be dismantled, but the Party was to maintain control, the obvious answer was that the *local* Party organs must exercise that control. So devolution of *economic* power to the enterprises was matched by a devolution of *political* power to the communes. Since the Party never abandoned the principle of democratic centralism, which means that all Party members everywhere are obliged to carry out the instructions of the Politburo or the Central Committee, the control of enterprises by the communes could be regarded as merely a more indirect way of exercising control over enterprises from the Party centre. But this method is undoubtedly more difficult, especially in a country like Yugoslavia with strong centrifugal tendencies. The local Party members, who control the communes, soon tended to identify themselves with the managers running the local enterprises. This gave rise to what the Yugoslavs call 'localism', or 'particularism', which is a sin. But the majority of the Party members are probably well pleased with this arrangement, which gives them more power, and more opportunities to benefit from the exercise of power, than the highly centralized Soviet system, in which only a few Party functionaries at the top have any power, while the rank-and-file members merely carry out instructions.

While the 1953 Constitution increased the role of the communes, it reduced that of the republics. The right to secede was dropped, and the Chamber of Nationalities, which had previously been a separate chamber of the Federal Assembly with significant powers, was merged with the Federal Chamber. In future it could meet separately only on special occasions. The Party leaders probably foresaw a danger that economic decentralization would encourage aspirations for political decentralization to the republics and provinces, which would weaken national unity and the central authority of the Party. Hence they tried to steer decentralized power away from the republics towards the communes. This manœuvre could not succeed. Within a few years the powers of the republics began to grow and eventually became dominant. The 1974 Constitution marked the final retreat from the 1953 attempt to reduce their status.

3. THE EFFECTS OF THE NEW SYSTEM: 1954–60

By the end of 1953 the framework of a decentralized and nominally self-managed system had been created. Central planning had been replaced by general indicative 'plans', or statements of intention, and enterprises were obliged to work for the market. There was still plenty of government intervention through price controls, wage controls, and investment allocations, and these interventions were often politically rather than economically motivated. But the managers had a good deal of scope for showing initiative. Theoretically, it was the workers' councils which made major business decisions and exercised substantial influence over the selection of directors. In practice, however, directors were selected by the Party, mainly on political grounds, and they continued to run their enterprises very much as they had done before. But they were at least obliged to submit their plans to the workers' councils and to answer questions. It was a small step towards industrial democracy, but a significant one.

The new system worked remarkably well. Decentralization of current operational decisions resulted in a rapid improvement in the quality of goods and services and rising productivity. As regards new investment, while the directors of enterprises had scarcely any funds under their direct control, they could propose new projects to the local commune, and bring pressure through the Party apparatus and in other ways to win approval for investment projects from higher levels of government and the banks. The communal authorities were intensely keen to attract funds for development, on which the prospects for local social sector employment, local tax revenues, local social services, and the prestige of the local officials so much depended. As a consequence of Yugoslavia's opening towards the West, the country could now draw on Western technology and Western (mainly United States) grants and credits to finance new investments and the import of raw materials and components. Industrial production grew between 1953 and 1960 at the astonishing rate of 13.7 per cent annum, and labour productivity at 3.9 per cent per annum. Over the same period the prices of industrial products rose at less than 1 per cent per annum and, although retail prices rose at 3 per cent per annum, real net personal income (wages) per worker in the social sector rose by as much as 6.2 per cent per annum.[8] Meanwhile, the number of people employed in the social sector rose from 1.84 million to 2.97 million, while the work-force in private agriculture declined from 5.25 million to about 4.55 million.[9] The number of persons registered for employment in 1960 (not all of whom were unemployed in the strict sense) was about 160,000, or 5.4 per cent of employment in the social sector and about 2 per cent of the total work-force.[10]

Despite these considerable successes, there were a number of problems. The most obvious was the persistent deficit in the balance of trade in goods and services, which averaged about 3 per cent of gross domestic product between 1953 and 1960. Fortunately, most of this deficit was covered in this period by foreign grants, especially from the United States. By 1959 the United States had given Yugoslavia over $1 billion of economic assistance, mainly in the form of foodstuffs, fuels, and raw materials (Hoffman and Neal 1962, 351). But foreign indebtedness was also rising and there was no guarantee that grants on the previous scale would continue to be forthcoming. During the preceding years it had been temptingly easy to set up new processing factories, using modern technology and imported machinery, materials, and components, mainly for the supply of the domestic market. As in other countries which have followed a similar policy, imports constantly tended to rise faster than exports, and there was a growing recognition that something needed to be done to change the balance.

[8] These rates are calculated from the index numbers given in YB80, 102 – 9.
[9] Ibid. 102 – 5, 102 – 7, and 104 – 9.
[10] Ibid. 102 – 6.

The second problem was that, although private consumption *per capita* had been increasing fast (6.6 per cent per annum between 1953 and 1960) the share of consumption in gross domestic product was still extraordinarily small (about 48 per cent in 1957-9). As a counterpart to this, the share of gross investment in GDP was very large. According to estimates made by the World Bank (World Bank 1975, Annex Tables 2.5 and 2.6) the share of gross investment—in both fixed assets and stocks—in GDP was more than 35 per cent in each year from 1953 to 1960, except in 1958 when it was 33 per cent. This is a high figure for a country like Yugoslavia, which in 1963 had a *per capita* GDP, at current exchange rates, of only one-quarter of the average for the European Community.[11]

As a consequence of the self-management system, the workers in Yugoslav enterprises are more conscious of, and more sensitive to, the division between consumption and investment than workers in centrally planned Communist countries. For the workers in Yugoslav enterprises are entitled to receive a full report on the annual accounts of their enterprise, from which they are able to see how income is allocated among different uses. The situation in 1959 in all 'productive' enterprises in the social sector (i.e. excluding those engaged in services such as health, education, and government administration and defence) was that 53 per cent of gross value added was paid in taxes, social security contributions, and interest on loans, 19 per cent was gross saving, and only 28 per cent was received in net cash incomes by the work-force.[12] Although much of the taxes and contributions went towards the financing of current government expenditure on administration, defence, and social services, a large part represented a compulsory levy for the finance of investment in the social sector. In the late 1950s about one-half of total gross investment in Yugoslavia was financed by funds under the control of the government.[13]

This enormous drain of funds from social sector enterprises inevitably provoked critical questions among both workers and managers, especially among the members of workers' councils. In the first place, it scarcely seemed compatible with the doctrine of self-management and the right of the workers to dispose of their own product. Secondly, it reduced the scope for workers to improve their standard of living. Thirdly, it gave the political authorities the final say in the use of more than half of the surplus generated within enterprises; and these funds could be diverted towards wasteful, prestigious, and politically motivated investments instead of towards more economically appropriate and productive purposes. There were a number of well-known examples of apparently wasteful uses of

[11] In 1960, when the dinar was greatly overvalued, the corresponding figure was about one-half. A comparison based on purchasing power parity rates would probably yield a figure of about one-third. Estimates for 1975 by Kravis and others (1982, Table 1–2) give Yugoslavia a *per capita* GDP compared with the United States of 23.2 per cent according to actual exchange rates and 36.1 per cent according to an estimated purchasing power rate. The latter figure would certainly be much lower in 1960.

[12] World Bank (1975), Appendix Table 6.5.

[13] Ibid. 6.2.

public funds, especially in Serbia and Montenegro, and it had become standard practice for political leaders—including even Tito—to refer to the existence of 'political factories'. The enterprises and areas which felt most aggrieved by this diversion of scarce funds were those which contributed most and received back least, i.e. the more prosperous enterprises and areas. While they accepted a responsibility for the richer areas to help the poorer, they considered that in many cases funds allegedly used for this purpose were being wasted. Hence it was necessary to establish closer control by the donors over the purposes for which these funds were used.

In view of the strong interest of the Party in retaining central political control over investment allocations, these grievances about income distribution would probably have come to nothing if it had not been for the influence of the national factor. The very wide differences in levels of social and economic development in the various parts of Yugoslavia meant that the most productive enterprises were located mainly in Slovenia and Croatia and the least productive in Macedonia and Kosovo. As Table 5.1 shows, in 1962 the social product (or gross value added) per worker in Slovenian enterprises was 1,385 thousand dinars while in Macedonia it was 863 thousand dinars and in Kosovo only 785 thousand dinars. Since net personal income per worker was kept more equal across regions by deliberate policy, the differences in gross surplus per worker between regions were relatively greater. With a system of proportional federal taxes on income the richer regions would clearly contribute more per worker to central funds than the poorer regions and, if taxes on income were progressive, the burden on the richer regions would be even greater. Data on federal tax revenues by region are not available for this period, perhaps because of their 'sensitive' nature, but some impression of the redistributive effects of federal fiscal policy can be obtained by comparing gross surplus per worker in each region with total expenditure on fixed investment in that region, divided by the number of workers in the productive social sector.[14] As Table 5.1 shows, total fixed investment per worker in 1962 was higher than average in Montenegro and Macedonia (and would also be very high in Kosovo if the figures were available). Hence, net surplus per worker, equal to gross surplus minus total fixed investment in the region, was very high in Croatia and Slovenia, negative in Montenegro and approximately zero in Macedonia. The final effects of fiscal redistribution depend on the allocation of the net surplus across regions. Various assumptions could be made about this allocation, but a simple and reasonably plausible one is that the allocation was made in proportion to the total net personal income in the productive social sector in each region.[15] The final column of the table gives the estimates of redistribution which result from the use of this assumption. It suggests that in 1962 total expenditure in Montenegro was nearly 50 per cent above the

[14] For the definition of the productive social sector see footnote[a] to Table 5.1.

[15] This implies that government expenditure—at all levels—on pensions, social services, administration, and defence is proportional to the sum of net personal incomes in the productive social sector.

TABLE 5.1

Social Product and Net Personal Income per Worker in the Productive Social Sector, Total Fixed Investment per Worker and Estimates of Redistribution, by Regions, 1962.[a]

(amounts in thousands of old dinars)

Region	Amount per worker				Final redistribution as per cent of social product[c]
	Social product	Net personal income	Total fixed investment[b]	Net surplus	
Yugoslavia	1,137	328	479	330	–
Bosnia-Herzegovina	1,044	305	447	292	1.5
Montenegro	1,023	313	884	−174	47.8
Croatia	1,215	345	445	425	−6.5
Macedonia	863	272	575	16	29.8
Slovenia	1.385	400	441	544	−10.1
Serbia proper	1,143	312	..	..	..
Vojvodina	952	303	..	..	..
Kosovo	785	253	..	..	..
Serbia total	1,066	306	494	266	4.0

Source: YB64, 204–3 and 215–3. The order of listing of the regions, down to Serbia, which follows the Serbo-Croatian alphabetic order of the names, is taken from the Yearbook.

[a] The 'productive' social sector consists of socialized enterprises engaged in the production of goods, and of certain services such as transport and distribution. Organizations providing mainly government and personal services are treated as non-productive. For further discussion of this distinction see pp. 91–2 below.

[b] Total fixed investment in the region divided by the number of workers in the productive social sector.

[c] Total net surplus is allocated across regions in proportion to total net personal income in each region. The column shows the estimated final percentage addition to, or subtraction from, regional social product resulting from production, income payments, fixed investment, and the assumed allocation of the net surplus.

social product of the productive sector (the gross material product of the region), and in Macedonia about 30 per cent above, while Croatia lost 6.5 per cent of its social product and Slovenia 10.1 per cent.

During the 1950s the inter-regional redistributive effects of federal fiscal policy and investment fund allocations began to become more apparent to Party leaders, directors of large enterprises, bank officials, and other informed people in each region, and this encouraged the re-emergence of the temporarily suppressed national conflicts between the republics and provinces. It was this factor which gave real impetus to the movement for reform. The Party could easily rouse public opinion against managers or workers of particular enterprises who demanded the right to retain more of their surplus product for themselves. But when these people coalesced as a 'national' group, or more strictly as a republic or province, the central Party's influence was weakened. For now the central Party apparatus was confronted by a republican or provincial apparatus within the party itself. In Stalin's Russia, where the Great Russians were always dominant, inner-Party national differences were ruthlessly suppressed. Indeed, on occasions whole nations were physically transferred to Siberia. But in Yugoslavia, with greater similarity of size between the nations, and with a sanctified wartime tradition of national equality, the central Party apparatus never had the same overwhelming power.

Although the movement for reform drew its real strength from the revival of nationalistic feelings, the reformers were careful to try to disguise this aspect. For example, Bakarić, the Croatian Party leader, succeeded in switching the demand of the reformers away from 'decentralization', with its nationalistic connotation, towards 'de-étatisation'. The latter demand, being firmly rooted in anti-statist Yugoslav ideology and the approved doctrine of self-management, was unchallengeable. But sophisticated managers, economists, or politicians knew well that the demand for de-étatisation was directed primarily against the power of the federal government, and was implicitly a demand for strengthening the power of republican and provincial governments and of groups of enterprises within each region. The reformers also made good use of academic economists, who developed the standard arguments in favour of a free market and against arbitrary central investment allocations. They were able to point to the distortions created by investments in 'political factories', which then had to be supported by subsidies or by favourable price control decisions. Indeed, the whole range of government controls over wages, prices, exchange rates, and foreign trade offered an easy target for an economic critique. As a consequence, the reformers were able to support their case not only with 'Marxist' arguments based on socialist self-management but with the traditional arguments of Western economic theory in favour of *laissez-faire* and a free market.

By the end of the 1950s all these strands were beginning to come together. The central government was concerned about the balance of payments; workers and managers in prosperous enterprises were getting tired of surrendering so much of the income of their enterprises to the government; the more advanced republics were becoming dissatisfied with the scale of transfer of resources to the less advanced, or at least to the allegedly wasteful use of such resources; and the economists were developing their own critique of a system which was supposed to be a market economy but which was severely distorted by government interventions, as well as by the monopolistic behaviour of many enterprises and the autarkic policies of many communes. The first steps towards reform were taken, hesitantly, in the late 1950s. But the year 1961 saw the first serious move in this direction. It was largely a failure, and there was a temporary reaction. but the wave gathered weight once more and finally broke through in 1965. The story of these events will be described in the next section.

4. THE ECONOMIC REFORM: 1961–5[16]

Although the decisive struggle over the question of reform took place during the years 1961–5, there were in earlier years a number of steps towards that goal, and there was—as we shall see later—a brief aftermath in 1966. In retrospect, the first stone was probably thrown by the Executive Committee of the Party in 1955, when it recommended a reduction in the share of investment and an increase in funds for consumer goods and agriculture. Two years later, at the First Congress of Workers' Councils, demands were raised for greater freedom of income distribution and more enterprise independence.[17] This was followed in 1958 by a change in the system of income calculation in enterprises. In future there was to be, in principle, no distinction between wages and profits. The net income of each enterprise (net value added minus taxes, contributions, and interest payments) was to be 'at the entirely free disposal of the enterprise, to be divided into personal incomes, investment and general funds, reserves, etc., as the workers' council should decide' (Rusinow 1977, 103). This new income system was essentially that which has obtained until the present time. In practice, however, in almost all years there have been restrictions on the rights of the workers to divide net income according to their own wishes.

The reform of 1958 was immediately followed, and largely negated, by the imposition of steeply progressive income taxes on personal incomes above a minimum, initially set at 80 per cent of the previous year's level of wages and salaries. The tax was opposed by the Federation of Trade Unions, who demanded that direct taxes should be levied only at proportionate rates on assets and net income respectively. Discussion of these questions continued during 1959 and 1960 in various bodies and in the press, with increasing concentration on the central issue of who should control the surpluses generated by enterprises. At the same time, the national, or inter-republican, implications of the question began to be more widely and publicly recognized. 'Thus it . . . was that the Yugoslav "national question", relatively dormant since the war, again became Yugoslavia's central question'. (Rusinow 1977, 118.)

In January 1961 a new Five-Year Plan was launched and simultaneously a number of economic reforms were introduced. The government once more gave enterprises complete freedom over income distribution and abolished progressive taxes. In addition, banks were made more independent, with the intention that they should no longer act simply as government agents in the distribution of credits. And, on the foreign trade side, the dinar was devalued, multiple exchange rates were abolished, and the number of products subject to quantitative restrictions was reduced.

[16] In this section I have drawn mainly on the admirable account by Dennison Rusinow (1977), especially pages 101–79.

[17] It is impossible to know whether these demands were spontaneous, or whether the Party, or a section of it, used the Congress as a platform from which to promote their own plans. It is a mistake to believe that any proposal is made in any forum in Yugoslavia without the prior approval of the Party.

Unfortunately, this mini-reform was unsuccessful. The devaluation raised costs and fed through into prices; the freedom granted to the banks resulted in a rapid expansion of the money supply; wages, under the control of the workers, followed merrily behind prices, and so perpetuated the inflation; and the foreign trade deficit increased. Within a few months the government imposed a wage freeze, cut back on investment, and partially reversed the liberalization of trade. The temporary boom turned into a recession, and both parties to the debate used this fact to give support to their own arguments.[18]

At this point Tito, who was in his heart a centralist of the old school, and who viewed all proposals for further decentralization and de-étatisation with considerable misgivings, made what turned out to be a serious tactical mistake. In May 1962, in the course of a strongly anti-liberal speech at Split, he referred to the need for 'a uniform socialist Yugoslav culture' (Rusinow 1977, 135). This resurrection of the idea of 'Yugoslavism', which had last been sponsored by King Alexander before the war, roused the fears of some of the national minorities, especially those which had suffered in the past under Great Serbian oppression—the Macedonians, the Albanians of Kosovo, and even the Muslims of Bosnia-Herzegovina. The result was to switch the sympathies of the party leaders of the less-developed regions away from the centralist to the liberal camp, despite the fact that the former gave them a better prospect for the maintenance of inter-regional economic transfers. Henceforward, the Croats and Slovenes were to receive strong support for the programme of reform, especially from the Macedonians. The Serbian centralists found themselves increasingly in a minority.

But two more years passed before a final decision was made. During this period there was a growing public debate about economic policy. The Party leadership was divided and unable to give any guidance. A conference of the Yugoslav Association of Economists, convened in December 1962 to discuss the economy, took on the whole an anti-liberal attitude; but a further meeting a month later showed that there was strong support for a freer market, especially among Croat economists but with some support from Serbian liberals. The debate among economists continued for the next two years and was eventually 'taken up by the mass media and in public speeches' (Rusinow 1977, 124). Thus the intellectual groundwork was prepared for the final political decisions.

An important event of 1963 was the adoption of a new constitution, which created, side by side with the Federal Assembly, which continued to include the Chamber of Nationalities as a separately elected component, four new specialized chambers: for economic questions, education and culture, welfare and health, and an 'organizational-political' chamber. These were all to be nominated by enterprises, institutions, or organiza-

---

[18] The 'recession' was, in fact, very mild—no more than a slowing down of the rate of growth. As so often happens, a few economic events or statistics were seized upon by political opponents to build a case for policies to which they were already committed on other grounds.

tions and elected by the communal assemblies. Many of the newly elected delegates to these chambers, although almost exclusively Party members, were specialists, including a considerable number of directors of larger enterprises. When these chambers were convened later in the year it turned out that the delegates had decided to take their responsibilities seriously, raising searching questions to the administration and entering into real debate on all matters of policy. It was an unheard-of situation in a Communist parliament. It reflected the mood of uncertainty and debate within the party itself and the growing support for a liberalizing reform.

The movement for reform gathered momentum during 1964. In January the question was debated in the Federal Assembly; in April the Fifth Congress of the Federation of Trade Unions gave its support to greater income retention by enterprises and greater enterprise control over investment policy. In his address to the Congress Tito showed that he had now moved closer to the liberal position, although still ambiguously. But when the Eighth Party Contress met in December, Tito came down firmly on the side of reform and Kardelj, in his usual fashion, developed a long ideological justification for it. Despite strong rearguard resistance by the centralists the Congress gave unanimous approval to the reform, and the matter was now settled, at least in principle. Significantly, the same Congress repudiated the concept of a single Yugoslav nation (Lendvai 1969, 159) and decided that in future the republican and provincial Party congresses should meet in advance of the Federal Congress (Shoup 1968, 212). Both decisions reflected the growth of nationalist divisions within the Party.

Now that the Party Congress had approved the reform, the government quickly went into action. Already in 1964 progressive taxes on enterprise incomes had been abolished once more, and the assets and liabilities of the General Investment Fund had been transferred to three federal banks. In March 1965 a new Law on Banks and Credit Transactions gave nominal control over bank policy to their major enterprise and institutional depositors, who became in effect shareholders, and the role of the political authorities was, in principle, reduced. But the banks were still placed under an obligation to adhere to 'social plans', which were ultimately a Party preserve. Finally, in July the Federal Assembly approved—in a single day—'a dozen laws, decisions, regulations and orders', which constituted the real Reform (Rusinow 1977, 176).

The Reform had five major components. First, there were to be lower taxes. Turnover taxes were in future to be levied only on final sales, at lower rates, and with less variation between products. Taxes on the income (net value added) of enterprises were abolished. The tax on fixed assets was reduced from 6 per cent to 4 per cent, subsequently to $2^1/_2$ per cent, and was finally abolished in 1971. And taxes and contribution rates payable on personal incomes of workers in the social sector were also reduced. Secondly, the role of the state in investment allocations was henceforward to be limited mainly to its control over the new Fund for the Development of Underdeveloped Regions. But the size of this fund, the list of contributing and beneficiary regions, the contribution rate, and the division of the fund between the beneficiary regions were all matters which would need to be agreed publicly and 'transparently'. Thirdly, there were very large adjustments in product prices designed to bring relative domestic prices closer to world parities, as a result of which raw material and agricultural prices rose sharply in comparison with industrial prices. Price controls were temporarily relaxed, but soon reimposed as the inflationary effects of the price adjustments began to be felt. Fourthly, the dinar was devalued from 750 to 1,250 to the dollar; customs duties, export subsidies, and the range of quantitative restrictions were reduced; and Yugoslavia became a full member of GATT. Finally, private peasants were at last given the right to buy farm machinery, including tractors, and the opportunity to obtain bank credits for this purpose. The liberal triumph appeared to be complete.

5. THE HIGH TIDE OF LIBERALISM: 1965–71

The immediate economic effects of the Reform were mostly bad. The sharp devaluation, coupled with the planned increases in prices of raw materials and farm products, produced an alarming rate of price inflation. In 1966 the material costs of manufacturing and mining rose by 28.0 per cent while gross value added (or 'social product') in this sector rose by only 15.4 per cent. Fortunately, this squeeze on incomes in manufacturing was offset by the decline in taxation. The share of gross value added in the whole productive social sector which was paid in taxes and interest charges fell from over 50 per cent in 1964 to 45.2 per cent in 1965 and 38.4 per cent in 1966.[19]

The price inflation, which was further perpetuated by the resulting wage (or income) inflation, was counteracted by a credit squeeze. This was one reason for the sharp check to the growth of output in 1965, and again in 1967 (see Table 5.2). But the other, and probably more important, reason was the fall in fixed investment. As the table shows, total fixed investment (in 1966 prices) fell by about 9 per cent in 1965, and by a further 5 per cent in 1966. This was partly a reaction to the excessively rapid growth of fixed investment in 1964 (nearly 22 per cent). But it was probably also much influenced by the redistribution of savings which followed the tax cuts. The share of gross value added which was saved by enterprises rose from 18.5 per cent in 1965 to around 25 per cent in each of the following three years;[20] and the share of enterprise saving in total saving rose from less than 30 per cent in 1963–4 to nearly 50 per cent in 1966–8. Meanwhile the share of government saving fell from over 55 per cent in 1963–4 to about 33 per cent in 1966–8.[21] It seems likely that this sudden switch in funds from

[19] World Bank (1975), Appendix Table 6.5.
[20] Ibid.
[21] Calculated from estimates of savings components given in World Bank (1975), Appendix Table 6.2, adjusted in the source for stock appreciation. It is not clear whether the totals refer to national or domestic savings, probably the former. The 1965 data in this source also show a large increase in the enterprise share of saving, but the figures in Table 5.2 (which are probably more reliable) suggest that enterprise savings did not increase sharply until 1966.

TABLE 5.2
Rates of Change of Selected Components of GDP at 1966 Prices
(percentage changes in each year)

Year	GDP at market prices	Gross fixed investment			Exports of goods and services	Imports of goods and services
		Total	Product-ive social sector	Non-pro-ductive social sector		
1963	10.2	8.3	6.5	10.9	15.0	13.8
1964	9.9	21.8	24.0	17.2	8.4	17.8
1965	1.4	−8.6	−17.8	−4.8	11.1	9.3
1966	5.0	−4.8	2.8	−28.0	12.6	22.7
1967	0.9	4.2	17.1	−39.0	5.2	8.3
1968	3.5	9.6	9.4	13.3	4.9	6.0
1969	9.3	10.3	12.5	5.5	11.2	12.9

Sources: GDP and exports and imports from World Bank (1975), Appendix Table 2.4.
Gross fixed investment in current prices from YB73, 119–1, deflated by deflators given in World Bank (1975), Appendix Table 2.12.

governments to enterprises led to a fall in government-financed investment which was not immediately offset by a rise in enterprise investment. As Table 5.2 shows, government investment in the non-productive sector (housing, social services, government administration, and so forth) was very sharply reduced in 1966 and 1967. Indeed, by 1967 it had fallen to only 42 per cent (in 1966 prices) of its 1964 level. Although one of the purposes of the Reform was to reduce investment, and the 'non-productive' sector might well have been expected to bear more than its proportionate share of the cut-back, such a large and rapid fall was unwise. It was a major cause of the severity of the recession.

On the foreign trade side, export volume rose well in both 1965 and 1966, and in the former year the growth in the volume of imports was satisfactory (see Table 5.2). But in 1966 there was a great new surge of imports. In current prices the trade results were somewhat better: the balance of foreign trade in goods and services, which had shown a deficit of $224 million in 1964, was slightly positive in 1965. In the following two years it fell back into deficits of $86 million and $136 million respectively.

The sharp fall in the rate of growth of real GDP during 1965 and 1967, together with the large adjustments in relative prices and the strengthening of the rights of enterprises to make their own investment decisions, led to a decline in employment in the social sector. During the period 1960–4 employment in the social sector had risen at an average rate of 5 per cent per annum. But in the following three years it fell by 2 per cent. The absolute fall from 1964 to 1967 was 69,000, of which 59,000 occurred in the productive sector and 10,000 in the non-productive sector. There was, in fact, no decline of employment in manufacturing and mining, but a rise of 38,000. Major falls occurred in agriculture (36,000), construction (75,000) and housing, public utilities, and artisan industries (33,000). In the non-productive sector, there was a rise in employment in social services of 34,000, offset by a fall in employment in government and other administration of 44,000. The number of people registered with employment offices as applicants for employment rose from an average of 212,000 in 1964 to 269,000 in 1967 (in 1968 it reached 311,000).[22] Meanwhile, the number of Yugoslav workers 'temporarily' employed abroad rose from 138,000 in 1964 to 296,000 in 1967 (and 401,000 in 1968).[23]

There were many complaints at this time in Yugoslavia that the introduction of stronger market discipline and the fall in employment opportunities was leading to an increase in inequality. The question will be examined in detail in Chapter 9 below. The general conclusion which emerges from that examination is that, while between 1964 and 1967 there was a temporary widening of inter-industry differentials (both in value added per worker and in net personal income per worker) there was only a slight temporary increase in overall inequality of earnings in the social sector. Against that, account should be taken of the fact that in the same period the prices received for their products by private farmers (about half the population) rose by 60 per cent, while the prices of industrial products rose by only 31 per cent.[24] So the farmers, who are the poorest section of the population, were better off.

Although the 1964 Party Congress had accepted the Reform unanimously, there was still considerable opposition to the policy within the Party, especially in Serbia. During the first twelve months after the July measures a section of the Serbian Party leadership and government adopted an attitude of passive resistance. While investment in other republics was being sharply reined in, investment in Serbia was less restricted. During 1965 expenditure on gross fixed investment (in current prices) in Serbia rose by nearly 12 per cent while in the rest of the country it fell by 3 per cent. In 1966 Serbian investment expenditure rose by 21 per cent, in the rest of the country by only 5 per cent.[25] Party leaders in Slovenia and Croatia, and to some extent elsewhere, became increasingly critical of the Serbian 'centralists', who in their view were trying to sabotage the Reform, and they began a campaign to break this opposition. The central figure of the opposition was Aleksandar Ranković, a member of Tito's wartime Politburo and since the end of the war in charge of Party organization (including appointments to all Party and government posts) and the State Security Service (UDBa). It gradually became clear that if the opposition to the Reform was to be overcome it would be necessary to remove Ranković and greatly to reduce the power of UDBa.

At first Tito was reluctant to move in this direction. But the Reformers had the sacred right of democratic centralism on their side. They were also fortunate enough to discover evidence that UDBa had been engaged in a wide range of 'dirty tricks', including wire-tapping of top Party leaders,

[22] All these data come from YB80, 102 – 5 and 102 – 6.
[23] Schrenk and others (1979), Table A.32.
[24] YB80, 102 – 9.
[25] YB68, 216 – 1.

among them even Tito. On 9 June 1966, wire-tapping devices were found in Tito's residence. A special investigating commission was appointed and reported to the Central Committee on 1 July. Ranković resigned his Party posts and his removal from the post of Vice-President of the Republic was recommended. It was further decided to reorganize the Security Service and to separate it to some degree from the Party apparatus.

The overthrow of Ranković and the defeat of the Serbian centralists, who were replaced in due course by Serbian liberals, gave enormous encouragement to the Reformers. It also brought further into the open the strongly nationalistic motives behind the movement for Reform. For the next five years, while the economic effects of the Reform were being digested, the tide of nationalism continued to rise. A series of constitutional amendments and legal changes gave more and more power to the republics and autonomous regions and less and less to the federation. The same process of 'federalization' was at work in the Party, and by the end of the period it was almost true to say that Yugoslavia had moved from being a one-party state to being an eight-party state (six republican parties and two provincial parties).

The main stages in this process were as follows. As mentioned earlier, in 1966 the tax on enterprise assets—an important source of federal revenue—was reduced from 6 per cent to 4 per cent. In 1967 firms were given the right ('temporarily') to retain part of their foreign exchange earnings from exports, thus reducing the amount of foreign exchange sold through the banks—predominantly in Belgrade—to other enterprises, often located in other republics (Rusinow 1977, 207–82). The demand that foreign exchange should belong to those who earned it was especially strong in Croatia, which was the republic with the largest foreign exchange revenue—from exports, tourism, and migrant remittances. The retention quota system was regarded by many Croats as only a first step towards giving Croatia the right to dispose independently of the whole of its foreign exchange revenue.

In the Party 'the power to appoint and dismiss higher and middle-rank functionaries, ostensibly elected but in fact for twenty years the prerogative of Ranković as Organizational Secretary, had now passed entirely to republican organs' (Rusinow 1977, 227). This was a key move towards the federalization of the Party. From 1969 onwards the primary loyalty of Party functionaries, and of Party cadres in all government and economic organizations, was to their own republican leadership. As a consequence, the quality of personnel appointed to federal posts began to decline.

In March 1967 a large group of Croat intellectuals, including many Party members, issued a 'Declaration on the Name and Position of the Croation Literary Language', in which they insisted on the separate identity of Croation and its exclusive use in schools, the press, and official documents (Rusinow 1977, 224–5). Although this proposal was officially denounced, and some of the signatories were expelled from the Party, this was the first overt sign of the wave of popular nationalism which was to rise up in Croatia during the following four years.

Later in the same year the Federal Assembly adopted six amendments to the 1963 Constitution, several of which strengthened the powers of the republics. One amendment gave the Chamber of Nationalities—the 'republican' chamber—the right to decide on almost all economic matters affecting inter-republican relations. Another amendment gave the republics joint responsibility with the federation in matters of public order, with republican prosecutors to be appointed in future by their own assemblies instead of by Belgrade (Rusinow 1977, 225–6). A further set of amendments, at the end of 1968, continued the process of federalization. The Federal Chamber was abolished and all its powers transferred to the Chamber of Nationalities, which would henceforward consist of twenty delegates from each republic—elected by its assembly—and ten from each autonomous province. Moreover, 'it was explicitly stipulated that the deputies must faithfully represent the views of the assemblies which had sent them' (Rusinow 1977, 228). The tax powers of the federal government were in future to be limited to the capital and turnover taxes, and the federation was no longer to have the right to impose taxes on income.

A significant amendment (No. XV) gave enterprises greater scope for determining their own internal organization. Most enterprises used this power to replace the managing board, a body elected by the workers' council from among non-managerial members of the work-force, by a 'business board' consisting entirely of managers (Comisso 1979, 110). This reflected the other aspect of the Reform, namely, the increased independence of enterprises, the greater opportunities for managerial initiative, and the heavier burden of responsibility for enterprise decisions, which now included investment decisions. But the growing influence of management was to be used later as a political argument by the Party for reimposing its own control.

The 9th Party Congress, which met in March 1969, was preceded, as previously agreed, by the congresses of the republican and regional organizations. In the conditions which now obtained in Yugoslavia, this meant that the republican and regional congresses were no longer rubber stamps for a centrally-determined Party policy but adopted their own standpoints, which they continued to press at the federal Congress. These congresses also made nominations for their representatives on the federal Party committees, which the federal Congress accepted without demur (Carter 1982, 57). The new committees, established by the Congress, consisted of a Presidency and a smaller Executive Bureau, each of which was to consist of an equal quota of members from each republic and smaller quotas from each of the two autonomous provinces. The degree of effective federalization of the Party is indicated by the fact that during the next two years the Executive Bureau of the Party abstained altogether from comment on internal republican affairs. According to Stane Dolanc, a leading official, the federal Presidency had become a place where republican bodies stated their views, and where the final decision was either a compromise or was deferred (Carter 1982, 59).

In April 1970 the Party Presidency 'adopted a resolution which recognized the "sovereignty" of the republics and provinces' (Rusinow 1977, 279). Federal powers were to be confined to foreign affairs, defence, and the responsibility for maintaining a unified internal market and equality between the nations and nationalities. Strict ethnic proportionality was to be applied in future to the staffing of the federal administration and the army. This tendency gained further impetus when in December Tito proposed that his position as President of the Republic should be replaced by a collective Presidency, which would consist of equal numbers from each republic, with smaller representation for the provinces (Rusinow 1977, 279–80).

While all these concessions to republican rights were being made, the nationalist movement in Croatia had been growing in strength and in public expression. Croatian representatives on federal government bodies increasingly attempted to block decisions which they believed to be adverse to their interests. The Croat Party leaders themselves supported this expression of Croat nationalism and refused to suppress popular manifestations of the same feeling. In November 1970 the *Matica Hrvatska*, a long-established organization for the encouragement of Croat culture, 'launched a membership drive and a new programme, in which it was declared to be its right and duty to interest itself in economic and political questions' (Rusinow 1977, 293). In the following March it launched a new weekly journal, *Hrvatski tjednik*, the circulation of which rapidly rose to over 100,000, while the membership of the organization rose from 2,323 to 41,000 (ibid.). In April the *Matica* captured the leadership of the Zagreb and Croatian student organizations. In May, Miko Tripalo, one of the Croat Party 'triumvirate', raised the demand for 'a radical revision of the Yugoslav foreign currency system' which then became the central demand of the Croat nationalists (Rusinow 1977, 296).

Until the middle of 1971, the response of the other Party leaders to Croat nationalism was to make more and more concessions to republican rights, both in the government and in the Party. The culminating point in this process was the adoption in June 1971 of twenty-three further amendments to the now almost unrecognizable 1963 Constitution. Most of these amendments were concerned with relations between the republics and the federation. The powers of the latter were restricted along the lines of the above-mentioned decision of the Party Presidency in the previous year. But even in these matters each republic was, in effect, to have a veto right when its own interests were seriously affected, and there was a list of questions—including virtually all economic questions—which could only be settled by unanimous agreement of the republics and the provinces. The federal government's own tax revenues were restricted to customs and stamp duties, but it was to receive part of the proceeds of turnover taxes collected by the republics and provinces, with their agreement. Proportional representation of the republics and provinces was to be applied in future to the membership of all federal organs, including the Federal Executive Committee, i.e. the council of ministers (Rusinow 1977, 284–5). The practical operation of the new system was facilitated by the establishment of a number of inter-republican committees at federal level, in which compromises and agreements on contentious issues were thrashed out. Although this system worked reasonably well, a side-effect was to deprive the Assembly, and even the Federal Executive Committee itself, of most of the independent authority which they had enjoyed since 1963.

Three of the amendments were the so-called 'workers' amendments', which had been proposed by the trade unions and adopted in April by the Second Congress of Self-Managers, but which had probably been drafted by Kardelj. They contained the germ of the new economic system, which was established three years later by the 1974 Constitution. Two key proposals were the disintegration of large and medium-sized enterprises into self-contained units (the so-called 'basic organizations of associated labour') and the introduction of 'self-management agreements' and 'social compacts', which were supposed to bind the whole economy together into a voluntary social plan. The new system will be described in detail in Chapter 6. What is significant, however, is that these ideas were brought forward simultaneously with the concessions which were being made to republican power. They were almost certainly an attempt by Party centralists, supported by Tito and Kardelj, to create a lever which would offset the effects of the concessions on political decentralization.

Despite the remarkable retreat from centralized power, or perhaps because of it, the nationalist fervour in Croatia continued to mount. In November the *Matica* published a series of demands, which included the demand that Croatia should be defined as 'the sovereign national State of the Croatian nation', in which the sole official language should be Croatian. The Croatian republic would control all tax revenues collected within its borders and make only voluntary contributions to the federation. It would have a separate central bank with its own monetary policy. Croatian members of the army would normally serve only in their own republic and there would be an autonomous Croatian territorial army (Rusinow 1977, 305). In November the students of Zagreb university called a strike in support of the demand for a new system of retention of foreign currency. Tito now reacted strongly and summoned a meeting of the Party Presidency, which on 1 December denounced the Croatian Party leaders as nationalists. Within another two weeks the triumvirate had resigned, and by the middle of January more than 400 of their supporters had resigned or been dismissed. With the Croatian national movement crushed, Tito determined to resurrect the central power of the Party. It was impossible to go back on the concessions to the republics. Instead, the scapegoats would be the managers, or the 'technocracy'. The short flowering of liberal market socialism was abruptly terminated.

CHAPTER 6

THE POST-REFORM SETTLEMENT

1. INTRODUCTION

By the end of 1971, Tito and the majority of the Party leadership were deeply dissatisfied with the results of the Reform. For the first three years the Reform, or the way in which it was carried out, had produced rapid inflation, a serious recession, and growing unemployment. After 1968 the economy got back into its stride, but unemployment continued to grow, and would have grown even more if it had not been for the large-scale emigration of Yugoslav workers to western Europe. Meanwhile, liberation in the political sphere, although modest by the standards of western democracies, had opened the door to leftism in the universities, a strike at Belgrade University, violent riots in Kosovo, and finally the nationalist upsurge in Croatia. It was clearly time to reassert Party authority.

While all the leaders would agree that a crucial requirement was to put the Party firmly back in the saddle, there must have been long debates about the other ingredients of the Party's response to the situation. The most difficult problem was how to deal with nationalism in Croatia. Nationalism in Kosovo could be met in the traditional manner by a combination of rhetoric, repression, and economic aid. In any case the Albanians of Kosovo had never been considered to be full members of the Yugoslav family. But Croatia was different. Clearly, those who had supported or tolerated nationalist 'excesses' in Croatia, whether inside or outside the Party, had to be punished. But it would be unwise to push this too far. After a quick surgical operation, involving the removal of a few of the top leaders, the Croats must be wooed back into the family. There would be no attempt to reverse the process of federalization. Indeed, there were still some steps to be taken in the same direction. At the same time, the attack on 'liberalism' should be extended into Serbia, partly to show the Croats that there was no discrimination against them.

But something more was needed to give weight to the Party's new line. As always when in difficulties, the Party's first thought was how to give the conflict a 'class war' flavour. It could be argued that the people who had strayed into leftism and nationalism were not the true working class but others, under the influence of capitalist ideas. The leftist intellectuals in the universities were an obvious target, but not a sufficiently convincing one.

So the Party decided to attack the managers and technicians—the 'technocrats'.

It was a natural and inevitable result of the Reform that the role of the managers and technicians in industry was enhanced. With greater freedom of choice of technology, markets, investment, and employment there was more scope for managerial initiative. The managers responded to these opportunities. But, in order to make efficient decisions, they needed on many occasions to act more quickly. Hence there was a tendency in the more successful firms for the managers to be given greater scope for independent decision-making. Many workers' councils left difficult business problems to the managers and their staffs, concentrating their own discussions on the smaller issues—although these were of considerable importance to individual workers—of entitlements to such things as promotion, holidays, or flats. It was easy to demonstrate, therefore, as sociologists had constantly done, that the real power over important business decisions was in the hands of a managerial élite.

Moreover, the Reform had special effects in the fields of banking and trade, which could also be regarded as reflections of the same 'managerial-technocratic' phenomenon. When the General Investment Fund, the major former instrument of federal finance and influence on the development of the economy, was closed down in 1965, its assets were transferred to three large banks with headquarters in Belgrade. These banks, which continued to collect interest and repayments of principal on earlier loans, now had considerable financial resources at their disposal, much of which was channelled back into the economy through other banks. Although banking policy was largely controlled, as it always had been, by the politicians, it now became easy to describe banks as 'centres of alienated power', another example of 'managerial-technocracy'. A further result of the Reform had been a large expansion in foreign trade and a growth in the importance of foreign-trade organizations. Quite naturally, some trade organizations made large profits so long as many industrial enterprises were still inexperienced in this area. These profits also became a target for criticism, and were attributed to the same cause.

It is difficult to know whether the Party genuinely wanted to curb the managers of industry, banks, and trade organizations, or merely to make them public scapegoats. There must have been some, including Kardelj, the perennial maker of new constitutions, who felt that the Party was confronted by a real threat to its power, and that radical measures were needed. At any rate, the Party got down to the job of completely reorganizing Yugoslav society from top to bottom. The outcome was the 1974 Constitution, the Associated Labour Act of 1976, and a number of other Acts dealing with specific problems. On paper at least, almost all the rules of economic and political behaviour were changed. Almost all the old terminology was also changed, so that nothing was easily recognizable; and everyone was obliged to learn a new vocabulary, which only a few Yugoslavs could properly understand.

There were three principal aims of the new constitution. The first was, so far as possible, to break down larger enterprises into smaller components, or divisions, within which the workers would exercise more direct control over management and the most important decisions. These 'basic organizations of associated labour' were also to be the nominal controllers of a major part of the political system, the banks and the social services, through a system of delegations. This was the Yugoslav version of 'the dictatorship of the proletariat'. The second aim of the constitution was to eliminate direct elections and the possibility of 'bourgeois democracy', i.e. of contested elections, which might open the door to political tendencies outside the Party's control. Every step in the electoral structure, in future, was to be under careful Party supervision, and the Party itself, either directly or through its subsidiary organizations, was to be represented as of right in all assemblies. The third aim was to introduce a new system of 'voluntary social planning', which it was hoped would solve the problem of reconciling a market economy with central political control.

Even before the constitution was approved the Party had taken steps to tighten its hold over the country. In September 1972 Tito sent a letter to all Party organizations calling for closer Party unity and a purge of deviationists. He denounced statism and unitarism, technocracy, nationalism, pseudo-liberalism and leftism; and he made a strong appeal for a 'class' approach. The Party must in future ensure that 'only true Communists held positions of responsibility in public life' (Singleton 1976, 273-4). As a result, editors were dismissed, Marxist studies were promoted in schools and universities, and directors of enterprises came under sharp attack (Comisso 1979, 131). At the Tenth Party Congress in May 1974, 'Tito called on the League of Communists to increase its activity in all organizations, strive to implement the new constitution, reorganise itself in conformance with democratic centralism, struggle against factionalism, and reaffirm itself as a specifically class-based political party' (ibid. 132).

The remainder of this chapter will be devoted to a description of (a) the new economic system, (b) the new political system, and (c) the new system of planning, as they are presented in the constitution itself and in subsequent legislation. Chapter 7 will contain an analysis of the underlying relationships in each of these areas, in a attempt to understand how the Yugoslav system really operates.

2. THE NEW ECONOMIC SYSTEM

The Yugoslav economy is divided into a social sector and a private sector, and simultaneously into a productive sector and a non-productive sector. The social sector is that in which assets are 'socially' owned and there is 'self-management'. In the private sector self-employed proprietors work with their own assets and may employ a limited number of other workers. The 'productive' sector, sometimes confusingly called 'the economy', consists of industries which produce goods, together with some which provide services, such as trade and transport, which are said to be part of the process of goods production. Most personal services, government administration, and the work of the 'socio-political organizations' (the Party, trade unions, Socialist Alliance, youth and veterans organizations) are classified as 'non-productive'.[1] This distinction, first made by Adam Smith in a famous passage of *The Wealth of Nations*, has somehow been carried down by Communists in the belief that it was endorsed by Marx. In fact, Marx defined a productive activity as one which created surplus value. Thus a peasant household's production of food for its own use would be non-productive, while a hairdresser who ran a business employing others would be productive. None the less, the Yugoslavs have taken over Adam Smith's distinction from the Soviet Union; it is part of the official ideology; and it has wide repercussions on laws, practices, attitudes, and statistics. Yugoslav 'national income', for example, excludes the incomes received by people working in the non-productive sector; and instead of the 'Western' concept of gross national product the Yugoslavs use the 'Eastern' concept of gross material product, which excludes the value of services produced in the 'non-productive' sector.

There are four possible combinations of these two classifications. Table 6.1 gives estimates of the number of people engaged in each of these four sectors. It will be seen that nearly 40 per cent of the Yugoslav active work-force is still employed in the private sector (if the hours worked by 'moonlighters' were also included, the figure might well be about 50 per cent). Of the total in this sector nearly 3 million are engaged in agriculture and fishing. The non-productive sector employs about one-eighth of the total active work-force. But this is not a true reflection of the importance of services, since the numbers employed in 'productive' services—trade, transport, catering, tourism, public utilities, and some minor services—amounted in 1980 to over 1.25 million. It must be remembered, also, that Yugoslav statistics contain no information about the defence forces and police, the total number of which may easily amount to half a million. Outside the active domestic work-force there are also about half a million unemployed (assuming about 60 per cent of those registered for employment are available for work) and about three-quarters of a million Yugoslavs 'temporarily' working abroad, mainly in western Europe.

We shall now outline the official system of organization of economic activities in each of these four sectors.

The productive social sector[2]

Before 1974 the business units in this sector were called 'enterprises'. They are now called by three different names. Most of the previous enterprises are called 'work organizations of associated labour'. For simplicity, however, we shall continue to call them enterprises. So far as possible, enterprises are now broken down into their divisional components called

[1] Banking and insurance are sometimes treated as 'productive' and sometimes as 'non-productive'. Compare, for example, in YB81, 105–3 where they are included in the 'economic' sector and Table 125–1, where they are listed in the 'non-economic' sector.
[2] In this section I have made considerable use of an article by Dr Dušan Jurić (1979). Other sources are given for specific points.

TABLE 6.1

Estimates of Numbers Engaged in Four Sub-sectors of the Yugoslav Economy, 1980

(thousands)

	Productive sector	Non-productive sector	Total
Social sector	4,826	972	5,798
Private sector	3,503[a]	200[b]	3,703
Total	8,329	1,172	9,501

Sources: Social sector: YB81, 105–1.
  Productive private sector: Vinski (1981).
  Non-productive private sector: a rough guess.

[a] Includes working proprietors, family workers, and paid employees. Excludes part-time student-workers. Covers farms, road transport, catering, and artisans, but apparently not shopkeepers.

[b] Intended to cover shops, private services (such as hairdressers), and self-employed professional workers such as doctors, lawyers, architects, and authors. The vast number of 'moonlighters' who do repairs and other jobs, are included in the social sector, where they are officially employed, although they may in some cases earn more from moonlighting than from their official jobs.

'basic organizations of associated labour'. (We shall call them basic organizations.) But many enterprises have not been divided up in this way, either because they were too small, or because the criteria for creating separate basic organizations could not be met. At the end of 1980 there were in the whole social sector 13,940 undivided enterprises (5,496 in the productive sector) and 4,321 enterprises consisting of two or more basic organizations (3,444 in the productive sector), with an average of nearly five basic organizations in each (YB81, 103 – 2). Since the rules applicable to enterprises are the same as those applicable to basic organizations, Yugoslav references to basic organizations usually implicitly relate also to enterprises.

An enterprise may be divided into component basic organizations if (1) each basic organization carries out activities which are technically separable, (2) the output of each base organization can be priced by reference to the market, and (3) the units are small enough to make self-management feasible. Workers have not only a 'right' but a 'duty' to set up basic organizations wherever possible. But, if one group of workers wishes to split off and others object, the matter is referred to a special 'court of associated labour'.

When an enterprise is divided into basic organizations, the latter do not become fully independent, but are obliged to enter into a 'self-management agreement' with one another so as to preserve the unity of the enterprise. A basic organization has the legal right to split off from an enterprise and become independent, or join up with other basic organizations in a new enterprise. But this right is hedged about with a number of conditions. The basic organization may not break away if this would 'substantially disrupt work in other basic organizations'. If it does break away, it must pay damages for any consequential losses imposed on other-basic organizations (Jurić 1979, 47). Since all basic organizations are tied down by innumerable 'self-management agreements', both within their enterprise and outside it, such separations would be extraordinarily difficult in practice. No information is available on their frequency.[3]

Many enterprises form parts of 'composite organizations of associated labour', of which there were altogether 373 at the end of 1980 (341 in the productive sector). These composite organizations tend, of course, to be large. Of the largest 220 organizations of all kinds operating in the productive sector in 1980, 160 were composites (*Ekonomska politika*, 28 September 1981). (These 220 organizations generated 48 per cent of the gross value added in the whole productive sector and employed 43 per cent of workers in that sector.) As an example, an electrical engineering firm called Iskra, with headquarters in Ljubljana, the seventh-largest firm in the country (in terms of gross value added) consists of 14 enterprises and 80 basic organizations. At the end of 1980 it employed nearly 30,000 workers and produced one-quarter of the value of output of the Yugoslav electrical industry. It is the fifty-eighth largest electrical products enterprise in the world, and the sixteenth largest in Europe. It employs 2,000 people on research and development and its 1980 exports were worth $145 million (ibid.).

Apart from basic organizations, most large enterprises and composite organizations contain another component called a 'work community'. A work community consists of the administrative, technical, marketing, and clerical staff, who provide services to several basic organizations within the same enterprise. It will be convenient to call it a staff division. Staff divisions are self-managed, but their rights (and duties) are in some respects restricted in comparison with basic organizations. These differences will be described later.

Organizations of all types may be associated in 'business communities' for specific purposes, such as research, training, exports, and other common interests. They are also usually shareholders in banks, which they thereby control. They may similarly control insurance organizations. All enterprises belong to industrial associations, which in turn are grouped into Chambers of the Economy, at republican, provincial, and federal levels. Chambers of the Economy are normally consulted about proposed legislation and other policy decisions which are likely to have an influence on economic conditions. They make representations to governments on all matters affecting their members' interests, and they sign social compacts committing their members (morally) to various 'norms' of behaviour.

All productive organizations and enterprises operate in the market, buying materials, selling their output, saving, investing, borrowing and so

---

[3] *Borba* (2 November 1982) describes some of the difficulties encountered by two basic organizations which wanted to separate from an agricultural 'work organization of associated labour'. The work organization was prepared to agree only if there was 'strict accounting' (presumably, an agreed division of the assets and liabilities) and an agreement on future technical co-operation.

forth. They do not 'hire' labour because the workers' incomes are not fixed by contract or agreement in advance but depend on the profitability of the organization or enterprise. So there is said to be no 'labour market'. In practice, however, newly recruited key workers often make special bargains about their wages and conditions.

All workers who have completed their period of probation are full members of their basic organization. They have an equal right to attend general meetings, to elect delegates to workers' councils and to serve on these and other elected bodies. Their incomes, however, depend on the total income of the organization, how much of that income is distributed, on their own qualifications, and on their estimated contribution to the success of the organization. The standard rule is that they are paid according to 'work and the results of work', but no one knows for certain what that means. Advances of income are paid out, after deduction of social security contributions, once a month; they may be adjusted each quarter in the light of the organization's degree of business success, and they are supposed to be adjusted finally at the end of each year when the accounts have been completed in February or March. In practice, when supplementary payments are due there is no problem, but when advance incomes have been too generous it is impossible to make an immediate adjustment, and excess payments made during the year are deducted during the following year.

There are elaborate rules for the computation of income. Sales and other revenues (including subsidies, interest receipts, and profits from investments in other enterprises) are supplemented by the change in the value of stocks. Sales are allowed to be counted only if cash or 90-day promissory notes have been received (Schrenk and others 1979, 130). Stocks are valued at current prices (so that capital gains or losses on stockholdings enter into accounting income, and also into national income), the current prices of finished products usually being estimated at their sale price rather than at cost of production. Stocks of unsaleable products are believed to be substantial in many cases.

From total revenue there is subtracted the cost of purchased materials and other non-labour input costs, depreciation at prescribed rates on the stock of fixed capital (valued at original cost, after adjustment at infrequent intervals for price changes) and taxes on turnover. This leaves 'gross income'. From this is then subtracted taxes on gross income, certain social security contributions, interest charges, insurance, legal costs, excess depreciation and similar outlays. The remainder, or 'net income' is then available to be allocated by the workers among three purposes: gross personal income (on which further substantial social security contributions are payable), fringe benefits in kind (meals, transport, sports facilities, holidays, housing, etc.), and saving ('accumulation' according to Marxist terminology). The last item includes compulsory contributions to reserve funds, both within the enterprise and at commune level, intended to cover losses and, in the case of enterprises in the richer republics, compulsory contributions, levied proportionately on the enterprise income, towards the Fund for Development of Underdeveloped Regions. The whole of the balance of 'free' savings will not necessarily be available for financing investment, since part of it, or even more, may be needed to repay the principal on loans or credits received in previous years. Since in recent years much investment has been financed by short-term suppliers' credits, mainly foreign, the turnover of loan capital is fairly rapid and most enterprises have been obliged constantly to raise new loans in order to maintain a desired level of investment.

In principle, it is only a basic organization which can make decisions about the final allocation of income. Each basic organization has its own balance sheet and income statement, and the worker-members have to approve proposals for income allocation by a procedure laid down in the by-laws of the organization, usually at a general meeting. These proposals will normally come from the workers' council of the organization; but, where the basic organization belongs to a wider enterprise or composite organization, such proposals are likely to have come down from the workers' council of the larger organization (and may well have been formulated initially by the management).

Basic organizations with thirty or more members have an elected workers' council, with delegates allocated in proportion to the number of workers in each unit and with due regard to the skill, age, sex, and nationality composition of the work-force. Delegates may not be elected for a term exceeding two years, nor may the same delegate be re-elected for more than two consecutive terms. The director and other senior managers are not eligible for election, although they are entitled to attend the council and participate in its discussions. Enterprises and composite organizations also have workers' councils elected in the same manner. Nominations for all these elections are drawn up by the trade union.

Workers' councils have very large nominal powers. They formulate business policy and plans, make investment and borrowing decisions, approve annual and interim accounts, and give final approval to the appointment of the director or the managing board, as the case may be. Each organization has a set of rules laid down in the self-managing agreement made at the time of its establishment and in subsequent by-laws, and these determine the precise powers of the workers' council and prescribe the circumstances in which any proposal needs to have the approval of the whole work-force, either at a general meeting or by secret ballot. Most workers' councils elect from their own membership or from other workers an executive committee, which has the responsibility for making proposals to the council and for supervising the implementation of its decisions.

Each organization or enterprise has either a sole director or a management board to perform the task of executive management. The director (or board) may make proposals to the workers' council, the meetings of which he has the right to attend. Once the council has made a decision, the director has the duty to carry it out, provided that it does not contravene the law. The post of director (or of a member of a board) must be publicly advertised. A nomination commission, consisting of representatives of the organization, the trade union and the relevant government authority (usually the local commune), selects one or more candidates by a two-thirds majority and proposes them to the workers' council for its final decision. In practice, they usually recommend only one candidate (in many cases, only one person applies for the job) and the workers' council automatically gives its approval. The director or board member is appointed for not more than four years. He can be relieved of his duties by the council in special circumstances, and he is eligible for reappointment at the end of each term of appointment.

Directors and managers are entitled to give workers instructions on how to work, subject to the general law and to the by-laws of the organization. Workers have a duty to carry out such instructions. A worker who is late or absent without leave, creates a disturbance, works badly, or refuses reasonable instructions can be disciplined. The matter must be referred by the management to a specially elected disciplinary commission, and the worker has the right of appeal to higher bodies. There is a graduated scale of possible punishments, leading up to the ultimate sanction of dismissal. In practice, dismissals are rare, although they were probably more frequent in the early days of self-management.

Standard working hours are forty-two a week, with a normal maximum of eight a day. This is usually operated in the form of five days of eight hours plus one Saturday in four. In one-shift enterprises the eight hours usually run from 6 a.m. to 2 p.m., or from 7 a.m. to 3 p.m. Since it is obligatory to give a break of thirty minutes, during which a hot meal is usually provided, the 'eight-hour' day is in fact no more that $7^{1}/_{2}$ hours of work, and often less. Annual holidays last for at least eighteen working days but may be as much as thirty-six working days. In addition, there are a considerable number of public holidays.

Workers are entitled to sickness or disability benefits, which commence on the first day of absence and last for a maximum of thirty days, at 80–90 per cent of their average net income during the previous twelve months (Toš 1980). This is paid by their basic organization. Thereafter, they receive benefits from the appropriate self-managing community of interest at 90 per cent of previous income.[4] Maternity leave is given for 180 days on full pay, with a right to work half-time thereafter until the child's first birthday, also on full pay. Retirement pensions, payable at or before 60 for women and 65 for men, are organized through self-managing communities of interest, which raise contributions on the personal incomes of working members to cover their cost. The maximum pension of 85 per cent of average earnings during the last ten years of work (after indexation on the cost of living) is received after forty years of service. Disability pensions for work-related disabilities may be as much as 100 per cent of previous earnings. Pensions are indexed on current earnings but, because shorter work periods yield lower pensions and there are some lags in the

---

[4] The communities of interest are discussed below.

adjustment of pension rates, average retirement pensions are about 75 per cent of average current earnings.[5]

There are also survivors' pensions, which depend on the age of the survivor and the number of dependants. Dependants include student children up to 26 years of age and previously supported parents and other relatives. Unemployment benefits are paid only to a small minority of the registered unemployed. In order to qualify, the unemployed worker must have worked continuously for twelve months, or for a total of eighteen months in the previous two years. In Slovenia, he receives 60 per cent of his average earnings in the previous twelve months, subject to a family means test.[6] Because of the security of tenure of established jobs in the social sector, very few of the unemployed have significant previous work experience. The unemployed are mainly former peasants, returned migrants, and young people who have recently completed their education.

Recruitment of new workers is supposed to be by advertisement and impartial selection of those most suitable. In practice, it is widely said that one gets a job in the social sector through personal influence and connections. Workers are free to leave a job at any time but, once a worker is accepted as a full member of an organization, he is entitled to security of tenure up to retirement age, except in the following circumstances: if he is no longer fit to work; if he has been sentenced to imprisonment for a period exceeding six months; or if he has been dismissed for disciplinary reasons. He cannot be dismissed because his services are no longer required, as a result of either a change in technology or a change in market conditions, and the basic organization is obliged to retain displaced workers or find new jobs for them. But there may be an agreement among basic organizations in an enterprise or composite organization to transfer redundant workers within the wider organization. There is, however, no guarantee that workers will be employed full time. When sales are slack, or there are shortages of raw materials or power, monthly incomes may fall to the legal (or locally agreed) minimum. When there are not sufficient funds to cover minimum incomes, the firm is regarded as making a loss and, in cases where the loss is not covered by internal or collective reserves or by special outside credits, the workers may temporarily receive no pay. Eventually, such a situation must be resolved either by a reorganization or by closure. In this last case, which is rare, the workers will, of course, have ceased to have guaranteed jobs.

Enterprises normally use their gross savings (depreciation plus net saving) to reinvest in themselves. In addition, they usually borrow as much as they can from the banks, from foreign sources, or on suppliers' credits. The division of available finance within an enterprise is a matter for discussion between the component basic organizations, each of which is

---

[5] This was the position in 1980. In 1981, when inflation was even faster, the average retirement pension was only 70 per cent of average earnings (*Ekonomska politika*, 24 May 1982).

[6] The 60 per cent figure comes from Toš (1980, 122) but OECD (1978, 31) gives a figure of only 35 per cent for 1976. The means test is mentioned by Thomas (1973, 38).

usually anxious to get as much as possible for itself. Where different basic organizations are located in different communes, there may also be strong political pressure from each commune to obtain a larger share. Enterprises are also allowed, and encouraged, to invest in other enterprises, especially if the recipient enterprise is making a loss, or is located in a backward area and needs extra finance or technical assistance. This is called 'pooling labour and resources'. There is not normally much pooling of labour, although managers and other skilled workers may be transferred to the subsidiary enterprise for a period. Investing organizations are entitled to a share of the residual income of their subsidiary, which is calculated after meeting all expenses, including the incomes of the work-force. Since the latter item usually has no predetermined upper limit, the rate of return on invested funds is usually low, and in recent years well below the rate of inflation. The investing organization cannot acquire any management rights, since this would deprive the workers in the subsidiary of their right to self-management. Moreover, the invested funds must be repaid over a definite period of time, so that the subsidiary eventually becomes fully independent.

Rules for the division of joint income within an enterprise among the component basic organizations are set out in the self-management agreement between them. There are two principal arrangements. According to the first, basic organizations trade in goods and services with one another at agreed transfer prices. Where possible, transfer prices are fixed by comparison with actual market prices. But there are obviously many cases—probably the majority—where no such market price exists. Presumably, in such cases transfer prices are fixed by bargaining, including reference to 'normal' costs of production. When prices of raw materials, energy, other inputs, or finished products change during the year, there must be much room for argument.

The second type of arrangement is, in effect, to pay each basic organization a total sum sufficient to provide an agreed rate of reward for each unit of labour and capital employed in the business. In this case, the enterprise as a whole, or even the composite organization, becomes the effective operating unit, and the division into basic organizations is largely nominal. It is believed that this arrangement is widely used. It is obviously an arrangement which is easier to operate in a period of rapidly changing prices and, for that reason alone, it is probably becoming predominant.

A basic organization does not own its assets, since all assets in the social sector are 'socially owned'. The basic organization has, in effect, the right of usufruct. Specific assets may be sold to other organizations and, if already fully depreciated, even to the private sector. But the organization cannot use the proceeds for income purposes. In Western (but not Yugoslav) terminology.it has a duty 'to maintain capital intact'. Many enterprises were originally established by their local communes, and communes are normally required to guarantee loans given to any organization in their territory. Apart from these direct financial obligations, communes have a general right to oversee all local enterprises and to intervene in their affairs, if they consider that they have been contravening the law or the numerous 'social compacts', which lay down 'norms' for enterprise behaviour. In a sense, therefore, the communes (or in some cases the republican or provincial governments) are the real 'owners' of enterprises. In any case, if an enterprise, or part of one, were closed down it would be the local commune which would inherit its assets and liabilities (and the responsibility to try to find alternative employment for its workers).

While all basic organizations have their own balance sheets and are entitled to 'accumulate', 'work communities' (or staff divisions) do not. A staff division is paid on the basis of so-called 'free exchange of labour'. This is not an exchange of labour for labour in a real sense but an exchange of services for money. The 'productive' basic organizations in an enterprise hire the 'non-productive' staff division (or divisions) to do the work of typing, keeping accounts, marketing, research, technical development and so forth. The terms of payment and the level of services to be provided are settled from time to time (at least once a year) and the workers in a staff division are, in effect, paid employees. A staff division has its own workers' council and it is represented on the enterprise (or composite) workers' council on an equal footing with basic organizations. Its manager, however, is appointed by the enterprise workers' council, after consulta-tion with the workers' council of the staff division itself. He is subject to overall control by the management board of the enterprise (Eames 1980, 150). A staff division is not entitled to separate from the enterprise without the consent of its basic organizations.

The non-productive social sector

This sector has two main sub-divisions. The larger part consists of the social services—education, health, social insurance and social welfare— and of banking and insurance and the activities of art, cultural, and research institutions. The smaller part consists of government administra-tion and the socio-political organizations. Units in the former group, such as schools, hospitals, theatres, and banks, are organized, in the same way as productive enterprises, into basic, work, and composite organizations, together with work communities where appropriate. They are managed by councils on which are represented not only the workers but also outside bodies such as governments or productive enterprises and, in the case of universities, the students. Units in the latter group, however, cannot be given full self-management rights, since they are carrying out directly the decisions of governments or socio-political organizations. Presumably, some attempt is made to give the staff of government departments and socio-political organizations the right to express their views about their own incomes and conditions of work. Jurić (1979, 56) says that workers in organs of government administration form work communities, but there is no mention of them in the relevant table of the Statistical Yearbook.[7]

[7] See, for example, YB81, 103 – 2.

Basic organizations in social services and in art, cultural, and research institutions are financed, and in part controlled, by so-called 'self-managing communities of interest'. Although many of these basic organizations sell some of their services on the market (theatres and museums are obvious examples, but other institutions such as schools sometimes raise income by renting their premises or in other ways) the bulk of their finance in total comes from 'contributions'. The intention of a community of interest is to provide a link between the organizations providing services on the one hand and the organizations or individuals paying for those services on the other, *without involving the government*. The finance of schools in a particular commune, for example, will be arranged through a self-managing community of interest. Normally, the community holds an assembly meeting once a year at which the delegates of the school employees form one chamber and the delegates of all basic organizations and work communities in the commune form another. At this meeting, a budget is drawn up for the coming year and a contribution rate is agreed. Contributions are levied proportionately on the personal incomes of all workers in the social sector (both productive and non-productive workers) and in some cases, e.g. for health services, on the self-employed. In principle, every basic organization or work community has to approve this rate, but it is difficult for it to avoid paying.

Basic organizations are members of many different communities of interest. They finance in this way not only schools, hospitals, universities, research institutes, theatres, and museums, but also pension funds, house construction, and some 'productive' activities, such as water supply, road maintenance, railways, and electric power. In December 1980 the total number of communities of interest was 7,826, or more than 15 per commune.

The workers in the service organizations—doctors, teachers, actors, and all the others from top to bottom—are supposed to have full self-management rights. But these rights are clearly more circumscribed than in the productive sector since the prices of these services are determined by bilateral bargaining. The communal and other governments have powers to enforce certain standards and, in the absence of voluntary agreement, to prescribe contribution rates. And the incomes of workers in the non-productive sector can be more directly controlled by government than those of workers in the productive sector.

The private sector

Since the distinction between productive and non-productive activities in the private sector has no effect on their methods of organization, the whole private sector may be treated under one heading.

As shown in Table 6.1 above, the private sector in Yugoslavia still employs a large proportion of the work-force. But the bulk of it consists of small farmers, most of whom are now in the older age groups. Farmers are not allowed to own more than ten hectares of arable land (except in mountain areas), and the great majority own considerably less. Some evasion of this rule can be practised, although it is probably not widespread. In some republics leasing of land is now allowed. Except for specialized producers of horticultural products, poultry products, and certain meat products most private farms are unable to provide an adequate full-time income for their existing work-force. For this reason a large number of farms are operated part-time by workers who have 'full-time' jobs in the social sector.

The non-farm private sector is not large but it provides some important services. It includes builders, truck and taxi drivers, bar and restaurant proprietors, shopkeepers, providers of personal services such as hairdressers, repairers of cars and durable goods, and professional people such as doctors and lawyers. No private business may employ, apart from the proprietor, more than five workers (ten workers in some republics). In fact, private firms normally employ much less than this: the total number of registered employees of private businesses is less than half the number of proprietors. There may, however, be a number of unregistered and family workers in addition to the registered employees.

Private farmers and other self-employed persons are encouraged to form co-operatives. Since the collapse of the drive for collectivization in 1953, virtually all collective farms have disappeared; but there are a certain number of other looser farm co-operatives for purposes such as purchasing of supplies and marketing. At the end of 1980 there were 342 artisan co-operatives, of which 157 were in building (YB81, 103 – 2).

The 1974 Constitution introduced a new scheme for association between a self-employed worker and a group of employed workers: the so-called 'contractual organization of associated labour'. Under the terms of the contract the self-employed worker contributes his own labour and the whole of the initial capital of the business. He automatically becomes the manager, but the organization is run on a self-management basis. The investor-manager is entitled to remuneration for his services and for an agreed return on his capital. The capital must be repaid over a limited period of time, after which the contract expires and the organization becomes a normal 'socially owned' basic organization. There is no limit on the number of workers who may be employed in a contract organization, but the scheme has not so far proved very successful. At the end of 1980 there were only eighty-two contract organizations in existence, of which only eleven were in industry (ibid.).

3. THE POLITICAL SYSTEM[8]

The assemblies

The 1974 Constitution abolished direct elections of members of legislative bodies at all levels—federal, republican, and communal. Direct elections, which offer the possibility of popular contests, are regarded as 'bourgeois

---

[8] In this section I have drawn mainly on *Constitutional System of Yugoslavia*, Belgrade 1980 (in English).

democracy'. Instead, Yugoslavia is now officially ruled by 'delegates', who are given mandates by 'delegations', who in turn are mandated by the voters. Delegates to communes elect delegates to republican and federal assemblies, so that republican and federal legislators are three stages away from their basic electorates. The electorate itself consists of workers, citizens, and members of political organizations. Workers elect delegations in their basic organizations, and citizens elect delegations in 'local communities'.[9] The members of socio-political organizations (the Party, trade unions, Socialist Alliance, etc.) do not elect delegations, but their delegates on government assemblies are appointed by their governing bodies.

Delegations of basic organizations and local communities are elected by secret ballot for a period of four years. Nomination lists are prepared by the trade unions and the Socialist Alliance, after giving some kind of opportunity for all electors to put forward nominations. Delegations are also elected by the armed forces. Local meetings of delegations are then held in order to elect delegates to two chambers of the commune assemblies. Delegations from basic organizations elect delegates to the 'chamber of associated labour'; delegations from local communities elect delegates to the 'chamber of local communities'. A third chamber consists of delegates appointed directly by the socio-political organizations.

Assemblies of the republics and provinces also consist of three chambers. The general rule is that the 'chamber of associated labour' is elected by the members of the corresponding commune chambers, from a nomination list drawn up by the Socialist Alliance. By way of exception, in Croatia members of the republican chamber of associated labour are elected by the *delegations* of associated labour, not by their delegates to the commune chambers. Delegates to the 'chamber of communes' of a republic or province are elected in different ways in different republics and provinces, but always by delegates of lower communal or city assemblies. Delegates to the 'socio-political chamber' are elected by the delegates of the corresponding commune chambers.

The federal assembly consists of two chambers, each of which is composed of equal quotas from each republic and smaller quotas from the provinces. The Federal Chamber consists of thirty delegates from each republic and twenty from each province—220 members in all. They are selected from basic delegations, nominated by the Socialist Alliance, and voted by the assemblies of communes in each republic or province. The Chamber of Republics and Provinces consists of twelve delegates from each republic and eight from each province—eighty-eight in all. They are elected by joint sessions of the three chambers in each republic or province from among their own members. Members of this federal chamber continue to sit also in their own republican or provincial assemblies, and thus provide a direct liaison between the federal and republican assemb-

[9] The total membership of such delegations exceeds one million.

lies. This also implies that the delegates to this federal chamber are likely to act as a pressure group on behalf of their own republic or province.

Executive bodies

At each level of government there is an executive council, elected by the corresponding assembly. The Federal Executive Council (FEC) which is in effect the Yugoslav council of ministers, is elected for four years by the Federal Assembly on the nomination of the Socialist Alliance (see below). Some members of the FEC are heads of administrative agencies while others have more general responsibilities. While the latter group are strictly allocated across the republics and provinces in accordance with the usual quota system (equal numbers from each republic and smaller numbers from the provinces), the former group are only roughly balanced by national composition. Members of the FEC may not take orders from their own republics, although in practice they may well have local sympathies. They may not be members of the Federal Assembly. As a result of what is called 'Tito's Initiative', a proposal which he made a year or so before he died, there have been some amendments to the 1974 Constitution mainly designed to ensure more rapid rotation of posts. The President of the FEC, who is in effect Yugoslavia's prime minister, can now serve for only one term of four years; and the other members of the FEC for only two terms (*Yugoslav Survey*, November 1981).

While the FEC has all the usual responsibilities of a council of ministers, including the right to propose laws to the Assembly, there is also another semi-executive body called the Presidency. This consists of one member from each republic and province, elected by their assemblies for five years, with a possibility of one further term, plus the President of the League of Communists of Yugoslavia, *ex officio*. The Presidency elects its own President and Vice-President. The former now acts also as President of the Republic, a post previously occupied by Tito during his life time.

The Presidency has certain important powers and also several formal duties such as are normally carried out by a head of state. It can propose legislation to the Assembly. It promulgates laws, appoints ambassadors, ratifies treaties, appoints senior army officers and certain judges, confers decorations, and grants pardons. It can order mobilization, declare war and, if necessary during an emergency, pass decrees with the force of law and temporarily take extra-constitutional measures. It can summon a meeting of the FEC, place an item on its agenda, and hold up the enforcement of an FEC decision while it is referred to one of the legislative chambers.

The republics and provinces also have presidencies, and in addition each of them except Montenegro has a Council of the Republic (or Province), elected on the nomination of the Presidency by the assembly from among prominent socio-political and other public figures. The role of these Councils is not very clear.

Division of powers

Broadly, the division of powers between the federation, republics, and communes follows the principle that specific powers are given to the higher bodies and that all residual powers belong to those lower down. The federal government is responsible for foreign affairs, defence, the criminal law, foreign economic relations, the preservation of the system of self-management, and general economic laws and policies, including federal economic plans, monetary policy, some price controls, exchange rates, customs duties, inter-regional aid, statistics, and weights and measures. It has the duty to preserve the unity of the Yugoslav market and to prevent monopolies and unfair competition. It is also responsible for state security and has the right to ban publications which are considered to be 'directed against the fundamentals of the socialist democratic order established by the SFRY Constitution, or which endanger the independence of the country, peace or international co-operation' (*Constitutional System of Yugoslavia*, p. 107).

Republican and provincial governments have considerable powers. In the economic sphere, they draw up social plans for their republic or province, regulate their banking system, exercise control over the prices of many goods and services, give financial assistance to their less developed areas, and levy taxes. They may intervene in the financial affairs of enterprises and communes, forcing them to assist other enterprises or communes which are in difficulty. They regulate the maintenance and use of roads, the system of town planning, educational and health services, the state security system, and law and order. They determine the territorial limits of communes and supervise all elections. They collect and publish their own statistical data.

The commune governments have much larger powers and responsibilities than similar levels of government in most other countries. At the beginning of 1981 there were 522 communes with an average population of about 40,000. They varied in size from 29 with a population of less than 10,000 to 42 with more than 100,000 (YB81, 3 – 1). Each commune has the responsibility to 'create and develop material and other conditions of life and work . . . for the self-management satisfaction of the economic, welfare, cultural and other collective needs of the working people and citizens' (*Constitutional System of Yugoslavia*, p. 79). It directs and co-ordinates economic and social development in its area and adopts a commune social plan. It controls local land use and town planning, housing, culture, education, and health services. Above all, it has a responsibility for ensuring the provision of employment for the local population. It also has a duty to use economic and tax policy to 'ensure the prosperity of farmers' and to 'encourage private work with privately-owned means of production' (ibid., p. 81).

Constitutional courts at both federal and republican and provincial levels have the responsibility of interpreting and applying the respective constitutions. Presumably, in cases of conflict the federal court has the final authority.

The Republican veto

An important provision of the constitution gives the Chamber of Republics
and Provinces of the federal assembly the exclusive power to decide all
major economic questions. These include: adoption of the Yugoslav social
plan, control of the monetary system, foreign exchange, foreign trade and
credit policies, methods of price control, financing of aid for the less
developed republics and provinces, division of the proceeds of sales taxes,
determining the federal budget, and ensuring a free internal market. All
proposals relating to these matters are voted on in the Chamber by the
delegations of the republics and provinces, acting on instructions from
their own assemblies. The normal rule is that no proposal is considered
carried unless it has received a unanimous vote from all delegations. But
the Chamber may pass 'temporary measures' by a two-thirds majority (*The
Constitution of the Socialist Federal Republic of Yugoslavia*, Articles 286
and 295). Such measures are proposed to the Chamber by the Presidency
and have a period of validity of one year.

The constitution can be amended only if the amendment receives a vote
of two-thirds of all delegates in the Federal Chamber and the agreement of
the assemblies of all republics and provinces (ibid., Articles 401 and 402).

CO-ORDINATION AND PLANNING

The principal method of co-ordination of Yugoslav enterprises—in both
the social and the private sectors—is the market. But the market is
supplemented, as in other market-economy countries, by agreements
between enterprises, by the general legal structure, and by government
interventions. In Yugoslavia, agreements between basic organizations,
enterprises, and other non-government social sector entities are called
'self-management agreements'. Laws are also supplemented by voluntary
'social compacts', involving at least one government authority, which are
intended to establish 'norms' of behaviour, similar to laws, but without the
legal right of enforcement. Government interventions are many and varied
and affect especially the allocation of finance, foreign exchange, imports,
or anything else in short supply, as well as prices, rents, and the rate of
interest. But on top of everything there is supposed to be a 'social plan',
which provides a framework within which the market, the agreements, the
social compacts, and government policy are to operate.

Self-management agreements

Any agreement or contract between basic organizations or other entities in
the social sector is called a 'self-management agreement'. It is legally a
voluntary act, but it can in principle be enforced in a 'court of associated
labour'. Agreements between basic organizations about the rules for a
proposed joint enterprise, between enterprises to establish a composite
organization, between two enterprises which agree to 'pool labour and
resources', between suppliers and their customers, between an industrial
enterprise and a wholesale or retail organization which sells its products,

are all examples of 'self-management agreements'. There is nothing unusual about any of this except the terminology.

Social compacts

Social compacts are made between entities in the social sector and one or more government authority, or between governments themselves, e.g. between the federal government and the governments of the republics and provinces, often with the participation of one or more socio-political organizations, especially the trade unions, as well as the chambers of the economy. They are nominally voluntary, but there is usually a great deal of moral and political pressure, emanating ultimately from the Party, to force the participants to enter the agreement. Social compacts are not legally enforceable. If they are broken, as they usually are, the most that can be done is to exert further moral or political pressure to bring the participants back into line.

Social compacts may be concerned with any aspect of public policy. They have been used to try to establish common policies in such fields as education, health, housing, prices, incomes, investment, allocations of finance, foreign exchange and imports, policies towards agriculture, energy, exports, the private sector, and so forth. Social compacts may be made at all levels of government and with various combinations of enterprises and socio-political organizations. The total number of compacts signed since they were first introduced in 1971 must be very large.[10] There seems to be no public register or digest of social compacts and it is doubtful whether most signatories can remember all the promises which they have made.

Social planning

It is an accepted Yugoslav dogma that socialism entails 'planning'. During the early 'administrative' period, ending in 1952, there was full central planning. Thereafter, until 1976, there were some years in which there was no plan at all, but in most years there were 'indicative' plans of an aggregative nature. These provided no detailed instructions to enterprises about their current operations but, at least until the 1965 Reform, attempted to give guidance on the allocation of investment funds between industries and for certain major projects.

The 1974 Constitution introduced the concept of 'self-management social planning', which was formalized in a 1976 law on planning. The intention is to combine decentralization and freedom of decision-making with order and planning. The solution to this puzzle is to persuade (or force) all social sector entities and governments to enter into 'voluntary' agreements and compacts which are consistent with an overall five-year plan for economic development. The first such plan covered the period

[10] According to one estimate there were in 1980 in the country as a whole about two million self-management agreements and social compacts (*Ekonomska politika*, 9 December 1980, repeated on 25 May 1981). *Borba* (21 November 1982) reports that in a meeting in Zagreb the figure was put at three million.

1976–80; the current plan (now abandoned) is for 1981–5. In addition, there is a less precise ten-year plan for 1976–85, and work is proceeding on a long-term plan for the period up to the end of the century.

The procedure for constructing a five-year plan is said to be as follows. During the year or two preceding the plan period every basic organization, work community, government, or other social sector entity is obliged to prepare its own plan. This is ultimately expressed in the form of a mass of statistical data giving forecasts for each year of the period of the entity's expected employment, outputs, inputs, investment, exports, imports, and so forth. In the meantime, the planning offices at federal and republican levels will have issued forecasts of corresponding macroeconomic variables. These two sets of data are then brought together in the planning offices—primarily at republican and provincial level—and studied for consistency. It is said that there then follows an iterative process of adjustment to all plans until they are made consistent. When this has been achieved, a large number of self-management agreements and social compacts are concluded, which embody the consistently planned relationships between the different entities and governments. That, at least, is the theory. What happens in practice will be considered in the following chapter.

CHAPTER 7

THE SYSTEM IN OPERATION

The previous chapter was concerned with the formal structure of the post–1974 system and it included only a few comments on the realism of the official description of that system. In this chapter we shall attempt to discover how the system operates in practice. Although Yugoslavia is not exceptional in exhibiting differences between its social theory and its social practice, the gulf between words and deeds, between theory and practice, seems to be wider in Yugoslavia than in most other existing societies.[1] This is a source of some confusion to those outside observers who rely mainly on official sources of information, and the result has been that some widely quoted descriptions of the Yugoslav system are seriously misleading. Fortunately, however, there have been a number of careful studies of the real situation, both by Yugoslav scholars and by outside investigators. In addition, the Yugoslav press publishes some remarkably frank news and comments on particular events; and politicians, directors of major enterprises, university professors, and other prominent persons frequently point out divergences between the theory of a socialist self-management market economy and its actual operation in Yugoslavia. In the preparation of this chapter I have drawn mainly on this voluminous and widely-scattered literature, but also an some general knowledge of the world, supplemented by discussions with a few well-informed individuals, both Yugoslavs and others.

This chapter will follow broadly the same pattern as the preceding one. We shall consider, first, the operation of enterprises in the productive social sector, and secondly the working of the self-managing communities of interest in the non-productive social sector. Discussion of conditions in the private sector will, however, be postponed until a later chapter, where it can be developed in greater detail. A number of particular aspects of the behaviour of social sector enterprises, such as their investment decisions, determination of prices, and the efficiency of labour and management, will also be reserved for more extensive treatment in later chapters. This chapter continues with an examination of the real functioning of the

[1] Yugoslavs themselves are well aware of this problem. A Slovenian member of the Federal Chamber, for example, in a debate on 13 April 1982, drew attention to the 'serious increase in the gap between the normative and the real, between declared policy and its implementation' (*Borba*, 14 April 1982).

political system, and concludes with an assessment of the effectiveness of 'self-management planning'.

1. THE ECONOMIC SYSTEM

The productive social sector

According to official doctrine, the assets of the social sector are socially owned but are managed by the workers employed in each organization. The workers have the right, either directly through mass meetings and secret ballots or through their representatives ('delegates'), to use those assets in order to maximize income. They also have the right to distribute that income—after paying taxes, interest charges, and social security and other contributions—as they see fit. They can, if they so wish, save and plough back part of the organization's income and use part for fringe benefits. The remainder is distributed as cash incomes. Workers also— either directly or indirectly—appoint their managers, and make major business decisions about expansion, diversification, investment, borrowing, 'pooling' income with other organizations and so forth. To what extent does this description correspond to the facts?

Before we attempt to answer that question it is necessary to consider the major social forces which operate within a Yugoslav enterprise. Apart from the manual workers, divided according to skill, there are the white-collar workers, the technicians, and the managers. All of these are arranged in a normal hierarchical structure, with the director, or general director, at the top and the unskilled workers at the bottom, and orders are passed downwards, as in any organization. Parallel with this, there is the structure of 'self-management', which gives the workers the right to receive information, make decisions, and elect the workers' council and the disciplinary and other committees. But this is by no means the end of the story. Both inside and outside the organization there are various highly organized groups, whose purpose is to ensure that the 'self-managed' organization carries out the plans and policies favoured by those groups.

First there is the Party, which has a 'basic organization' of its own within each basic organization. Since there are now over two million Party members, of which more than half are probably working in the productive social sector, on the average about a quarter of all workers in that sector must be Party members. Members are obliged to pay quite large membership dues and to spend a great deal of time at meetings.[2] The members of the Party group within a basic organization will not normally have much influence as individuals on the policy of the organization, but they can be used by higher Party committees and functionaries to support the Party's policy on specific issues, which do not run too directly against the interest of the workers in that organization.

---

[2] Zukin (1975, 185) reports that Party dues in 1973 were 600 dinars a year. This was equivalent to about $40 at the current exchange rate. On a membership at that time of a little over one million, this would yield $40 million, a very large sum for a country of only 20 million people on a fairly low standard of living.

Secondly, there is the trade union. There are different trade unions for different industries, but there will normally be only one trade union in a given enterprise. Since virtually all workers are members, the trade unions have large incomes and a multiplicity of full-time officials. In a self-managed enterprise trade unions have no role to play as mobilizers of the workers against the employer, and the occasional strikes which occur in Yugoslav enterprises are not organized by the trade unions. Indeed, trade union officials do their best to bring such strikes to an end. Since there is little for the trade unions to do about wages and conditions, they tend to concentrate on providing holiday homes and other fringe benefits for their members. But the officials are carefully selected Party members, who have been told that they have an important role to play in making the socialist self-management system work. Under the Constitution and the Associated Labour Act the trade unions are given considerable powers. The trade union appoints one-third of the members of the selection committee for the nomination of candidates for the post of director, and it has the right to propose his resignation. The trade union nominates all the candidates for election to the workers' council (as well as to the associated labour chamber of the local commune); it has the right to be kept informed about all major decisions of the workers' council; and it prepares the ground for all discussions at mass meetings of the work-force. Trade unions are directly represented in the socio-political chamber of the commune, and their officials sign social compacts on many matters, especially those concerned with incomes, employment, and prices (Radević 1981). The trade union secretary inside an enterprise is a key member of the 'informal structure', or political *aktiv*, an élite group of political activists within the enterprise.[3]

In some basic organizations there will also be a 'youth brigade', consisting of members of the League of Socialist Youth of Yugoslavia, whose secretary will be a further member of the *aktiv*. Sometimes also there will be a veterans' organization with a similar function. All these organizations will be brought into action to campaign for a 'self-management' decision which the Party considers to be important. A number of small meetings will be held and individuals canvassed with a view to winning a majority. The 'relatively rare large meetings of the whole Workers' Collective . . . tend merely to confirm the success (or failure) of the preceding campaign' (Schrenk 1981, 39).[4]

Each of the socio-political organizations has an apparatus of local, republican, and federal officials, any or all of whom may wish to intervene in the affairs of an enterprise, either directly or through the indirect channels of government bodies, the banks, and the communities of interest. The most pervasive influence is usually that of the commune, the officials of which can exert great influence over the policies of local enterprises. The commune has a one-third representation on the nomina-

[3] For the 'informal structure' see Kalogjera (1981, 110). For the political *aktiv* see below.
[4] Granick (1975, 379) gives an example of this process in an enterprise which he visited.

tion committee for the post of director of each of the basic organizations in its area. It is usually required to guarantee loans made to local enterprises, and it keeps a close watch on enterprise policies in relation to such matters as investment, employment, imports from other communes, incomes, and prices. Republican governments and their officials play a similar role in relation to some of the larger enterprises. No doubt the Party at commune and republic level previously discusses all major questions and instructs the relevant government officials accordingly.[5]

Apart from the socio-political organizations, which are ultimately only different representatives of a single organization, there are several other groups which have a strong interest in the policies of enterprises. These are (1) the managers, (2) the technicians, (3) other white-collar workers, and (4) the manual workers. All of these have a common interest in the success of the business, provided that they are not expected to contribute too heavily, or 'unfairly', to that success. There are many business decisions which promise, or seem to promise, substantial benefits to all members of the enterprise, particularly those which involve the making of investments financed by cheap outside loans. But there are other decisions which give rise to some conflict of interest. The managers and technicians, for example, are likely to be more favourable to a policy of general expansion, even if it means taking on more workers, while manual workers may be more reluctant to see their share of enterprise income diluted.[6] Similarly, managers and technicians may be more disposed to increase enterprise saving and plough-back, while manual workers, especially the older ones, may prefer higher immediate cash incomes (Neuberger and James 1973, 270). There are also differences between these groups which do not arise from a conflict of interest, but from differences in their decision-making abilities and opportunities. By the nature of their education and work experience manual workers and non-technical white-collar workers are not well equipped to analyse complex business problems, nor do they have in the course of their work the opportunity to participate in discussions about technical aspects of those problems. Managers and technicians have a higher level of education, are constantly required to study and discuss complex managerial and technical problems, and naturally see themselves as having the primary responsibility to resolve such problems. Moreover, they receive in the course of their work a large amount of information which is not similarly available to other workers. As a consequence, managers and technicians tend to play a dominant part in discussions at self-management meetings about major business decisions, not necessarily because they have a difference of interest, but because they have a difference of aptitude, experience, information, and conception of their role.

[5] The role of the Party in relation to the enterprise is discussed at length in Carter (1982, Chap. 3). Her description refers mainly to the period of the 1960s, and the role of the Party will have increased since then.

[6] This reluctance may, however, be more than offset by the expectation that most of the newly recruited workers will be their own relatives.

In the final analysis, the various groups and interests operating within and around a Yugoslav self-management enterprise resolve themselves primarily into three: the Party, the managers, and the workers. The Party has the sole responsibility for the whole of society, for the success of the economy, and for a politically acceptable distribution of the fruits of production among its constituents, the workers in the social sector. Since no other party is allowed to exist, the Party can never relax: it must involve itself in everything, seem to be able to solve every problem, constantly demonstrate its incomparable powers of leadership. Moreover, since the Party is the only reliable ladder to power and privilege its more ambitious members are always looking for opportunities to demonstrate their abilities and energy. No economic system in a one-party state, whether centrally planned or of the Yugoslav type, can operate without the constant intervention of the Party, directly or through its satellite organization. Managers, on the other hand, are primarily interested in being allowed to do what they are employed to do—to make a success at their businesses. This gives them psychic satisfaction, justifies their superior status and pay, and opens avenues to future promotion. For all these reasons, their natural preference is to be allowed both to make and to implement their own decisions, without constant interference and questioning by the socio-political organizations on the one side or the workers on the other. Finally, the workers, who are supposed to be the real rulers, do not want to have the responsibility for major business decisions, for which they know that they are not well qualified and which impose a burden of anxiety which they would prefer to leave to others.[7]

The interplay between these three groups in the Yugoslav system is highly complex. Having chosen 'self-management' and a market economy, the Yugoslav Party was obliged to surrender some of its directing role to the managers. Up to 1965 the transfer of power was slow and halting; but for the next six years the managers were given much greater scope and the Party tried hard to follow a policy of *laissez-faire*. But it could not last. The strains on the Party were too great. How can the 'vanguard' of a socialist society hand over major responsibility for the economy—the basis of everything according to Marxist theory—to a group of managers? It made no difference that the great majority of managers were Party members.[8] Under *laissez-faire* conditions this was a formality, since by definition the Party managers would not be receiving direct orders from the Party. The Party—or in particular its leading personnel, the political establishment—was in danger of becoming redundant, the fifth wheel on the coach. Hence the reaction in 1972. The pretext was Croat nationalism, but the real reason was the dangerous loss of Party power during the period of the Reform. This was made clear in Tito's letter of September of that year.

Meanwhile, what of the workers, in the name of whom the whole system

[7] Differences in interest and attitude between managers and workers will be discussed in greater detail later in this chapter.

[8] In 1972, 70 per cent of directors of large and medium enterprises were Party members and 83 per cent of bank directors (Eames 1980, 179).

is supposed to function? The Yugoslav workers never asked for self-management.[9] Indeed, it is doubtful whether manual workers would willingly choose to accept the responsibilities of management in any society, whether capitalist or socialist. Self-management is a propaganda slogan, a convenient piece of ideology, hurriedly chosen by the Yugoslav Communists in a critical moment of their history. For the workers, self-management has some agreeable features. It means a relaxed state of discipline and a reduction in managerial power. It means less time on the job and more time at meetings (although this sometimes has some disagreeable aspects). It means more opportunity for the individual worker to raise issues which directly concern him; his relative pay, his working conditions, his prospects of promotion, his chance of getting a flat.

There is abundant evidence from empirical studies of self-management enterprises, by both Yugoslav and foreign investigators, that at meetings of the workers' councils most proposals for major business decisions come (as one would expect) from the management; that the discussion of these issues is dominated by managers and technicians, with some participation by the chairman; that manual workers, who are usually under-represented in relation to their numbers in the enterprise (especially the unskilled), confine themselves mainly to raising detailed points about the likely effects of any change on the group which they represent; and that the discussions only come alive when they focus an a question such as the treatment of an individual worker or the allocation of a flat.[10] This is all quite natural. The idea that workers want to manage their own enterprises is an illusion of certain intellectuals, most of whom have never done any manual work and have little conception of the attitudes of ordinary workers. The management of a modern enterprise, even one of medium size, is a complex and specialized task, or group of tasks, requiring the full-time attention of a management team of specially qualified people. The ordinary worker can no more take responsibility for managerial decision-making than he can perform a surgical operation, write a symphony, or play in a champion football team.[11]

Despite all the rhetoric about 'workers' self-management' the real position is that major business decisions are taken by one or other (or both) of two groups: the Party and the managers. The history of Yugoslav self-management can only be understood correctly if it is viewed as a series of shifts in the relative strength of these two groups. The purpose of the 1972 reaction, embodied subsequently in the 1974 Constitution, was to re-establish the predominance of the Party over the managers. Apart from

[9] Marković (1982, 187) writes: 'Self-management was not imposed on [the Party leaders] under the pressure of the masses. They themselves reintroduced [sic] it.'

[10] See, for example, Eames (1980, 66–9 and 261), Granick (1975, 337–8 and 382), Horvat (1976, 160–1), Jerovšek and Možina (1978, 285), Neuberger and James (1973, 280), Rus (1978, 210–11), Vejnović (1978, 267-76), Wilson (1979, 235), and Zvonarević (1978, 176–96).

[11] Workers in a Belgrade factory in the period of the Reform said to a foreign visitor: 'I wish someone would tell me what to do and I would not have to worry why', and 'Let someone else manage; I want good pay' (Adizes 1971, 219).

Tito's 1972 'call to arms', and the resulting increase in Party membership and Party activity, a principal aim of the Constitution was to weaken the power of managers by breaking up enterprises into basic organizations. But, although the rhetoric and the letter of the law says that power should be in the hands of the workers, the real fact is that the power lost by the managers was transferred, not to the workers, but to the Party.

The exercise of power

By what methods, and to what extent, was the Party able to re-establish its authority over enterprises in the social sector? Among the great variety of levers at the disposal of the Party, there are two which are of crucial importance for this purpose. The first is Party control over the banks; and the second is Party control over the 'informal structure', the political *aktiv* within each organization.

A major purpose of the 1965 Reform was to strengthen the financial independence of enterprises by reducing taxation, so allowing enterprises to retain, if they wished, a larger proportion of their incomes for reinvestment. There is some doubt as to whether this aim was in fact achieved, except temporarily for the first few years after the Reform. The evidence is incomplete and to a certain degree contradictory. One of the difficulties is that an often-quoted set of figures refers to the financing of investment in fixed assets.[12] But the statistical allocation of investment funds to different purposes is arbitrary. A more meaningful figure is the ratio of gross enterprise saving to total enterprise investment. On this basis, Table 7.1 suggests that the share of self-finance of social sector enterprise investment did indeed increase after the Reform. But these figures are unadjusted for stock appreciation, which was of increasing

TABLE 7.1

The Finance of Gross Investment in Social Sector Enterprises

Percentage of gross investment of social sector enterprises financed by:	1961–5	1966–70	1971–5
Own gross savings	62.3	68.4	74.0
Financial savings of:			
Investment loan funds	35.6	20.6	5.1
Households	2.6	11.2	18.3
Rest of world	3.2	4.2	5.6
Others[a]	−3.7	−4.4	−2.9

Source: Schrenk and others (1979), Table A.6.
Notes: The data are derived from flow-of-funds accounts, which record payments for investment, not the value of work done. Investment includes the change in value of stocks, not adjusted for stock appreciation. Financial saving of each sector is equal to its gross saving minus its gross investment.
[a] Governments, other social sector organizations, and unclassified.

[12] See, for example, *Društveno planiranje i proširena reprodukcija* (1980), Table 1 on p. 307.

importance after 1965, and especially in 1971–5. A rough adjustment for stock appreciation can be made with the help of estimates by the World Bank for the periods 1966–70 and 1971–5.[13] After this adjustment the percentages of self-financing of social sector enterprises for these two periods fall back to 63.6 and 63.1 respectively, virtually unchanged from 1961–5.

Thus, approximately one-third of adjusted gross investment by social sector enterprises continued to be financed from outside sources. The table shows that the ultimate sources of these outside funds have changed radically since the Reform. In 1961–5 investment loan funds supplied almost the whole amount (in the sense that their contribution to the total pool of financial savings was almost sufficient to cover the financial deficit of enterprises), and the contributions of households and the rest of the world were small. During the following ten years, however, the contribution made by the investment loan funds fell away, especially after 1970, and the contribution of household financial savings increased dramatically. There was also a steady growth in the contribution made by foreign borrowing.[14]

These changes in the sources of external finance are important for a number of reasons, and they have been much discussed in Yugoslavia. But for the present purpose the crucial question is: what are the channels through which external finance reaches social sector enterprises? And in this respect there has been no significant change since 1961–5. For, throughout this period, virtually all external finance was channelled to enterprises through the banks. As a result, almost all enterprises are deeply indebted to the banks, and depend on them to provide large amounts of supplementary funds, to cover not only the increase in their current assets but also their investments in fixed assets. Indeed, the *gross* flow of bank loans to enterprises in any year is much larger than their net requirement of bank finance, partly because bank loans are constantly being repaid and reborrowed, and partly because much of the flow of bank loans to enterprises is ultimately financed by increases in enterprise deposits in banks.[15]

Thus, those in Yugoslavia who control the banks have a lever of enormous importance for controlling enterprise investments. According to the law, Yugoslav commercial banks (so-called 'basic' banks) are controlled by their founder members, who may be basic organizations, communi-

[13] The estimates are derived from Schrenk and others (1979), Table A.9.

[14] It must be borne in mind that these figures do not measure the direct flow of funds from each sector to social sector enterprises but the relation between the contribution of each sector to the total pool of financial savings and the total demand of social sector enterprises on that pool.

[15] The reasons include: (1) enterprise money holdings tend to increase automatically with the increase in the money value of their turnover; (2) enterprises are obliged to hold some of their reserves, e.g. for housing investment, in special deposits; (3) there are always some enterprises with temporary surplus funds, which they keep in the banks; (4) banks sometimes require enterprises to make deposits as a condition for obtaining loans, thus increasing the effective interest charge on the loan. For the last practice see Granick (1975, 397).

ties of interest, and 'other social legal entities', but not governments.[16] A bank is established by a self-management agreement between its founders, who 'pool resources' for this purpose, i.e. make the initial investment. Each member, irrespective of size, is entitled to one delegate at the bank's assembly, where decisions are made by equal votes about the bank's annual and medium-term plans, the upper limit of its indebtedness, and the distribution of its income. All the bank's income must be distributed; it is not allowed to accumulate funds of its own, so as to avoid the growth of 'anonymous capital'. The assembly elects an executive committee to make day-to-day decisions and a credit committee to allocate loans. The professional management participates in meetings of these bodies but has no vote. Most important of all, the banks are obliged to integrate their plans with the general social plan and with the self-management agreements and social compacts signed by their founder members. In principle, therefore, the banks' loan allocations should be consistent with the social investment plan.

As might be expected, there is virtually no published information about the inner workings of the banking system. But some inferences can be made from a few facts and a multitude of comments on the results. At the end of 1980 there were 162 'basic' banks. Except in Croatia, these were all combined into 8 'associated' banks, designed to handle large loans and to undertake foreign exchange transactions.[17] On the same date there were 34,390 basic organizations.[18] If all of these basic organizations were founder members of basic banks there would be, on the average, over 200 basic organizations per basic bank and over 4,000 per associated bank. Since there is a perennial shortage of bank credit in relation to the demand for credit at the existing artificially low interest rates (real interest rates have been negative for many years and in recent years heavily negative), there is a constant struggle for influence over credit allocations. It is impossible, therefore, for the banks' credit committees fairly to represent the founder members who elect them; and this situation creates an open invitation for intervention by some 'higher interest', which is inevitably the Party, speaking in the name of the working class as a whole, and legally supported by references to the social plan, in the framing of which it has already played a predominant role.

That this is the real position is easily demonstrated by innumerable public references to the control of bank finance by governments and socio-political organizations. The weekly journal *Ekonomska politika*, for example, repeatedly states, as if it were an axiom, that bank loans to enterprises are provided under pressure from governments and socio-political organizations.[19] The same inference can be drawn from the

[16] Banks are now governed by the Law on the Fundamental Principles of the Credit and Monetary System, which entered into force on 7 January 1977.

[17] *Ekonomska politika*, special supplement, 16 November 1981.

[18] YB81, 103–2.

[19] Recent examples can be found in the issues of 22 March 1982, p. 18 and 17 May 1982, pp. 18–20.

resolution of the Third Congress of Self-Managers of Yugoslavia, held in Belgrade in June 1981, and attended by 1,693 delegates. Among other things, the resolution declares that 'it is indispensable resolutely to overcome, through the activities of organized forces of society, the practice that factors outside associated labour, in informal tandems with managing boards of basic organizations of associated labour, banks and executive organs of socio-political communities [governments] and organs of socio-political organizations [the Party and its satellite organizations], make decisions regarding the means of expanded reproduction [finance for investment]'. It is also 'indispensable to prevent organs of socio-political communities and other factors outside associated labour from interfering, beyond their authorization, in decision-making in organizations of associated labour and banks' (*Yugoslav Survey*, August 1981, pp. 6–7).

The second major lever of Party influence on the policy of basic organizations is the political *aktiv*. The *aktiv* is an unofficial group, normally small, consisting of Party members holding key positions in the socio-political organizations (such as Party secretary, trade union secretary, and secretary of the youth organization), in the workers' council, and among top management (Adizes 1971, 99).[20]

In a Zagreb engineering firm in 1974 Comisso (1979, 242) noted that the *aktiv* met in private in the director's office. In a Belgrade firm in 1977 Eames found that discussions at meetings of the workers' council were frequently foreclosed when a member drew attention to the fact that the matter had already been agreed by the Party, the trade union, or the political *aktiv* (Eames 1980, 227, 230, 242). The occupants of the different posts in the Party, trade union, and workers' council are changed at intervals—usually 2–4 years—under the rules of rotation. But, since it is largely the same group who move around from one position to another, in so-called 'horizontal rotation', the composition of the *aktiv* remains fairly constant. According to Zukin, who interviewed a small sample of Belgrade families in 1972, her respondents considered that leading positions in the Party, trade unions, and workers' councils 'have become restricted, in effect, to professional activists and their dependants'. She also reported the comments of a young metalworker, interviewed in a survey by the weekly journal *NIN* in 1971, who said: 'On the management-committee-union circuit the same people are constantly moving back and forth' (Zukin 1975, 128, 137).

Although higher Party functionaries regard the political *aktiv* as one of their essential levers for influencing enterprise policies, this lever, like others, can often be made to work in opposite or other directions. For example, the director may call on the *aktiv* to persuade officials of the commune, the republican government, the Party, or the trade union to help the enterprise to obtain a bank loan, a foreign exchange allocation, or an increase in its product prices. Indeed, under a vigorous and popular director, the *aktiv* may become more a means of lobbying on behalf of the

[20] See also Carter (1982, 238–9).

enterprise than an instrument of outside Party control over the enterprise. There are many complaints that workers' councils, and even Party organizations, think only of the private interest of the enterprise to the exclusion of consideration of general social policy and 'solidarity'.[21] Even when the *aktiv* is not being used in this direction it is an important managerial instrument for influencing worker opinion inside the enterprise and for ensuring support by self-management bodies and the workers generally for managerial initiatives.

While the Party uses the banks and the *aktiv* to influence the policies of enterprises, it does not have complete control over enterprise policy. By virtue of the fact that the Party long ago abandoned full central planning, and has given enterprises considerable 'self-management' rights, and placed them under the necessity to respond to the market, the members of those enterprises—both workers and managers—have a real degree of power such as they would not enjoy in a centrally planned economy. The managers, in particular, occupy a key position in the economy. The Party cannot give managers detailed orders if it wants enterprises to compete successfully in the market. But there is always a temptation to intervene for political reasons, and the boundary between the spheres of influence of the Party and the managers is constantly shifting. In recent years, to judge by unanimous public comment, it seems to have shifted a long way in favour of the Party and the government and to the detriment of managerial autonomy.[22]

Managers, of course, are in no position to put up a strong resistance to Party pressures. Directors are nominated by commissions on which Party influence is overwhelming.[23] If a director loses the confidence of the local commune leadership, the Party as such, or the trade union, he may easily be removed and will certainly not have his contract extended at the end of his four-year term. His career prospects will be seriously damaged. The Party can bring pressure on him also in other ways, by creating difficulties for the enterprise's credit applications, or by whipping up criticism of him among the workers. So long as a director sees eye to eye with local Party officials he can concentrate on his real job, which is to organize his enterprise efficiently. But it means that directors need to be politicians first and foremost, and this reduces the probability that the best potential directors will be appointed.[24]

---

[21] The Serbo-Croat phrase for 'organization of associated labour' is *organizacia udruženog rada*, the acronym for which is *OUR*, and the deviation complained of is known as '*ourizacia*'.

[22] In public statements this is not described as a loss of autonomy for managers, but for 'self-managers', i.e. the workers. But the reality is otherwise, as Yugoslav politicians, business men, and publicists must know.

[23] *Ekonomska politika*, 13 July 1981, cites a recent social compact in Belgrade under which every election of a director by a workers' council 'will be cancelled if it is not based on the previously obtained "opinion" of the co-ordinating committee of the commune'.

[24] Directors and other senior staff are required, in addition to their technical qualifications, to demonstrate that they have satisfactory 'moral and political qualities'. Although it is sometimes stated that Party membership is not necessary to satisfy this requirement, in practice it almost certainly is. The question is discussed further in Chapter 12 below.

Normally the director of an enterprise works closely with the Party and its representatives in government, the banks, and the trade unions. Such a director would keep in regular telephone contact with influential officials of these organizations.[25] In this situation, the current of influence flows in both directions: the Party uses the director to carry out policies which it favours, and the director uses the Party to get what he wants, on behalf of his enterprise, from the commune or republican governments, the banks, the price control authorities and so forth.[26] So long as the director has the support of the Party, he can normally make the 'self-management' system work in the way in which he, and the Party, want it to work. Such a director will be able to appoint to senior staff positions the people whom he prefers, since the workers' council will ratify his choices.

He and his senior staff form the 'collegium', an informal group which meets regularly to discuss organization and planning.[27] Proposals for changes of policy usually come to the workers' council from this group. If they are thought to be controversial, the director will first discuss them also with the political *aktiv* (Granick 1975, 367). The result, as Eames (1980, 252) noted, is that 'detailed discussion of important business matters does not take place' in the self-management meetings, since 'this work has already been carried out by commissions, or at the meetings of experts, managers and socio-political organizations, held prior to the meetings of the self-management bodies themselves'.[28]

[25] There is a well-known story about a leading Yugoslav official who was asked at a lecture in Stockholm what were the main instruments used by Yugoslavs to implement their plans. His answer was: 'Telephones!' (Horvat 1976, 43).

[26] Of course, managers cannot always get what they want from the outside authorities, even when they have the full support of their own workers, self-management bodies, and Party and trade union secretaries, because there is a scarcity of aggregate resources. An example is given by Comisso (1979, 192) of persistent failure of a firm to get the funds which it considered necessary, even when 'meetings were held with the municipal and republic economic chambers, the city trade union federation, the industrial associations of the mining industry for which [the firm] was a major equipment supplier, and the city and republic legislatures'.

[27] Comisso (1979, 236) found in the Zagreb firm which she studied in 1974 that the collegium included 'all supervisory personnel above the foreman level as well as the crew of university-trained engineers and economists in the R and D Department'. According to Schrenk (1981, 32) the collegium may also include the president of the workers' council and the chairman of the trade union. The director can vary the composition of the meeting to suit the agenda.

[28] Comisso (1979, 188–9) noted that plans for annual production, investment, and financing were drawn up by executives, discussed at the collegium, and then submitted for approval by the self-management bodies. Individual members of these bodies sometimes made comments and suggestions, but there was never any group conflict, since 'everyone wanted the firm to make money, everyone wanted it to increase productivity, and everyone was in favor of higher incomes'. Moreover, the workers did not want management to spend time preparing alternative plans, just for discussion, since there was 'too much talking' already (ibid. 190). And 'like business policy, the legitimacy of managerial influence on questions relating to the organization of work was virtually unquestioned'. 'Job and shift assignments, the organizational flow of authority, equipment purchases, making up for delays, work hours, plant safety, and other technical and on-the-job issues were routine questions that rarely provoked any disputes in the self-management bodies' (ibid. 191).

The lack of worker influence on business decisions arises from several causes. In the first place, as mentioned earlier, manual workers have insufficient knowledge, training, and experience to make a confident contribution to the discussion of such decisions.[29] Even those who are elected on to the workers' council or the management board have little time to become acquainted with all the relevant facts, and the rotation system ensures that new groups of inexperienced workers are constantly being brought on to such bodies. Secondly, the managers and technicians, who have greater knowledge, training, and experience, usually also have more verbal ability and persuasive powers.[30] And, because they prepare all proposals for discussion, they have many opportunities to frame the proposals in such a way as to win the support of the workers (Zvonarević 1978, 184). Occasionally, also, they may engage in a little 'manipulation', as in the example cited by Schrenk (1981, 40) where the management, with the support of the workers' council, proposed that the annual accounts should include 'sizable voluntary depreciation and low allocation to business funds (undistributed profits)' in order to 'discourage claims for higher personal incomes from the rank-and-file'.

But the third reason for lack of worker influence on major decisions is the most important. It is that most workers *do not want* to take responsibility for such decisions (Neuberger and James 1973, 280).[31] Those who take such decisions implicitly accept the risks which flow from them. A good decision will raise future incomes; but a bad one will reduce them, and may even lead to the threat of bankruptcy and the loss of jobs. The workers are glad to support decisions recommended by those whom they trust. But they do not want to be saddled with the prime responsibility for business decisions, since they know that some decisions turn out badly and that, if they themselves have taken them, they will be expected to bear the consequences. In other words, workers are 'risk-averse'. So the workers, or their delegates, go to the 'self-management' meetings, listen to the management's proposals and, if they sound good, vote for them. Thus, they almost invariably endorse proposals for more investment, especially if

[29] Granick (1975, 337–8) points out that a workers' council is more handicapped in this respect than the members of a board of directors of a capitalist firm, who also usually accept management advice.

[30] The enormous number of laws, regulations, self-management agreements, and social compacts, which are a feature of the Yugoslav system, are so complicated that only people with expert knowledge, sometimes only a lawyer, can interpret them and try to determine their relevance to a particular business decision (Eames 1980, 260). The profession of lawyer is in great demand and the number of students enrolling in law faculties has grown rapidly.

[31] Rus (1979) gives the following results of a sample survey of workers employed in seven industrial plants and two commercial organizations in Slovenia in 1974: 12.5 per cent of workers wanted to decide on long-term plans, 17.1 per cent wanted to decide about investments, and 18.3 per cent wanted to decide on the introduction of new products. Since there were positive correlations between these aspirations and such variables as education, income, and status, the percentages of manual workers who wanted to make strategic decisions must have been smaller. This, then, was the position in the most advanced republic in Yugoslavia after more than twenty years of intense propaganda in favour of self-management.

most of the finance is to come from bank credits. The points on which they are likely to express differing views are cases of discipline, housing allocations, and the distribution of income. The workers as a whole may want more cash income and less 'accumulation' than is wanted by the Party and the managers. And particular groups of workers may have a grievance about their own incomes, especially when some change in market conditions or working practices has resulted in a fall in earnings in one or other department (or in one basic organization within an enterprise). It is in situations like this that groups of workers go on strike. Lacking confidence in the effectiveness of self-management bodies as channels for remedying their grievances, and receiving no support from the trade unions, they resort to direct action.[32] The effects are immediate and dramatic. The political *aktiv* is galvanized, and Party and trade union officials rush around looking for solutions. Almost invariably the strike lasts only for a few hours and the workers win their demands (Granick 1975, 387).[33] It speaks much for the tolerance and sense of solidarity among Yugoslav workers that they resort to strike action so rarely.[34]

Conclusions

According to Yugoslav ideology it is crucially important that the workers, especially the manual workers, should be in control of productive enterprises in the social sector. This is where value is produced and where socialist accumulation takes place. Unless the workers control this sector, there is no effective working-class power—no socialism. But, as we have seen, the workers do not control the most important decisions of the self-management system. These decisions are, in fact, controlled on the one hand by the Party, working through government agencies, the banks, and the other socio-political organizations, and on the other by the managers. Most of the time these two groups work closely together, even when Party and government officials are publicly attacking 'managers and technocrats', while journalists speaking for the managers are criticizing the interventions of governments and the socio-political organizations.[35]

Even if the workers do not enjoy the benefits (and burdens) of 'real' self-management, there are other advantages of the self-management

[32] The trade unions are often used by the Party and government as a channel for putting pressure on the workers to adhere to social compacts on income distribution or to work harder. See Schrenk (1981, 38). The Zagreb newspaper *Vjesnik* (14 October 1981) reported that the president of the Croatian Council of Trade Unions, Mirko Mećava, in the course of a visit to an enterprise in one district of Zagreb, had strongly emphasized the need for work discipline and the strengthening of the activities of enterprise disciplinary committees.

[33] Comisso (1979, 196) quotes a case where the workers' council of a firm called a strike to force the bank to guarantee its credit for an agreed import transaction. The bank quickly signed the required form shortly before the strike was due to start and apologized for its six-week delay in doing so.

[34] During 1980 there were 245 'work stoppages', as they are euphemistically called. The average number of workers involved was about 50 and the average period only a few hours (*Ekonomska politika*, 29 June 1981, p. 22).

[35] A Belgrade banker, asked by a visitor whether he did not feel worried by the frequent public criticism of bankers by politicians, replied: 'Pay no attention'.

system. Firstly, self-management requires, and provides the political justification for, a market economy, from the existence of which the people of Yugoslavia have derived great economic and political benefits. Secondly, even partial self-management gives the workers in an enterprise opportunities to ask questions and to raise particular issues about which they feel strongly. As a consequence, they enjoy a higher status than the wage-earners in either capitalism or Soviet-type state socialism. Thirdly, the workers have the power to remove a director whom they dislike. This power is not often used—but it exists. Fourthly, in the absence of employers, who can be made a scapegoat for all grievances, together with the great volume of propaganda about the virtues of self-management, Yugoslav workers are probably more willing to adjust to new conditions, more co-operative and less obstructive of technical change than workers under capitalism (except perhaps in Japan).

But there are other features of the self-management system which are less satisfactory. First, the reduction in managerial disciplinary power, and the almost complete abolition of the risk of dismissal, has helped to create much slackness, absenteeism, lateness, and general unwillingness to respond to orders. Secondly, the self-management system is very time-consuming and increases the volume of paperwork and the number of administrative staff. Thirdly, the attempt to strengthen self-management, or rather to weaken the managers, by breaking enterprises into basic organizations, has accentuated the complexity of the system, increased the time spent at meetings, and imposed greater burdens on managers.[36] While capable managers, who have the confidence of their workers, have been able to surmount these difficulties, mainly by short-circuiting official procedures, the less capable have been dragged down by them. Finally, there is a danger that the lack of correspondence between theory and practice, between high rhetoric and known reality, will breed increasing cynicism, leading to a progressive reduction of efficiency and job satisfaction.

The non-productive social sector

This section will mainly be concerned with the organization of the social services. The control of banks has been touched on in the previous section, and there is little available information about the role of 'self-management' within government departments and among the staffs of the Party and the other socio-political organizations.

The avowed purposes of the present Yugoslav method of organizing the social services, through self-managing communities of interest, are that (1) the workers engaged in providing these services should enjoy self-management rights, (2) workers in the social sector as a whole, who provide the finance for these services by their 'contributions', should have an influence over the determination of the quality and quantity of services

---

[36] It is reported, also, that one of the effects of the breaking up of enterprises into basic organizations has been to reduce flexibility and the willingness of workers to make adjustments which they expect to affect different basic organizations differently.

provided and on the size of budgets, and (3) except in cases of deadlock between the above two parties, there should be no government intervention. The reason for treating social services differently from productive industry is said to be that social services cannot be sold on the market. Instead, they are supplied and paid for by the process known as 'free exchange of labour', by bilateral bargaining.[37]

Although the intentions behind this system are good, the logic is not entirely clear. If goods or services cannot be traded in the market, as in the case of strictly collective goods, such as national defence, the right answer is to give the responsibility to the government (as happens, of course, in the case of national defence in Yugoslavia). The argument for treating social services, such as education and health services, differently from other goods and services is not that they are collective goods, i.e. goods which cannot be attributed to individuals, but that politicians (or the community which they represent) wish to ensure that selected groups should receive such services, whether they can afford to pay for them (or in some cases even wish to have them) or not. They are 'merit' goods, and their social provision is, in part, a method of redistributing income. This being so, there does not seem to be any way of avoiding political responsibility for the determination of the quality and quantity of such services, the entitlements of different groups, and the methods of raising the funds to pay for them. There is much to be said for allocating this political responsibility so far as possible to local or regional bodies, but it does not seem practicable to give the responsibility to enterprises.

The truth is that the burden of 'self-management' responsibilities on Yugoslav enterprises is beyond their capacity. The workers have more than they can cope with in trying to participate in decisions about the operation of their own enterprises. On top of this, they are obliged to send delegates to the communes, to the banks, and to all sorts of communities of interest—for schools, universities, scientific research, culture, health services, roads, water supply, transport, electric power and so on. In every case they are supposed to act as the 'masters', who decide policy and allocate funds by raising levies on their own income. The task is impossible; and, not surprisingly, the communities of interest are in fact controlled by their administrative staffs, acting on behalf of governments (and the Party). There have been isolated cases in which enterprises have refused to contribute towards particular services on the grounds that they can provide them more satisfactorily themselves.[38] But the universal complaint is that both the policies and budgets of communities of interest are decided by governments.

[37] In fact, Yugoslav communities of interest for social services raise quite substantial amounts of their revenue from commercial sales. Drulović (1978, 74–5) gives the following proportions: for the health service 22 per cent, for schooling 14 per cent, for the arts 46 per cent, and for scientific activity 68 per cent.

[38] *Ekonomska politika* (9 March 1981) cites two examples of large enterprises, one in Serbia and the other in Zagreb, which have established their own technical schools—for 700 and 370 students respectively—and negotiated a corresponding reduction in their contribution to the local community of interest.

By way of illustration, there follow two typical quotations from *Ekonomska politika*:

. . . in spite of all social decisions, and also explicit legal rules, the financing of communities of interest is carried out in a purely budgetary fashion. Instead of making compacts about the forms, volume and quality of services, from which there ought to emerge an optimal development of these activities and a rational expenditure of resources, new self-managing communities of interest are being created (at the end of last year there were 3,842 with more than 40,000 employees and they had all the practical attributes of government power) (2 November 1981).

Contributions to the social activities of self-management communities of interest have not the least in common with the proclaimed so-called free exchange of labour, but rather they have in essence the character of taxes (they are fixed by the assemblies of the socio-political communities), besides which neither the bases nor the rates satisfy even the basic demands which are presented to the mechanism (8 June 1981).

Similar views were expressed in the previously quoted resolution of the Third Congress of Self-Managers of Yugoslavia, one paragraph of which demanded:

To put an end to the practice of determining the rate of contributions and the purpose for which resources for collective needs are to be used by decisions taken in the assemblies of socio-political communities, instead of determining them through self-management agreements (*Yugoslav Survey*, August 1981, p.8).[39]

Apart from this, it is widely believed that the system of communities of interest is both costly and inefficient. During the period 1973–81 the total number of government officials rose from 108,000 to 127,000 while the number of officials employed in communities of interest rose from zero to 43,000 (*Ekonomska politika*, 1 June 1981, quoting Professor Dušan Bilandžić of Zagreb University). By early 1981 there were more than 3,700 self-managing communities of interest and more than 5,500 laws, regulations, decisions, rule books, decrees, self-management agreements, and so on, which regulated the financing of general and community needs (*Ekonomska politika*, 30 March 1981, p. 28).

It is often said that the system has failed to give power to the workers who pay for the social services, but has given excessive power to those employed in the social services, and to the administrative personnel of the communities of interest. Since each social service is under a separate community of interest, it can be argued that there is too little, not too much, budgetary control over expenditure on the social services as a whole. The administrators of the community of interest for schools, for example, will propose a certain level of staffing and other costs, and a

---

[39] See also an article in the November 1981 issue of *Yugoslav Survey* on 'Free Exchange of Labour' where it is said that decision-making in communities of interest is 'preponderately guided by policies defined by socio-political communities' (p. 61). *Ekonomska politika* (13 December 1982, p. 24) has written bluntly: 'The parts of income which are set aside for financing general and collective social needs have never been the subject of genuine decision-making by the workers.'

corresponding levy on workers' incomes. It is virtually impossible for a single enterprise to reject this demand, and there is no way in which it can organize opposition, since this would be contrary to the rules of the communist one-party system. So this levy has to be paid.[40] Then there is a levy for pensions, for the medical service, for scientific research, for museums, art galleries, and libraries, for the theatre and other cultural activities, for local transport, for the water supply, and so on. While many of these levies are quite small, the total grows to a high figure, usually in the range of 40–70 per cent of gross workers' incomes. It is no wonder that there are constant complaints that the burden is too great. But attempts to solve the problem by forcing the 'self-management' system of communities of interest to work according to the law seem to be misconceived. In the end, the Yugoslavs will probably be obliged officially to give back the responsibility for controlling and financing the social services to governments.

2. THE POLITICAL SYSTEM

In this section we shall consider, first, the effects of the delegate system, secondly, the control of the socio-political organizations, thirdly, the state of civil liberties and, fourthly, the effects of federalization.

The effects of the delegate system

At no time since the establishment of Communist government in Yugoslavia have other political parties been allowed to exist. Indeed, the suggestion that an alternative party should be allowed to contest elections would be regarded as counter-revolutionary. For a brief period during the Reform years there were some electoral contests between different Communist candidates representing different points of view, and parliamentary debates were lively.[41] But both these phenomena were brought to an end by the 1974 Constitution, in the name of greater democracy. Under the system of delegations and the pyramid structure of elections to higher bodies, coupled with a complete ban on organized opposition, there is no possibility of any candidate with an independent viewpoint and popular support entering a commune assembly, let alone the Federal Assembly.[42] In the words of Carter (1982, 8), 'the adoption since 1974 of the "delegate" system for all elections has in practice undermined the degree of electoral choice that existed briefly in the late 1960s and strengthened party control over delegates in the assemblies, under the

---

[40] If 51 per cent of enterprises covered by a community of interest agree to a contribution rate, it becomes a law for all.

[41] In 1967 there were on the average 2.3 nominations per seat in communal elections, and for the Federal Chamber 82 candidates for 60 seats, nominated by communal assemblies. In several cases it was in fact an old Partisan, representing the views of Party conservatives, who was victorious in these federal elections (Rusinow 1977, 223–4).

[42] In a random check on the election of delegations in Croatia in 1978, Rusinow (1978, 13) found that two-thirds of candidate lists contained exactly the number of posts to be filled, and in the remainder only a few extra, e.g. 28 names for 25 places.

guise of eliminating political élitism'. Wilson (1979, 234) has also remarked that since 1974 'The excitement of public elections like those of 1964 and 1968 are things of the past, and the "general political deputy" as representative of the people has disappeared'.

Two other changes in the 1974 Constitution had the effect of further guaranteeing the dominance of the Party. The first is the creation of separate 'socio-political' chambers in commune and republic assemblies, consisting of delegates chosen by the Party and its satellite organizations. The second is the rule that delegates to assemblies are no longer to give up their normal occupations. 'This was designed to ensure that all except the "socio-political" delegates should be part-time politicians' (Wilson 1979, 219).[43]

One of the virtues of the delegate system is supposed to be that delegates regularly consult with their electors and are 'mandated' by them. In practice, however, Yugoslavs have discovered that the mandate system, if taken seriously, is disruptive of effective government. Recently, Zvone Dragan, Vice-President of the Federal Executive Council (equivalent to Vice-Premier) said on a television programme: '. . . often it happens that representatives of the competent organs of the republics and provinces come to meetings of committees without authority, with so-called imperative mandates. No one gives way by a single millimetre and when he has announced his opinions he goes home, and we—the FEC—have then to square the circle, which is impossible' (*Ekonomska politika*, 7 December 1981, p. 6). According to Zukin (1975, 181) meetings of electors, both in enterprises and local communities, are dominated by 'Establishment activists' who 'put down criticism'. The vision of workers and citizens telling their delegates how they want them to vote is an illusion.

Even the delegates from basic organizations, the heart of the proletariat, who go to their own 'chambers of associated labour' in communes and republics, have proved to be unable to play an effective part in formulating government policy. As Comisso (1980, 204) explains: 'In part, internal instability and enterprise insularity were responsible for low participation: enterprises and [basic organizations] were hesitant to assume too high a political profile and to defend publicly potentially controversial positions. More profoundly, however, enterprises remained essentially productive and economic entities; as such, they were ill adapted to perform the tasks of interest aggregation and policy formulation the new system expected of them.' They 'lacked the time and personnel to devote to the working-out of broad legislative proposals and policy initiatives [which] their delegates might present before government assemblies—especially since any individual proposal they presented ultimately might not be adopted. As a result, the burden of preparing legislation fell to full-time political leaders and bureaucrats, much as in the past.' And the same applies to the delegates from basic organizations to the assemblies of the communities of interest (ibid. 205).

[43] See also Rusinow (1977, 332).

With the best of intentions, delegates are given great masses of information, to the point where they simply cannot digest the material received. 'With the ostensible purpose that participants in self-management activities and in the delegate system should be better and better informed, the administration produces a mass of printed matter, which even the most conscientious delegate cannot read through. For the session of the Education Council of Croatia, for example, each member of that body received by post a packet of material weighing three and a half kilograms' (*Vjesnik*, 31 October 1981). Eames (1980, 264) quotes a delegate to a commune chamber of associated labour, who said in a television discussion that over a period of four years he had received 100,000 pages of documents, weighing 420 kilograms. (That represents about 100 pages per weekday!)[44]

The delegates to assemblies are predominantly non-manual workers. Even in the commune assemblies, only 32 per cent of delegates in 1978 were 'non-farm manual, sales and service', although a further 17 per cent were from farms. In the republican assemblies in the same year only 11 per cent were miners and industrial workers, and in the Federal Assembly only 20 delegates out of 303 were in this category.[45] A large proportion of delegates are full-time officials of socio-political organizations. In the Federal Assembly as a whole 45 per cent of delegates were from socio-political organizations, and in the Chamber of Republics and Provinces, which has decisive power on all economic questions, the proportion was 74 per cent (*Yugoslav Survey*, August 1979, pp. 16–21).

Virtually all delegates are members of the Party. From a scrutiny of biographical details of members of republican chambers elected in 1967 Carter (1982, 125) found that all the 120 delegates in Serbia were Communists, all but one in Croatia, and all but seven in Slovenia.[46] But the few non-Communist delegates would have been sponsored, along with the others, by the Socialist Alliance, and would be subject to pressure from that quarter if they failed to 'toe the Party line'. In the Federal Assembly in 1968–9 Denitch (1976, 216) reports that out of 65 delegates interviewed in a survey all were members of the Party.

Despite the one million or more members of 'delegations', elected with much publicity every four years, the concentration of power in Yugoslavia is very great. Horvat (1976, 41) quotes Stipe Šuvar, a Croat academic-politician, as writing in 1972: 'Socio-political power . . . is still possessed and exercised by narrow ruling groups. . . . For instance, all essential functions in the Federation and the states are performed by at most a

[44] *Ekonomska politika*, 18 May 1981, reports that delegates to the Federal Assembly have received pages of material marked 'government secret' or 'strictly confidential'. 'Many of these pages, it is suggested in [the official] report, have remained secret even to the Delegates because they often do not manage to read them . . .'.

[45] There was only one manual worker delegate to the Federal Assembly from each of Croatia, Macedonia, and Slovenia.

[46] In some cases the fact of Party membership may have been omitted from the biography, especially in the case of delegates not having official positions in the Party.

hundred-odd people.' Even at the level of the commune, Comisso (1979, 93) quotes the views of Professor Eugen Pusić: 'To see [the commune] as an autonomous community embodying the free consensus of the citizens . . . is an elusive ideal . . . Not only is the commune still very much defined by its power role, but there is a tendency toward the formation of local élites, centralized within the communal area, looking toward the central government instead of toward the local population . . . '

The socio-political organizations

If the ordinary worker or citizen has no method of influencing government policy by action outside the approved socio-political organizations, what opportunities are there for influencing the policies of those organizations? In 1980 there were just over 2 million members of the Party, 14.2 million members of the Socialist Alliance (approximately the same as the number of persons in the population aged 20 and over), 5.4 million members of the Federation of Trade Unions, 3.5 million members of the League of Socialist Youth, and 1.1 million members of the Veterans' Federation (Yearbook 1981, Table 103-21). It is obvious from these numbers that membership of all organizations (other than the Party itself) is virtually compulsory, and therefore no more than a formality. The large size of the Party also indicates that it is no longer accurate to describe it as a 'vanguard' of dedicated revolutionaries. A great many Party members must have joined for opportunist or careerist reasons.[47]

The satellite organizations have scarcely any life in them. This is especially true of the trade unions and the Socialist Alliance. The youth organization includes a number of enthusiastic young people, and the veterans' organization acts as a pressure group on behalf of its members.[48] But neither the trade unions nor the Socialist Aliance is anything more than a subservient agent of the Party, which appoints their officers and determines their policies. Even in the relatively liberal period of the Reform the Party openly treated the Socialist Alliance as no more than a subsidiary organization. In October 1969, for example, the Montenegrin Central Committee of the Party criticized the Socialist Alliance for acting independently of the Party and insisted that the Secretary of the Alliance should be dismissed. The Alliance Conference submissively accepted this demand and the President also resigned, being replaced by the Secretary of the Central Committee of the Montenegrin Party (Carter 1982, 108).[49]

[47] A 1982 public opinion survey in Macedonia, with a sample of 1,200 respondents, found that many people consider that a large number of Communists are members for careerist reasons (*Borba*, 31 October 1982).

[48] But a delegate at the Seventeenth Conference of the Youth Organization of Vojvodina criticized the professionalization of youth leaders. 'The same candidates go from one job to another, which leads to professionalization. . . We all know that a young person is negatively affected by five or six years of professional work' (*Borba*, 21 November 1982).

[49] In a discussion among federal leaders of the Socialist Alliance in May 1982, prior to the Twelfth Congress of the League of Communists, various suggestions were made about the content of the Congress resolution. One speaker remarked that the Socialist Alliance is

For a few years the trade unions appeared to show some independence under the leadership of Vukmanović-Tempo, a leading but somewhat eccentric Party member, who was asked by Tito to take over the presidency of the Trade Union Federation in 1958. From Tempo's description, the trade unions were at the time 'treated entirely as a wing of the party. Tito told him briskly that working in the party and in the trade unions were the same thing "in self-management conditions" and the decision to appoint Tempo as the new trade union head was made at a meeting of the Party Executive Committee' (Carter 1982, 159–60). Tempo made the trade unions an important pressure group on behalf of the Reform, in line with the increasingly dominant section of the Party itself. But in 1967 he was removed, probably by the Party liberals, who found his continued emphasis on trade union independence inconvenient (ibid. 160). At congresses of the trade union federation there is often a good deal of rhetoric about the role of the unions in protecting workers' rights, and even some hints of criticism of the government on certain issues. But it never leads to any practical action. A Yugoslav expert on industrial relations, when asked about the benefits and costs to an individual of becoming a trade union official in his enterprise, replied that the benefits are higher status, consultation by the management, occasional trips to conferences, and perhaps a better chance of getting a flat or a free holiday, while the cost is ostracism by his fellow workers.[50]

While no sensible person in Yugoslavia would expect to exert any independent influence on social or political policy through participation in the satellite organizations, is there not some hope of doing so through the central power house, the Party? The answer is that one might as well hope to influence the policy of the Catholic Church by becoming a Catholic. It is true that the Party, unlike the Church, has all the trappings of democracy. There are Party congresses, committees are elected, resolutions are passed. But the reality is that everything is decided by the top leadership, as in all Communist Parties. 'Yugoslav Party Congresses . . . do not actually make policy decisions or choose the Party's leaders, although theory and the Party Statutes say they do. These things are done elsewhere and beforehand' (Rusinow 1978, 1).

The Party is supposed to be governed by the Leninist principle of 'democratic centralism'. This says that, before a decision is taken, there should be complete freedom of discussion and voting, but afterwards every member must loyally carry out the decision and express his support for it.

mainly run by pensioners and housewives and proposed that it should in future be obligatory for Party members to attend their local meetings of the Alliance (*Vjesnik*, 18 May 1982). Mirko Bošković, a member of the Croatian Conference of the Socialist Alliance, said that the meetings of the Alliance are becoming closed gatherings, dominated by officials. The Communists do not bother to draw in 'the masses', and fewer and fewer people participate in serious discussions at Alliance meetings.

[50] A delegate to the Ninth Congress of the Federation of Yugoslav Trade Unions said (*Borba*, 13 November 1982): 'There are many trade union officials who want to be obedient, because by that means they receive important material benefits. Most often they obtain large and pleasant flats and, of course, move on to higher positions.'

What has never been resolved, however, is whether members are entitled to try to modify a decision, or reverse it, on a subsequent occasion; and, if so, at what point they are allowed to express their views freely without being accused of failing to support an already taken decision.[51] The rules of democratic centralism are supplemented by a rule that members of the Party are not allowed to form 'factions'. This means that people who disagree with a proposed, or previously taken, decision are not allowed to get together and organize a campaign against the decision within the Party. (Lenin, of course, never agreed to any such rule in the early days, when he frequently carried on campaigns within his party against the majority). When these two sets of rules are further combined with the Communist policy of suppressing all alternative political parties, and any independent organization which might become even partially involved in politics, the basis is laid for a fully totalitarian system. For, if people are not allowed to organize either a separate party or a separate group within the monopoly party, they are totally subordinate to those who control that party.

Even a monopoly party, however, has to modify its policies in response to some forms of public pressure. This is especially evident in Yugoslavia, where two factors allow such pressures to reveal themselves more easily than in Soviet-type communist states. Firstly, the genuine federalization of Yugoslavia, and even, to a considerable degree, of the Party itself, means that the the republican or provincial parties sometimes express different points of view, especially on questions which affect local interests. For example, Milka Planinc, who was elected President of the Federal Executive Council (i.e. Premier) in May 1982, made a veiled criticism only a few days previously in Zagreb, in her capacity as President of the Central Committee of the Croatian Communist Party, of a proposal of the outgoing FEC for a change in the foreign exchange system which was strongly opposed in Croatia. Indeed, differences between the republics and provinces have become almost an everyday occurrence in Yugoslavia. The second factor is that Yugoslav enterprises are 'self-managed', i.e. they are not centrally planned but have a certain, although limited, degree of independence. This again means that there are opportunities for representatives of enterprises, usually directors but sometimes also members of workers' councils or even trade unions, to express different points of view, both in private and in public.

Because of these greater opportunities for public expressions of criticism of government policies, Yugoslavia is not a fully totalitarian state.[52] Indeed, in some respects the Yugoslav Party is even more sensitive to

[51] The Yugoslav Party tried to clarify this question somewhat in the Party Statute adopted at the Ninth Congress in 1978, where it is laid down that 'a Party member who finds himself in the minority on a specific issue when it comes to the vote is entitled to keep his opinion, and by implication to argue for a subsequent reversal of the decision he opposed, although he is still obligated to do his part, loyally and energetically, in implementing it as long as it stands' (Rusinow 1978, 11).

[52] One of the characteristic features of a fully totalitarian state is that its citizens are not allowed freely to cross its frontiers. Since 1967 Yugoslavs have enjoyed almost complete freedom in this respect.

public opinion than parties in bourgeois democratic states. For a democratic party is accustomed to the idea of losing power to the opposition and, on some issues, it would rather risk the loss of an election than abandon what it believes to be its essential principles. But to a Communist party the loss of power, even temporarily, is an unthinkable disaster. Because of the greater degree of freedom of criticism in Yugoslavia, the Yugoslav Party, which equally abhors the thought of losing power, is obliged to walk more carefully than in other communist states. It is noticeable, for example, how weak and hesitant the federal government is in dealing with major economic problems, such as inflation or the shortage of foreign exchange. It is less willing to take a 'hard line' than many governments in democratic states or, of course, than any government in a Stalinist state.[53]

Despite the above-mentioned opportunities for freedom of criticism in Yugoslavia, public expressions of opinion are severely shackled. Yugoslavia is officially a Marxist state; Marxism is taught compulsorily to all schoolchildren and students;[54] many subjects—such as Tito, the leading role of the Party, 'brotherhood and unity' of the peoples of Yugoslavia, and the virtues of self-management—are taboo; many key jobs are reserved exclusively for Party members, so that a member who incurs Party displeasure faces the risk not only of expulsion but of losing his job.[55] Party members belong to the élite, the only people who officially have the right to lead. But most of them dare not make use of that right, except to carry out the instructions of the leadership.

The truth is, of course, that it is impossible to maintain genuine democratic rights within a monopoly party. The only guarantee of democracy is the right to leave an established party and start a new one. If this right is denied, and denounced as counter-revolution, anyone who tries to organize a 'faction' within the monopoly party can be accused of breaking the rules and supporting counter-revolution. This was the fate of Djilas, as it had been of Trotsky. But Djilas never actually organized a faction and, although he has spent many years in prison for his writings, mainly published outside Yugoslavia, he is at liberty and draws his

[53] The paralysis of the Party and government in Poland during the period of the independent activity of Solidarity is a further example of the weakness of totalitarian parties where there is even a partial relaxation of their control over public opinion.

[54] Section V of the Basic Principles of the 1974 Constitution specifies: 'The system of upbringing and education shall be based on the achievements of modern science, especially of Marxism as the foundation of scientific socialism . . . ' (*The Constitution of the Socialist Federal Republic of Yugoslavia* (p. 68).

[55] A much publicized recent example occurred in a small town in northern Vojvodina, near the Hungarian frontier, where a group of schoolteachers were expelled from the Party for attending a Bach organ concert given in the local church, and automatically lost their jobs. One woman teacher was eventually reinstated after a year, during which she was engaged in manual work, because she made a full apology and promised never to do such a thing again. A male teacher of mathematics and Marxism, however, who also appealed, was not reinstated because he continued to maintain that a Communist had a right to enter a church for a secular purpose.

pension. Tito never murdered any of his closest collaborators. This, also, is a mark of Yugoslavia's difference.

It must be recognized that there is a real political dilemma in a country like Yugoslavia. Because of the national differences and the scope for national discord, there can be little doubt that if people were allowed to form alternative parties there would soon be 'national' parties; and this would lead to a danger that the country would fall apart, or at least become a field for foreign meddling. Nevertheless, Yugoslavia suffers from the lack of genuine opportunities for democratic expression of opinion. A theoretical, but perhaps utopian, solution would be to allow two communist parties, provided that they had substantial branches in every republic. But this would mean forswearing a basic teaching of Marxism, that the proletariat can be truly represented by only one party, whose policy is based on a 'scientific'—and hence uniquely valid—theory of socialism.[56]

Civil liberties

Some aspects of civil liberties have been touched on in the previous section. But there remain a few further points to be considered.

Chapter III of the Constitution contains an impressive list of rights and freedoms of the citizen. These include 'freedom of thought and opinion' (Art. 166), 'freedom of the press and other media of information and public expression, freedom of association, freedom of speech and public expression, freedom of gathering and public assembly' (Art. 167), freedom of 'scientific, scholarly and artistic creation' (Art. 169) and freedom of religion (Art. 174). It is further provided that 'a man's life is inviolable', except that capital punishment may be imposed for 'a grave criminal offence' (Art. 175); 'The inviolability of the integrity of the human personality, personal and family life and of the other human rights shall be guaranteed. Any extortion of a confession or statement shall be forbidden and punishable' (Art. 176); 'Man's freedom is inviolable. No one may be deprived of liberty except in cases and by the procedure specified by statute' (Art. 177). A person arrested must be given a statement of the grounds for his arrest within twenty-four hours, and may appeal against arrest to a court, which must decide within forty-eight hours. Detention can be ordered only by a court, or exceptionally by another authority for a maximum of three days (Art. 178). 'No one shall be punished for any act which before its commission was not defined as a punishable offence by statute or a legal provision based on statute, or for which no penalty was threatened' (Art. 181). 'Homes shall be inviolable. No one may enter without a warrant any dwelling or other premises of others or search them against the will of their tenant.' In the case of a search, the owner or a

---

[56] Fundamental differences between the Soviet, Chinese, and Yugoslav Parties sufficiently prove—although not to each party separately—that the dogma of the unique 'interpretation of Marxism' is false. The right of different nations to follow different paths to communism is now reluctantly accepted, at least in words. But it is so far unthinkable that different parties within a single state should be allowed to advocate different paths.

member of his family has a right to be present. But in special cases a search without warrant is permitted (Art. 184). 'Secrecy of mail and other means of communication shall be inviolable.' But exceptions are allowed 'if this is indispensable for the conduct of criminal proceedings or for the security of the country' (Art. 185).

There seems to be no doubt that the Yugoslav Party and government genuinely want to maintain the rule of law and civilized methods in the conduct of (non-political) criminal investigations and proceedings. There is no obvious evidence in Yugoslavia of police surveillance nor is there a system of organized spying by neighbours as in other communist countries. But the citizen's constitutional rights and freedoms are heavily qualified in practice. The legal basis for this is provided in Article 203, which reads in part:

No one may use the freedoms and rights established by the present Constitution in order to disrupt the foundations of the socialist self-management democratic order established by the present Constitution, to endanger the independence of the country, violate the freedoms and rights of man and the citizen guaranteed by the present Constitution, endanger peace and equality in international cooperation, stir up national, racial or religious hatred or intolerance or abet the commission of criminal offences, nor may these freedoms be used in a way which offends public morals.

There is also a special clause to Article 174 which reads: 'Abuse of religion and religious activities for political purposes shall be unconstitutional.'

It would be unrealistic, therefore, to say that in Yugoslavia there is genuine freedom of thought and opinion, speech, association, and the press. So far as the press is concerned, all editors are Party members and are carefully monitored. In June 1969, for example, the editor-in-chief of *Tanjug*, the Yugoslav news agency, was forced to resign for allowing publication of critical comments on the international meeting of communist parties in Moscow (Carter 1982, 189). In 1968, the editors of *Književne Novine* were hounded by the Serbian Party and the Federal Party Executive for publishing criticisms of a Central Committee member, and eventually the principal editors were expelled from the Party. Editors of major papers in Serbia and Croatia were dismissed during the 1972 reaction (ibid. 189–90). In 1965 about 65 per cent of journalists in the Yugoslav Journalists' Association were Party members (ibid. 187) and the figure is probably higher now. A journalist who is expelled from the Party will almost certainly lose his job.

Although there is no prior censorship of published material, all publications must be submitted to the authorities for inspection; and specialist lawyers devote themselves to the task of discovering whether there is anything in them which is contrary to the law. If they believe this to be so, the publication can be banned by the public prosecutor, subject to later approval by a court. Banning is not always fully effective. In three months of 1971, Carter (1982, 187) reports, the Supreme Courts of Serbia and Croatia refused to confirm bans in seven out of ten cases. But there are many informal forms of pressure. In 1975 *Praxis*, the well-known journal of leftist sociologists and philosophers which had long been a thorn in the side of the Party leadership, was finally closed down when the Party persuaded the printers' union not to handle it (Carter 1982, 194).

In Yugoslavia almost any independent act of speech or writing may be punishable for 'disrupting the foundations of the socialist self-management democratic order', for 'endangering international cooperation', or for 'stirring up national, racial or religious hatred'. On these kinds of general grounds Djilas was condemned to long terms of imprisonment, many Croat leaders of the period of the 'national euphoria' were held in prison for many years, and Kosovo students who demonstrated in 1981 in support of a separate Kosovo republic were arrested and sentenced.[57] But these are only the ultimate sanctions. Much more important are the economic sanctions against those who express themselves too freely or try to organize any kind of opposition. Tito formulated the Party's attitude to the use of economic sanctions very clearly in a speech at Labin on 1 May 1971:

I am not going to appeal to you to economize . . . But I do appeal to those people who occupy responsible posts in the economy, in banks, and in other sectors of our economic life—and these are mainly occupied by communists—to behave in the way laid down in the decisions of the League of Communists, and not in the way they themselves decide. Otherwise we shall have to act decisively. This will not just mean that they will be expelled from the League of Communists and keep their posts. I am sorry, no, they will have to leave their positions, too, not only the Party (*Yugoslav Survey*, August 1971, p. 13).

Especially since 1972, there has been strong Party pressure on intellectuals. The best-known case is that of the Belgrade professors of philosophy who were accused of encouraging the student revolt of 1968. Tito set the tone for dealing with them also in his speech of May 1971:

Our young people are good. But some of them are a little misled by various stories, lies and slanders and are somehow vacillating. We have decided to pay the youth greater attention and give them the right bearings. I am, for example, against our universities keeping and tolerating teachers who work against our system, who educate our youth against our society, who slander our leaders . . . We decided to do something about that, too, regardless of all kinds of autonomy, because it cannot be otherwise (op. cit. p. 14).

---

[57] Amnesty International reports that in 1980, before the Kosovo riots of 1981, nearly 600 people were prosecuted in Yugoslavia for criticizing the government, almost twice as many as in the previous year. The offences were usually 'hostile propaganda' or 'maliciously and untruthfully representing conditions in Yugoslavia'. Dr Fanjo Tudjman, a Croat historian, was sentenced to three years of imprisonment, with a five-year ban on public expression, for giving interviews to foreign journalists, in the course of which he said that Croatia's economic interests were not guaranteed. Father Nedjo Janjić, a twenty-three-year-old Serbian orthodox priest, was given a four-and-a-half-year prison sentence for singing nationalist songs at his son's christening (*The Times*, 10 February 1981). *Borba* (29 July 1982) describes, without comment, an incident which occurred at a youth demonstration in Belgrade in support of the Palestinians, attended by 70,000 people. During the meeting a small group held up posters with the Polish word for 'Solidarity'. They were promptly arrested and later sentenced to between 25 and 50 days of imprisonment for 'offending in a public place the socialist, patriotic and national feelings of the citizens and the social-political order'.

It took another four years before Tito's objective was achieved. Finally, in 1975, after the Serbian assembly had passed special legislation, eight members of Belgrade's Philosophy Faculty were 'suspended indefinitely'. But they continued to receive full pay until new jobs, if any, were found for them (Wilson 1979, 242). This is another sign of the difference between Yugoslav and Soviet-type communism.[58]

The effects of federalization

The growth in federalization of the Yugoslav government, and hence also to a large extent of the Party, has already been described. The most important development has been the granting of a veto power to the delegates from each republic or province in the Chamber of Republics and Provinces, which alone can decide on all major economic questions. Although the Federal Party could, in principle, use its right of democratic centralism to give instructions to the Party members composing each delegation, or even to the members in each republican and provincial assembly which mandates its delegation, there is no evidence that this has happened so far, or at least not in such a brutal manner. There is probably from time to time a certain amount of arm-twisting. But it must be remembered that the federal Party bodies themselves are composed of quotas of members from each republic and province who, although not officially 'delegates', may easily come to behave as such. The difficulty is that, since the death of Tito, there is no 'Yugoslav' leader who is above suspicion of favouring his own nation. Even Tito, when he used the 'firm hand', as for example in bringing down Ranković, or in suppressing Croat nationalism, was always careful to balance the main action by attacks on corresponding forces in other republics.

Conditions may change in the future. But, for the time being, the Party's authority is considerably weakened by federalization. From innumerable examples of inter-republican differences and deadlocks it may be sufficient to quote two, which were both reported in a single issue of *Ekonomska politika* (19 April 1982). The first concerns a loan of $2 million granted to Yugoslavia in June 1980 by the World Bank for the construction of motorways. By April 1982 not a cent had been used, because the relevant communities of interest for roads in Serbia, Croatia, Slovenia, and Vojvodina had not yet been able to agree on a way of dividing the money amongst themselves. The second concerns a proposal made by the Executive Council of Serbia that the price of coal should be raised by 5 per cent in order to raise funds for developing the mines. Despite a shortage of coal and the enormous burden to the country of the cost of imported oil, this proposal also has failed to be implemented for a period of two years, because of lack of agreement among the republics and provinces.

The position has been well summarized by Rusinow (1980, 11). Except for the occasions when Tito intervened, on special issues or appointments, or in foreign affairs,

---

[58] Dr W. Brus, however, informs me that in Poland in 1949–56 'bourgeois professors' were excused from teaching duties but kept on full pay.

for more than a decade macro-economic and regional or local political and social policies have been the product of frequently tortuous and sometimes stormy public or private negotiations within and among economic enterprises and sectors, institutionalized interest groups, state organs, and a variety of 'socio-political organizations' (always including but not always dominated by the chief of these at every level, the relevant Party organization).

This is a good description of the state of affairs at the federal level on any issue which has economic implications. But the situation is different within each republic and province. Here the Party has greater control, and both organizations and individual members are more likely to toe the Party line.

Thus Yugoslavia is, in effect, a federation of one-party states. Since Tito's death, these states are held together by a comon fear of outside intervention and by the legacy of Tito's teachings, especially the doctrine of 'brotherhood and unity'. The former influence will remain strong under all circumstances, but the latter may lose some of its force as time passes. In a crisis, the unity of the country will always command enormous popular support, with the help, if necessary, of the Yugoslav Army and the federal police. This is, of course, a long way from the theoretical model of political self-management and the dictatorship of the (nationless) proletariat through the delegate system. The reality is a great deal more complicated.

3. SELF-MANAGEMENT PLANNING

According to the official doctrine, planning in Yugoslavia starts, like everything else, from the bottom.[59] Each basic organization, work community, and commune prepares its own provisional plan. These provisional plans, or lists of 'indicators', are circulated to all interested bodies, including higher authorities, and then 'harmonized'. Once consistency has been achieved, self-management agreements are made between enterprises, and social compacts between governments and other bodies, and these are intended to crystallize the achieved set of relations. The 'plan' is merely a document which summarizes the aggregate implications of these agreements and lists some of the more important investment projects included in them.

Although there is a considerable Yugoslav literature about self-management planning, it is written in very general terms and gives scarcely any details about the actual content of the plans of basic organizations, the process of harmonization, and the precise forms in which self-management agreements and social compacts are drafted. It is necessary, therefore, to rely mainly on inference from comments made in various sources about the nature of these processes. The discussion will be arranged under five headings: (i) the plans of productive basic organizations; (ii) the process of

[59] Stojanović (1982, 26) maintains that the planning process starts with a statement of national priorities by the Federal Executive Council. She also asserts that each planning entity prepares 'at least two variants' of its initial plan 'to allow for changes should it need to co-ordinate its plans with other subjects' (p. 28). It is difficult to reconcile these statements with descriptions from other sources.

harmonization; (iii) enforcement of plans; (iv) the cost of self-management planning; and (v) an assessment of the advantages and disadvantages of the system.

The plans of productive basic organizations

Although productive basic organizations are not the only basic units which make plans, it is their activities which are of dominant importance for economic development; and, since productive basic organizations trade on the market, it is in this sector that the problems of integrating the roles of planning and the market are most acute. Each productive basic organization is obliged to prepare, a year or more before the end of each Five-Year Plan, a set of 'indicators' or forecasts for a wide variety of variables relating to its own business. These include values of outputs, inputs, exports, imports and investment, all in constant prices, and employment and productivity. Separate estimates are required for each year of the forthcoming five-year plan period.

The first question which arises in this connection is: How do basic organizations make these forecasts? More particularly, what considerations do they have in mind when they compile their figures? It seems probable that all basic organizations want to expand. This will almost certainly be true of the managers, whose reputation, from both an economic and a political point of view, depends on the successful expansion of their business. The workers might be expected to take a more critical attitude to plans for expansion, since their main interest is in increasing their own income, and not all plans for expansion will necessarily have that effect. But there are three factors specific to the Yugoslav environment which will usually tend to make expansion and rising real income per worker mutually compatible objectives. The first is that, since most Yugoslav firms are of less than optimum size, expansion will lead to economies of scale and hence to a higher level of income per worker. The second is that, since most Yugoslav firms are using a technology which is less efficient than the best available, there is a strong desire to introduce more advanced technology, and this usually requires an expansion of output. The third is that the Yugoslav loan interest rate has always been kept low, and for many years now has been negative in real terms (less than the rate of inflation). This gives a strong incentive to increase the use of capital which, when associated with the previous two considerations, is more likely to lead to an expansion of output (and employment) than to a simple substitution of capital for labour.

Apart from these economic reasons for expansion, there are powerful political pressures on enterprises to plan for growth in output, employment, and productivity. These pressures will come from the local commune and possibly also from the political *aktiv* and party organization within each enterprise. Although it is obligatory for the plans of basic organizations to be endorsed by the workers as a whole, either at a general meeting or through a ballot, it is doubtful whether the workers fully understand the implications of the large amount of statistical material which describes their 'plan'. According to one informant it is believed that in most large enterprises the preparation of the plans for the component basic organizations is done by the central technical staff, and largely by extrapolation of previous trends.

In a capitalist economy one would expect that firms with a record of good profitability would tend to plan for a more rapid rate of expansion than those with poor profit records (although there will always be exceptions, since some firms with good past profits will have sound reasons for slowing down their rate of growth while others with poor past profits will consider themselves on the verge of seizing important new opportunities). But in Yugoslavia there are several reasons why firms with poor 'profit' records, i.e. low rates of accumulation, will put forward plans for rapid expansion. Firms in less developed areas benefit from cheap and plentiful loans, and receive special encouragement to expand even in spite of previous poor performance. Firms in priority industries are supposed to receive preferential treatment and are under pressure to make bold plans for expansion. And many communes, even outside the officially designated less developed areas, are anxious to expand local production and employment, and will encourage local enterprises to plan accordingly. Finally, because enterprises know that there is always a shortage of funds for financing investment, and that the allocation of such funds depends to some extent on the 'plan', they will tend to inflate their planned investment requirements in the hope of obtaining a larger share of the available funds. The consequence is that, when all plans of basic organizations are aggregated, there always emerges an excess demand for investment (and possibly an insufficient demand for extra employment).

The process of harmonization

It has been suggested that the process of harmonizing plans of basic organizations in Yugoslavia is analogous to a comprehensive system of forward markets leading to a general equilibrium (Schrenk and others 1979, 78). If this were so, it would be an exciting economic experiment which would provide a test of the practicability of the theoretical proposals of Arrow (1964), Debreu (1959), and others. But the Yugoslav planning system deviates from the Arrow-Debreu model in a number of crucial respects. In the first place, there are large areas of the Yugoslav economy which are not covered by self-management planning. These include supplies from the private sector and the rest of the world, and demands from both these sectors and from final consumers. Secondly, relative prices play no systematic role in the Yugoslav planning process, which is essentially physical (or constant price) planning. So there is no method of adjusting supplies and demands towards equilibrium, as in forward markets, by changes in relative prices.[60] Thirdly, the main objective of

[60] As a consequence, output plans and prices are often inconsistent. For example, the tobacco growers announced in March 1981 that they could not guarantee to increase output at the rate of 6.6 per cent per annum as prescribed in the plan for 1981–5, unless there were an increase in their prices or subsidies. Since the government has said that they have no more

Yugoslav planning is not to establish a set of consistent contracts for current supplies, i.e. for purchases of materials from specific suppliers and for sales of products to specific customers. Although some contracts of this sort may be made, they are merely by-products of the planning system, and would probably have been made in any case in the absence of planning. Yugoslav planning is essentially investment or development planning, i.e. an attempt to determine the extent to which productive capacities need to be increased, how much of available resources can be allocated to each industry, and how much to certain large projects.

In the absence of a system of forward markets leading to the achievement of equilibrium—if feasible—through price adjustments, the only other logical method of planning is through a centrally estimated input-output model, or the Soviet method of 'material balances', followed by some rational system of allocating each industry's production target to specific enterprises. The Yugoslavs regularly prepare input-output tables, but they do not seem to use these to any large extent for planning purposes.[61] An input-output based plan would, of course, owe nothing to 'democratic', or 'bottom-up', self-management planning, and would, almost certainly yield results inconsistent with the results of such a system. The most that could be done would be to allocate the input-output determined capacity for a given industry among the enterprises in that industry with some regard to their individually-expressed desires, or 'plans'. But, since in almost every case there would have to be some reduction in total claims for expansion, a method which paid regard to enterprise plans would be unlikely to lead to the most efficient allocation of resources. Under Yugoslav conditions, the allocation of investment resources to individual enterprises is a very politically sensitive operation, and in practice the federal authorities are not able to cut back the investment plans of the republics and provinces so as to correspond to aggregate required capacity.[62]

Even in the absence of a full input-output prediction of capacity requirements for a given set of final demands, Yugoslav planners probably have a fairly good idea of what capacities will be needed, at least in certain key industries such as electric power, rail transport, and iron and steel. But it is not clear how much influence they have on the 'harmonization' of enterprise investment plans. As a consequence of political federalization

finance for subsidies, and presumably the producers have no expectation of an improvement in their prices, the producers regard the plan as ineffective (*Ekonomska politika*, 30 March 1981). Another example concerns the social sector farms in Vojvodina, which in the autumn of 1981 sowed 5,000 ha. of winter barley and somewhat less of sugar beet, although they were not supposed to sow either of these crops according to plan. They were induced to 'break their word' because the prices encouraged them to do so (*Ekonomska politika*, 26 October 1981).

[61] The systematic use of input–output methods has been advocated by a number of economists, including Babić (1980) and Bazler-Madžar and others (1981, 65–9).

[62] Petroleum refining capacity is about twice as great as required, because every republic wants to have its own refinery. In iron and steel, a new cold rolling mill which was being constructed at Smederovo in 1981–2 was expected to raise cold rolling capacity to more than double requirements for 1982, although existing capacity was already more than sufficient (*Ekonomska politika*, 23–9 November 1981, p. 24).

the influence of federal planners is especially weak, and, so long as this is so, the uses of an all-Yugoslav input-output model are limited. Within each republic and province, the central planners have more influence because they are supported, and prompted, by the regional Party organizations. Moreover, there are sometimes only one or two enterprises engaged in a particular industry within a republic or province, and in any case the number of enterprises competing for investment allocations in a republic or province is almost always smaller than in Yugoslavia as a whole. This simplifies the problem, but only by creating a dangerous tendency towards regional autarky.[63]

The actual process of 'harmonization' of self-management plans in Yugoslavia seems to be a very rough-and-ready business. Representatives of enterprises in the same industry within a republic or province are brought together to consider the proposals for expansion which have been put forward by the members of the group. Presumably, the planning office has made an estimate of the total capacity required in that industry, although the method of arriving at that figure is unknown. A rational method would require a rational decision not only about domestic consumption but also about imports and exports, from and to the rest of the world, and from and to the other republics and provinces, matters on which rational calculations are difficult to make in Yugoslav conditions. But some figures must be put on the table. Then the assembled representatives presumably enter into lengthy arguments and bargaining sessions to try to determine the allocation of extra capacities between them. It is said that discussions continue at various levels and in various groups with a view to arriving at a consistent plan. This is sometimes said to be a process of iteration; but a leading Yugoslav economist has offered the following comment (Madžar 1979, 422):

Prolonged bargaining and delayed enactment of the agreements created serious problems relevant to their coordination. Brought at different times and shaped more-or-less separately, without taking systematic account of the wider repercussions of the proposed sectoral development, the agreements do not quite guarantee the reaching a consistent and socially-rational overall path of development of the economy. The planning procedure which could duly encompass all relevant interdependencies in the system—had not yet been worked out. Another problem of coordination is how to succeed in describing overall social plans, and the agreements on the foundations of these plans, from an enormous multitude of lower-level plans and agreements, Usual iterative procedures are not envisaged as integral parts of the planning process and the solution of the coordination of the really large number of planning decisions remains to be found.[64]

---

[63] Complaints about local and regional autarky are innumerable. In most industries the unified Yugoslav market, which it is a prime responsibility of the federal government to preserve, simply does not exist. According to *Ekonomska politika* (20 April 1981, p. 10): 'Since 1970 the volume of trade in goods and services between republics and regions has fallen.'

[64] Another group of economists have expressed their doubts whether so-called 'democratic' planning is really possible, because of the 'exceptionally large number' of planning agents, because of the large number of methods of harmonizing individual and collective interests,

Although full harmonization of plans is evidently not achieved, a special effort is made to reach consistent plans for selected 'priority' industries. In the 1976–80 plan period these included electricity, coal and uranium mining and processing, oil and natural gas, most other heavy industries, tourism, transport, and post and telecommunications (Blagojević 1980, 49). In the 1981–5 plan the food industry has also been made a priority industry. According to Schrenk and others (1979, 80) 'For priority activities, harmonization is required by law to lead to a programme that is agreed upon by a predetermined date and codified in legally binding obligations'. But this does not seem to have had the desired results. In electricity, for example, it is reported that persistent shortages of power are due to failure to fulfil plans for expansion of capacity, 'sometimes not even as much as 50 per cent' (*Ekonomska politika*, 7 June 1982, p. 12). The director of a large steel enterprise said in an interview with the same paper (19 April 1982, p. 25): 'You know, as a steel man I feel frightened when I see in some documents that the iron and steel industry is a priority industry, because I know that nothing will come of that.' Even if one allows for a certain Yugoslav penchant for exaggeration, it seems clear that even in priority industries harmonization is far from complete.

In practice, the planners for any five-year period do not start with a blank sheet of paper, even in relation to investment. At the beginning of the period, there will already be a large number of partially completed investment projects, started in the previous period (or sometimes in the one before that). Normally, the arguments in favour of completing such projects are overwhelming. Often, also, full advantage from these projects can be obtained only if other supplementary projects are put in hand. Within the remaining area the priority industries will exert a strong pull, and there will also be many political pressures in favour of particular projects in particular locations. Speaking about the Croatian plan for 1981–5, which was still being discussed in the Croatian parliament in June 1981, Gojko Steković, President of the Chamber of Associated Labour of the Croatian parliament, said (*Ekonomska politika*, 29 June 1981, pp. 25–6): '. . . the earlier plan was a "patchwork" of many temporary and short-term elements', and 'it is not easy to upset the logic of inherited "priorities" and to break the resistance of industries and groups which have for a long time been "registered" for priority social attention and privilege'. He added that: 'it is not at all easy to use the plan to impose generally valid "rules of the game" under which the decisive criteria for all programmes and projects would be the extent to which they increase income, how far they accelerate our inclusion in the international division

and because of the large number of decisions which have to be reached (Bazler-Madžar and others 1981, 17). In another passage they add: 'The plans of organizations of associated labour cannot be the source of all other plans because such organizations only can and should concern themselves with their own income, not with the proportions and possibilities of the economy as a whole. Every attempt to construct plans from the bottom upwards leads either to complete failure or to an endless process of harmonization which makes efficient management of the economy impossible' (ibid. 40).

of labour, how far they strengthen the technical and economic independence of the country together with the rational inclusion of forcign accomplishments, how far they contribute to a uniform regional development and to similar socially justified development interests'. It should come as no surprise, therefore, to learn that at a meeting of the Council of the Federation of Trade Unions it was reported that more than a year after the commencement of the 1981–5 plan 'many collectives [i.e. enterprises] still do not have any plans, or have imprecise or inconsistent plans' (*Borba*, 3 February 1982).

Enforcement of plans

Even if a perfectly consistent output and investment plan were to be discovered, there would be no compulsion on enterprises in non-priority sectors to accept their assigned roles in it. They can be encouraged to sign self-management agreements, but they cannot be forced to do so. If an enterprise is strongly opposed to a proposed agreement, it can find many pretexts for postponing its signature, and if the agreement involves enterprises in more than one republic it is quite likely to receive the support of its own political authorities in this course of action. There seem to be no published figures on what proportion of national output is fully 'harmonized', and on what proportion of the harmonized output is covered by satisfactory self-management agreements.

In a complete system of self-management planning all plans would be harmonized, all harmonized relations would be crystallized into fully specified and precise self-management agreements and social compacts, and all self-management agreements and social compacts would be fully enforceable. In practice, none of the self-management agreements or social compacts arising out of the Yugoslav planning process appears to be enforceable. In general, no social compacts of any kind are enforceable, and the only self-management agreements which seem to be effectively enforceable are those concerning the establishment and rules of operation of basic and other organizations. Self-management agreements about plans are not usually in the form of contracts, which might be enforceable in principle, but are rather agreements about desirable increases in output, and hence capacity, in different enterprises within an industry. Clearly, that which is merely agreed to be desirable cannot be enforced.

The lack of enforceability of plan agreements is a crucial weakness of the Yugoslav planning system. A social 'plan' which is unenforceable is no plan and, not surprisingly, there have been many complaints about this aspect. A report in *Vjesnik* (13 October 1981) on a discussion at the Executive Board of the Economic Chamber of Yugoslavia reads:

Many self-management agreements and social compacts, on which our social and economic life is largely based, do not always yield in full their expected results. Well-formulated documents, although they would in essence be possible and necessary for controlling many current and long-term matters, are not everywhere equally respected and faithfully applied. By the nature of things, they do not contain any penalty or similar clauses, because it is a question of documents which are composed on the basis of voluntarily accepted obligations, but there is also lacking almost all moral responsibility for their implementation.

More brusquely, Luka Bročilo, director of steel firm, in an interview with *Ekonomska politika* (19 April 1982, P. 20) pointed out that his firm spent a long time in participating in the process of reaching agreements and making compacts, but 'scarcely anything of that has been carried out . . . So, dare we pose the question of what use are all these documents, all that wasted time and the involvement of hundreds of people, from working groups to various inter-republican conferences, if we have been unable later to bring these documents to any effect?' Another director of a steel firm said (ibid., p. 24): 'We have some very fine documents, some beautiful compacts adopted at the highest level in Yugoslavia, by the highest government agencies, and out of all that nothing is achieved.' Similarly, *Ekonomska politika* (22 March 1982, p. 11), discussing self-management agreements in the petroleum and coal industries wrote: 'What was written in those self-management agreements and what actually happened last year are two quite different things'.

Influenced, presumably, by such experience, the Third Congress of Self-Managers in June 1981 resolved, *inter alia* (*Yugoslav Survey*, August 1981, p. 15):

The Congress demands greater responsibility and consistent fulfilment of obligations assumed through self-management agreements and social compacts on the foundations of plans. That should be a general rule for all obligations also under other self-management agreements and social compacts, which must be legally binding on parties to them, while the failure to fulfil them should entail corresponding sanctions.

But such demands are self-contradictory. If self-management planning is genuinely 'democratic' and 'bottom up', it must be voluntary. And voluntary agreements which do not take the form of contracts, i.e. for the signing of which there is no *quid pro quo*, will not be signed at all if there is a threat to make their implementation compulsory. Planning can either be voluntary, leading to enforceable contracts, or centrally imposed. It cannot combine the voluntary, but non-contractual, Yugoslav type of agreement with compulsion. And 'moral' compulsion is, of course, an evasion of the problem.

Despite the lack of enforceability of plan agreements, there is much pressure on enterprises and other bodies to sign them. This is partly pressure from the Party and its satellite organizations, as well as through government agencies, but also takes the form of a rule that the allocation of bank finance should be governed by the 'plan'. If an enterprise wants to obtain finance for a project, it should make sure that the project is 'in the plan', which means that it has made an approved self-management agreement with other enterprises in the same industry about the total expansion of capacity and its allocation among the different enterprises.[65] To be 'in the plan' is a necessary, but not a sufficient, condition for obtaining bank finance for a project. The final decision on the allocation of finance rests with the banks, and ultimately with the Party.

The cost of self-management planning

Self-management is extremely time-consuming. Babić (1980, 466) has pointed out that at the end of 1978 there were 19,203 basic organizations, 14,269 enterprises without basic organizations and many thousands of work communities and other organizations, making a total of more than 95,000 planning agents. 'That fact causes enormous problems of multi-level planning, where exchange of information . . . is the central problem.' In fact, exchange of information is only part of the problem. The central problem is how to arrive at consistency between the plans of 95,000 planning agents.

According to Schrenk and others (1979, 79) 'The full cycle of planning, involving time-consuming iterations within and among numerous planning agents, takes two to three years. The costs of planning, particularly those associated with the absorption of scarce managerial and administrative talent, are thus likely to be high.' Moreover, planning is intended to be a continuous process, with constant revisions in the light of changes in circumstances. So the absorption of talent occurs not only during the two to three years preceding each five-year period but, to a smaller extent, continuously.

An example of the burden placed on enterprises by the planning process is given in a report *Ekonomska politika* (25 May 1981, p. 6) about the combine *Borovo*, which produces a wide range of rubber products, including shoes. *Borovo* sent copies of its combine plan, without showing separate figures for each of its basic organizations, to the communes, the republics, and the federation. But it received a demand that copies of the plans of each basic organization must also be sent. The president of the business board of the combine commented:

It is clear to us that each basic organization must have a plan, but why is it so important for the Skupština of the Federation to know how many shoes each of our basic organizations produces? Demands like this burden us with a large number of non-productive workers, hence lowering our productivity. We have 2,000 workers in our administration, but it could be much less. Chambers, communes and various republican organs ask us for a series of statistics which they most often never read. Ten years ago we had fewer administrative staff, and people could go out for a walk, because they had too little to do. Today, with twice as many administrative staff, we cannot complete our work on time.[66]

[65] It is not known whether enterprises sometimes make self-management agreements to allocate expansion of capacity among themselves to an extent and in proportions which are contrary to the wishes of the republican planning officers or politicians. Presumably, a flagrant deviation from centrally approved behaviour would mean that the agreement would not be considered a valid part of the plan.

[66] A similar comment was made by a director of an enterprise who was interviewed early in

Madžar (1979, 416) has drawn attention to the fact that, as the number of units participating in a bargaining process increases, 'the difficulties of reaching a solution which will be acceptable to everybody multiply at a progressive rate', so that 'the amount of time required to . . . complete the bargaining becomes prohibitive. This important aspect was very frequently disregarded in the present system.' It is not clear, however, how agreement can be reached even among a few participants when there is no provision for price adjustments as part of the bargaining process. Nevertheless, the search for the philosophers' stone of harmony among planning agents is clearly likely to be more complex and more prolonged when tens of thousands of agents are involved.[67]

One result of the time-cost of the planning process, but also perhaps of the inherent difficulty of finding a consistent solution, is that the agreements and compacts and final plans of enterprises, which are essential for the implementation of the social plan, are not concluded in time. Indeed, there is some suspicion that some are never concluded. Madžar (1979, 421) reported that in May 1978, halfway through the 1976–80 plan period, two out of seventeen 'agreements on the foundation of the social plan' between the republics and the federal government, which were all considered to be essential for the operation of the plan, had not yet been concluded. For the 1981–5 plan, *Ekonomska politika* (28 September 1981, p. 10) reported that the 'so-called third part' of the plan required the conclusion of forty-four social compacts; but up to September 1981 only two of these had been concluded. Six more were currently under discussion. A Slovenian delegate to the Committee of the Republics and Autonomous Provinces on the Social Plan and Development Policy had said that 'without these compacts there is in practice no social plan.'[68]

General assessment of the self-management planning system

Because the Yugoslav Cummunists are opposed to state socialism, they have introduced self-management and a market economy. But, because they are in control of a one-party socialist state, and intend to remain in

1981, in the course of a survey of 72 general directors and presidents of management boards of major enterprises throughout Yugoslavia. He said that every year nearly 400 pages of reports are sent from his commune to the federal government regarding the work of basic organizations in the commune. 'They do no one any good. I am free to say that no one reads them. But an army of officials makes up the estimates, fills up the forms and makes the analyses' (*Ekonomska politika*, 12 January 1981, p. 19).

[67] Bazler-Madžar and others (1981, 11) make the same point about the exceptional amount of time required to operate a 'democratic' system of planning, both on the account of the time required for each planning agent to prepare its own plan, and the time taken after that to try to reach agreements with every other planning agent.

[68] In a later issue (*Ekonomska politika*, 15 February 1982, p. 14) it was reported that the producers and processors of lead, zinc, and antimony were currently discussing a proposed self-management agreement about 'the foundations of the plan of development' for the period 1981–5. The journal considered that the plan proposals were unrealistic, because they would require an investment of 40 billion dinars at 1980 prices, of which the enterprises in the industry could finance less than one-tenth from their own savings.

control, they must also have 'planning'. So they have invented 'self-management planning'.

Self-management planning is an attractive idea. It seems to solve the fundamental social problem of how to reconcile freedom and order. But one step in the argument is missing. No satisfactory method has been suggested for reducing 'democratic' freedom of choice to a single 'harmonized' social plan. The only known way of approaching such a result is a free market, with freely fluctuating prices as the method of achieving equilibrium. But this would mean accepting *laissez-faire* market socialism. Although the Yugoslav Communists moved a considerable way in that direction during the years of the Reform, they pulled back abruptly in 1972. Now they are left with the problem of reconciling the unreconcilable.

Self-management planning is supposed to start from the bottom, with each planning agent preparing its own provisional plan. In the meantime, the planning offices—at federal, republic, and provincial levels—work out rough perspective plans for each area, giving estimates of probable rates of growth of capital, labour and output, imports and exports, and the implied requirements for expansion in each industry to meet the total growth in domestic demand.

From this point onwards there can be indefinitely complicated negotiations between large numbers of alternative groups of planning agents, arranged by industry or activity, type of consumer, commune and republic, or any combination of these. While no general solution is possible to the problem of harmonization of plans subject to a set of fixed prices, it does not follow that all the documents, meetings, and discussions will be fruitless. If the representatives of a group of enterprises supplying one category of products are brought together to discuss how to share out the proposed increment in total supply among themselves, and strong political and financial pressures are brought on them to reach agreement, in many cases some agreement will be reached. These are partial building blocks for an overall social plan, which may be duly recorded in the form of self-management agreements. In so far as such agreements are reached and implemented, it can be argued that there is a significant social benefit, since the total expansion in capacity for the groups of products covered by these agreements will be in line with the requirements of the economy. But there are also some disadvantages.

In the first place, there is obviously a considerable risk that the meetings to share out capacity will tend to encourage monopolistic behaviour. In the judgement of Bazler-Madžar and others (1981, 31) 'Social compacts, and especially self-management agreements, are often drawn up in such a manner that they include monopolist and particularist elements'. Madžar (1979, 415) remarks that 'nothing in the system precludes making agreements at the expense and to the detriment of the interests of third parties'. Although monopolies are prohibited by the constitution, 'there is no trace of practical and workable institutional solutions which could prevent making such arrangements'. The Third Congress of Self-Managers (*Yugoslav Survey*, August 1981, p. 13) expressed vigorous opposition to 'the creation of monopolistic positions of individual manufacturing or trading organizations, through self-management agreements', but offered no suggestions about how to prevent this within a framework of self-management planning.

Secondly, under Yugoslav conditions of federalization, there is a strong probability that self-management planning will encourage autarkic tendencies at the republican and provincial levels, and even at the level of communes. There is general agreement that this has in fact happened. Capacity is duplicated in different republics — every republic wants its own steel plant, its own refinery, even its own airline—and communes encourage local enterprises to buy supplies from other local enterprises. Enterprises which are making losses turn to their own republics or communes to give them subsidies, or to help them to obtain bank credits. In the words of Vladimir Bakarić, the veteran leader of the Croatian Party, 'when a product is manufactured then the bank finances it regardless of what success it has on the market . . . The second [obstacle to free competition] is the system or manner of agreement-making where everyone protects his own and therefore protects the whole and, by extension, the basic organization of associated labour—regardless of what condition it is in' (*Socialist Thought and Practice*, 1981, No. 4, p. 4).

Thirdly, as already mentioned, the system is very costly, especially in terms of scarce managerial skills which might otherwise be used to improve enterprise efficiency.

Fourthly, the intrinsic inability of the system to achieve harmonization by voluntary methods encourages intervention from government and Party authorities. To quote Bakarić again (ibid.), 'the motive force of progress becomes a political factor. This is what all of us are now condemning on the one hand but putting into practice on the other. There are no development plans or programmes without the socio-political organizations . . . ' Marijan Korošić, a leading Yugoslav economist, is reported in *Ekonomska politika* (2 November 1981, p. 25) to have said:

Self-management in this country is in a state of stagnation, perhaps even retreat. The influence of government, or actually of several governments, and of semi-government agencies is constantly increasing. At the same time the autonomy of working collectives is constantly being reduced . . . The economy is being re-bureaucratized and at the same time the market is being significantly restricted . . . In the institutional reforms such as we have had from 1974 until now bureaucracy has seized a place for itself, broadened it and, so it seems, much consolidated its position thereon.

And a more recent article in *Ekonomska politika* (7 June 1982, p. 21) adds:

Probably it is not controversial to say that today the basic organizations are more and more becoming branches or organs of the socio-political communities (the latter make decisions about investments, prices, management personnel, exports, regional pooling of resources and so on), just as it is not controversial to say that exactly this characteristic has contributed to the fact that the financial results of productive basic organizations should be such as they are [with many making losses].

Yugoslav economists have added a number of other complaints about the present system of planning, or its operation. The system is too complex and needs to be simplified (Madžar 1979, 422); it provides no remedy for unexpected changes in conditions; it needs to be enforceable (Bazler-Madžar and others 1981, 179–80); and there is need for better statistical data (ibid., Chapter IV). But these criticisms do not go to the root of the problem. There is no way in which self-management planning can be simplified without squeezing out its self-management component; no economic system of any kind can avoid the losses caused by unexpected changes in conditions; voluntary non-market agreements cannot be made enforceable without undermining the voluntary basis; and more and better data would only increase the cost without solving the fundamental problems of the system.

Against the real disadvantages of the system are there not some important advantages? One argument in its favour by a leading Yugoslav economist is that self-management planning forces the bureaucrats to think about the implications of their decisions. This may be true. But it seems to be a rather costly way of reaching the desired objective. Some might be tempted to argue that self-management planning has raised the rate of growth. But it would be difficult to sustain this argument. Unfortunately for self-management planning, its introduction has coincided with the growing world inflation and recession caused by the OPEC-induced rises in petroleum prices. During this period, the rate of growth in Yugoslavia has declined as elsewhere, the balance of payments has deteriorated, and massive foreign debts have accumulated. Many Yugoslav economists are not convinced that self-management planning has made any significant difference to the behaviour of the economy (Bazler-Madžar and others 1981, 175); and the only correct conclusion seems to be that the advantages of self-management planning, if any, are so small as not to compensate for the very considerable costs which the system imposes.

4. GENERAL CONCLUSIONS

This has been a long and difficult chapter, because the problem with which it has been concerned is intrinsically difficult. No economic or political system in the world works exactly as it is supposed to work and it would be unfair to expect the Yugoslav system to reach an unusually high standard in this respect. But the evidence suggests conclusively that the real content of the Yugoslav system deviates sharply from its official description. Part of the reason for this is that the Yugoslav Communists have depicted their system in very emotive and propagandist terms. The liberal use of a highly value-loaded terminology, in which such words and phrases as 'socialist', 'self-management', and 'associated labour' are repeated over and over again, creates the impression that social relations in Yugoslavia are far removed from the experience of other countries. It is all the more disturbing, therefore, to find that in many respects Yugoslavia is not so different from other countries after all.

The Yugoslav system does differ in some important ways from both the capitalist system and the Soviet-type socialist system. On the one side there is very little private ownership of productive assets except in agriculture, where the size of farms is severely restricted; on the other, there is no complete system of central planning. But Yugoslavia shares with capitalism one very important characteristic, namely, a market economy; and it shares with the Soviet Union another very important characteristic, namely, a monopoly Marxist Party. The fundamental Yugoslav problem is how to reconcile these two disparate elements, and especially how to reconcile them within the framework of a quite exceptional degree of federalization. The solution which has been chosen is 'self-management' which, on the one hand, provides a rationale for a market system and, on the other, gives the Party almost unlimited scope for controlling the system.

The problems of managing this complex system are enormous. The apparatus of self-management—inside enterprises, in the political arena, and in social planning—is cumbersome and costly. The enterprise part of it probably gives some real satisfaction to the workers, but much less than is claimed for it, and at the expense of a substantial weakening of discipline and of the work-efforts of a considerable section of the labour force. The political system of 'self-management' is at best a formality, at worst a cruel deception. Its only significant element is the republican right of veto which, although ideologically consistent with self-management, was introduced for other reasons. And 'self-management planning' seems to be little more than a time-consuming charade.

In view of all the high hopes and sincere beliefs associated with the idea of self-management, it is disagreeable to have to conclude that it has turned out to be not much more than a vast public relations exercise. Unfortunately for its promoters, many Yugoslavs are beginning to see self-management in this light. But the phrase itself and in a vague sense the idea behind it, if not the particular institutions through which self-management is now supposed to be realized, will probably survive for a long time to come, perhaps indefinitely. It is a potent idea, and the Yugoslavs deserve high credit for being the first to try to take it seriously and on a large scale. But a good deal of hard thinking and frank assessment of results is still needed before it can be said that 'self-management' has added a unique and workable component to humanity's knowledge of methods of economic and political organization.

PART III

Appraisal of Results

CHAPTER 8

MAJOR ECONOMIC ACHIEVEMENTS

In this chapter we shall summarize the record of Yugoslav economic achievement under self-management, as measured by aggregate data. Changes in the distribution of the benefits of economic progress will be examined in Chapter 9. The topics for review in this chapter are: growth rates of output, employment, and productivity; changes in the distribution of the labour force; the growth of real personal incomes and consumption; changes in prices; the balance of payments; regional development; and a brief comparison of the record of Yugoslavia's growth with that of some other comparable countries.

Before we begin, it is necessary to decide what period should be covered by the study. Since Yugoslav growth rates have fluctuated from time to time, and especially during the 1950s, this is not a trivial problem. As can be seen from Figure 8.1, if the growth of gross material product were measured from 1952, a different impression would be given from that which would arise from using 1949 as the base year. Since 1950 was the year in which self-management was first introduced, and since that year was more typical of the previously attained level of economic development than the next few years of severe economic difficulties (resulting from the tightening of the Cominform blockade and the effects of collectivization and droughts in agriculture), it seems best, in an analysis of long-term trends, to start from 1950.

A second problem is to decide on the terminal date of the study. At the time of writing this chapter (1982), many statistics were not complete beyond 1979. In addition, the Yugoslav economy has been under exceptional stress since that year, as a result of the further rise in petroleum prices and the gathering world recession. For both these reasons, it seems preferable to carry the long-term analysis only up to 1979. However, an appendix to this chapter will contain a discussion of changes in economic conditions since that year.

Thirdly, it is necessary to decide how to divide the whole period 1950–79 into sub-periods. Some authors have selected particular sub-periods to correspond with what they regard as periods in which different economic polices were in operation. For example, Horvat (1982) reproduces some earlier results in which he identified the period of self-management as starting in 1954. Estrin (1981) compares the period 1952–65 with 1965–73,

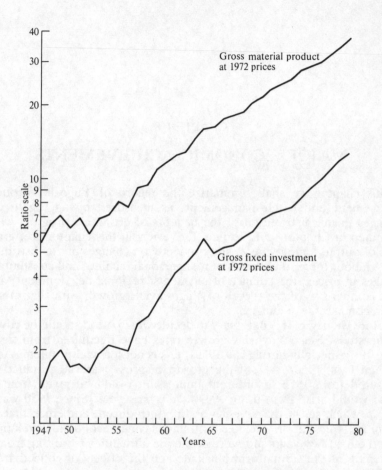

FIG. 8.1. Yugoslav Economic Growth 1947–79

on the grounds that the 1965 Reform marked a substantial change in 'legal methods of allocating resources'. Sapir (1980) compares 1955–65 with 1966–74. Both these latter authors attempt to estimate in this way the effects of the Reform on growth and other variables. As Figure 8.1 shows, if one chooses 1952, 1954, or 1955 as the base date for a study of Yugoslav growth up to 1965, one will inevitably obtain different results from those which would emerge from from using 1950 as the base date. While there is no doubt that the growth of gross material product between the early 1950s and 1965 was very rapid, part of this was due to the recovery of momentum after the setbacks of 1950–2. According to estimates by Puljić (1980), the level of utilization of fixed capital assets in industry rose from about 65 per cent in 1955 to over 90 per cent in 1964. This is consistent with the view that a significant part of the rapid growth in output in these years represented a recovery towards the long-term growth path of the economy. In addition, the second diagram in Figure 8.1, showing the growth of gross fixed investment, suggests that the rate of growth of investment from the 1956 recession up to the 1964 boom was too great to be sustainable under any institutional arrangements. It is unwise, therefore, to regard this period, or something like it, as the 'ideal', and to conclude, from a simple comparison of this period with one or other subsequent period, that the Yugoslav economy could have been more successful if the pre-Reform system had been left unchanged. The correct interpretation of the historical record is certainly more complex than that.

In the light of the above considerations, it seems that the most neutral method of dividing the whole period 1950–79 is to choose three approximately equal sub-periods, namely, 1950–60, 1960–70, and 1970–79. Comparisons of rates of growth in these three sub-periods will not lead to strong conclusions about the effects of particular Yugoslav institutional changes, but they will offer some information about changes in trend rates of growth during the operation of the self-management system in Yugoslavia.

1. OUTPUT, EMPLOYMENT, AND PRODUCTIVITY

A summary of average annual rates of growth of output, employment and productivity is given in Table 8.1. The first line, however, deals with a more fundamental statistic, namely, the rate of growth of the resident population. Over the period as a whole the natural rate of increase of the population was steadily falling—from 17.2 per thousand in 1950 to 8.5 per thousand in 1979—but the growth of the resident population has also been affected by migration. During the latter part of the 1960s there was a large outflow of workers from Yugoslavia to western Europe, predominantly to the Federal Republic of Germany, and during the 1970s some of these migrants returned.[1] As a consequence, the growth of the resident population was lower in the 1960s than in the 1970s. This, of course, has had implications for the rate of growth of domestic employment and unemployment, as well as for the standard of living of the domestic population, who have received substantial remittances from abroad to support a diminished number of people. These remittances have also contributed significantly to the Yugoslav balance of payments and have helped to increase the levels of both household saving and household investment (the latter mainly in houses).

The measurement of the growth of domestic real product depends in part on the definition of that variable. In Yugoslav official statistics domestic product is measured by the 'Marxist' concept of gross material product, which excludes personal services other than trade, transport,

---

[1] The total number of Yugoslav workers 'temporarily' resident abroad rose from about 100,000 in the early 1960s to a peak of over 1 million in 1973, since then it has declined, reaching 770,000 in 1980. See Schrenk and others (1979), Table A. 27 and OECD (1981), Table H. There has also been a small amount of emigration of dependants.

TABLE 8.1

Rates of Growth of Output, Employment, and Productivity, Yugoslavia
(average percentage per annum)

Line	Variable	1950–79	1950–60	1960–70	1970–79
1.	Resident population	0.92	1.19	0.59	0.88
2.	Gross domestic product, 1966 prices	5.70	5.64	5.42	6.07
3.	Gross material product, 1972 prices	6.30	6.46	6.30	6.13
4.	GDP per capita, 1966 prices	4.74	4.39	4.80	5.05
5.	GMP per capita, 1972 prices	5.34	5.20	5.68	5.10
6.	GMP in social sector, 1972 prices	7.03	6.79	7.52	6.77
7.	GMP in private sector, 1972 prices	2.58[a]	2.67[b]	2.24	2.84
8.	Social sector employment: Total	3.75	4.36	2.63	4.31
9.	Productive sector	3.85	4.70	2.63	4.27
10.	Non-productive sector	3.31	2.86	2.67	4.53
11.	Fixed capital, productive social sector, 1972 prices	8.33[c]	8.69[d]	8.51	7.90
	Productive social sector:				
12.	Labour productivity	3.06	2.00	4.76	2.40
13.	Capital productivity	−1.20	−1.75	−0.91	−1.05
14.	Combined factor productivity	1.84	0.89	3.13	1.41
	Industry and mining:				
15.	Gross material product, 1972 prices	8.45	9.47	8.10	7.71
16.	Employment	4.43	5.83	3.15	4.31
17.	Fixed capital, 1972 prices	8.86[e]	9.88[f]	8.55	8.31
18.	Labour productivity	3.85	3.44	4.80	3.26
19.	Capital productivity	−0.38	−0.37	−0.41	−0.55
20.	Combined factor productivity	2.69	2.43	3.33	2.20

[a] 1949–79. [b] 1949–60. [c] 1954–79. [d] 1954–60. [e] 1952–79. [f] 1952–60.

Sources:

Line 1   Total mid-year population from YB81, 102 – 4. Workers temporarily abroad in 1970 and 1979 from OECD (1981) Table H. Dependants resident abroad estimated at 10 per cent of workers.

Line 2   1950 – 70: World Bank (1975), Appendix Tables 2.3 and 2.4. 1979 GMP at 1972 prices from YB81, 102 – 7, converted to 1966 prices by the ratio of GDP in 1966 prices in 1971 in World Bank (1975), Appendix Table 2.4 to GDP in 1972 prices in the same year in Schrenk and others (1979), Table A.13, and grossed up to estimated GDP by comparing GDP : GMP ratios in 1966 prices in previous years.

Line 3   YB77, 102 – 6 and YB81, 102 – 7.

Lines 4–5   Derived from previous data.

Lines 6–7   YB77, 102 – 6 and YB81, 102 – 10.

Lines 8–10   YB77, 102 – 4 and YB81, 102 – 5. Annual average data.

Line 11   YB81, 102 – 12. End-of-year data.

Line 12   Derived from Lines 6 and 9.

Line 13   Derived from Lines 6 and 11.

Line 14   Line 3 minus (0.7 × Line 9) minus (0.3 × Line 11).

Line 15   YB77, 102 – 6 and YB81, 102 – 10.

Line 16   YB81, 102 – 5. Annual average data.

Line 17   YB81, 117 – 1. End-of-year data.

Line 18   Derived from Lines 15 and 16.

Line 19   Derived from Lines 15 and 17.

Line 20   Line 15 minus (0.7 × Line 16) minus (0.3 × Line 17).

catering, and banking. The main services excluded are government-provided social services, administration and defence. Alternative estimates, based on Western concepts, of Yugoslav gross domestic product have been made by the World Bank for the period 1950–75. These can be roughly extrapolated to 1979 with the help of official statistics of gross material product. The result of these calculations are shown in Line 2, with the Yugoslav official estimates of gross material product in Line 3.

The series of gross domestic product (GDP) differs from the series of gross material product (GMP) in two main respects (apart from the fact that the former is in 1966 prices and the latter in 1972 prices). In the first place, GDP covers most of the services excluded from GMP, but probably not the security services and defence. Since the 'volume' of such services has tended to grow more slowly than the volume of output of goods and 'productive' services, GDP tends to grow more slowly than GMP. In addition, Yugoslav estimates of GMP are not corrected for stock appreciation so that, when they are deflated by a price index for current goods and services, the resulting constant price estimates still contain most of the effects of capital gains or losses on stockholdings. In years of rapid inflation this leads to a significant overestimate of the rate of growth of real product.[2] Since inflation has, on the average, been accelerating in Yugoslavia during the past twenty years, the failure to adjust GMP for stock appreciation leads to an upward bias in the estimate of the average rate of growth of real product. For both these reasons, therefore, it can be expected that the estimated growth of GMP will exceed the estimated growth of GDP. This expectation is confirmed by a comparison of Lines 2 and 3 of Table 8.1.

Whether one judges Yugoslav performance by the growth of GDP or of GMP the record of growth over the period 1950–79 has been very impressive. Moreover, it has been remarkably stable over three sub-periods (although not in particular years, especially in the 1950s). An economic system which can generate such a rapid and stable rate of growth is be envied, especially when one finds the same trends continued right through the 1970s. Moreover, per capita real product has also grown very fast—over the full period at 4.74 per cent per annum on a GDP basis and 5.34 per cent per annum on a GMP basis (Lines 4 and 5).

Real product has consistently grown much faster in the social sector than in the private sector (Lines 6 and 7). The latter sector consists predominantly of private agriculture. From 1953 to 1979 (the only available earlier figure relates to 1952, which was a year of agricultural disaster) GMP in

[2] For example, if (1) at the end of each of two consecutive years the value of stocks were equal to one-quarter of gross domestic product during the year, excluding the change in stocks, (2) the price of both GDP and stocks were to rise by 10 per cent (between the averages of the two years for GDP, and between the two year-ends for stocks), (3) the volumes of both GDP and stocks remained constant, then the two alternative estimates of the growth of GDP at constant prices would be: before adjustment for stock appreciation, 2.3 per cent; after adjustment for stock appreciation, zero. With other assumptions the same, but the price rise equal to 30 per cent, the corresponding figures would be 5.8 per cent and zero.

private agriculture rose by 2.09 per cent per annum. Since the active work-force in private agriculture declined during this period at an average rate of 2.01 per cent per annum, labour productivity in private agriculture rose by 4.18 per cent per annum, which is more than in the social sector, or even in industry (Lines 12 and 18).[3]

Employment in the social sector rose at a remarkable average rate of 3.75 per cent per annum over the whole period 1950–79. This means that it was nearly three times as large in 1979 as in 1950. The rate of growth was faster in the productive sector than in personal services, except in the 1970s when the rate of growth of the latter sector was slightly faster. There was a considerable slow-down in both sectors during the 1960s, as a result of the Reform, but a remarkable recovery during the 1970s, in spite of the world recession and of increasing balance of payments problems (Lines 8–10).

The volume of fixed capital in the productive social sector is officially estimated to have risen by 8.33 per cent per annum between 1954 and 1979. Despite some decline in this rate during the latter part of the period, it was still nearly 8 per cent in 1970–9 (Line 11).

Labour productivity in the social sector rose by 3.06 per cent per annum from 1950–79. The rate was considerably lower in the first decade than in 1960–70, and low again in the 1970s (Line 12). Capital productivity has consistently fallen, by 1.2 per cent per annum over the whole period but faster in the first decade (Line 13). The estimates of combined factor productivity in Line 14 have been made on the arbitrary assumption that the appropriate weights are 0.7 for labour and 0.3 for capital.[4] No adjustments have been made for the qualities of either factor or for their degree of utilization. The results suggest that 'technical progress' was most rapid in the 1960s, which is consistent with the expected effects of the Reform.

Separate estimates for the industry and mining sector are given in Lines 15–20. Gross material product, employment, and fixed capital all grew faster in industry than in the productive social sector as a whole. Labour productivity has also grown faster, and capital productivity has fallen more slowly. The result is that the growth of combined factor productivity has been higher in industry than in the whole productive social sector, and it seems to have been more stable.

---

[3] GMP in private agriculture at 1972 prices is given in YB81, 102 – 17. Estimates of the active work-force in private agriculture have been made by Vinski (1981).

[4] These are approximately the weights used in studies of Western economies. No division can be made in Yugoslavia between the earnings of labour and capital, since all workers in the social sector receive incomes from both sources, and so do almost all the workers in the private sector. Estimates of the elasticity of industrial output with respect to labour and capital have been made from time series by Sapir (1980) and Puljić (1980). The former used a CES production function with separate estimates for 1955–65 and 1966–74, and found that technical progress contributed 4.8 per cent to industrial growth in both periods. The latter, after making adjustments for the level of utilization of both labour and capital and the quality of labour, used a Cobb-Douglas production function and estimated that technical progress contributed 4.5 per cent to the growth of industrial output in 1955–64 and 3.7 per cent in 1964–74.

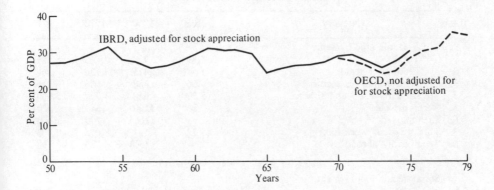

FIG. 8.2. Gross Fixed Investment as Percentage of GDP at Market
Prices

In concluding this section it is of some interest to examine the behaviour
of gross fixed investment. The share of gross fixed investment in GDP in
Yugoslavia has averaged about 28 per cent over the whole period 1950–79,
fluctuating in the range of 25–31 per cent from 1950–75 but rising to 35 per
cent or more in the years 1978 and 1979.[5] On the average the increase in
the value of stocks, after adjustment for stock appreciation, has added
nearly 5 per cent to gross investment, but this rate fell from over 7 per cent
in the period 1952–9, to 4.7 per cent in 1960–9 and 2.3 per cent in 1970–5.[6]
Figure 8.2, which shows the movements in the share of gross fixed
investment over the whole period, suggests that there have been cyclical
movements in this ratio. Peak periods were 1954, 1961–3, 1970–1 and 1978,
at approximately eight-year intervals. Trough years were 1957, 1965, and
1973, exactly at eight-year intervals. It seems that the investment ratio has
an underlying tendency to rise, reaching every eight years or so an
insupportable level, when it has to be checked by institutional or policy
changes. The underlying reasons for the tendency of investment to grow at
an excessive rate will be considered in Chapter 10.

2. DISTRIBUTION OF THE LABOUR FORCE

A broad picture of the size and distribution of the labour force in selected
years is given in Table 8.2. In a country with a large peasant population it is
always difficult to decide how many people should be included in the

[5] Estimates for 1978 and 1979 are derived from OECD (1981), Table B. Since the GDP
estimates in this source are not adjusted for stock appreciation, the shares of fixed
investment, given as 35.3 per cent and 34.6 per cent must be regarded as underestimates.
[6] These are averages of the annual percentages derived from current price estimates in
World Bank (1975) Appendix Tables 2.5 and 2.6 and Schrenk and others (1979), Table A. 12.

TABLE 8.2
Distribution of the Labour Force, Selected Years, Yugoslavia
(annual average in thousands)

Line	Category	1950	1960	1970	1979
	Social sector employment:				
1.	Total	1,894	2,903	3,765	5,506
2.	Productive sector	1,526	2,415	3,130	4,560
3.	Non-productive sector	368	488	635	946
4.	Private agriculture and fishing	(5,000)	4,368	3,720	3,009
5.	Other private	(200)	(160)	(340)	(520)
6.	Unemployed	(30)	(100)	(190)	(460)
7.	Total resident work-force	7,124	7,531	8,015	9,495
8.	Temporarily abroad	–	(50)	783	790
	Percentages of total resident labour force				
	Social sector employment:				
9.	Total	26.6	38.5	47.0	58.0
10.	Productive sector	21.4	32.1	39.1	48.0
11.	Non-productive sector	5.2	6.5	7.9	10.0
12.	Private agriculture and fishing	70.2	58.0	46.4	31.7
13.	Other private	2.8	2.1	4.2	5.5
14.	Unemployed	0.4	1.3	2.4	4.8
15.	Temporarily abroad	–	0.7	9.8	8.3

Sources:

Lines 1–3   YB81, 102 – 5.

Line 4   Vinski (1981). 1950 figure extrapolated back from 1953.

Line 5   Vinski (1981), rounded off. 1950 figure extrapolated back from 1953.

Line 6   60 per cent of persons registered as seeking work, as given in YB81, 102 – 6. 1950 figure extrapolated back from 1952.

Line 8   Schrenk and others (1979), Table A.27 and OECD (1981) Table H. 1960 figure extrapolated back from 1961.

labour force. Moreover, in Yugoslavia many people have jobs in more than one sector. Workers in the social sector, who usually finish work at 2.00 p.m. or 3.00 p.m. and have most Saturdays and Sundays free, plus other holidays, can, if they wish, take on other work. If they have a family farm or plot, as many do, they may work on it, perhaps for almost as many hours as they work in their social sector job, and often harder. Many social sector workers also engage in 'moonlighting', which is a form of unregistered private sector employment. The estimates in Table 8.2 are accurate for the social sector—although they exclude the armed forces and police—but are only approximate for the other categories. Lines 4 and 5, which are based on recent estimates by Vinski (1981), are intended to include all active family workers. The estimates in Line 6 of the number of unemployed are very approximate. Official figures record the number of persons who are registered as desiring jobs in the social sector. But it is well known that this includes a considerable number of schoolchildren and students, as well as people working on farms or in other jobs (some even in the social sector). The official figures, therefore, exaggerate the number of people who are currently both out of work and available for work. Surprisingly, scarcely any attempts seem to have been made to arrive at better estimates of unemployment. It is often said that only about 60 per cent of registered job-seekers are currently unemployed, and this assumption has been made in the present case.[7]

During the period 1950–79, the total resident work-force increased from 7,124,000 to 9,495,000, or by 33 per cent. In the same period the total population, including persons temporarily abroad, increased by 36 per cent. The main feature of the distribution of the work-force has been the rise in the proportion in the social sector from 26.6 per cent to 58.0 per cent and the decline in the proportion in private agriculture from 70.2 per cent to 31.7 per cent. At the same time there has been a significant increase in the proportion of workers in private non-agricultural occupations (from 2.8 per cent to 5.5 per cent), in the unemployed (from 0.4 per cent to 4.8 per cent), and in the number of workers temporarily abroad (from zero in 1950 to 8.3 per cent of the resident work-force in 1979). If all the migrant workers had stayed at home, and if all of them, or others whom they replaced in jobs, had been added to the unemployed, the unemployment rate in 1979—expressed as a percentage of the hypothetical resident work-force—would have been 12.1 per cent. But it is unlikely that this would have been allowed to happen in practice.

The 'job-seeker rate', measured by the percentage of job-seekers to those already employed in the social sector, is higher for females than for males in all regions, and higher for both sexes combined in Macedonia and

TABLE 8.3
Job-seekers by Sex and Region, 1980

Region	Job-seekers, annual average (000)			Per cent of job-seekers to workers in social sector employment (annual average)		
	Males	Females	Total	Males	Females	Total
Yugoslavia	350.3	435.2	785.5	9.6	21.6	13.8
Bosnia-Herzegovina	60.9	76.0	136.9	10.8	29.7	16.7
Montenegro	7.9	14.3	22.2	9.1	36.4	17.6
Croatia	29.2	49.3	78.5	3.5	9.1	5.7
Macedonia	53.4	63.8	117.2	18.3	50.0	27.9
Slovenia	4.9	5.9	10.8	1.1	1.7	1.4
Serbia proper	114.2	159.5	273.7	11.9	32.9	19.0
Kosovo	53.4	14.1	67.5	38.8	39.6	39.0
Vojvodina	26.7	52.2	78.9	7.6	27.0	14.4

Source: YB81, 204 – 3, 204 – 4 and 204 – 7.

[7] In a recent article in *Borba*, 13 April 1982, it was remarked that out of almost 800,000 registered job-seekers only 400–500,000 were estimated to be really unemployed. But the article admits that there is no firm basis for this conclusion.

TABLE 8.4

Job-seekers by Skill Qualification Level, 1978

Qualification	Number of registered job-seekers, average 1978 (000)	Number employed in the social sector, end 1978 (000)	Percentage of job-seekers to number employed in social sector
Secondary or higher education	155.0	1,493.2	10.4
Skilled or highly skilled workers	142.7	2,150.2	6.6
Semi-skilled or elementary education	92.7	1,010.7	9.2
Unskilled	344.4	971.5	35.5
Total	734.8	5,325.5	13.8

Source: YB81, 105 – 5 and 105 – 16.

Kosovo (see Table 8.3). The job-seeker rate is much lower in Slovenia, only 1.4 per cent for both sexes combined in 1980, and moderate in Croatia, 5.7 per cent for both sexes combined in the same year. The demand for jobs by women is particularly pressing, with more than 25 per cent of job-seekers to existing employment in all regions except Croatia and Slovenia, rising to 50 per cent in Macedonia.

Table 8.4, relating to 1978, also shows that the job-seeker rate is higher among the unskilled without elementary education than among those with better qualifications. The bulk of these poorly qualified job-applicants are presumably peasants trying to get out of farming and into secure, and relatively well-paid, jobs in the social sector.

3. REAL PERSONAL INCOMES AND CONSUMPTION

The level of real personal income per worker in the productive sector depends primarily on output per worker, but also on the proportion of enterprise income which is distributed as personal income, and on the ratio between producer and consumer prices. During the period 1952–79 output per worker in the productive social sector rose by 3.2 per cent per annum while, according to Table 8.5 below, net real personal income per worker in the same period rose by 4.7 per cent per annum. The precise explanation for this difference is not easy to find. According to the official price indexes, discussed in detail in the next section, industrial producer prices rose over the full period by 6.6 per cent per annum, while the consumer price index rose by 11.7 per cent per annum. This implies a severe fall in the industrial terms of trade. But the implicit price deflator of gross value added in the non-agricultural productive sector (which includes a small amount of non-agricultural private activity) increased over the same period by 11.4 per cent per annum, i.e. at virtually the same rate as the consumer price index; and this was true also in each sub-period. The main explanation seems to lie, therefore, in changes in the proportion of value

TABLE 8.5
Changes in Real Personal Incomes and Consumption
(average annual percentage changes)

Line	Category	1952–79	1952–60	1960–70	1970–9
	Gross personal income per worker:				
1.	Productive social sector	..	..	6.6	1.3
2.	Private agriculture	..	..	2.8	3.3
	Net personal income per worker, social sector:				
3.	Total	4.5	5.0	6.3	2.1
4.	Productive sector	4.7	5.0	6.7	2.1
5.	Non-productive sector	3.9	4.9	4.9	2.3
6.	Personal consumption per capita	5.3	5.7	5.7	4.5
7.	Consumption of meat per capita	4.4	6.7	1.8	5.4
8.	Consumption of milk per capita	2.1	3.8	0.2	3.2
9.	Consumption of sugar per capita	5.1	8.1	4.5	1.1

Sources and notes:

Line 1   Net personal incomes, including 'personal incomes out of material expenses', plus contributions levied on personal incomes, per worker and deflated by the consumer price index. Income data from YB63, 105 – 5; YB73, 105 – 13; YB81, 107 – 6. Number of workers from YB81, 102 – 5. Consumer price index from YB76, 102 – 29 and YB81, 102 – 33.

Line 2   Net value added per worker, deflated by the consumer price index. Income data and price index as for Line 1. Number of workers in private agriculture from Vinski (1981).

Lines 3–5   YB76, 102 – 29 and YB81, 102 – 33.

Line 6   YB81, 102 – 8. Consumption of goods and 'productive' services, deflated by the consumer price index and divided by the resident population.

Lines 7–9   YB79, 102 – 15 and YB81, 102 – 15. Kilograms per head of resident population and visitors.

added distributed as personal income. Data are not available on this matter prior to 1958, but between 1960 and 1970 there was a significant increase in the proportion of net value added in the social sector which was distributed as net personal income: it rose in ten years from 30.6 per cent to 41.4 per cent. This alone would be enough to raise real personal income per worker by more than 3 per cent per annum, and it more than accounts for the difference between the growth of output per worker in the productive social sector of 4.8 per cent per annum and the growth of net personal income per worker in the same sector of 6.7 per cent per annum. During the following nine years the share of net value added in the social sector which was distributed as net personal income fell from 41.4 per cent to 37.4 per cent, which would account for 1.1 per cent of the difference between the increase in output per worker in this sector of 4.3 per cent and net real personal income per worker of 2.1 per cent.[8]

Table 8.5 shows that over the period 1952–79 real consumption per capita (of goods and 'productive' services) rose at an average rate of 5.3 per cent per annum. The rate was 5.7 per cent in each of the first two sub-periods, and declined to 4.5 per cent in the third. Over the period as a

[8] Sources: YB63, 105 – 5; YB73, 105 – 13; YB81, 107 – 6.

whole, and in the first and third sub-periods, consumption per capita rose
faster than net personal income per worker in the social sector. There are a
number of possible reasons for this difference, and the more important of
them are identified in Tables 8.6 and 8.7.

TABLE 8.6

*Some Factors Relevant to the Relation between Net Personal Income per
Worker in the Social Sector and Consumption per Head of the Total
Population*

Line	Description	1952	1960	1970	1979
1.	Per cent of population employed	43.3	40.4	40.1	42.4
2.	Per cent of employees in social sector	26.7	39.1	48.1	60.9
3.	Per cent of net personal income per worker in private agriculture to net personal income per worker in the social sector	..	38.8	31.0	34.4

Sources:

Line 1   Table 8.1, Line 1 and Table 8.2.

Line 2   Table 8.2.

Line 3   Incomes in the productive social sector and private agriculture from YB63, 105 – 5, YB73, 105 – 13 and YB81, 107 – 6. Employment from YB81, 102 – 5 and Vinski (1981). Income per worker in the productive social sector converted to income per worker in the whole social sector by the ratio of column 1 to column 2 of YB81, 102 – 33.

TABLE 8.7

Sources and Uses of Household Income
(percentages of total income)

Line	Description	1952	1960	1970	1979
1.	Total net labour income, of which:	78.7	81.3	78.9	69.6
2.	Social sector income	23.5	41.1	57.8 ⎤	
3.	Private sector—money income	25.2	21.3	11.5 ⎦	63.5
4.	Private sector—income in kind	30.0	18.9	9.6	6.1
5.	Social security transfers	19.3	15.3	13.2	15.7
6.	Other domestic transfers	0.7	2.1	1.0	3.7
7.	Foreign transfers	0.9	0.7	6.2	8.1
8.	Interest, etc.[a]	0.4	0.4	0.7	2.9
	Total income	100.0	100.0	100.0	100.0
9.	Taxes and contributions[b]	0.3	1.1	2.0	2.4
10.	Saving: Total	1.3	3.7	13.7	16.2[c]
11.	Financial saving	0.9	2.6	6.8	9.4[c]

Sources: 1952–70: Nikić (1979), Table 3.

Lines 6 and 8 separated by taking interest, etc. from YB63, 105 – 7 and YB73, 124 – 1.

1979: YB81, 106 – 2 and 108 – 1, except Line 10, which is from Nikić (1979), Table 3.

[a] Interest on savings deposits plus some minor items.

[b] Taxes and contributions paid after receipt of net personal income.

[c] 1977.

There might have been a significant change in the proportion of the resident population who are employed. In fact, this proportion was slightly lower in 1960 and 1970 than in 1950, but largely recovered by 1979 (Table 8.6, Line 1). There has, however, been a major change in the proportion of the employed work-force who are in the social sector. Over the full period 1950–79 this rose from 26.7 per cent to 60.9 per cent (Table 8.6, Line 2). Since net income per worker in private agriculture (where most of private sector workers are employed) has always been much lower than in the social sector (Table 8.6, Line 3), this transfer of workers between sectors is alone responsible for personal income per worker in both sectors rising faster than income per worker in the social sector. For example, the transfer of workers from private agriculture to the social sector during the period 1960–79 was responsible for increasing net personal income per worker in both sectors combined by nearly 1 per cent per annum.

Other factors which have caused consumption to grow faster or slower than labour income are identified in Table 8.7. On the positive side, there has been a significant growth in the importance of income from foreign transfers (mainly migrant remittances) and, to a smaller extent, in other domestic transfers and interest on savings deposits. As a consequence, the share of labour income in total household income has fallen, especially since 1970. Indeed, between 1970 and 1979 it fell from 78.9 per cent to 69.6 per cent. This is probably the main explanation for the divergence between the growth of personal income per worker and consumption per capita in this period. This effect was partly offset by a rise in the saving ratio (from 13.7 per cent in 1970 to 16.2 per cent in 1977). In the previous decade the rise in the saving ratio was much larger, and more than offset the small decline in the share of labour income. This was more than enough to account for the difference between the growth of net personal income per social sector worker in this period (6.3 per cent per annum) and the growth of consumption per capita (5.7 per cent per annum).

The growth in the proportion of non-labour sources of income in Yugoslavia, especially in recent years, has important implications. As in many other countries, there has been a trend towards reducing the role of current labour and increasing the opportunities for obtaining income from transfers, in the Yugoslav case especially from foreign transfers. The share of income from interest is also growing. Moreover, if information were available about incomes from 'moonlighting',it would probably show that the share of income received from social sector employment in recent years has stabilized or has even fallen. These matters will be discussed further in Chapter 13 below.

Yugoslavia now has a high personal saving ratio (16.5 per cent of disposable income in 1977). Much of these savings are invested in property, mainly in 'weekend' houses. Of the remainder, the population aims to deposit as much as possible in foreign exchange deposits rather than in dinar deposits. The unusual system of foreign exchange deposits allows any person to open an account in any bank in a wide range of foreign currencies, in practice mainly in Deutschmarks or dollars. These deposits were until recently earning interest at 7–8 per cent, and both the deposit and the interest are repayable in dinars when required, at the rate of exchange ruling at the time of repayment.[9] This is an exceptional opportunity to hedge against the rapid rate of Yugoslav domestic inflation. Since 1970, the ratio of household cash (including a trivial amount of current deposits) to household income (the former measured at the end of the year, the latter during the year) has fallen slightly from 14 per cent in 1970 to 12 per cent in 1980. Meanwhile, interest-earning dinar deposits have risen slightly from 17 per cent to 18 per cent of household income, so that the percentage of total dinar cash and deposits has remained about constant. Foreign exchange deposits, on the other hand, valued at current exchange rates, have risen during this same period from 3 per cent to 22 per cent of household income. As a result, total cash and deposits have risen from 34 per cent of household income to 52 per cent.[10] Holdings of foreign exchange deposits must now be worth considerably more than holdings of dinar deposits.[11]

4. PRICES

Like many other countries, Yugoslavia experienced fairly stable prices in the 1950s, followed by accelerating inflation in the 1960s and 1970s. The nearest to stability in the 1950s were the prices of industrial products. As shown in Table 8.8, in the period 1952–60 (data for the previous two years are not available) producers' prices of industrial products rose at 0.7 per cent per annum, wholesale prices at 0.2 per cent per annum, and retail prices at 0.5 per cent per annum. However, the prices of farm products, construction, and services were already rising quite rapidly in this period (around 7 per cent for farm products and construction, and as much as 12.3 per cent for services at retail). As a consequence, the retail sales index rose by 2.6 per cent per annum, and the consumer price index (which covers some services not included in the retail sales index) by 4.9 per cent per annum.

During the period 1960–70, all rates of growth of prices were higher than in the previous period. At the producer and wholesale level, growth rates were up by 4 to 7 per cent; but the growth rate of the retail price index rose by 8 per cent and catering services by 9 per cent. The exception was the services component of the retail sales index which rose from 12.3 to 12.8

[9] Foreign exchange deposits may also be withdrawn in foreign exchange, i.e. without conversion into dinars, and used for foreign travel or other purposes, such as the import of household goods. This right was restricted in October 1982 to $250 a month. At the end of 1979 there were estimated to be about three million foreign exchange accounts, worth about $7 billion. The gross inflow in that year was about $3.4 billion, but withdrawals amounted to about $1.7 billion. Total interest of about $0.5 billion was credited to these accounts during the year. For 1979 data see Čolanović in Stojanović (1982, 138).

[10] 1970 income from Nikić (1979), Table 3. 1980 income estimated from preliminary information about GMP in that year and the ratio of household income to GMP in 1979 (YB81, 106 – 2 and 107 – 5). Household assets from YB80, 111 – 1 and YB81, 111 – 1.

[11] The sharp fall in the value of the dinar during 1981 and 1982 will have at least doubled the dinar value of foreign exchange deposits.

TABLE 8.8
Changes in Prices
(average annual percentage changes)

Line	Category	1952–79	1952–60	1960–70	1970–9
	Industrial products:				
1.	Producers' prices	6.6	0.7	4.9	14.0
2.	Wholesale prices	8.3	0.2	7.6	16.9
3.	Agricultural products				
	(private farmers)	13.1	6.8	13.8	18.2
4.	Construction	13.1	7.3	13.1	18.3
	Retail sales:				
5.	Total	10.4	2.6	10.6	17.6
6.	Industrial goods	9.2	0.5	9.2	17.7
7.	Agricultural goods	12.9	5.9	14.1	18.1
8.	Services	14.0	12.3	12.8	17.1
9.	Catering services	15.3	8.9	17.9	18.5
10.	Consumer price index	11.7	4.9	12.0	17.7
11.	Imports	4.9	−0.9	3.5	12.1
12.	Exports	5.1	−0.4	3.0	12.8

Sources: YB78, 102 – 28, 102 – 29 and 112 – 6; YB81, 102 – 9, 102 – 27, and 102 – 33.

per cent, bringing its rate of growth more closely into line with the rates of growth of retail goods prices.

During the period 1970–9 there was a further—and greater—increase in the rate of price inflation. The rate of growth of industrial goods prices rose to 14.0 per cent per annum and the rate of growth of wholesale prices rose to 16.9 per cent per annum. Rates of growth of farm products, construction, and services rose by smaller amounts, and as a result most rates tended to converge to about 17–18 per cent per annum for the period as a whole.

Over the period 1952–79 as a whole producers' prices of industrial goods are estimated to have risen at 6.6 per cent per annum, while their wholesale prices rose at 8.3 per cent per annum, and their retail prices at 9.2 per cent per annum. These differences may be due in part to the increasing relative cost of services at wholesale and retail level, but they are large enough to suggest that there may also have been an increasing tendency to understate producer prices in official returns.[12]

The prices paid to private farmers have risen faster than industrial product prices throughout the period, the difference being especially large in the first two sub-periods. This was the result of official recognition that the early policy of squeezing the peasants for the benefit of socialized industry was counterproductive, especially in view of the collapse of

[12] A report in *Borba* (12 July 1982) draws attention to the widespread practice among producers of 'surcharging' prices for the cost of investment, foreign exchange, losses, loans for development, and 'special orders'. It is unlikely that these surcharges are included in the prices reported to the statistical authorities. Wholesale and retail prices, however, will include the cost of these surcharges.

collectivization. Even now official purchase prices for farm products are set too low to stimulate adequate farm output. In the hope of shielding the consumer from increases in food prices, there is a considerable lag in the adjustment of official farm prices to changes in farm costs. The consequence has been an unnecessary dependence on imports of some farm products, such as sugar and vegetable oils, and even occasionally maize, and a failure to develop export markets for other products.

Construction prices have risen very closely in line with the prices of farm products, at 13.1 per cent per annum over the whole period 1952–79. Especially in the first two sub-periods construction prices rose much more rapidly than the prices of industrial products. It is widely recognized that the costs of construction are now grossly in excess of what they should be. For example, it is estimated that the cost of a new social sector flat, of quite modest size, is equivalent to twelve years of average net personal incomes in the social sector.[13] If depreciation and repairs require at least 3 per cent of capital costs, and interest is charged at 5 per cent, the economic rent for such a flat would absorb the whole of average net personal income. In practice, rents are heavily subsidized, repairs are neglected, and inflation has made the real rate of interest negative. But this is an unstable situation (which will be discussed further in Chapter 10). The principal causes of the problem are the inefficiency of construction—arising in part from excessive investment demand which leads to a chronic shortage of materials—and insistence on building high-rise blocks of flats.

The price indexes for both imports and exports have risen more slowly than all the other price indexes, over the whole period and in each sub-period. At first sight this may seem to be inconsistent with the theoretical prediction, based on Chapter 3, that world prices, in terms of dinars, are likely to be the main determinant of Yugoslav domestic prices, at least for tradable goods. But the domestic price indexes are base-weighted, with a constant base, while the import and export price indexes are chained indexes of annual changes, with a new base each year.[14] This technical difference in method of calculation is almost certainly responsible for a considerable part of the difference between the domestic and foreign trade price indexes, and perhaps for virtually the whole of the difference between the price indexes for foreign trade and the index of producers' prices of industrial products. If the import and export price indexes, which are calculated by the same method, are regarded as comparable price indexes of imports and of Yugoslav output of tradable goods respectively, the close similarity in their movements is consistent with the previously mentioned hypothesis.[15]

---

[13] *Borba* (16 July 1982). In Belgrade, the corresponding figure in 1981 was about 16 years (*Ekonomska politika*, 13 September 1982, pp. 18–20).

[14] See the 'Explanations on Methodology' at the beginning of each Yearbook.

[15] Since throughout this period the dinar has not been freely convertible, both the true dinar value of exports and the true dinar cost of imports should reflect, at least in part, the black-market rate for dinars. An article in *Borba* (5 November 1982) quotes an estimate from a survey of major exporting enterprises that 80 per cent of products exported to the

5. THE BALANCE OF PAYMENTS

Yugoslavia's current balance of payments has been negative in all but a few years of the period 1950–79. Expressed as a percentage of gross domestic product at market prices the current deficit was, on the average, only 0.8 per cent in the years 1950–4, but it worsened steadily over the next two five-year periods (see Table 8.9). In the first five years after the Reform the current deficit was on average only 0.4 per cent of gross domestic product. But once more it began to deteriorate, and in the five-year period 1975-9 it reached 2.8 per cent.

The balance of trade in goods and services has always been more negative than the current balance as a whole. In the 1950s the trade deficit was about 3–4 per cent of GDP, and this continued into 1961. From 1962 to 1969 the trade deficit was smaller, in the region of 1–3 per cent of GDP. But from 1970 onwards the trade balance seriously deteriorated: except in

TABLE 8.9

Exports, Imports and the Current Balance as Percentages of Gross Domestic Product at Market Prices

(average of annual percentages in each period)

Period	Goods and non-factor services			Balance of transfers and factor services	Current balance
	Exports	Imports	Trade balance		
1950–4	6.27	9.97	−3.70	2.91	−0.79
1955–9	13.26	16.30	−3.04	1.47	−1.57
1960–4	14.70	17.58	−2.88	0.74	−2.14
1965–9	19.23	20.53	−1.30	0.87	−0.43
1970–4	20.25	25.83	−5.58	4.70	−0.88
1975–9	17.51	24.81	−7.30	4.54	−2.76

Sources:
GDP   1950–65: World Bank (1975), Appendix Tables 2.5 and 2.6.
           1966–75: Schrenk and others (1979), Table A.12.
           1976–9: Estimates by author.
Exports and imports: 1950–65: World Bank (1975), Appendix Tables 2.5 and 2.6.
                        1966–75: Schrenk and others (1979), Table A.12.
                        1976–9: YB81, 106 – 6.
Current balance: Dollar estimates in World Bank (1975), Appendix Table 3.1 and Schrenk and others (1979), Table A.18, converted to dinars by ratio of exports valued in dollars in previous sources and exports valued in dinars in these sources. 1975–9 values in dinars from YB81, 106 – 6.
Factor service and transfer balance: Difference between current balance and trade balance.

convertible currency area are sold at prices below domestic prices, including 43 per cent at discounts of 31 per cent or more. These latter, it is said, must be sold at a loss, since subsidies and refunds would be insufficient to cover such discounts. 'In fact, many enterprises make up for their losses on exports by increasing the prices charged on the domestic market.' Clearly, changes over time in the ratio of black-market to official dinar values could be responsible for some of the differences between changes in official indexes of domestic and foreign trade prices; but they should not significantly affect a comparison between rates of change in import and export prices, both of which are likely to be biased to a similar degree by this factor.

1972, it was at least 4 per cent in deficit, and in most years it was between 6 and 10 per cent in deficit (9.9 per cent in 1974, 9.5 per cent in 1979). The worst years were those in which petroleum prices increased sharply, but the change in the trade balance was clearly apparent before 1974. Between 1965–9 and 1970–4 the ratio of imports to GDP rose by 5.8 per cent (from 20.5 per cent to 25.8 per cent) while the export ratio rose by only 1 per cent (from 19.2 per cent to 20.2 per cent). In the next five years the import ratio fell by 1 per cent, but the export ratio fell even more, by 2.7 per cent to 17.5 per cent. In 1979 this latter ratio was down to 16.1 per cent while the import ratio was up to 25.7 per cent, a most ominous development.

Trade in services, mainly tourism and associated transport services, has made a small positive contribution to the trade balance as a whole. Although there is a significant import of services, including expenditure on foreign tourism and travel, the net contribution of the service item has been in the region of 1–3 per cent of GDP during the period 1975-79. Trade in merchandise has, therefore, been even more in deficit than the trade in goods and services as a whole. In the period 1975–9 the deficit on merchandise trade averaged 9.4 per cent of GDP, ranging from 6.7 per cent in 1976 to 11.5 per cent in 1975. In no year since 1969 have merchandise exports covered more than 70 per cent of the cost of merchandise imports, and in most of these years this percentage has been in the range of 50–60 per cent.[16]

The difference between the balance of trade and the current balance has been bridged by payments for factor services and the receipt of transfers. Factor service payments have consisted predominantly of outward interest payments, so that this item has slightly increased the gap to be bridged. The major inflow has consisted of workers' remittances. These have become of increasing importance since 1968, and throughout the 1970s they were equivalent to about 5 per cent of GDP.

Over the period 1952–79 the value of merchandise exports rose at an average rate of 13.1 per cent per annum, while the volume index rose by 7.7 per cent per annum (see Table 8.10). On the import side, over the same period the value rose by 14.4 per cent per annum and the volume by 8.8 per

TABLE 8.10
Growth of Merchandise Trade
(average annual percentage changes)

Merchandise trade	1952–79	1952–60	1960–70	1970–9
Exports - Value	13.1	11.0	11.5	16.8
Volume	7.7	11.9	7.7	4.2
Imports - Value	14.4	10.5	13.3	19.3
Volume	8.8	10.9	10.0	5.7

Source: YB81, 102 – 27, 102 – 28, and 102 – 29.

[16] YB81, 102 – 8.

cent per annum. The growth in the volumes of both exports and imports was greatest in the first sub-period, 1952–60, when the volume of exports rose by 11.9 per cent per annum and the volume of imports by 10.9 per cent per annum. During the 1960s and 1970s, however, these growth rates declined, especially on the export side; and in each decade the volume (and value) of imports rose faster than the volume (and value) of exports.

The commodity composition of Yugoslav merchandise trade has changed out of all recognition since before the second world war. In 1939 Yugoslavia exported no machinery or transport equipment and virtually no chemicals. The bulk of its exports (measured in tonnage) consisted of food and raw materials.[17] Even as late as 1956 there had been little change in this respect (see Table 8.11). In that year 59 per cent of the value of exports consisted of food and raw materials, only 4.5 per cent consisted of chemicals, and only 4.6 per cent consisted of machinery and transport equipment. But by that time 32.1 per cent consisted of other—less complex—manufactures. During the next quarter-century the composition of exports changed radically, with a steady decline in the share of food and raw materials, reaching 21.6 per cent in 1980, and a rise in the share of chemicals, machinery, and transport equipment. By 1980 this latter group of products represented 39.7 per cent of the value of exports. By the

TABLE 8.11
Commodity Composition of Merchandise Trade, 1956–80
(percentages of total values of exports and imports respectively)

	1956	1960	1965	1970	1975	1980
Exports						
Food, drink and tobacco	33.8	33.1	25.6	18.7	11.7	11.4
Raw materials	25.0	16.8	11.1	10.7	7.7	10.2
Chemicals	4.5	4.1	5.4	5.9	9.3	11.3
Machinery and transport equipment	4.6	15.0	23.5	22.7	28.0	28.4
Other manufactures[a]	32.1	31.2	34.3	42.1	43.2	38.8
Imports						
Food, drink and tobacco	31.8	9.1	14.7	7.2	5.5	6.6
Raw materials	27.0	21.2	23.4	15.9	23.2	34.4
of which: petroleum and products	9.9	5.5	5.6	4.8	12.3	23.6
Chemicals	7.0	8.6	9.2	9.3	10.8	12.1
Machinery and transport equipment	19.9	36.8	27.6	33.2	34.0	28.0
Other manufactures[a]	14.3	24.2	25.1	33.9	26.5	18.9

Sources: YB60, 2 – 234 and 2 – 235; YB64, 113 – 13 and 113 – 14; YB68, 113 – 11 and 113 – 12; YB72, 113 – 11 and 113 – 12; YB76, 114 – 11 and 114 – 12; YB81, 121 – 12 and 121 – 13.
[a] Includes unclassified items.

[17] YB64, 113 – 13.

middle of the 1960s Yugoslavia was predominantly an exporter of manufactures, and by the middle of the 1970s the share of manufactures in total exports had reached more than 80 per cent.[18]

On the import side, in 1956 Yugoslavia was still heavily dependent on foreign supplies of foodstuffs, which accounted for virtually the whole of the 31.8 per cent of imports described in the table as food, drink and tobacco. Imports of chemicals, machinery and other manufactures were on a much more modest scale than they would be in later years. By 1960, however, both these proportions had changed dramatically: imports of food, drink, and tobacco were down to 9.1 per cent and imports of chemicals, machinery, and other manufactures were up to 69.6 per cent. Although these two proportions fluctuated somewhat during the following two decades, they have not changed radically. The most distressing development, however, has been the growth in the cost of petroleum imports, which rose from about 5 per cent of the total in the 1960s and early 1970s to as much as 23.6 per cent in 1980. It is this factor more than any other which has thrown Yugoslavia's balance of payments, and all other aspects of its economy, into a critical condition.

Since the time of the Cominform blockade Yugoslavia has done most of its foreign trade with Western countries, and to a lesser extent with the less developed countries. But, as political relations with the Soviet Union

TABLE 8.12

*Yugoslavia's Dependence on Merchandise Trade
with CMEA Countries*

(percentages of total exports and imports respectively)

Year	Exports to:		Imports from:	
	CMEA	USSR	CMEA	USSR
1970	32.1	14.4	20.5	6.7
1971	36.5	14.8	23.7	8.6
1972	35.1	14.7	24.5	8.8
1973	32.1	14.3	24.2	9.0
1974	38.2	17.7	22.5	10.0
1975	46.0	24.9	23.9	10.5
1976	41.6	23.4	29.2	13.6
1977	38.9	21.7	28.2	13.5
1978	35.5	18.1	28.8	13.8
1979	39.2	20.6	24.6	12.8
1980	44.3	27.7	29.3	17.9

Sources: YB75, 114 – 10; YB78, 121 – 11; YB81, 121 – 11.

[18] If semi-processed foods, beverages, and materials are included in manufactures, this figure would be about 90 per cent. Despite the growth of total manufactured exports, these exports are widely dispersed over different commodity groups. This failure to specialize in particular fields of manufactured exports is a source of weakness in Yugoslavia's export effort, and reflects the fact that few enterprises really want to be bothered with exports.

improved, trade with the Comecon countries revived. By 1970 32.1 per cent of Yugoslavia's exports went to Comecon countries, of which 14.4 per cent went to the USSR, and 20.5 per cent of Yugoslavia's imports came from Comecon countries, of which 6.7 per cent came from the USSR (see Table 8.12). Since Yugoslavia's Comecon trade is bilaterally balanced, with little overall surplus or deficit in individual years, and since Yugoslavia's total merchandise exports cover only part of its imports, the Comecon share of Yugoslavia's exports is bound to be higher than the Comecon share of Yugoslavia's imports. Following the 1973 rise in petroleum prices Yugoslavia's dependence on trade with Comecon countries has increased, mainly but not exclusively because a large proportion of Yugoslavia's imports of petroleum come from the USSR. By 1980, 44.3 per cent of Yugoslavia's exports were going to the Comecon countries, including 27.7 per cent to the USSR. Apart from the need to pay for petroleum and other raw materials, such as cotton and coking coal, Yugoslav enterprises find that it is relatively easy to sell their products in the Comecon countries, where there is always excess demand, and quality standards are low.[19] In the West, on the other hand, market competition in quality and price is much stronger, and in addition there is now a severe recession. Recent changes in the structure of trade have created a difficult problem for the Yugoslav government, which wants to avoid becoming too dependent on the Comecon countries, partly for political and partly for economic reasons. But, if the recession continues, it will be almost impossible for Yugoslavia to avoid a further increase in its trade dependence on the Soviet bloc.

Despite persistent deficits in the current account, Yugoslavia's level of international indebtedness was not excessive in the mid-1970s. In 1975, for example, the gross debt service ratio (ratio of all debt service payments to total receipts from exports of goods and services and workers' remittances) was 17.6 per cent, and the net ratio (after deducting debt service credits) was 15.6 per cent. The ratio of gross debt service payments to gross domestic product was 4.4 per cent. These ratios were all somewhat higher than in 1966, but not dramatically so (the gross debt service ratio in 1966 was 13.2 per cent). A World Bank team which visited Yugoslavia in 1976 expressed the opinion that 'in comparison with other developing countries active in the international capital markets, [Yugoslavia's] current indebtedness, although high, is not excessive', and that 'the debt service ratio in recent years does not indicate any significant problems'.[20] But by 1982 the position had sharply changed for the worse. As shown in Table 8.9 above, the average current account deficit in the five years 1975–9 was 2.76 per cent of GDP, and the deficits in 1980 and 1981 were probably about the same. In mid-1982 it was estimated that Yugoslavia's indebtedness had

[19] As the economist, Mladen Kovačević, said to *Ekonomska politika* (9 November 1981), exports to the eastern European countries are easier because their criteria of prices, quality, and competitiveness are more appropriate for Yugoslav enterprises.
[20] Schrenk and others (1979), 221–2, and Table 9.13.

reached about $20 billion, much of it in the form of supplier credits, with an annual debt service cost of about $5 billion. This probably represents a debt service ratio of about 35 per cent. The government has also come to realize the grim fact that receipts from about half of its merchandise exports go through bilateral clearing accounts with the Comecon countries, and that these are not available for the settlement of debts to Western banks or commercial suppliers. So the debt service ratio, calculated on the basis of total foreign receipts, is not a good measure of the country's ability to meet its obligations. A debt service ratio calculated on the basis of convertible currency receipts would probably be at least 50 per cent.

Yugoslavia is one among a group of countries which tried to avoid fundamental adjustments in face of the petroleum price rises and their further consequences. The government kept its foot firmly down on the accelerator, investment was allowed to continue to rise as a proportion of GDP, the balance of payments deteriorated, and debts soared. Finally, in 1982 the government began to take strong measures to curb expenditure, especially investment expenditure, to restrict imports and to expand exports. But the task now facing the country is extremely onerous and may well precipitate internal divisions.

Some fundamental reasons for the weakness of Yugoslavia's balance of payments will be discussed in Chapter 10.

6. REGIONAL DEVELOPMENT

The country which was created in 1918 by the amalgamation of a number of very disparate components inherited enormous differences in regional levels of development. At one extreme was Slovenia, which had been part of the Austrian empire for centuries, where both literacy and the degree of industrialization were quite high. At the other extreme were Macedonia and Kosovo, which had both been under Turkish rule for centuries, where both the levels of literacy and industrialization were abysmally low. The relative span of differences did not change much during the inter-war years and, when the Communists took over in 1945, they recognized that they faced a heavy task in trying to lift the backward regions up towards the level of the more advanced regions. But they did not appreciate the full seriousness of the problem. According to Marxist ideology large differences in economic development, like all other major ills, are due to capitalism. Hence the Yugoslav Communists genuinely believed that within a few years after the revolution, at most within two or three decades, the wide regional differences within their own country would be eliminated. Experience has shown that this belief was an illusion. Despite rapid rates of growth in the less developed regions, partly attributable to very substantial economic assistance from the more advanced regions, relative differences in levels of income per capita have *increased*. The evidence for this phenomenon, and some of the reasons for it, will be discussed below. A deeper analysis will be made in later chapters.

Table 8.13 gives estimates of the resident population in each republic

TABLE 8.13
*Population and Relative Net Material Product per Capita,
by Regions*

	Resident population 1979 (millions)	Net material product per capita[a] (Yugoslavia=100)			
		1953[b]	1961	1971	1979
Yugoslavia	21.5	100	100	100	100
Bosnia-Herzegovina	4.0	84	73	67	66
Montenegro	0.6	62	65	72	60
Croatia	4.4	114	122	127	130
Macedonia	1.8	61	62	66	67
Slovenia	1.8	174	195	187	197
Serbia proper	5.4	94	95	96	97
Kosovo	1.5	47	33	32	30
Vojvodina	2.0	109	102	118	123

Sources: Net material product ('national income'): YB63, 203 – 5; YB69, 203 – 2; YB73, 204 – 6; YB81, 205 – 6.
  Resident population: YB81, 203 – 1 and 203 – 2, adjusted for estimated number of workers and dependants temporarily abroad.
[a] Net material product (called 'national income' in Yugoslavia) equals gross material product minus depreciation. It is divided by the estimated resident population in each year.
[b] Measured in 1960 prices.

and autonomous province in 1979, and of relative levels of per capita net material product in each region in selected years from1953 to 1979. In 1953 the average level of real output per head was very low in comparison with later periods (it was still affected by the agricultural crises of the early 1950s) and, in general, inter-regional differences in output per capita were smaller at that time than subsequently. From 1953 to 1961 the relative positions of the most prosperous regions—Croatia and Slovenia—increased, and the relative positions of two of the most backward regions—Bosnia-Herzegovina and Kosovo—declined. (One of the reasons for this, as shown in Table 8.14, was the more rapid rate of growth of population in the less developed regions.) After 1961 the relative positions of Bosnia-Herzegovina and Kosovo continued to decline, although more slowly, while the relative positions of Croatia and Vojvodina steadily improved. In 1979, therefore, there remained very wide differences between the levels of per capita output in different regions. At the extremes, Slovenia produced nearly twice the average, Kosovo less than a third of the average. Croatia and Vojvodina were both producing about twice as much per capita as Bosnia-Herzegovina, Montenegro, and Macedonia, and four times as much as Kosovo.[21] As will be seen later,

[21] If the ratios for Slovenia and Kosovo are applied to the estimates by Kravis and others (1982) of the purchasing power equivalent levels of GDP per capita in Yugoslavia and some

inter-regional differences in per capita consumption levels are usually smaller than differences in per capita output levels, especially when collective consumption is taken into account.

Rates of growth of net material product and of the resident population are shown separately in Table 8.14. For Yugoslavia as a whole, net material product rose less rapidly in the 1960s and 1970s than in the period 1952–60 (which was biased upwards by the low level of output in 1952). In general, each region experienced rather similar rates of growth in each sub-period (the rapid growth of Vojvodina's output in 1952–60 is a reflection of the great importance of agriculture in that province and the influence of the agricultural recovery). In Slovenia, output consistently rose faster than the average, especially in the 1970s, and in Bosnia-Herzegovina output consistently rose less fast than the average, but not much less in the 1970s.

There were wider differences between regions in the rates of growth of the resident population. Natural rates of increase have always been higher in the less developed regions than in the more advanced regions (in 1970, for example, the rates per 1,000 population were 14.3 in Bosnia-Herzegovina, 13.6 in Montenegro, 15.6 in Macedonia and 27.6 in Kosovo, as against 3.9 in Croatia, 5.9 in Slovenia, 5.7 in Serbia proper, and 2.8 in Vojvodina).[22] The resident population was also affected by the emigration

TABLE 8.14

Rates of Growth of Net Material Product at 1972 prices and Resident Population, by Regions

(average annual percentage rates of growth)

	Net material product at 1972 prices			Resident population		
				1953–61	1961–71	1971–9
	1952–60	1960–70	1970–9			
Yugoslavia	8.8	6.2	6.1	1.1	0.7	0.9
Bosnia-Herzegovina	7.3	5.4	6.0	1.8	1.0	1.3
Montenegro	5.7	8.2	4.6	1.5	1.0	1.2
Croatia	8.9	6.2	5.8	0.7	0.1	0.5
Macedonia	8.0	7.7	6.2	0.9	1.3	1.4
Slovenia	9.0	6.8	6.6	0.7	0.5	0.6
Serbia proper	8.7	6.0	6.1	1.0	0.6	0.6
Kosovo	8.1	6.6	5.6	2.1	2.4	2.6
Vojvodina	12.2	5.6	6.3	1.3	0.3	0.3

Sources: Net material product ('national income'): YB81, 205 – 2.
　　　　Population: as for Table 8.13.

other countries, the inference may be drawn that in the 1970s Slovenia had a level of per capita output of about 70 per cent of the United States level, and Kosovo about 11 per cent. This would put Slovenia approximately on the same level as Austria, and Kosovo on approximately the same level as the Philippines, Thailand, or Zambia.

[22] YB81, 203 – 2.

of workers during the late 1960s, which was especially important in Croatia. As a result of this emigration, the annual rate of growth of the resident population was slightly less in the 1960s than in the 1970s, especially so in Croatia where it fell to 0.1 per cent in the 1960s. In Vojvodina, also, the resident population rose at a very slow rate throughout the 1960s and 1970s. But in Kosovo the resident population has been rising at an increasing rate, reaching 2.6 per cent per annum in the 1970s. This has imposed a brake on the growth of per capita output in Kosovo, and it has had a number of other important economic and political effects.

The wide differences in net material product per capita between the regions are the result of many influences. Probably the most fundamental are differences in culture, technical knowledge, and experience; but these are difficult to measure. There are, however, some more easily measured influences which are identified in Table 8.15. First, there are differences between regions in the proportion of the population in the active work-force. In 1971, the latest year for which regional estimates of the active work-force are available until the 1981 Census results are published, the activity rate varied from 75 per cent of the average in Kosovo up to 121 per cent of the average in Serbia proper. Montenegro was also near the bottom of the range, and Slovenia near the top. This factor alone is responsible for much of the difference between the regional levels of NMP per capita (for 1971) in Table 8.13 and of NMP per worker in the same year in Table 8.15.

Secondly, output per worker in the whole economy depends on output per worker in different sectors and the proportion of the work-force engaged in each sector. Here we distinguish only the productive social sector on the one hand and private agriculture (which represents the overwhelming part of the private sector) on the other. Inter-regional differences in labour productivity in the productive social sector are smaller than differences in labour productivity for the whole economy. In 1971, social sector productivity ranged from 69 per cent of the average in Kosovo up to 117 per cent of the average in Slovenia, much less than the corresponding figures for the whole economy, which were 54 per cent and 165 per cent respectively. The main reasons for these changes were inter-regional differences in the proportions of workers engaged in private agriculture and the extremely low level of productivity in that sector. On the average, in 1971 NMP per worker in the productive social sector was 6.4 times as great as in private agriculture, and this ratio varied from 3.3 in Vojvodina—where private farms are relatively prosperous—up to 7.6 in Serbia proper.[23] Given this wide difference in productivity in the two sectors, average productivity for the whole economy clearly depends to a considerable extent on the proportion of the work-force engaged in private

[23] The reasons for this enormous difference will be discussed further in Chapter 13. For Yugoslavia as a whole, the ratio was 5.5 in 1961 and about 6.1 in 1979, when the percentage of the Yugoslav work-force engaged in private agriculture had fallen to about 32 per cent.

TABLE 8.15

Some Influences on the Level of Output per Capita, by Region, 1971

	Active work-force as proportion of resident population	Net material product per worker		Value of fixed capital per worker in productive social sector[a]	Ratio of NMP per worker in PSS to NMP per worker in private agriculture	Per cent of active work-force in private agriculture
		Whole economy	Productive social sector			
		(Yugoslavia = 100)				
Yugoslavia	100	100	100	100	6.4	44
Bosnia-Herzegovina	83	81	88	107	7.1	48
Montenegro	76	95	97	145	6.6	42
Croatia	104	122	109	102	6.1	38
Macedonia	87	76	78	83	5.5	43
Slovenia	113	165	117	95	5.5	24
Serbia proper	121	79	96	99	7.6	54
Kosovo	75	54	69	129	5.5	54
Vojvodina	102	119	101	90	3.3	38

Sources: Resident population: YB73, 202 – 3.
Work-force: YB72, 202 – 1 and 202 – 2; YB73, 202 – 3.
Net material product: YB73, 204 – 6.
Value of fixed capital at current value: YB73, 205 – 1.
[a] Active fixed capital per worker in the social sector: YB73, 205 – 1.

agriculture. In 1971 this varied from 24 per cent in Slovenia up to 54 per cent in Kosovo and Serbia proper.

Productivity within the social sector depends in part on the amount of fixed capital per worker. In 1971 this varied from 83 per cent of average in Macedonia up to 145 per cent of the average in Montenegro. (In 1979, this range was similar—81 per cent in Macedonia, 143 per cent in Montenegro—but the figure for Kosovo had fallen to 105 per cent.)[24] In general, as we shall see, there has been a large net transfer of capital towards the less developed regions, especially to Kosovo. But the level of capital-intensity in the productive social sector in these regions depends on how such funds are used. In Montenegro a large proportion has been used for a few highly capital-intensive projects, and a similar tendency has been at work in Kosovo. In Macedonia, on the other hand, greater priority seems to have been given in this period to the growth of employment.

We pass now to consider how policies have affected inter-regional differences in relative levels of personal income per worker and in consumption and investment per capita. As will be shown in more detail in Chapter 9, there has been considerable pressure on enterprises not to distribute out of net income as much in the form of personal incomes as the workers would prefer. And this pressure has been especially strong in the case of the more prosperous enterprises, which have more to distribute. The effect has been to reinforce what would probably have been a spontaneous tendency for the more prosperous enterprises to have a higher saving ratio. As a result, inter-regional differences in the level of personal income per worker are smaller than the corresponding differences in output per worker. This is demonstrated for the years 1962 and 1975 in Table 8.16.[25] In general, relative net personal income per worker is higher than relative GMP per worker in the poorer regions, and vice versa.

Another way in which inter-regional differences in consumption per capita have been reduced has been through government-organized assistance from the more developed to the less developed regions. Since 1965 this assistance has taken two forms. First, there is the Federal Fund, to which all enterprises contribute a certain proportion of their GMP as a compulsory loan, and which is distributed in the form of soft loans to the less developed republics (Bosnia-Herzegovina, Macedonia, and Montenegro) and to the autonomous province of Kosovo. Secondly, there are budgetary transfers from the federal budget to the same regions for the support of social services. During the 1971-5 plan period the Federal Fund levy was fixed at 1.94 per cent of the GMP of social sector enterprises, and the total amount of budgetary assistance was fixed at 0.83 per cent of total GMP. During the 1976-80 plan period the corresponding figures were 1.97 per cent and 0.93 per cent.[26]

The effects of these transfers on total available resources in each region

---

[24] YB81, 201 – 2, measured in 1972 prices.

[25] At the time of writing, 1975 was the latest year for which these figures were published.

[26] See Schrenk and others (1979, 303 and 308).

TABLE 8.16

Output per Worker and Personal Income per Worker in the Productive Social Sector by Region, 1962 and 1975

(Yugoslavia= 100)

	1962		1975	
	Output per worker[a]	Personal income per worker[b]	Output per worker[a]	Personal income per worker[b]
Yugoslavia	100	100	100	100
Bosnia-Herzegovina	92	93	88	94
Montenegro	90	95	90	89
Croatia	107	105	109	104
Macedonia	76	83	77	85
Slovenia	122	122	125	117
Serbia proper	101	95	91	96
Kosovo	69	77	76	86
Vojvodina	84	92	103	101

Sources: 1962: YB64, 204 – 3.
    1975: YB77, 205 – 1.
[a] Gross material product per worker.
[b] Net personal income per worker.

can be roughly estimated, on the following assumptions; (1) the legally prescribed rates of levy and allocation of funds were exactly implemented, and (2) the budgetary contribution of each region to the cost of the budgetary transfers was proportionate to its GMP. Estimates for the year 1974, based in part on World Bank estimates, are given in Table 8.17. These show that the effect of the assistance programme was to raise available resources in Kosovo by 36.1 per cent of initial GMP, and in Montenegro by 13.0 per cent. Macedonia and Bosnia-Herzegovina, however, benefited by only 6.7 per cent and 4.5 per cent of their GMP respectively. The other republics each made a net contribution of between 2.4 per cent and 2.6 per cent of their GMP. Since loans distributed from the Federal Fund are made on highly concessionary terms (in 1971–5 at 4 per cent rate of interest, with a grace period of three years and a maturity of 18 years, with even better terms for Kosovo), and since inflation has always been faster than the nominal rate of interest, and in recent years at 30–50 per cent per annum, loans from the Fund contain a large grant element. In total, therefore, the more advanced republics—including Serbia, which is only on about the same level as the country as a whole—have been donating about 2 per cent of their GMP each year towards these assistance programmes. This is no mean achievement, especially when one considers how much difficulty has been encountered in trying to reach the United Nations target of 1 per cent of GNP for assistance to the less developed countries.

In addition to the inter-regional transfers arising from the official programme all regions have received important benefits in the past fifteen

TABLE 8.17
Domestic and Foreign Transfers, by Region, 1974

	GMP (billion dinars)	Transfers as percentage of GMP		
		Domestic (net)	Foreign remittances	Total
Yugoslavia	407.2	–	7.3	7.3
Bosnia-Herzegovina	50.6	4.5	12.6	17.1
Montenegro	7.1	13.0	4.8	17.8
Croatia	107.8	– 2.5	9.1	6.6
Macedonia	23.2	6.7	10.8	17.5
Slovenia	66.9	– 2.6	3.4	0.9
Serbia proper	98.7	– 2.4	5.2	2.8
Kosovo	8.5	36.1	12.5	48.6
Vojvodina	44.5	– 2.4	5.2	2.8

Sources: GMP: YB76, 204 – 5.
Domestic transfers: Budget and federal fund transfers from Schrenk and others (1979), Table A.39 minus 0.83 per cent of each region's GMP, assumed to be its contribution to federal budget transfers.
Foreign remittances: Total workers' remittances from YB76, 106 – 2, divided in proportion to workers living abroad in 1971 Census from YB76, 202 – 4.

years from workers' remittances. In 1974 these added 7.3 per cent to the total GMP of Yugoslavia. If the remittances are distributed by region in proportion to the number of its workers reported as living abroad in the 1971 Census, the results (shown also in Table 8.17) indicate that Bosnia-Herzegovina, Croatia, Macedonia, and Kosovo benefited most in relation to their GMP. In combination with the domestic transfer programme these foreign transfers brought the level of increase in available resources in Kosovo up to nearly 50 per cent, and in the three less developed republics to 17–18 per cent.

It cannot necessarily be assumed that all the contributions from the Federal Fund served to increase investment above the level which would have been attained in the absence of the Fund. Nor can it necessarily be assumed that the budgetary transfers served only to increase expenditure on social services. There is always the possibility that part of the benefits of assistance programmes designed for one type of purpose will be shared by other purposes. It would be interesting, therefore, to be able to examine relative levels of per capita consumption in different regions. In the absence of published estimates of personal consumption by region, some rough estimates may be made by adjusting GMP in each region for transfers, investment, and collective consumption expenditure on government and social services. The results of this exercise are shown in Table 8.18.[27]

[27] Apart from the errors which inevitably arise when aggregate figures from different sources are subtracted from one another, the table omits the effects of private domestic transfers, e.g. by workers who have migrated to other regions. These would probably somewhat increase the flow from the richer to the poorer regions.

TABLE 8.18

Output, Consumption, and Investment per Capita by Region, 1974
(Yugoslavia=100)

	GMP per capita	Consumption per capita			Gross investment per capita
		Total	Collective	Private	
Yugoslavia	100	100	100	100	100
Bosnia-Herzegovina	67	67	73	66	90
Montenegro	75	68	89	63	120
Croatia	127	132	118	135	110
Macedonia	70	79	70	82	67
Slovenia	196	175	189	172	212
Serbia proper	95	94	103	92	82
Kosovo	32	39	50	37	55
Vojvodina	117	115	96	120	102

Sources: Population: Total population from YB76, 202 – 2 minus 1.1 times workers resident abroad in 1971 Census, from YB76, 202 – 4.
GMP: YB76, 204 – 5.
Gross investment: GMP multiplied by estimate of percentage of gross investment to GMP in Schrenk and others (1979), Table A.39.
Total consumption: GMP plus workers' remittances and foreign lending plus net budget transfers and transfers from the federal fund minus gross investment. Total workers' remittances from YB76, 106 – 2, divided in proportion to workers abroad from YB76, 202 – 4. Foreign lending (current deficit) from YB76, 106 – 2 divided in proportion to GMP. Budget transfers and federal fund transfers from Schrenk and others (1979), Table A.39 minus 0.83 per cent of each region's GMP, assumed to be its contribution to the federal budget transfers.
Collective consumption: Expenditure on government and social services (excluding banking and insurance) from YB76, 216 – 2. Does not include social transfers.
Private consumption: Total minus collective consumption.

TABLE 8.19

Household Ownership of Durable Goods, by Region, 1978
(percentage of households owning each item)

	Refrigerator	Television		Washing machine	Motor car	Holiday home
		Black and white	Colour			
Yugoslavia	70.0	62.9	8.6	49.3	28.7	2.4
Bosnia-Herzegovina	63.5	56.6	5.3	37.8	19.9	1.4
Montenegro	64.9	56.2	4.6	35.5	20.9	1.6
Croatia	73.2	64.4	9.1	57.6	31.6	3.8
Macedonia	67.1	64.5	7.2	39.8	31.0	1.0
Slovenia	78.7	63.8	18.2	80.1	49.8	3.0
Serbia proper	71.3	62.9	9.0	45.7	29.3	2.6
Kosovo	37.7	51.4	4.1	22.6	13.1	0.3
Vojvodina	78.5	73.9	7.3	52.2	23.2	2.4

Source: Statistical Bulletin of the Federal Statistical Office no. 1125, Table 4.

While these figures show that, as one would expect, inter-regional differences in collective consumption per capita are smaller than differences in per capita GMP, differences in private consumption per capita are not all in a similar direction. Croatia benefits from its larger-than-average receipts of worker remittances. Montenegro's per capita consumption is reduced by its relatively low receipt of worker remittances and, despite its gains from the official assistance programmes, its high level of investment. Kosovo's relative level of per capita private consumption is higher than its relative level of GMP per capita, but not by as much as might be expected in the light of the huge inflow of official assistance.

Comparisons of standards of living can be made more concretely, and to some extent with more realism, by means of specific indicators. Accordingly, Table 8.19 shows the proportions of households in each region which owned selected durable goods in 1978, and Table 8.20 gives a few social indicators for 1975. With the major exception of Kosovo, the level of ownership of durable goods is remarkably high. It is especially notable that already in 1978, 50 per cent of households in Slovenia owned a motor car, and about 30 per cent in Croatia and Serbia proper.[28] The proportion of households owning holiday homes is unusually large for a semi-developed country. The social indicators show a high degree of uniformity in life expectancy and in the proportion of dwellings with electricity. Inter-regional differences are wider for secondary education and for dwellings with water and sewerage; and indicators expressed on a per person basis tend to show low levels for Kosovo and, to a lesser extent, for Bosnia-Herzegovina, in both of which the rate of population growth has been higher than elsewhere.

7. AN INTERNATIONAL COMPARISON

From what has been said previously, it is clear that Yugoslavia, under its system of 'socialist self-management', has achieved a high rate of economic growth of both output and consumption. The average standard of living has changed out of all recognition in the past thirty-five years. But many other countries, with a variety of economic and political systems, have had similar experiences. How do their rates of growth compare with that of Yugoslavia? Obviously, such a comparison cannot provide a complete test of the effectiveness of alternative systems. There are many dimensions of social life which are not covered by gross domestic product; and the accuracy of measurement of the economic product itself varies between countries. Nevertheless, such a comparison is of some interest. It is at least a first step towards an assessment of the effectiveness of alternative systems.

It is useful to start by considering the level of per capita GDP already achieved in Yugoslavia in comparison with some other countries. For this purpose we may use the results of a careful study by Kravis and others

[28] It is not known whether these figures also include official cars, which are very plentiful, often with chauffeurs.

TABLE 8.20

Selected Social Indicators, by Region, 1975

(Yugoslavia = 100)

	Bosnia-Herzegovina	Montenegro	Croatia	Macedonia	Slovenia	Serbia proper	Kosovo	Vojvodina
Life expectancy at birth								
Males	98	104	100	100	100	103	99	101
Females	97	104	103	96	104	102	95	103
Population over ten years with secondary or higher education	70	94	121	76	144	103	46	111
Area of dwellings per person	77	81	118	82	127	100	63	125
Dwellings with electricity	87	90	103	104	109	102	86	104
Dwellings with water and sewerage	68	99	122	111	133	97	37	119
Doctors per person	66	76	114	91	133	120	35	109
Hospital beds per person	75	130	118	91	127	108	48	101

Source: Schrenk and others (1979), Table 11.2.

TABLE 8.21

Per Capita GDP at Purchasing Power Rates, Selected Countries, 1975

Country	Per cent of United States
Yugoslavia	36.1
Austria	69.6
Hungary	49.6
Italy	53.8
Poland	50.1
Romania	33.3
Spain	55.9

Source: Kravis and others (1982), Table 1–2.

(1982) in which estimates were made for a selected group of countries of gross domestic product converted at purchasing power rates of exchange. Results for Yugoslavia and some other countries of central and southern Europe are given in Table 8.21. These show that in 1975 Yugoslavia's per capita GDP was still only 36 per cent of the United States level, and not much more than half that of Austria.[29] Romania is placed a little below Yugoslavia, but Hungary, Poland, and Spain are estimated to have been in 1975 already at or above 50 per cent of the United States level. Thus Yugoslavia is still a relatively poor country by European standards, as it has been for the whole of its existence. The main incubus is Yugoslavia's large proportion of poor peasants—still about 30 per cent of the work-force. But in the longer term this is also a valuable resource for further growth, provided that appropriate policies are applied.

Table 8.22 presents the results of calculations for a group of countries of average rates of growth of GDP (or NMP) at constant prices and of per capita GDP (or NMP) over the periods 1960–70 and 1970–9. The countries included are those which border on Yugoslavia or which were at fairly similar levels of economic development in 1960. The figures show that high rates of growth of GDP and NMP were achieved by all these countries during the 1960s. Yugoslavia's growth rate in this period was, in fact, below the median rate. But in the 1970s the position was different: only Brazil, Turkey, Bulgaria, and Romania had higher rates of growth of total product. On a per capita basis, Yugoslavia's growth rate in the 1960s was approximately at the median, but in the 1970s it was exceeded only by Brazil, Bulgaria, and Romania.[30] The conclusion from this rough test

[29] As mentioned earlier, a comparison of Slovenia with Austria would place them on approximately the same level. This shows how much Yugoslavia's remaining backwardness arises from the backwardness of its southern and eastern regions.

[30] Rates of growth of net material product in Comecon countries are not strictly comparable with similar rates for market-economy countries, since both the quality and the product-mix of outputs in the former group of countries are usually inferior, as a result of central decision-making and the lack of response to consumer (and producer) demand.

TABLE 8.22
Rates of Growth of Yugoslavia and Some other Countries

Gross domestic product at constant prices	Total product		Per capita product	
	1960–70	1970–79	1960–70	1970–79
Yugoslavia	5.4	6.1	4.8	5.1
Austria	4.5	3.7	3.9	3.6
Brazil	5.3	8.7	2.3	5.7
Greece	7.6	4.7	7.0	4.1
Italy	5.3	2.9	4.6	2.3
Japan	10.5	5.1	9.4	3.9
Mexico	7.3	5.2	3.9	1.8
Portugal	6.3	4.1	6.3	2.9
Spain	7.2	4.1	6.0	3.0
Turkey	6.0	6.4	3.4	3.8
Net material product at constant prices				
Yugoslavia	6.2	6.1	5.7	5.0
Bulgaria	8.2	7.2	7.4	6.6
Hungary	5.4	5.8	5.1	5.3
Romania	8.6	10.2	7.6	9.1

Sources: Yugoslavia: YB81, 102 – 8 and 107 – 2.
Other countries: UNCTAD (1980), Table 6.2.

seems to be that Yugoslavia's economic system has worked well, especially during the increasingly difficult conditions of the 1970s.[31] To make a more complete assessment one would need to take into account the distribution of income (which will be discussed in Chapter 9) and the nature of the political system. On the latter point, Yugoslavia is clearly not a full democracy; but it allows its citizens a great deal more freedom of debate and civil rights than any of the Comecon countries, and at least as good conditions in this respect as in many of the less developed countries of Latin America, as well as in some periods in the countries of southern Europe.

Gross domestic product is only a first approximation to a measure of economic welfare, which depends also on how the product is spent. Some comparative figures on this aspect for selected OECD countries are given in Table 8.23. It will be seen that Yugoslavia allocates a low share of its GDP to personal consumption; in 1979 it was the lowest of the group. This

---

[31] But the price for this has been accelerating inflation and a great accumulation of foreign debts. Other countries in a similar position have had similar experiences, as the well-known problems of Poland, Mexico, and Brazil testify.

TABLE 8.23

Shares of Consumption and Fixed Investment in GDP, Yugoslavia and Selected OECD Countries, 1970 and 1979

Country	Private final consumption		Government final consumption		Gross fixed capital formation	
	1970	1979	1970	1979	1970	1979
Yugoslavia[a]	53	52	17	18	28	35
Austria	55	55	15	18	26	25
Greece	69	64	13	16	24	26
Italy	63	61	14	16	21	19
Japan	52	58	7	10	36	32
Portugal	69	73	14	15	18	19
Spain	68	69	9	11	23	19
Turkey	70	68	13	14	19	19

Source: OECD (1982b).
[a] GDP not adjusted for stock appreciation.

is partly compensated by a high level of government final consumption, although it would be necessary to look more closely at the composition of such expenditure before making a final judgement. The main reason for the low consumption share, however, is the high allocation to investment.[32] Of the group of countries shown in the table, only Japan has achieved a similar proportionate allocation to investment; most of the other countries have managed with an investment share considerably below that of Yugoslavia.

A high rate of investment is, in general, a good augury for future growth. But there is a good deal of evidence that much of Yugoslavia's investment has been wasteful. This is, indeed, one of the costs of the self-management system, at least as it has been operated hitherto in Yugoslavia. This problem will be discussed further in Chapter 10.

8. CONCLUSIONS

During the 1960s and 1970s Yugoslavia achieved a high and fairly stable rate of economic growth, at least as good as in many other comparable countries, and in the 1970s better than in most. The current level of output is depressed by the existence of a large proportion of private farmers, whose activities have been hampered by official policies. Despite this, productivity in private agriculture has grown as rapidly as in the social sector, partly as a result of labour leaving the farms.

Although employment in the social sector has expanded greatly, it has not provided sufficient jobs to absorb the growth in the work-force and the

[32] This is for fixed investment only, and the estimate is biased downwards by the fact that Yugoslav GDP is not adjusted for stock appreciation.

migration of farm labour. The problem was alleviated in the late 1960s and early 1970s by a large-scale migration of labour to western Europe. But since the mid-70s unemployment has grown, and now stands at an uncomfortably high level.

During the 1960s personal consumption grew in line with gross material product, but in the 1970s somewhat less rapidly. The standard of living has risen since 1950. This is reflected in the high current level of ownership of durable goods, including cars, as well as in various social indicators.

Prices were rather stable in the 1950s, especially the prices of industrial goods, but in the next two decades they were accelerating, and in recent years the rate of inflation has become extremely serious. This is a problem with which the government is struggling, but without very much success. It may well be that a self-management system has an inflationary bias.

Deficits in the balance of payments were generally moderate in the 1950s and 1960s, but in the 1970s, especially since the energy crisis, they have been large and increasing. A weak growth in exports has been partly offset by receipts from tourism and workers' remittances, but since the mid-70s very large foreign debts have accumulated, and they have now reached crisis proportions.

Yugoslavia had from its inception a very difficult regional problem, which was later inherited by the Communists. Despite large transfers of resources from the richer regions, which have helped the poorer regions to maintain a high rate of growth, inter-regional differences in per capita product have continued, and even widened. This is partly the result of a higher rate of growth of population in the poorer regions, but it is also the result of using too much of available resources for capital-intensive projects. In some of the poorer regions there is still a dead weight of inefficient agriculture and cultural backwardness which it may take a long time to overcome.

APPENDIX TO CHAPTER 8

DEVELOPMENTS SINCE 1979

After nearly thirty years of rapid and fairly stable growth, the Yugoslav economy, like that of many other countries, began to falter and stagnate in 1979. During the next three years the rate of growth of output (both social product and industrial output) steadily diminished, unemployment continued to rise, and inflation moved into the range of 30–40 per cent per annum. Table 8.24 contains a summary of these and other indicators of economic performance in 1970–9 and 1979–82 respectively.

The main source of the country's troubles was the second (1979) major increase in world petroleum prices. This not only imposed a new direct burden on Yugoslavia's balance of payments but, by provoking the world recession, brought further serious difficulties. At a time when it was a matter of urgency to increase foreign exchange revenue Yugoslav exports encountered increasing competition in Western markets, while the growth of receipts from migrant remittances and tourism slowed down. Meanwhile, the rise in world interest rates added a heavy burden to the payments side of the foreign accounts, with net interest payments increasing from $0.6 billion in 1979 to $1.8 billion in 1982 (OECD 1983, 24).

In retrospect, it is clear that Yugoslavia would have been in a better position to cope with these problems if it had not allowed its foreign debt to grow at such a rapid pace during the previous six years. Net foreign debt, which amounted to about $4 billion in 1973, had by 1979 reached nearly $14 billion (ibid. 27). Like many other countries Yugoslavia had tried to ride out the effects of the first great petroleum price rise of 1973 by allowing domestic demand, especially investment demand, to continue to grow rapidly. From 1973 to 1979, consumers' expenditure rose by 40 per cent, collective consumption by 53 per cent, and gross fixed investment by 66 per cent, all in 1972 prices (ibid. 62). Not surprisingly, except in 1976, the current account of the balance of payments was in serious and increasing deficit, reaching a level of $3.7 billion in 1979 (ibid. 74).

When in 1980 the magnitude of the problem at last became apparent—and the political authorities had summoned enough courage to face it—strong measures were taken to reduce demand (mainly by a tight monetary policy), the dinar was sharply devalued, and imports and foreign exchange allocations were restricted. But by that time the world situation had become even more difficult. The current deficit was still $2.3 billion in 1980, and although it declined in the next two years, net foreign debt rose from under $14 billion in 1979 to over $18 billion in 1982 (ibid. 27 and 74). For some reason, the net foreign debt in recent years has always grown by more than the amount of the current deficit. The balance-of-payments estimates are probably not very reliable, and even the size of the foreign debt is difficult to measure accurately. These phenomena are both causes and consequences of weaknesses in economic management at the federal level.

Since fixed investment had clearly become excessive in 1979, and since it is difficult—and more politically dangerous—to reduce consumption, the brunt of demand restriction fell on investment, and especially on construction. But government current expenditure was also severely squeezed, and both consumers' expenditure and collective consumption in 1972 prices were slightly lower in 1981 than in 1979 (ibid. 62). By mid–1983 gross fixed investment in 1980 prices was estimated to have fallen from its 1979 peak by a third (ibid. 47). Meanwhile, there was growing pressure on enterprises to export, almost 'at any price', while supplies of imports were curtailed (both directly and through a shortage of foreign exchange allocations). In 1980 and 1981 the volume of exports rose satisfactorily, but in 1982 it appears to have fallen somewhat, despite continuing devaluation of the dinar. Import volumes were severely restricted in 1980 and 1982, but less so in 1981 (Table 8.24). These changes in net foreign demand in volume terms helped to maintain the growth of total output. But by 1982

TABLE 8.24
Rates of Growth, 1970–82
(average percentage per annum)

	1970–9	1979–82	1979–80	1980–1	1981–2
Gross material product (1972 prices)	6.1	1.6	2.3	1.5	0.9[a]
Industrial production (index)	7.7	2.8	4.6	3.9	0.0
Agricultural production (index)	2.8	(0.5)	0.0	1.3	(7.0)
Employment in social sector:					
Productive sector	4.3	2.8	3.3	3.0	2.2
of which, Industry	4.3	3.2	2.9	3.7	3.2
Non-productive sector	4.5	2.7	2.7	2.7	2.7
Labour productivity in industry	3.3	−0.4	1.7	0.2	−3.1
Consumers' expenditure (1972 prices)	5.6	0.1	0.7	−1.0	0.5[a]
Gross fixed investment (1972 prices)	7.9	−7.3	−5.9	−9.8	−6.2[a]
Cost of living (index)	17.5	34.3	30.3	40.7	31.7
Real net personal income per social sector worker	2.1	−5.3	−7.5	−5.0	−3.3
Exports of goods and services (1972 prices)	4.2	5.1	11.0	12.2	−3.7[a]
Imports of goods and services (1972 prices)	5.7	−8.8	−10.0	−2.3	−13.5[a]

Sources: 1970–9: Most items taken from previous tables in this chapter. Industrial and agricultural
      production and cost of living from OECD (1983). Consumers' expenditure from OECD (1982).
      1979–82: OECD (1983). Where 1982 estimates are preliminary, average growth for the whole
      period was obtained by cumulation of the annual figures, and to that extent is also preliminary.
[a] Preliminary estimates, at 1980 prices.

the shortages of essential imports of fuel, materials and components
were placing a direct obstacle in the way of maintaining industrial
production.

One remarkable achievement in this period was the continued increase
in social sector employment, at an average annual rate of nearly 3 per cent
overall, and at over 3 per cent in industry. As a result, the number of
registered job-applicants rose by only 64,000 between 1979 and 1982,
although in the latter year it reached a total of 826,000. The other effect,
however, was to depress labour productivity, especially in industry, since
the social sector was increasingly absorbing the unemployed into unnecessary jobs. While there is much to be said on social grounds for
work-sharing rather than open unemployment, the risk is that overmanning and slackness, which were already problems in self-managed
enterprises and organizations, may become ingrained habits.

The problems of adjustment to the rise in petroleum prices and to the
world recession would have been very great in any circumstances. But they
were made more difficult by the inner complexities and contradictions of
the Yugoslav economic and political system. As will be shown in
subsequent chapters, the Yugoslav system is weak on exports, weak on
inflation, weak in its control and allocation of investment, weak in
promoting competition and a unified market, and weak in providing
political leadership for macroeconomic policy. In the 1970s there was a

failure to come to terms with the energy shortage, and aggregate investment was allowed to grow at an irresponsible rate. After 1979, however, the government gradually began to get a grip on the situation, although it was still hampered by its own indecisiveness and the high degree of federalization of economic policy. In late 1982 and early 1983 severe measures were taken to strengthen the balance of payments, and interest rates were raised sharply, reaching in some cases a level approximately equal to the rate of inflation. There was much talk about reducing inflation and controlling money incomes, but not much sign that anything effective would be done. In a non-wage economy, with a government which is extremely sensitive to unemployment, it is difficult to find a solution to this problem. The money supply was being kept under tight control and some loss-making enterprises had been allowed to fail. But political pressures seemed likely, as before, to soften the effect of even the harshest measures.

Early in 1982 the government appointed a Commission on Economic Stabilization which produced a number of useful and challenging reports. The main thrust of the Commission's recommendations was towards the re-establishment of a genuine market economy, which may be regarded broadly as a demand for a return to the principles of the Reform. Since the days of the Reform, however, the devolution of power to the republics and provinces has gone so far (partly, indeed, to compensate for the abandonment of the Reform) that the way back to a unified market economy may now be blocked, unless federalization were to be reversed. The immediate problem of the balance of payments in 1983 was being solved by additional foreign loans amounting to about $5 billion, of which about half was apparently new money (and hence added to the accumulated debt). But, with severe shortages of many important consumer goods, there was a growing sense of economic crisis, and a possibility that this might precipitate a political crisis.

CHAPTER 9

THE DISTRIBUTION OF INCOME

The question with which this chapter is concerned is to ascertain how the benefits of Yugoslav economic progress have been distributed among the population. We shall also attempt to compare the distribution of income in Yugoslavia with similar data for other countries. Some of the advantages and disadvantages of the self-management system in this respect will be touched on as we proceed.

It must first be remarked that the distribution of the benefits of a given socio-economic system cannot be measured only by the distribution of income. Other important dimensions of inequality are the distributions of wealth and of political and economic power. Moreover, income itself can be measured in a wide variety of ways, each of which may yield a different conclusion. If we leave the last point aside for the moment, we may focus briefly on the distributions of wealth and power.

In Yugoslavia the distribution of wealth is much restricted in comparison with the situation in capitalist countries. No private business may employ more than a few non-family members (in most republics no more than five); no private farmer may own more than 10 hectares of arable land (except in mountain areas), and no one may own more than three houses or flats. Although there is probably a small amount of evasion of these regulations, it is obvious that no one in Yugoslavia can be a (dollar) millionaire. It is true that there is no restriction on the accumulation of savings deposits, including deposits in foreign exchange, which have the advantage that they retain their foreign exchange value. Much of the value of dinar deposits has been wiped out during the past few years of extravagant inflation. But workers employed in western Europe have in many cases made large savings—by hard work and careful spending—and built up considerable foreign exchange deposits in Yugoslavia. In addition, many of them have invested in small businesses or in housing, including some large houses on the Adriatic coast which are used partly for private tourist accommodation. But all of this amounts to very little in comparison with the inequalities of wealth which arise in the course of economic development under mainly free enterprise conditions.

As regards the distribution of power, it is difficult to make precise comparisons. Nominally, Yugoslav workers have complete power over their own enterprises. In practice, as we have seen, this power is much circumscribed. The power rests predominantly in the hands of the managers and the Party élite, partly inside the enterprise but mainly outside. Because of official propaganda, many Yugoslav workers may have an illusion of power; but the more sophisticated know that on all important issues they are systematically 'manipulated'. In the political sphere, there is, on the one hand, overt discrimination against the private peasants—still nearly one-third of the population—and, on the other, complete domination of decision-making in the social sector by the Party. There are no free elections; there is no right to organize an alternative party; there is no right to propose alternative policies. The press publishes a good deal of criticism on detailed matters, but it never develops clear proposals for reform. At best, there is an endless repetition of the demand that the principles of self-management should be consistently applied in practice.

In comparison with a Soviet-type country, the distribution of wealth in Yugoslavia is a little more unequal (mainly as a result of allowing freedom of migration across the frontiers), but the distribution of economic and political power is more equal (perhaps mainly as a result of federalization). In comparison with a democratic capitalist country at a similar level of development, the distribution of wealth in Yugoslavia is a great deal more equal, the distribution of economic power is not very different, and the distribution of political power is more unequal. But there is, of course, no guarantee that, if Yugoslavia had remained a predominantly free enterprise country, it would have been able to preserve democratic institutions, especially in view of the internal national tensions, which have been suppressed under Communist rule but which would probably have increased under conditions of democratic freedom.

After these general comments, we may turn to the analysis of the distribution of income, on which subject there are more 'hard facts' (although as we shall see, many of these facts are not as hard as they seem). The discussion will be divided into three sections: (1) the distribution of household income; (2) the distribution of earnings in the social sector; (3) the distribution of income between communes.

1. THE DISTRIBUTION OF HOUSEHOLD INCOME

As was seen in the last chapter, Yugoslavia suffers from two major sources of structural inequality: the inequality between the average level of incomes in the social sector on the one hand and in private agriculture on the other; and the inequality of average incomes between regions. (These two sources of inequality are also partly interactive.) With personal income per worker in private agriculture only about one-third of the average in the social sector, and social sector income itself quite widely dispersed between the richest and the poorest regions, it would not be surprising to find that the overall level of inequality of household income in Yugoslavia was higher than in more homogeneous countries. But there are some other influences at work within the social sector. First, there are no accumulations of private capital, with corresponding incomes; secondly, the political system, and perhaps also self-management itself, exerts considerable pressure to reduce earnings differentials within enterprises.[1] On the other hand, as a result of the self-management system, those groups of workers who are employed in enterprises with an efficient organization, more or better capital equipment, or other advantages, receive higher incomes than those employed in the less efficient or less well-equipped enterprises. They receive, in other words, part of the rents of efficient organization and other advantages, and part of the net product of invested capital. This sometimes leads to very wide differences between earnings for approximately the same job in two enterprises in the same area. There are no published statistics on this phenomenon, but many casual comments can be found, including comments by well-informed people in high positions.[2]

Of the factors which make for a widening of personal income inequality, inter-regional differences in productivity are partially offset by budgetary transfers to the poorer regions for the support of social services. Peasant households, however, have been left to find their own solutions as best they can. Hundreds of thousands of peasant families have managed to pull themselves out of the pit of poverty by sending their sons and daughters to work in social sector enterprises. As a result, only a minority of households owning agricultural land are now purely agricultural households, i.e. without a single member with a regular job outside agriculture or a pension from the social sector. The majority of land-owning households are 'mixed', with at least one member receiving a regular non-agricultural income. In 1979, among peasant families as a whole, net income from non-agricultural sources was almost as important as income in cash and kind from agriculture.[3] The other solution to peasant household poverty

---

[1] There have been many complaints about excessive egalitarianism, especially from managers, but also from trade union officials and others who allege that workers are not paid in accordance with the principle of 'the results of work', and that idlers are often paid as much as those who work hard. This problem will be discussed further in Chapter 11.

[2] Granick (1975, 337) asserts that there is a wide variation in earnings of workers of similar skills in different enterprises. He reports (p. 419) that in Split in 1972 'average salaries in the bank, the Chamber of Commerce, and the foreign trade enterprises were ten times as high as the average in the commune as a whole'. Although this is not a comparison between workers of equal skill, it does lend support to his previous comment. Horvat (1976, 185) quotes Šefer as saying that in Belgrade in 1967 pay rates for the same job in different enterprises differed by as much as 1:4. The inclusion of fringe benefits would widen this range even further. At a meeting of economists in November 1982 it was said that, while the inter-industry range in cash personal incomes is 2.4 to 1, the inclusion of enterprise fringe benefits other than housing raises it to 6.8 to 1, and, with housing also included, it becomes 14 to 1 (*Borba*, 5 December 1982). An article in *Borba* (23 April 1982) asserts that there are large differences in incomes between basic organizations in the same industry. 'In spite of many years of experience, and the making of social compacts and self-management agreements about incomes, it turns out that it is more important where you work than how you work.' A similar comment was made by Peter Kostić, former Federal Secretary of Finance, in an interview with *Ekonomska politika* (22/29 November 1982). An article in *Borba* (25 October 1982) gives figures for average monthly income per worker in basic organizations in Croatia during the first half of 1982. In many organizations the average was less than 8,000 dinars, while the average for the highest-paying organization in the republic was over 88,000 dinars.

[3] YB81, 114–49. For households with small areas of land (up to 3 ha.) most of net income came from non-agricultural sources. Even among those with more than 8 ha. nearly 30 per cent of income was from off the farm.

has been large-scale emigration of young peasants to western Europe. As a consequence many peasant households now receive a substantial part of their incomes from remittances. But there is a residue of older peasants who have no sons or daughters still living with them or sending them remittances. These are the poorest of the poor.[4]

The only available statistics on household income distributions in Yugoslavia are those collected at five-year intervals since 1963 in income and expenditure surveys organized by the Federal Statistical Office. These are two-stage sample surveys and, as far as can be judged, they have been efficiently planned and implemented. But they have two main weaknesses. The first is that the variable which measures a household's 'disposable resources' includes a number of lump-sum receipts from such sources as the sale of durable goods or real estate, loans received, and the proceeds of insurance policies. On the other hand, it does not include any allowance for imputed rents of owner-occupied accommodation, or of accommodation provided free of charge by employing organizations, or indeed for the large implicit subsidy on flats rented from social sector organizations. Other fringe benefits are also excluded, as they usually are in other countries. But fringe benefits in Yugoslavia are often a large component of total real earnings, and they vary widely in importance between enterprises and between individuals within enterprises.[5]

The second weakness, which could easily be corrected, is that the published tables refer to household characteristics within groups ranked according to total household resources. But a group of households in the same range of resources will include a variety of different types of household, as measured by their size and composition. What is needed for a study of resource (or, strictly, income) inequality is a distribution of households or persons ranked by per capita income, or by income per equivalent unit (or 'consumption unit'). Most countries fail to provide such distributions, and Yugoslavia is one of them. The problem is especially important in a country such as Yugoslavia where average household size varies considerably with total household resources. Rough estimates can be made of per capita distributions from tables showing the numbers of households of different sizes in each resource class, and some results of such estimates are given below.

Before we consider the estimates of overall household resource inequality it is useful to take note of the information provided by the surveys on differences in average resources per household, or per person,

---

[4] In recent years a scheme has been created for providing peasants with retirement pensions in return for the surrender of their land. But not much progress seems to have been made in this direction, partly because it is left to each republic or province to set up its own scheme, which they have been reluctant to do, since the value of the land surrendered is usually not sufficient to cover the cost of the pension. Much of the land which has been surrendered is in small and scattered plots, which it is difficult for the social sector to use, and it has consequently been allowed to run to waste.

[5] Apart from houses and flats, the most important are food, transport, and holidays. But there is a wide range of expenditures by enterprises on so-called 'collective consumption'. One advantage of spending money in this way is that it largely evades the social compacts restricting the distribution of cash income.

TABLE 9.1

Average Resources in Three Types of Household, Yugoslavia, 1973 and 1978

		Per cent of households	Mean number of persons per household	Relative resources	
				per household	per person
All households	1973	100.0	3.9	100	100
	1978	100.0	3.8	100	100
Agricultural households	1973	21.5	4.1	75	70
	1978	17.4	3.9	65	64
Mixed households	1973	27.5	4.7	109	89
	1978	29.9	4.6	106	87
Non-agricultural households	1973	51.0	3.3	106	125
	1978	52.7	3.3	108	124

Sources: Statistical Bulletin of the Federal Statistical Office, nos. 833 and 1125.

in different types of household (agricultural, mixed and non-agricultural) and in different regions. Table 9.1 gives a breakdown by household type for Yugoslavia as a whole in 1973 and 1978; and Table 9.2 shows a simultaneous breakdown by household type and region in the latter year. The results show that the proportion of purely agricultural households (those with some land and no outside source of regular labour income or pension) was only 17.4 per cent in 1978, and had fallen from 21.5 per cent in 1973. In 1978 nearly 30 per cent of households were 'mixed' (with some land but also one or more member regularly employed off the farm, or with a pension), and this percentage had risen slightly between 1973 and 1978. Thus, nearly half of all Yugoslav households in 1978 still owned some land, although nearly two-thirds of such farm households received some kind of regular non-farm income. Looked at from the side of employment, it is a remarkable feature of Yugoslavia that a large proportion of workers in the social sector are still 'peasant-workers' who retain some connection with a family farm.

Table 9.1 also shows how relative resources vary across these three types of household. Because mixed households are larger than the average and non-agricultural households smaller, differences in per capita resources between the three types of household are greater than differences in total household resources. In terms of both total and per capita resources, agricultural households appear to have fallen quite considerably in relation to others between 1973 and 1978. In the latter year, on a per capita basis, agricultural households had only about half the level of resources of non-agricultural households.

Table 9.2 shows how inter-regional differences operate within each type of household. Per capita resources are highest in Slovenia for each type of household, and lowest in Kosovo. Households with an agricultural interest

TABLE 9.2

Average per Capita Resources by Region and Type of Household, 1978
(Yugoslavia = 100)

Region	Type of household			
	Agricultural	Mixed	Non-agricultural	All
Yugoslavia	64	87	124	100
Bosnia-Herzegovina	59	71	105	81
Montenegro	59	81	100	85
Croatia	77	106	139	119
Macedonia	51	65	86	72
Slovenia	101	134	176	157
Serbia proper	63	90	132	105
Kosovo	35	45	54	45
Vojvodina	96	117	118	114
Coefficient of variation (%)	31	31	30	33

Source: Statistical Bulletin of the Federal Statistical Office, no. 1125.

(pure or mixed) are relatively better off in Vojvodina, in comparison with other regions, than non-agricultural households in the same province. The (unweighted) coefficient of variation between regions is slightly higher for agricultural and mixed households than for non-agricultural households, and distinctly higher for all types of household. This reflects the fact that the proportion of non-agricultural households is positively correlated with the per capita resources of such households in different regions, while the corresponding correlation for agricultural households is negative. In other words, richer regions usually have higher per capita resources in each type of household *and* a higher proportion of non-agricultural households, while poorer regions have lower per capita resources in each type of household *and* more peasant households.

Overall household inequality can be measured in a number of different ways, and Table 9.3 shows three alternatives. The first is to classify (or rank) households by total household resources and to examine the dispersion of households between such classes. This common method takes no account of variations in household size and composition and, where such variations are large, may give a misleading impression of the degree of inequality. The second is to classify households by their per capita resources and to examine the dispersion of households between such classes. This method almost invariably yields a lower estimate of the degree of inequality than the first method. This method, or a closely similar one in which incomes or total expenditures are expressed per equivalent unit, or per consumption unit, is used in most income distribution statistics published by Comecon countries, and by a few other countries, such as India and Indonesia. The third method shown in the table is to classify households by their per capita resources and to examine

TABLE 9.3

Alternative Measures of Household Inequality, Yugoslavia, 1978

	Households ranked by household resources	Households ranked by per capita resources	Persons ranked by per capita resources
Percentage resource shares of:			
Top 10%	23.5	17.9	25.2
Top 20%	40.6	31.6	41.5
Bottom 20%	6.5	12.9	6.2
Bottom 10%	1.7	5.1	2.3
Percentiles as per cent of median Percentiles:			
10	36	41	38
20	55	60	50
80	163	184	173
90	209	200	232

Sources and methods: All data are derived from Federal Statistical Office, *Statistical Bulletin*, no. 1125. For the first column the Bulletin gives the required distribution of households by household resources. For the second and third columns, use was made of the information given in the Bulletin about the percentage of households of each size within each household resource class. It was assumed that each household with n members in a class with average household resources of y received exactly y/n resources per capita, and that $n = 10$ for households with 7 or more members. Households were ranked by the variable y/n and their total resources, number of households and number of persons were each accumulated. All the parameters shown in the table were estimated by graphic interpolation.

TABLE 9.4

Shares of Selected Inter-Percentile Groups in Total Household Resources, Yugoslavia, 1968, 1973 and 1978

(Percentages)

Group of households ranked by household resources	1968		1973	1978
	A	B		
Top 5 per cent	16.5	15.1	14.7	15.7
Top 10 per cent	24.0	25.3	25.0	23.5
Bottom 25 per cent	8.8	..	9.0	8.8

Sources: 1968: A estimate from World Bank (1975), Appendix Table 9.21.
            B estimate from Jain (1975), Table 80.
        1973: *Statistical Bulletin of the Federal Statistical Office*, no. 833, Table 2. Estimates made by graphic interpolation.
        1978: *Statistical Bulletin of the Federal Statistical Office*, no. 1125, Table 2. Estimates made by graphic interpolation.

the distribution of *persons* between such classes. This method is scarcely ever used in official statistics, although it is clearly preferable on theoretical grounds. (A close alternative would be to show the dispersion of persons after ranking households by income per equivalent unit.) The third method often shows a lower degree of inequality at the bottom end of the scale than the first method (because households at the bottom of the scale are usually smaller than average) but often shows a higher degree of inequality at the top end of the scale. A study of the three columns of the table will show that the characteristics mentioned above are exhibited in the present case.

The only method of measurement which is readily available for a series of years in Yugoslavia is the first, and some estimates of resource shares on this basis are given in Table 9.4. These figures suggest that relative household resource inequality remained rather stable between 1968 and 1978. In the absence of major political or economic changes, this is a typical finding for most countries in which a consistent time series of inequality measures is available.[6]

How does inequality in Yugoslavia compare with inequality in other countries? International comparisons of inequality are very uncertain, because of the use of different measurement techniques in different countries, as well as possible differences in reporting biases and other errors.[7] In Part I of Table 9.5 inequality in Yugoslavia is compared on the basis of distributions of households by household income (or resources) with a number of other countries which use the same technique of measurement. The countries included in the comparison are either from southern Europe or countries which are believed to use fairly reliable survey methods. In Part II, Yugoslavia is compared with countries from eastern Europe on the basis of distributions of households by per capita income. In Part I, most of the data for the other countries are pre-tax. In Part II, all the data are post-tax.

The general impression from the comparisons is that Yugoslavia is more equal than Spain or Turkey (especially the latter), slightly more unequal than Australia, Canada, and the United Kingdom, and significantly more unequal than the three Comecon countries. It must be remembered, however, that the Yugoslav data refer to resources, not income, and this may slightly increase the Yugoslav measured degree of inequality. The other important consideration to bear in mind is the extreme regional heterogeneity of Yugoslavia. If one were to compare Slovenia alone with the Comecon countries the differences would probably not be very great.[8]

---

[6] There is some evidence that household inequality in Yugoslavia increased between 1963 and 1968. World Bank (1975, Table 4.2) shows an increase in the Gini coefficient of 'household income' between these two years from 0.32 to 0.34. Nikić (1979) estimated, by a different method, that the Gini coefficient increased between 1963 and 1973 from 0.33 to 0.36, the main increase being among agricultural and mixed households. A definite conclusion on this matter would require a thorough study of the basic data and a review of the results of using alternative techniques of measurement.

[7] See Lydall (1978) for more detailed discussion of these problems.

[8] A comparison of distributions of households by household income in Slovenia and

TABLE 9.5

*International Comparisons of Household Income Inequality, Yugoslavia
and other Countries*

I. Households ranked by household income

Country, year, and income type	Percentage income shares				Gini coefficient
	First 10%	Second 10%	Ninth 10%	Top 10%	
Yugoslavia, 1968, post-tax	2.3	4.3	16.1	25.3	0.35
Australia, 1967–68, pre-tax	2.4	4.7	15.4	23.5	0.32
Canada, 1965, pre-tax	2.3	4.4	16.0	24.0	0.33
Spain, 1964–65, pre-tax	2.2	3.8	16.2	29.3	0.39
Turkey, 1968, pre-tax	1.0	1.9	15.9	44.7	0.57
United Kingdom, 1969, pre-tax	2.2	3.7	15.2	24.5	0.34
United Kingdom, 1969, post-tax	2.6	4.2	15.1	23.1	0.32

II. Households ranked by per capita income

Country, year and income type	Percentiles as percentage of median	
	P10	P90
Yugoslavia, 1978, post-tax	41	200
Czechoslovakia, 1973, post-tax	56	167
Hungary, 1969, post-tax	58	164
Poland, 1973, post-tax	60	181

Sources: Part I : All countries except United Kingdom from Jain (1975). United Kingdom from Royal
Commission on the Distribution of Income and Wealth (1977) Tables D9 and D14.
Part II: Yugoslavia from Table 9.3 above. Others from Michal (1978).

2. THE DISTRIBUTION OF MONEY EARNINGS IN THE SOCIAL SECTOR

Regular annual series are published in Yugoslavia on the distribution of
earnings in the social sector. The figures for recent years refer to
permanent employees who worked for between 160 and 200 hours in the
month of September, and the income measured is 'net personal income',
i.e. money income paid out in the month, after contributions for social
security and excluding compensation for travel and other business
expenses.[9] Separate figures are not published for different age, sex, or
occupational groups, but there is a breakdown by industry.

Another source of information about income differences is the annual
accounts of enterprises in the social sector. From the published tables it is

Yugoslavia as a whole in 1978 gave the following results for P 10 and P 90 (as percentages of
the median of each distribution): Slovenia 37 and 175; Yugoslavia 36 and 209. This suggests
that the figures for P10 and P90 for Slovenia in Part II of Table 9.5 might be about 40–5 and
165–70.

[9] Members of the army and police are not included in the distribution.

possible to derive average gross value added per worker and average net personal income per worker in each industry. Since these figures are based on the annual accounts, the personal income figures should be more reliable than those reported to the statistical authorities for a single month. They are also larger, for two reasons: first, the annual figures include end-of-year bonuses, or balancing payments, while the monthly figures measure essentially 'income advances'; secondly, the published statistics derived from the annual accounts show a single figure for net personal income and 'other personal receipts', the latter including compensation for business expenses.

The dispersion of individual earnings can conveniently be measured by two parameters: the tenth percentile and the ninetieth percentile, each expressed as a percentage of the median. The first ratio (P10/P50) indicates the relative dispersion of the lower tail of the distribution; the second ratio (P90/P50) indicates the relative dispersion of the upper tail of the distribution. From the results for selected years, shown in Table 9.6, it appears that earnings inequality increased slightly from 1964 to 1967 (the initial period of the Reform), but by 1971 it had returned approximately to the 1964 position, and in subsequent years it declined.

Income differences between industries are often measured by the (unweighted) coefficient of variation between industry averages in the manufacturing sector. In the second part of Table 9.6 such coefficients are given for manufacturing and mining industries in Yugoslavia. Out of twenty-two industries for which data are available for the period 1964–75, the film industry is so small and unusual in its behaviour that it has been excluded. In addition, for the coefficient of variation of gross value added per worker alternative estimates are given, in the first of which the petroleum industry is included and in the second excluded. Comparable

TABLE 9.6

Distribution of Personal Incomes in the Social Sector, 1964–79

Quantile ratios of net personal incomes, whole social sector (%)[a]	1964	1967	1971	1975	1979
P10/P50	62	60	62	64	63
P90/P50	173	175	174	167	170
Inter-industry coefficient of variation, manufacturing and mining (%)					
GVA per worker[b]	46.2	55.0	42.7	61.1	..
GVA per worker[c]	33.9	42.3	29.7	32.6	..
Net personal income per worker[b]	18.2	25.9	21.1	18.5	..

Sources: YB66, 106 – 8 and 121 – 9; YB69, 106 – 7, YB70, 122 – 7; YB72, 122 – 5;
YB73, 106 – 4; YB76, 123 – 6; YB77, 107 – 6; YB80, 105 – 20.
[a] 1964 incomes are for the whole year; the remainder for September only.
[b] 21 industries, excluding films.
[c] 20 industries, excluding films and petroleum.

data are not available for 1979, since a more detailed breakdown of industries has been used in the published statistics for recent years.

These figures show that during the early Reform years, up to 1967, there was a considerable increase in the inter-industry dispersion of both gross value added per worker and personal income per worker. But by 1971 the dispersion of gross value added per worker had fallen back below its 1964 level, and by 1975 the dispersion of personal income per worker had fallen back to approximately its 1964 level.[10] The temporary widening of dispersion of personal income per worker during the Reform has been previously noted by Popov (1972) and Estrin (1981). Popov considered that it was the result of an association between the level of activity and inter-industry income differences: the prosperous industries continue to raise their income payments regardless of conditions, but the less prosperous fall behind in a slack period and catch up during booms. Estrin, on the other hand, regards the widening of inter-industry dispersion of personal incomes during the Reform period as being the result of a relaxation of central control over labour earnings, and the subsequent reduction of dispersion as being the result of a re-establishment of control after 1972. He also maintains that since 1961 the level of inter-industry dispersion of personal incomes has been higher than in some other countries.

While it is true that the Reform gave enterprises greater freedom in distributing income to their members, and this may well have been one reason for the widening of inter-industry dispersion after 1964, it is important to remember that one of the major features of the Reform was a radical realignment of prices, intended to bring them closer to international parities. Inevitably, any sudden change in price-ratios will affect different industries differently. This is probably the main reason for the widening dispersion of gross value added per worker between 1964 and 1967. (When the petroleum industry is included in the sample, a similar, widening of this coefficient occurred in 1975, presumably reflecting the sharp increase in petroleum prices in 1974.) Since it is a standard principle of Yugoslav incomes policy that relative personal incomes should move in the same direction as (but to a smaller degree than) changes in value added per worker, it is not surprising that between 1964 and 1967 there was a widening dispersion of personal income per worker, followed by a reduction during the next few years.

As regards the question whether the inter-industry dispersion of personal incomes has been greater in recent years in Yugoslavia than in other countries, Estrin's comparisons are not conclusive, because he apparently uses data on the inter-industry dispersion of earnings of manual workers (wages) in the other countries with which to compare the Yugoslav dispersion of earnings of all employees. That the latter type of distribution is normally more widely dispersed than the former can be seen

---

[10] The decline in dispersion between 1971 and 1975 was due at least in part to a 'wage freeze' in 1972–3, which turned out in fact to be a squeeze on increases in higher incomes.

from data on the United States and Canada in OECD (1965, 152-9). In any case, the inter-industry coefficient of variation is not a very reliable statistic for making international comparisons of the level of dispersion of earnings, since its size depends on the number of industries in the sample, i.e. the degree of fineness with which industries are broken down, and the exact definition of each industry.

It would be more interesting to make an international comparison of the dispersion of earnings of individual employees. Unfortunately, however, not many countries report data of precisely the same kind as those which are available for Yugoslavia. The Yugoslav figures cover all permanent employees, irrespective of age, who worked approximately full-time during the given period (in recent years the month of September). The nearest approximation to this is two sets of data reported in Saunders and Marsden (1981) for the Netherlands and Great Britain in October 1977 and April 1978 respectively, the relevant figures from which are shown in Table 9.7. The best approximation to the Yugoslav definition seems to be the first set of Netherlands figures. The second set, and the figures for Great Britain, exclude young workers and, in the Netherlands case, also overtime pay. It is difficult to draw precise conclusions from this comparison, but it seems that the Yugoslav disperison is not very different from those existing in these two countries.[11]

In interpreting the results of any international comparison it is necessary to take account of several further considerations. In the first place, the Yugoslav statistics refer to earnings after tax, whereas in most other

TABLE 9.7

International Comparison of Dispersion of Earnings of Full-time Workers in Whole Economy

Country, year, and type of distribution	Period of measurement	P10/P50 (percentages)	P90/P50
Yugoslavia, 1979, all social sector employees working 160–200 hours in the month	Month	63	170
Netherlands, 1977, all employees, including overtime pay	Week	64	180
Netherlands, 1977, employees aged 23 and over, excluding overtime pay	Week	78	156
Great Britain, 1978, men aged 21 and over, women aged 18 and over	Week	60	164

Sources: Yugoslavia: Table 9.6 above.
   Others: Saunders and Marsden (1981, 55–6).

[11] An earlier comparison in Lydall (1968, 153) suggested that the 1963 Yugoslav dispersion of earnings was about the same as in Sweden, Poland, West Germany, Canada, Belgium, and the United States, but greater than in Czechoslovakia, New Zealand, Hungary, Australia, and Denmark.

countries the statistics refer to earnings before tax. In countries which have a progressive system of taxation the dispersion of pre-tax earnings is clearly not a reliable indicator of the degree of inequality of effective post-tax earnings. Secondly, almost all published distributions of earnings exclude the value of fringe benefits. There is reason to believe that such benefits (especially the provision of free or cheap housing) are more unequally distributed in Yugoslavia than in many other countries.[12] To that extent, the Yugoslav earnings distribution underestimates the dispersion of total employee benefits. Thirdly, the Yugoslav distribution is slightly widened by the influence of inter-regional differences in earnings, which are greater in Yugoslavia than in most other countries. On balance, therefore, the Yugoslav statistics probably slightly underestimate the degree of inequality of real employee benefits in that country in comparison with the statistics available for most other countries.

3. THE DISTRIBUTION OF INCOME BETWEEN COMMUNES

In Yugoslavia great importance is attached—both in theory and in practice—to the role of the communes as centres of local government and of economic and social planning and control. It is presumably for this reason that each year a considerable quantity of statistics for each commune is published in the Yearbooks. Since there are more than 500 communes, these data provide a valuable source of fairly detailed information about some aspects of economic development, in particular about changes in the dispersion of income per worker and other variables between communes. Moreover, with the help of such a large sample of observations it is possible to estimate some interrelations between different economic characteristics by means of regression techniques.

The years selected for study in the first instance were 1971 and 1978, and communes in all regions were included in this analysis. At a later stage, it was decided that it would be more useful to make a year-by-year analysis for two regions (Slovenia and Serbia proper) over the whole period 1971–8. Detailed scrutiny of the data suggested the necessity of excluding a few communes from both these analyses. In the case of some of the capital cities, where data were given both for the whole city area and for its component communes, the preferred choice was to retain the communes and exclude the city data; and this rule was followed in Belgrade, Ljubljana, and Sarajevo. For Zagreb and Skopje, however, where there was no division into smaller communes in 1971, it was necessary to exclude such data also for 1978, keeping these two cities as single units of observation in both years. Twelve communes were excluded because their

---

[12] Comisso (1979, 105) reported that 'depending on their financial capabilities, enterprises supplied their employees with housing, transportation subsidies, low-cost meals, individual loans for education, consumer credit, and other fringe benefits. As these items constituted a significant portion of individual household budgets, their impact on wage differentials could be substantial.' Richer enterprises, for example, provided more and better apartments, which were sometimes sublet in whole or part for substantial rents.

data were either very unstable or extreme (often because they were rather small communes).[13] And in three other cases, communes which were amalgamated or divided between 1971 and 1978 had to be treated in each year as if they were undivided throughout.[14] The final sample contained 490 communes, of which there were 59 in Slovenia and 108 in Serbia proper.

An overall view of changes in the degree of inter-commune dispersion of value added, income, and fixed assets per worker for the whole country is given in Table 9.8. The degree of dispersion is measured by the coefficient of variation, and the coefficients are based on weighted distributions of communes. The results show that the relative dispersion of each of the five variables declined significantly between 1971 and 1978. The degree of equalization over this period was greater for fixed assets per worker, especially in the productive sector, than for value added or personal income per worker. Even so, the dispersion of fixed assets per worker in the productive sector was still very large in 1978. This is not surprising, since some highly capital-intensive enterprises, such as power-generating stations and heavy metal and chemical processing industries, are inevitably concentrated in a few locations.

TABLE 9.8

Inter-Commune Coefficients of Variation, Yugoslavia, 1971 and 1978
(percentage coefficients)

Sector and variable	1971	1978
Productive social sector:		
Net value added per worker	26	23
Net personal income per worker	21	18
Fixed assets per worker	89	61
Non-productive social sector:		
Net personal income per worker	26	23
Fixed assets per worker	39	33

Definitions:

Net value added is gross value added during the year minus obligatory depreciation.

Net personal income is income paid out in cash during the year, after contributions for social security but including compensation for travel and other business expenses.

Fixed assets are equal to the undepreciated value of such assets at the end of the year. Values are revised from time to time to compensate for inflation.

Number of workers is the number employed on 30 September.

The coefficient of variation, defined as the standard deviation divided by the mean, is a measure of relative dispersion which is independent of the original units of measurement. For these estimates each commune was given a weight proportional to the number of workers employed in the relevant sector in the given year.

[13] These were four communes in Belgrade (Barajevo, Čukarica, Rakovica and Sopot), Crna Trava, Glogovac, Kladovo, Lastovo, Obrovac, Postojna, Pregrada, and Vrgorac.
[14] The communes affected, as described by their undivided names, were: Buje, Čapljina, and Sarajevo Centar.

The figures are consistent with the proclaimed policy of levelling up, both between and within regions. As was shown in the previous chapter, there has not, in fact, been much levelling between regions. So, most of the levelling must have occurred within republics and provinces. This is confirmed for most regions by a study of changes in the regional coefficients of variation. The major exception is Montenegro, in which the inter-communal dispersion of both net value added per worker and fixed assets per worker (in both sectors) increased between 1971 and 1978.

It will be noted that in both years net personal income per worker in the productive sector is more equally distributed across communes than net value added per worker. This is in accordance with official policies on income distribution as well as with a probably spontaneous tendency for the more productive enterprises to have a higher saving ratio. A comparison of the productive and non-productive sectors shows that for personal incomes inter-commune dispersion is greater in the non-productive sector while for fixed assets per worker it is less. The explanation for the former result is that highly paid non-productive workers (political functionaries, administrators, and cultural and medical workers) tend to be concentrated in certain communes, especially in the capital cities. The explanation for the latter result is that the technically determined range of capital-intensity in productive activities is normally much wider than the corresponding range of capital-intensity in non-productive activities.

A closer study of changes in inter-regional dispersion can be made with the help of the eight-year series for Slovenia and Serbia proper. Because the observations for individual years are subject to temporary fluctuations which may partly obscure the underlying changes, the data used for the analysis of dispersion within Slovenia and Serbia are trend estimates for each variable, the trend values being derived from regressions of the logarithm of each variable on time. The results of this analysis, summarized in Table 9.9, show that in almost all cases the major decline in the dispersion of these variables, in both Slovenia and Serbia, occurred between 1971 and 1974, with a more moderate further decline in the next two years.[15] Between 1976 and 1978, on the other hand, there was a slight increase in dispersion for the majority of the variables. Because Serbia proper is a much larger and more heterogeneous region than Slovenia it is not surprising that the degree of dispersion of all variables is greater in Serbia than in Slovenia. Serbia is, from an economic point of view, a sort of microcosm of Yugoslavia as a whole; indeed, the range of variability of economic development between Serbian communes is in many cases wider than the range of variability in Yugoslavia as a whole (compare Tables 9.8 and 9.9).

The above results are consistent with the view that during this period there was a conscious policy designed to reduce inter-communal economic

[15] As mentioned earlier, there was a 'wage freeze' in 1972–3, which had more restrictive effects on the growth of higher incomes.

TABLE 9.9

Inter-commune Coefficients of Variation, Slovenia and Serbia, 1971–8
(percentage coefficients)

Region, sector, and variable	1971	1974	1976	1978
Slovenia				
Productive social sector:				
Net value added per worker	19.8	16.2	14.4	13.6
Net personal income per worker	11.3	10.2	9.9	10.1
Fixed assets per worker	67.1	48.1	39.2	38.8
Non-productive social sector:				
Net personal income per worker	27.8	20.6	17.2	18.0
Fixed assets per worker	35.1	26.1	23.2	24.9
Serbia proper				
Productive social sector:				
Net value added per worker	30.3	25.2	22.9	23.3
Net personal income per worker	24.2	19.8	18.2	18.4
Fixed assets per worker	103.2	60.8	49.9	73.7
Non-productive social sector:				
Net personal income per worker	30.4	29.2	29.1	30.7
Fixed assets per worker	44.7	38.7	36.4	35.6

Notes and definitions: The estimates are based on trend values of the variables, derived by fitting semi-logarithmic regression equations to the eight-year series. For calculating the coefficient of variation each trend value was weighted by the number of workers employed in the sector in the given year.

The variables are as defined in Table 9.8.

inequality. The results could also be explained, at least in part, by a natural tendency for industry to spread outwards to the less developed areas, encouraged by the efforts of communal authorities to attract industry and to secure their fair shares of available bank credits and other funds. All of these influences would work in the direction of a systematic tendency towards inter-communal equalization. The extent to which there was such a tendency can be measured by regressing the trend values of the variables for 1978 on the trend values for 1971. The results for three variables in the productive sector are shown in Table 9.10.

By regressing the logarithms of the beginning and end-of-period values of the variables one obtains an estimate of the systematic reduction in relative inequality of each variable during the period. For example, the coefficient of 0.54 for Slovenia in the first line indicates that, in the absence of other influences, the degree of inter-communal dispersion of net value added per worker in that republic would have fallen in the period 1971–8 by 46 per cent. In the case of fixed assets per worker the systematic reduction in dispersion is more than 80 per cent in both regions. Actual dispersion, as we have seen, did not decline to the same extent, and the discrepancy between these two findings must be attributed to the influence of other factors unrelated to the initial level of each variable.

TABLE 9.10

Regression Slope Coefficients of 1978 Logarithmic Values on 1971 Logarithmic Values, Productive Social Sector, Slovenia and Serbia

Variable	Slovenia	Serbia
Net value added per worker	0.54	0.52
Net personal income per worker	0.67	0.54
Fixed assets per worker	0.19	0.17

Notes: The estimates are based on unweighted regressions of the trend values of the variables, as defined in Table 9.9.

For any variable, X, the regression equation was in the form $\ln X_{78} = a + b \ln X_{71}$, where the subscripts refer to the year of observation. The coefficients given in the table are the estimated b-coefficients. All the estimates are highly significant in the statistical sense.

We have noted already that the dispersion of net personal income per worker is always less than the dispersion of net value added per worker. From the samples of communes in the two regions we can also examine the cross-section regression relation between these two variables. Table 9.11 gives the results of such an analysis. The slope coefficients indicate how the inter-communal pattern of distribution of net personal incomes per worker is related to inter-communal differences in net value added per worker. The pressures towards equalization of personal incomes are evidently greater in Slovenia than in Serbia. Although the average ratio of net personal income to net value added was 0.39 in Slovenia in each of these years, and 0.40–0.41 in Serbia, the marginal propensity to distribute income, measured across communes, was only 0.21 to 0.24 in Slovenia and 0.26 to

TABLE 9.11

Coefficients of Regressions of Net Personal Income per Worker on Net Value Added per Worker in the Productive Social Sector, Slovenia and Serbia, 1971–8[a]

Year	Slovenia		Serbia	
	Slope coefficient[b]	Elasticity[c]	Slope coefficient[b]	Elasticity[c]
1971	0.21	0.53	0.26	0.67
1972	0.21	0.55	0.26	0.68
1973	0.22	0.57	0.27	0.70
1974	0.23	0.59	0.28	0.71
1975	0.24	0.60	0.29	0.71
1976	0.24	0.60	0.29	0.71
1977	0.24	0.60	0.30	0.70
1978	0.23	0.59	0.29	0.69

[a] Based on unweighted regressions of trend values of the variables, as defined in Table 9.9.
[b] Regression coefficients of natural values.
[c] Regression coefficients of logarithmic values.

0.30 in Serbia. The elasticity coefficients measure the relation between a 1 per cent difference in value added per worker and the accompanying difference in personal income per worker. The changes in the slope coefficients over time suggest that between 1971 and 1975 there was some relaxation of the egalitarian pressures but that this was increased again in 1978.

4. CONCLUSIONS

The distribution of household income in Yugoslavia, as measured in the official surveys, is more equal than in some other southern European countries but more unequal than in some of the eastern European countries. It must be remembered, however, that Yugoslavia is a very heterogeneous country, especially because of differences between regions and differences between private agriculture and the social sector. If a relatively homogeneous and developed republic such as Slovenia were compared with, for example, Czechoslovakia or Hungary there would probably not be a great deal of difference in the dispersion of income.

Hence 'self-management' in the Yugoslav context does not seem to have generated an especially wide dispersion of personal incomes. But this may be at least partly the result of strong pressures on 'self-managed' organizations to conform to politically determined norms of behaviour. Yugoslav experience, therefore, does not tell us what the distribution of income would be like in a purely *laissez-faire* self-managed economy.

Inequality of household income may have increased between 1965 and 1968, but since that year it seems to have remained quite stable.

The dispersion of labour earnings in the social sector widened during the early Reform years, but after 1967 it began to return towards its previous level. By 1975 it was virtually the same as it had been in 1964, both between individual workers and between manufacturing industries.

The dispersion of individual labour earnings in the social sector seems to be about the same as in some more developed and more homogeneous countries, such as the Netherlands and Great Britain.

The dispersion across communes of value added per worker, personal income per worker, and fixed assets per worker in the social sector declined between 1971 and 1978, mainly in the first five or six years. This probably reflects a systematic policy to level up communes, especially within republics and provinces. The effects of pressures on enterprises to exercise restraint in the distribution of personal incomes can also be seen in the inter-commune analysis of the relation between value added per worker and personal income per worker.

CHAPTER 10

THE ALLOCATION OF RESOURCES

In the previous two chapters we described the record of Yugoslav economic achievements during the period of self-management. In this chapter and the following chapter we shall consider the economic efficiency of the Yugoslav system. Economic efficiency has two main components: allocative efficiency and organizational efficiency. Allocative efficiency is achieved when available resources of land, labour, capital, enterprise, and foreign exchange are allocated to their most productive uses, i.e. when the last unit of each resource employed in each activity produces the same amount of value. (The method of determining the relative value of each product is an important matter; but, for the purpose of measuring allocative efficiency, the method, or the scale of values which it generates, can be taken as given.) Organizational efficiency, sometimes called X-efficiency, is measured by the ability of members of the work-force of an enterprise—managers, technicians, skilled and unskilled workers—to use the technology and resources at their disposal to the best advantage. The productivity of human beings is not simply a matter of the equipment available to them, nor of the amounts of formal education or training which they have received, but also of something else—certain *esprit de corps*, attention to quality and detail, responsiveness to demands from outside the enterprise and from managers and other workers within the enterprise. Economists often assume that organizational efficiency is the same in all enterprises. But this is an unwarranted assumption. Organizational efficiency can vary enormously, depending on the quality of management, the attitudes of workers, and the system of incentives. The question of the degree to which organizational efficiency is affected by the existence of a self-management system is of considerable importance for judging the desirability of such a system.

The present chapter is concerned with the allocative efficiency of the Yugoslav system; the following chapter will be devoted to its organizational efficiency. So far as possible, in both chapters an attempt will be made to separate the effects of self-management as such from the effects of other features of the Yugoslav environment.

In this chapter we shall start by considering the mobility of resources in general between enterprises and regions. Secondly, we shall examine the efficiency of allocation of three specific types of scarce resource: labour, capital, and foreign exchange. Thirdly, there will be a review of the allocative aspects of Yugoslav housing policy. Finally, an assessment will be made of the effects of a self-management system on the efficiency of resource allocation.

1. MOBILITY OF RESOURCES BETWEEN ENTERPRISES AND REGIONS

It was argued in Chapter 3 that there is a strong inducement for most Yugoslav enterprises to expand their scale of production in order to take advantage of further economies of scale. On grounds of allocational efficiency this tendency is justifiable up to a point, since it results in lower costs of production. But the tendency has been accentuated by government policy. With a view to restricting the inequality of distributed incomes, the federal and regional governments (and the Party and its subsidiary socio-political organizations) have insisted on the conclusion of social compacts designed to oblige the more prosperous enterprises to retain a larger proportion of their incomes for reinvestment than the less prosperous enterprises. Although many kinds of social compacts are not rigorously observed, the social compacts on income distribution seem to have had some effect, probably because income distribution is a very sensitive matter in a communist country. The outcome, however, has been to increase the degree of concentration of investible funds; and this tendency has been strengthened by the policies of the banks, which allocate most of their credits to enterprises which supply a significant part of the cost of investment out of their own resources.[1] In any case, the banks are officially controlled by their enterprise shareholders (or 'founders'), and this must create a bias towards giving more generous credits to the larger enterprises.

In spite of the high degree of concentration of investible funds in the hands of existing enterprises, many Yugoslav economists express concern at the fact that so much of investment is financed out of bank credits, and advocate a strengthening of self-finance. Their arguments in favour of increasing self-finance are twofold. On the one hand, this is regarded as an ideological necessity, because it is essential that the workers should control the 'means of expanded reproduction.'[2] A different sort of argument is that

[1] Neuberger and James (1973, 260) state firmly that 'the amount a bank is willing to lend is directly related to the amount the members themselves are providing, in the form of reinvested earnings'. Granick (1975, 390) says that 'retaining enterprise income for investment purposes is usually a precondition for receiving bank loans', and reports (p. 402) that one large bank in Slovenia has a rule that long-term loans are given only to enterprises which supply 70 per cent of their investment needs from internal finance.

[2] A report by a group of Yugoslav economists (*Društveno planiranje i proširena reprodukcija*, Informator, Zagreb 1980, p. 6) refers to the 'well-known Marxist saying' that whoever controls expanded reproduction controls the whole of society. However, it does not follow from this that the workers can only exercise such control directly within their enterprises. There is, after all, an elaborate political structure in Yugoslavia, which is said to be designed precisely for the purpose of giving the workers control over their government. On the problems of reconciling self-management with government economic control see Brus (1975) ch. 2.

self-finance is much favoured in capitalist countries as a means of improving investment efficiency, and that this consideration should apply also in Yugoslavia.[3] No specific reasons are given for believing that self-finance promotes investment efficiency, but it seems that the main argument is that existing enterprises are better qualified to make an accurate appraisal of investment projects. In any case, the discussion leads up to a proposal that each enterprise should be obliged to save a certain proportion of its income.[4]

There are three reasons for regarding a high level of self-finance as undesirable. The first is that, as shown in Chapter 3, income which is reinvested in the Yugoslav-type of co-operative tends to increase income per worker; and this has the effect of raising the cost of labour in relation to the cost of capital. Hence, the greater the volume of accumulated self-finance in Yugoslav-type enterprises, the greater the bias towards capital-intensive investment decisions.

The second objection to a high level of self-finance is that it is likely to reduce the number of new entrants. A steady stream of a new entrants is important for preserving a healthy level of competition, for encouraging flexibility of technique and product design, and for promoting employment in less capital-intensive enterprises. For the past twenty years Yugoslav policy has neglected these objectives by giving more encouragement to enterprise concentration.[5] This policy began with the movement towards economic reform, which culminated in 1965. The number of enterprises in industry and mining reached a peak of 2,787 in 1961; ten years later it had fallen to 2,398. In 1961 there were 215 enterprises employing less than 30 workers, and in 1971 only 158.[6] Since there have never been many bankruptcies, these figures are sufficient to demonstrate that during this period there were very few new entries.[7]

The third objection to self-finance under Yugoslav self-management conditions is that it creates a serious barrier to the regional mobility of resources. If an enterprise reinvests within its existing structure in such a way that the extra income created by the investment (and by any associated

[3] Ibid., p. 11.

[4] The proposal is described as 'programmed accumulation'. See, for example, ibid., 15. The influential federal Commission on Problems of Economic Stabilization, in its report on the 'basic prerequisites' (strictly, 'starting bases') of stabilization comes down firmly in favour of increasing self-finance as a means of improving the efficiency of investment (*Borba*, special supplement, 27 April 1982).

[5] The break-up of enterprises into basic organizations since about 1971, and especially since the Associated Labour Act of 1976, was almost entirely a formal exercise. It has not hindered the process of industrial concentration, as can be seen in the results of the annual surveys of the 'top two hundred' enterprises in *Ekonomska politika*.

[6] YB63, 109 – 5 and YB73, 109 – 5. Similar statistics are not available for subsequent years, because of the re-organization of enterprises into basic and other organizations.

[7] For further confirmation, up to 1968, see Sacks (1973, 82–3); see also the comments of Granick (1975, 414). More recently, Sacks (1979, 334) has written: 'Although Yugoslav law does include antitrust statutes designed to protect competition, there has been virtually no enforcement of them. On the contrary, official statements by leading politicians always seem to encourage mergers (both horizontal and vertical).'

factors of production) is shared by the workers within the enterprise, the existing workers will have no reason to object, provided that the extra income is sufficient to give the additional workers an equal share of the enterprise income and leave some surplus for raising average incomes all round. But if the investment is in a new plant located at some distance from the rest of the enterprise, and especially if it is in a different republic or province, there will be a serious risk that the workers employed in the new plant will eventually demand the right to separate from the main enterprise. In any case, the new plant will become a separate basic organization, will full self-management rights. There will probably be a self-management agreement which obliges the new basic organization to remain part of the enterprise and to pool its income with the other basic organizations in that enterprise. But, if the workers in the new plant are determined to break away, as they may well be at some stage, and they are supported in that demand by the political authorities in their commune, republic or province, it will be virtually impossible to prevent them from doing so. Even if the funds invested by the main enterprise in the new plant are eventually repaid with interest, under inflationary conditions the investing enterprise suffers a loss of the real value of its capital, and in addition it loses the benefits which it would have received from reinvesting within its own original structure.

This is, indeed, one of the fundamental economic problems of a self-management system of the Yugoslav type. Any system which gives the workers in a particular plant the right to manage, and to enjoy the fruits of, the capital equipment of that plant, without paying those who invested in that plant the full value of the extra income generated by that investment, creates a powerful bias against the transfer of capital and technology from one plant or enterprise to another. The obstacles to the transfer of capital and technology from one region to another within Yugoslavia are much greater than the obstacles to such transfers by capitalist firms across international boundaries. In a world of guaranteed private property rights, such as existed in the latter part of the nineteenth century, private capital was extremely mobile across regions and frontiers; but in a world of self–managed organizations there would be enormous obstacles to the mobility of capital, and most of such transfers would be made only as acts of charity.

The Yugoslavs have tried to overcome the problem of inter-regional mobility of capital by two methods. The first is the Federal Fund for the Underdeveloped Regions, which is an institution for providing economic aid. As shown in Chapter 8, the flow of funds through this channel has been impressively large. But experience has shown in Yugoslavia, as it has also shown in respect of similar transfers of funds between nations, that soft loans are often spent wastefully, and that the benefits are often received mainly by selected minority groups. Hence the Yugoslav government has tried to encourage financial transfers by a second method, namely, by direct investment across regional boundaries.

Direct investment by one enterprise in another is called in Yugoslavia 'pooling labour and resources', which we shall call, for convenience, PLR. PLR is recommended officially as a means of transferring finance and technology between enterprises generally, not only between richer and poorer regions. Indeed, efforts are constantly made within regions to persuade more successful enterprises to agree to PLR with less successful enterprises, especially those which are on the verge of bankruptcy. Not surprisingly, these efforts are not often successful. As one Yugoslav commentator wrote, 'It is a well known phenomenon that organizations of associated labour which operate better are reluctant to associate with those which operate on the verge of profitability or even operate at a loss'[8]. Similarly, in the words of a group of economists, 'Those . . . organizations of associated labour . . . which are in a favourable position do not exhibit a tendency to pool labour and resources with those organizations of associated labour with which, according to the logic of technological and income relations, they are interdependent, but which have an unfavourable position in the acquisition and distribution of income' (Vojnić 1979, 98). The richer enterprises prefer 'short-term commercial and credit relations to long-term income relations from pooling labour and resources with "poorer" partners' (ibid. 106). The result is that only about 4 per cent of total investment is financed by PLR, and much of this arises from obligatory contributions towards the financing of infrastructure and energy production.[9]

Although PLR has not been a successful policy within regions, it was thought that it might become a useful method of promoting inter-regional investment, if the investing enterprises were given a special inducement to agree to such arrangements. The inducement offered was that funds invested through PLR in the less developed regions should count towards the compulsory loans made to the Federal Fund, to the extent of 20 per cent of the total in 1976–80, and to the extent of 50 per cent in 1981–5. This is an ingenious idea, because loans to the Federal Fund yield a negligible return (especially in conditions of rapid inflation) and there might be some inter-regional investments which the investing enterprises would regard as preferable. But the obstacles to inter-enterprise investment under self-management conditions are formidable, and the volume of inter-regional PLR has to far been disappointingly small. In the 1976–80 plan period only about 2 per cent of the amount eligible for offset against Federal Fund loans was used for inter-regional PLR.[10] In the first eighteen months of the 1981–5 plan period the authorities succeeded in getting 22 PLR agreements signed betweeen enterprises in Kosovo and other enterprises in developed regions; but these agreements are planned to create only 6,700 extra jobs, and, if experience is a guide, there is no guarantee that all of this will be achieved.

[8] Article in the official journal *Socialist Thought and Practice* (August 1981) on 'Income based relations in the agricultural complex "Beograd" '.
[9] *Društveno planiranje i proširena reprodukcija*, Informator, Zagreb 1980, p. 9.
[10] *Yugoslav Survey*, May 1982, p. 15.

Inter-regional mobility of capital in Yugoslavia is hampered not only by the difficulties already referred to but also by other influences. There are persistent complaints of autarkic tendencies in republics, regions, and communes. Although the federal government has a constitutional duty to maintain the unity of the Yugoslav market, it seems to have been unable to resist these tendencies. It is reported that the proportion of total turnover of goods and services which crosses republican and provincial boundaries fell from 27.7 per cent in 1970 to 22.9 per cent in 1978 (*Borba*, 8 August 1982). According to another source, the proportion of total money payments made across republican and provincial boundaries fell from 14 per cent in 1976 to 10 per cent in 1981, while investments across the same boundaries were said to be only 'of symbolic value' (*Borba*, 27 April 1982, quoting the deputy director-general of the Federal Social Accounting Service).

Among the reasons for this disturbing trend one should probably include the tradition of Balkan local loyalties. But the special Yugoslav combination of political and economic self-management systems seems to be the major reason. As shown in Chapter 5, when the Party adopted the self-management principle for enterprises it also gave important supervisory powers to the local communes, since in this way the Party could retain effective control over enterprise policy. But this devolution of economic control to local authorities, and after 1965 increasingly to the republican and provincial governments, created a strong basis for autarkic tendencies. Local and regional governments, which have the major responsibility under this system for promoting investment and employment within their own areas, and which are closely allied with local enterprises, are tempted to follow an autarkic policy, thus reproducing on a local level the usual tendency of communist national governments to be highly protectionist and suspicious of free trade.

The economic consequences of these local and regional autarkic policies have been deplorable. The mobility of capital is restricted, there is much duplication of productive facilities, imports from other areas are discriminated against, and local enterprises are encouraged to take their supplies only from local sources. Granick (1975, 419–20) reports the case of a Slovenian enterprise which 'had great difficulties in selling in Croatia . . . because wholesalers would not carry its products'. It retaliated by establishing its own retail outlets and by aiding a wholesaler to enter the Croatian market. A leading economist, Zoran Popov, interviewed by the weekly journal *Ekonomska politika* (17 November 1980), remarked that 'the republics and provinces are almost exclusively in control of economic policy. The consistent implementation of this arrangement in the practical development of the system has made our system inflexible, sluggish and inefficient.' In particular, it has limited the unity of the market and the mobility of the factors of production. In Popov's opinion, the position was made worse by the division of enterprises into basic organizations since, if different basic organizations are located in different communes, there is pressure from the commune authorities to control the investment decisions of their own basic organizations, regardless of the point of view of the whole enterprise.[11]

The Commission on Problems of Economic Stabilization declared that in recent years autarkic tendencies have manifested themselves 'at all levels, from the basic organization of associated labour up to the federation'.[12] Resources are kept within regional boundaries by decisions of governments and quasi-governmental authorities (p. 19). The free movement of capital within the Yugoslav market is 'imperative' (p. 12) and it is also important to have free movement of labour and knowledge, including scientific and technical achievements (p. 13). The Commission recognized that PLR has not so far been very successful and suggested that one reason for this is 'the present discouraging arrangement and criteria for distributing joint income between the associated partners' (p. 15). This is a theme which was previously expressed by the Third Congress of Self-Managers of Yugoslavia when it declared that for the development of PLR 'it is indispensable to determine objectified criteria for sharing jointly created income, such as the standards for current and past labour, which will express the contribution of each organization of associated labour to the realization of joint revenue or joint income'.[13] But this touches on delicate ideological issues and raises some extraordinarily difficult measurement (or accounting) problems. It is hard to see how PLR will ever create satisfactory conditions for the mobility of capital so long as self-management rights are treated as sacred.

2. THE ALLOCATION OF SPECIFIC RESOURCES

Labour

Labour in general is not in short supply in Yugoslavia. On the contrary, the major problem is that much of it is wasted in unemployment, in underemployment on small farms, or in overmanning in the social sector. It would be facile to suggest that Yugoslavia could have completely avoided the problem of unemployment, but the problem has been accentuated by an excessive concentration on capital-intensive investments in established enterprises. This aspect of the use of labour is, therefore, best considered in relation to the allocation of capital, which will be discussed below.

Despite the general surplus of labour supply, there are some types of

[11] In an interview with *Ekonomska politika* (22/29 November 1982), Petar Kostić, formerly Federal Secretary for Finance, said: 'One of our economists says that there is a built-in motivation in our system for each government authority to have its own factories. As a result, investments are made in less efficient local enterprises instead of in more profitable enterprises elsewhere.' According to *Borba* (5 November 1982) in all leading branches of industry—such as base metals, machinery, electronics, chemicals, and automobiles—capacity is constructed on the formula of 'six plus two', i.e. one plant for each republic and province. Similarly, in the 'non-productive' sector *Borba* (5 December 1982) alleges that almost every town in Serbia has or wants to have a university.

[12] *Borba*, special supplement, 27 April 1982, p. 14.

[13] *Yugoslav Survey*, August 1981, p. 10.

labour for which there is an excess demand. There are frequent reports of shortages of workers in coal and other mining, building, and social sector agriculture (e.g.*Borba*, 5 August 1982). In some areas there is also a shortage of skilled workers, because school children refuse to enter special technical schools (ibid.); and the non-ferrous metals industry has a considerable number of unfilled vacancies (*Ekonomska politika*, 22 June 1981, p. 16).[14] In general, young people in Yugoslavia are moving away from manual occupations, especially those which are heavy, dirty, or dangerous. There is an enormous pressure of demand for academic qualifications, which is excessively concentrated on such fields as medicine, law, and sociology. This is a problem which is common to many countries, and it would be unreasonable to attribute it to the existence of a self-management system. But the 'flight from the factory' suggests that the psychological compensations of self-management and the official emphasis on the superior role of 'productive' in comparison with 'non-productive' activities have not outweighed other more material considerations in determining young people's choice of occupation. The Yugoslav authorities are aware of the need to shift differentials in favour of deficit occupations, but it is difficult to overcome resistance to changes in traditional differentials, especially since the people who should be cut back are those who take most of the decisions.[15]

Governments, especially at the commune level, have tried to overcome the problem of general unemployment by putting pressure on local enterprises to take on more workers than they really need.[16] This pressure seems to have been successful, but at the expense of depriving enterprises of their self-management rights to make their own economic decisions.

[14] *Borba* (20 July 1982) complains that in a certain area which has a long tradition of coal-mining the new generation refuses to enter the industry. In a subsequent issue (4 November 1982) *Borba* reported that in Vojvodina there were 81,500 registered job-seekers but 72,000 vacancies in productive work. The young people were unwilling to take jobs in manufacturing, building, and agriculture. They all wanted office jobs. Similarly, it reported (14 December 1982) that the 'Red Flag' automobile plant in Kragujevac had been able to fill only 70 of the 130 apprentice scholarships offered in 1982, even although these lead to a guaranteed job in the enterprise. An organization in Belgrade invited eleven unemployed workers for interviews, but only four turned up and were given jobs (*Borba*, 7 December 1982). Young people stay at universities for long periods of time. In Serbia, only 3 per cent of students complete their degree course in minimum time; the average period (of students completing?) in 1980 was 7.4 years; and 24 per cent of the same group took 10 years or more (*Borba*, 14 July 1982).

[15] Thomas (1973) maintains, on the basis of a 'human capital' analysis, that already in the early 1970s university education had a negative net present value on almost any reasonable assumption about the discount rate. He concluded (p. 197): 'Technical higher education and university education both for private and social purposes are highly inefficient.' But he was not taking into account the fact that for a lucky minority such types of education are the avenues to power and prestige, as well as to above-average earnings.

[16] See Schrenk (1981, 56). In Serbia it was proposed in early 1982 that each basic organization should take on two half-time beginners in place of each full-time beginner. Under the existing law they are obliged to take one beginner each year for each 40 workers already employed. The proposed scheme would double this intake (*Borba*, 8 April 1982). But the paper draws attention to a number of practical difficulties.

This is one aspect of the increasing intervention of political agencies in enterprise affairs which we shall discuss at greater length in connection with the allocation of capital.

In the Yugoslav type of self-managed enterprise the workers' incomes depend to a considerable extent not only on their own abilities and efforts but also on the volume of capital at their disposal, much of which is available free of charge, since it was either inherited or accumulated out of enterprise income in previous years. Because there are no individual property rights in these funds, a worker who transfers from one enterprise to another loses the benefit of this accumulated capital. If he moves to an enterprise which has less capital per worker, he will usually suffer a fall in his earnings, even although the marginal productivity of his labour in the new enterprise is higher than in the previous one. In this way, the Yugoslav type of self-management system imposes a brake on the mobility of labour and on its allocation to its most productive uses.[17]

Capital

The wasteful allocation and use of capital is the most serious defect of the Yugoslav self-management system. Indeed, all the weaknesses of the system seem to converge in this area. There are three main causes of these weaknesses. In the first place, as pointed out previously (especially in Chapter 3, pp. 40–1) a Yugoslav-type of labour-managed enterprise has a bias towards capital-intensive investment decisions, even when there are large numbers of unemployed.[18] This bias also seems to be strengthened by the attitudes of the local political authorities who, although keen to absorb the local unemployed, are also anxious to increase the incomes of the workers already in social sector employment. Politicians have a natural tendency to be big spenders, especially out of loans or grants from other agencies, and they like to see the construction of economic monuments, or 'political factories'.[19]

Secondly, despite high rates of inflation during the past two decades, the nominal rate of interest on bank credits to social sector enterprises has been kept low; and the real rate of interest in most years, especially recently, has

---

[17] This problem has been carefully analysed by Meade (1980, 93–6). It must be remembered, however, that workers in modern capitalist industry also receive part of the rents of the more profitable firms and are often deterred from moving for other reasons, such as non-transferrable pension rights.

Despite the above-mentioned braking effect of the system on labour mobility between social sector enterprises, there has been a good deal of labour migration between republics and provinces, mostly from peasant households in the poorer regions.

[18] Tyson and Eichler (1981, 164) write: '. . . the evidence supports the view that Yugoslavia's investment efforts have been focused on capital-intensive projects and have thus been less effective in job creation than smaller investment efforts' in other countries.

[19] In the words of Stevan Doronjski, then President of the League of Communists, excessive investments are due to 'the technocratic and bureaucratic stubborn heads' who 'permanently think of nothing else but of grandiose projects, and turn a deaf ear to, and neglect the real needs of the people' (*Socialist Thought and Practice*, 1980, No. 12, p. 16). These 'technocratic and bureaucratic stubborn heads' are, in fact, the local Party bosses.

been negative. The result has been a large excess demand for credits, which has obliged the banks to allocate available funds according to other criteria. In effect, it is the established enterprises, or those which have the support of local politicians, which tend to receive the lion's share of available loan finance.[20] Once again, potential new entrant enterprises and the unemployed fail to receive sufficient support. One of the reasons for keeping the rate of interest low is the desire of the politicians to avoid paying higher rates to private savers. There is an ideological objection to the payment of *rentier* incomes in a communist society, and perhaps a fear that higher interest rates would lead to an increasing dispersion of income. It does not seem to be recognized that a simple way to meet these objections would be to levy an income tax on interest paid to private households.

The third source of inefficiency in the allocation of capital is the most fundamental, and the most difficult to overcome within the existing system. The problem is that under the Yugoslav system social sector capital belongs to nobody.[21] Nominally, all social sector capital belongs to 'society'. But the location of society is indefinite. It is certainly not intended to mean 'the government', for this would contradict the basic anti-statist philosophy of Yugoslav self-management. Nor are the workers in an enterprise entitled to regard themselves as the representatives of 'society', for this would encourage tendencies to 'group ownership', which is also ideologically taboo.[22] So the workers in enterprises are invited to take decisions about the use of large amounts of capital which are not owned by them. It is true that, in principle, the future level of their own incomes depends on the efficiency of these decisions, but only in a rather indirect fashion. There is a qualitative difference between making decisions about one's own money, or about the use of credit which, if the result turns out badly, will directly reduce the value of one's own investment in an enterprise, and making decisions about the spending of other people's money. For in the latter case, if the project turns out badly, it is the other people who will bear most of the cost.

This lack of motivation for taking sufficient care in the spending of 'social' resources is reinforced in Yugoslavia by the reluctance of the government (i.e. the Party) to allow enterprises which make bad investment decisions to bear the consequences. Bankruptcies, although allowed in principle, are almost always avoided by measures of special

[20] See Schrenk and others (1979, 182).

[21] A self-management attorney, speaking at a conference in Zagreb, said, 'Social property is, in principle, everybody's and nobody's' (*Borba*, 7 February 1982). The same definition was already used some years previously, when a speaker at a congress of self-managers remarked that some people 'interpreted "everybody's" to mean "mine" when it was to their advantage, but "nobody's" was the operative word when damage, losses and responsibility was in question' (Drulović 1978, 72).

[22] While 'group ownership' is regarded in Yugoslavia as a deviation from true self-management principles, Soviet commentators use the phrase pejoratively to describe any kind of self-management system.

assistance.[23] Additional bank credits are produced under political pressure, or there is compulsory PLR with a more successful enterprise.[24] The latter enterprise may itself be partially compensated with a grant of cheap credit.

Increasingly, workers and managers in Yugoslav enterprises have come to feel that they need not worry about the risk of business losses. The press is full of complaints about the number of enterprises running at a loss. In 1978 Stane Dolanc (1978, 19), then Secretary of the Executive Committee of the Presidency of the Central Committee of the League of Communists, reported that enterprises working at a loss, which included many large ones, employed about one-fifth of the total work-force.[25] It is often alleged that firms making losses continue to pay out personal incomes at, or even above, the previous level. Indeed, it is said that in some cases such firms pay higher personal incomes than profitable firms.[26] The conclusion of the journal *Ekonomska politika* (7 September 1981, p. 5) is that associated labour has little motivation to make better use of social capital since 'it carries no real responsibility for economic risk, since this has, in the last resort, been socialized'.[27]

An irresponsible attitude towards investment decisions is fostered not only by the 'socialization of risks' but also by an increasing tendency, especially since 1974, towards government or Party intervention in the affairs of 'self-managed' enterprises. This is a recurrent theme of comments in the press, and even in speeches by leading politicians. The general director of a large enterprise in Novi Sad, in an interview with the journal *Ekonomska politika* (26 July 1982, pp. 19–21) said: 'Decisions about what should be produced and what investments to make are the result of decisions taken in some superstructure. Few development decisions are made within the enterprise; instead, development tasks emerge from various social compacts at the level of the sub-region, region, province or republic.'[28] *Ekonomska politika* itself frequently expresses the same

[23] Moore (1980, 11) writes, 'The most important institutional fact is that enterprise bankruptcy, although legally provided for, in fact rarely occurred.'

[24] Sirc (1979, 157) states that credits to loss-making firms are sometimes given on very favourable terms such as 2 per cent interest and delayed repayment. See also Granick (1975, 412).

[25] In 1982 the situation was even worse. According to *Ekonomska politika* (22 November 1982) in the first six months of 1982 about 52 per cent of basic organizations operated at a loss.

[26] *Borba* (18 May 1982) reports the case of an enterprise in Vojvodina which made losses in both 1980 and 1981, but which increased its payments of personal incomes in spite of this. Part of the observed association between losses and higher personal incomes must be a purely statistical (or accounting) result, since in determining whether an enterprise has made a loss distributed personal incomes are treated as a cost.

[27] In a federal parliamentary debate a delegate from Slovenia said that 'in this country . . . we still engage superbly in the issuing of various rights and the incomprehensible tolerance of unfulfilled obligations'. Among the rights which he listed were the right to borrow without guarantee of repaying the debt, and the right to make losses and to have guaranted personal incomes. *Ekonomska politika*, 13 July 1981, pp. 17–18.

[28] It is interesting to note that he did not mention the federal government as a source of such decision. This well illustrates the decline of the economic authority of the federal government.

opinion. In an article on 26 July 1982, p. 5, it wrote: ' . . . everyone agrees that major investment decisions are taken in practice by the most influential presidents of organs of socio-political communities and organizations'. Hence 'in the great majority of cases decisions are made about the investment of other people's capital so that there is no material or any other kind of risk'. Formerly, there was a connection between personal income and the income of the enterprise, but that 'has gradually disappeared, because the level of income increasingly depends on concrete actions of the government administration, while the level of personal incomes depends on the level previously achieved, on the cost of living, and so forth'. On an earlier occasion (9 November 1981, p. 5) it wrote: 'It is worth noticing, however, that both the expansion of investment and the "mistaken locations" are merely the result of the existing position in the area of the financing of investment, of relations in which there is no real market economic dependence between the makers of investment decisions and their effects, just as the manner of using these resources does not create for anyone an economic risk or a material interest.'

Ivan Laća, writing in the journal *Socialist Thought and Practice* (1981, No. 1, p. 42), was even sharper in his comments: 'The present situation in regard to investments is a textbook example of administrative, statist and similar tendencies as well as of the damage caused by statist inability to resolve problems. It is certain that many investment decisions are made outside and irrespective of the framework of associated labour, and when these investments prove to be a failure (so-called political factories) no one was held responsible.' He added (p. 43) that ' . . . the dismantling of federal statism . . . had the undesired effect of strengthening statist tendencies in other socio-political communities i.e. republics, provinces and communes'.

Dirlam and Plummer (1973, 240–1) quoted a Yugoslav economist, who wrote in 1970: 'No answer has been discovered in our system to the important question of personal responsibility for unsuccessful performance of the management.' And they themselves commented that, while there is need for 'stricter standards of financial performance', 'no strong political support can be mustered for a program that would actually cost managers and workers their jobs if the enterprise engaged in financially reckless investment'.

Vladimir Bakarić, the leading Croat Communist, wrote bluntly (*Socialist Thought and Practice*, 1981, No. 4, p. 4): 'When a product is manufactured then the bank finances it regardless of what success it has on the market'. The Commission on Problems of Economic Stabilization was equally forthright (*Borba*, special supplement, 27 April 1982): 'Decisions about investment expenditure have been predominantly beyond the control of workers in organizations of associated labour' (p. 6). 'In this connection, it is necessary to emphasize that the worker in the basic organization of associated labour has not been up to now, and is not now, in a position to be able directly to influence decisions on the direction of development and the harmonization of relations with the market, nor to have any influence on the social plan and on the economic and other measures for its implementation' (p. 14). Decisions about investments are made in the lightest fashion, and the bad results are easily passed on to society as a whole by 'covering losses, violations, rehabilitation, writing off of debts, and so forth' (p. 17). 'Under present conditions we behave towards social capital as if, because it is social, it has no price and there is no value to be replaced in the process of production,' so that the rational use of capital loses significance, and differences in factor composition are not reflected in prices and incomes (p. 17). 'The practice, which has continued for many years, of writing off losses at the end of the year and of covering them in a non-selective way or transferring them to the next year . . . obstructs the normal process of appearance and disappearance of specific products.' This undermines efficiency and burdens efficient enterprises with the cost of supporting the inefficient (p. 23). The Commission had the courage to add that 'We are still enslaved by the prejudice or dogma that no organization should be allowed to fail' (p. 23).[29]

Irresponsibility in the making of investment decisions has many undesirable consequences, of which two are particularly important. The first is that there is a constant pressure towards excessive investment, which Bakarić described in 1979 as 'a kind of "investment mania" ' (*Socialist Thought and Practice*, 1979, No. 2, p. 26). The results are reflected in the tendency, which we noted in Chapter 8, for the share of investment in gross domestic product to rise to an insupportable level, thus adding to inflationary pressure and worsening the balance of payments. The second is that the productivity of investment is lower than it might be. Bakarić again (1979, p. 27) stated: 'The effectiveness of investments is declining, too, with the direct result of relatively low rates of productivity.' *Ekonomska politika* (29 June 1981) declared that 'One of the basic characteristics of the development of the whole Yugoslav economy is the exceptionally low efficiency of investment.' This is especially so in the less developed regions. For example, in 1976–9 the simultaneous marginal capital-output coefficients in Montenegro and Kosovo were twice as great as in the country as a whole. Professor Aleksander Bajt from Ljubljana, in an interview with *Ekonomska politika* in 1980 (17 November 1980), pointed out that negative real rates of interest have encouraged capital-intensive investments and industries, and have led to 'the almost complete socialization of risks, because of which one is less and less surprised by the judgement that the efficiency of our investments is little more than half as much as in other countries'. An econometric analysis by Mates (1981), based on a cross-section regression over 326 sectors of the economy,

---

[29] Ratko Svilar, former Vice-President of the Yugoslav Economic Chamber, said in an interview with *Ekonomska politika* (11 October 1982): 'We have arrived at such a situation that no one any longer takes account of costs or technology . . ., no one takes account of the way in which staff are used, . . . all because the influence of the economic factor, of the factor of the market, has simply ceased, or has greatly weakened.'

appears to confirm that the rate of return on capital in Yugoslavia is very low, possibly as little as 4 per cent.

Foreign exchange

Yugoslavia is persistently short of foreign exchange, and has been critically so during the past few years. Some shortage of foreign exchange is an almost inevitable accompaniment of the economic development of a less developed country in the modern world; and a period of acute shortage in Yugoslavia—as in many other countries—was precipitated by the rise in petroleum prices and its consequences for world trade. Under the pressure of the current foreign exchange crisis the Yugoslav government have taken desperate measures to restrict imports and to stimulate exports, at almost any cost. But such emergency measures are not a satisfactory basis for a longer term policy. There seems to be a growing recognition that the country has given insufficient attention to exports and that a new approach is needed.

Despite Yugoslavia's acceptance of a market system and of the need to maintain an open economy, trading relatively freely with the outside world, there have been a number of ideological obstacles to the pursuit of a genuinely export-oriented policy. The most important of these obstacles is the 'heavy industry' dogma, inherited from Stalinist Russia and never completely abandoned. Every republic and province wants to have its own steelworks, oil refinery, and cement factory, in the belief that only when they have established these 'heavy' plants will they have a secure base for future economic development. The truth is, in fact, almost entirely the opposite. The areas which have poured most of their resources into heavy investments at the expense of more labour-intensive industries have imposed a heavy burden on themselves, and missed a major opportunity to stimulate employment and faster economic growth. The lesson has been learnt during the current recession. In the words of *Ekonomska politika* (19 October 1981, p. 11):

While everyone is searching for an answer to the foreign exchange shortage, in Croatia five industries are highly successful in exports: textiles, wood products, leather and footwear, food products and shipbuilding. Each one earns much more in exports than it uses of imported materials. Yet these are the industries which have been held back by discrimination in favour of giant enterprises and by criticism that they are inappropriate for our level of development, that they do not pay well, etc. But it is the giants which rely heavily on imports and foreign credits, while these traditional industries earn the foreign exchange.

One does not wish to suggest, of course, that Yugoslavia needs no steelworks, no oil refineries, no cement factories and so forth. But there has been an irrational passion for these monumental plants and there is now much excess capacity in some of these industries.

The second main ideological obstacle to a healthy export trade, as well as to a reduction of import dependence, has been the bias against private agriculture. This topic will be pursued further in Chapter 13.

Among institutional obstacles, it seems likely that the system of social planning creates a bias in the direction of (apparent) import-replacement and against export expansion. When planning starts by each enterprise setting out its own targets for inputs and outputs, followed by an attempt to 'harmonize' these aspirations, it is almost inevitable that the main criterion for harmonization will be the satisfaction of domestic demand rather than the development of profitable export markets. As a result 'Relatively few enterprises in Yugoslavia are . . . oriented primarily toward the export market by means of long-term supply contracts and tied outlets' (OECD 1978, 16).

Another institutional difficulty arises from the way in which a self-managed economy responds to devaluation. Devaluation is a useful method of correcting a foreign deficit, provided that domestic incomes and prices are not immediately, or very quickly, adjusted upwards in line with the new world price level in terms of local currency. In capitalist countries a brake on wage rises can be imposed to some extent by the time-lags in the wage adjustment process, by an explicit incomes policy, or by a deliberate deflation of domestic demand, which may be needed in any case to make room for the increase in export demand. But in Yugoslavia there are no wage contracts in productive industry, incomes policies have been directed primarily towards the maintenance of relativities rather than the absolute level of money incomes, and the deflation of demand, while it reduces output, does not have much effect on prices.[30] The consequence is that, at least under existing Yugoslav policies, devaluation is not an effective remedy for a structural weakness in the balance of payments, although it may well be necessary in order to prevent further deterioration of the balance when domestic inflation is occurring for other reasons.

In addition to periodic devaluations (which have recently become a fairly steady downward float of the dinar) the Yugoslav government uses two other major instruments for influencing the foreign balance. The first is a system of tariffs on imports and subsidies on exports; and the second is a system of allocating foreign exchange, one of the principal elements of which is the granting of foreign exchange retention quotas. In the background, there is also an apparatus of quantitative import controls which, although not normally exerting an important influence on the commodity composition of imports, can be used in an emergency.

The average level of import tariffs is not high, but the level of protection for finished products is greater than for raw materials and intermediates, so giving an even higher rate of effective protection for the former group. Expenditure on export subsidies represents more than half the amount raised by customs duties (more than 57 per cent in 1980). The 1982 federal budget provides for an expenditure on this item of 46.5 billion dinars (approximately $1 billion) compared with estimated revenue from customs duties of 71.2 billion dinars.[31] Since export subsidies are concentrated on

---

[30] These problems will be discussed further in Chapter 12.
[31] *Ekonomska politika*, 7 December 1981, pp. 10–11.

exports to the convertible zone, i.e. to non-Comecon countries, which represent about half the total value of exports, the average rate of subsidy may be close to 20 per cent.[32] Both tariffs and subsidies can be tailor-made to suit the preferences of the authorities and thus influence the commodity composition of imports and exports. People can always find arguments in favour of discriminatory policies of this sort, especially when they yield benefits to industries in which those who advocate them have an interest; but it is doubtful whether such policies are good for the country as a whole.

Under conditions of domestic inflation, tariffs and subsidies gradually lose their effectiveness, unless they are accompanied by regular devaluation. As mentioned above, devaluation under Yugoslav conditions is not a powerful weapon for correcting a foreign deficit, and the combination of devaluation with tariffs and subsidies is also insufficient to overcome a fundamental weakness in foreign trade. But the third instrument which the Yugoslavs employ, namely the system of foreign exchange retention quotas, is much more potent. In the words of Schrenk and others (1979, 226): 'The right of enterprises to discretion in the disposition of their foreign exchange earnings has been the principal official device for export promotion since 1965.' This system has a number of peculiar characteristics, and it has also had an increasingly damaging effect on the whole economy. We shall therefore devote more space to its discussion than to the previously mentioned instruments.

The retention quota system goes back to the earliest days of self-management. Over the years, retention rates have been changed, and differences in the rates allowed to different industries have been adjusted, but the essential principle has been kept, that exporters are allowed to keep part of the foreign currency proceeds of their exports to be used at their own discretion.[33] A number of features of this system should be noted. First, the influence of the system is entirely dependent on the under-pricing of foreign exchange at official rates. If foreign exchange were freely convertible at a market-clearing rate, no one would want to retain foreign exchange except for speculative reasons. The influence of the retention ratio, and the strong attachment of Yugoslav enterprises and republican governments to the maintenance of the system, are proof that the dinar has been persistently overvalued, or at least that people expect it to be overvalued in the future. The retention ratio is like a drug, which has potent effects so long as the fundamental disease is uncured, but which would be of no value to a healthy organism.

The second main feature of the system is that it tries to place the responsibility for financing imports on the firms which use the imports.

[32] According to Granick (1975, 421) export subsidies in 1970 were equal to the 22 per cent of the total value of exports of industrial and mining products.

[33] According to Granick (1975, 422) export retention quotas vary widely, changing from year to year. They even differ for different firms within an industry. *Ekonomska politika* (30 September 1982, p. 7) reports that the retention ratio for processors of copper varies across republics from 24 per cent in Croatia to 40–50 per cent in Serbia.

Although retained foreign exchange can be sold, and is in fact sold at a black market rate, the main incentive to enterprises to obtain foreign exchange through the retention system is to pay for their essential imports. There is no doubt that this is a powerful means of putting pressure on enterprises to make a serious effort to export, and there seems to be a kind of justice about it. But eventually, as we shall see, it has the most undesirable consequences.

The practical effect of the foreign exchange retention system, like that of any administrative displacement of the price system, depends crucially on its rules of operation. It starts from the simple proposition that 'he who does not export, neither shall he import'. But what is meant by 'import' and 'export'? If the words refer only to *direct* imports and exports there will be a strong incentive for producers to export rather than supply the domestic market, and to buy 'home produced' materials and components rather than imported materials and components. This sounds excellent until it is recognized that the diversion of supplies from the home market to exports can sometimes cause serious damage to other domestic industries or to consumers.[34] It soon becomes obvious that the enterprises which are the final exporters are not alone responsible for producing the exported commodities, but are indebted—to greater or less degree—to those who supply them with their materials and components or, indeed, to those enterprises which supply the home market in order that they may have the privilege of supplying the foreign market. Equally, those who supply the home market may argue that they are doing so at the expense—to themselves—of withholding supplies for export. At the very least, if their products have an import content, they may insist that it is not they alone who should be responsible for finding the necessary foreign exchange but also their customers. If the logic is pursued far enough, it becomes clear that everyone in the economy is responsible to some degree for the total import bill, and everyone deserves to be rewarded to some degree for the results of the export drive.

The Yugoslavs have accepted the logic of joint responsibility for exports but not for imports. In the 1974 Constitution there was a hint—in Article 43—that all who contribute towards generating income through the export or import trade should share in the benefits. But it was a law of 1977 which created the institutional framework for collective responsibility for the balance of payments. The law provides for the establishment of communities of interest for foreign economic relations at federal level and in each republic and province, with representatives from enterprises, other communities of interest, economic chambers, banks, and other organizations. These bodies make plans for the balance of payments of each

---

[34] During the spring of 1982 two Yugoslav petroleum producers asked permission to export nearly one million tons of petroleum in order to cover their essential foreign exchange costs of oil exploration in Angola and spare parts for local oil drilling (*Ekonomska politika*, 1 March 1982, p. 11.) The absurdity of this proposal is, of course, that Yugoslavia is a major importer of petroleum and was suffering from an acute shortage at that time. Yet this is the kind of behaviour to which enterprises are logically driven by the foreign exchange retention system.

republic and province, as well as for the federation;[35] they allocate targets for exports and imports; they determine retention ratios; and they agree on the distribution of centrally controlled foreign exchange, i.e. the part which is not retained by enterprises, as well as that arising from workers' remittances and foreign grants and loans. One of their main tasks also is to supervise the conclusion of agreements ('self-management agreements') between final exporters and the domestic enterprises which supply them with materials, components, and services, directly and indirectly, for the division of retained foreign exchange.[36] But there is no provision for making similar agreements with domestic customers to share the foreign exchange cost of the import content of their supplies. Indeed, such arrangements are illegal.

The task of allocating retention ratios and then dividing the retained foreign exchange between the final exporter and its direct and indirect suppliers must be incredibly complex and arbitrary.[37] Moreover, since all these agreements are made within the framework of republican and provincial communities of interest, there is no simple way in which suppliers of materials or components from other republics or provinces can be compensated. The effect of the whole arrangement is to encourage regional autarky. According to *Borba* (26 April 1982) 'One republic exports and acquires foreign exchange while another imports the same goods, but at a considerably higher price.' It reports that a speaker at a 'round table' which the paper organized said that each republic and province has its own balance-of-payments position, which it clings to, despite the need for adjustments. It was also pointed out at the meeting that there is no organized system for ensuring that republics or enterprises which receive products from other republics or enterprises reimburse them for their import content. On another occasion, a delegate to the Federal Parliament from Montenegro said that 'each republic and province . . . has its own balance of payments. That is almost the legal position' (*Ekonomska politika*, 13 July 1981, p. 17). A delegate at the Third Congress of Self-Managers from a large enterprise which has factories in four republics described how, since the division of enterprises into basic organizations in 1976, each basic organization is obliged to work within its own republic's foreign exchange system. As a result, the foreign exchange earnings of the four factories can no longer be put at the disposal of the whole enterprise (*Ekonomska politika*, 22 June 1981, p. 11).

---

[35] The plans are not enforceable, merely indicative. Not surprisingly, they are usually not fulfilled.

[36] See OECD (1980, 38–9) and Tyson and Eichler (1981, 178).

[37] During 1981 more than 420 self-management agreements were made in Croatia for the distribution of foreign exchange between trade-linked enterprises (*Ekonomska politika*, 28 September 1981, p. 6). The paper also reports that in Yugoslavia as a whole 60 per cent of such agreements provide for the sale of foreign exchange at a rate above the official rate of exchange. The Governor of the National Bank of Yugoslavia himself admits that there is a black market for foreign exchange, often covered by self-management agreements (*Ekonomska politika*, 17 November 1980, p. 25).

Although enterprises selling on the home market are not legally entitled to demand any foreign exchange from their customers, this practice has been growing (*Ekonomska politika*, 7 September 1981, p. 12). 'In Vojvodina, many cases have been noted of basic organizations which blackmail others to provide foreign exchange, or loans on privileged terms, or to pay prices above the levels set by social compacts, in return for supplies of scarce raw materials and components' (*Borba*, 5 February 1982). In May 1982 the Zagreb newspaper *Vjesnik* was put under extreme pressure by its newsprint supplier to make partial payment for its supplies in foreign exchange. Deliveries were held up and the paper was reduced to three days' supply before some solution was found (*Vjesnik*, 8 May 1982). During 1980 the Croation producer of X-ray films, which is the sole domestic supplier of the whole Yugoslav market, was unable to obtain from the Croation community of interest enough foreign exchange to maintain its normal level of output. Supplies to hospitals in other republics were cut and X-ray examinations were postponed. In this way the other republics were put under pressure to allocate foreign exchange for this purpose (*Ekonomska politika*, 16 February 1981, pp. 27–8).

During the past few years the scarcity of foreign exchange has become so acute, and the arrangements for distributing it so unsatisfactory, that enterprises are beginning to resort to barter. The journal *Ekonomska politika* (22 February 1982, p. 7) reports that increasingly there are such stories as: 'If you want cellulose for your paper factory, you will get it on condition that you supply us with newsprint for newspapers in our region', or 'No oil, then no castings', or 'You can have our steel only in return for food'. On another occasion, it reported (8 March 1982, p. 7) that in Vojvodina cattle-breeders delivering animals for fattening demand 300 kg. of ready-mixed stockfeed, or 40 kg. of soyabean meal, or 12 kg. of fishmeal. More recently, a large enterprise which required cables was told that it could have them in return for copper. Fortunately, the firm was able to obtain the copper by supplying the copper producer with coal, which it produces itself (*Ekonomska politika*, 18 October 1982, p. 8). Even government authorities are reported to use this technique. In one locality of Vojvodina it was reported that peasants were being offered supplies of petrol by the government in return for maize (*Ekonomska politika*, 16 November 1981, p. 6).

The directors of enterprises, desperately trying to maintain production and to meet targets for supplies to home and export markets, are deeply disillusioned with the present system of allocating foreign exchange. The general director of a major steel firm, Peter Dodik, expressed his frustrations in the course of an interview with *Ekonomska politika* (19 April 1982, p. 23). 'When its a question of the foreign exchange system, it is completely irrational. We are a market economy. We have decided on that. Recent congresses have taken the same position. Therefore, we ought to develop further that concept of a market economy. But now there is more administration and étatistic involvement in that area than ever.' In other market economies, even when they have a shortage of foreign exchange, 'a firm can to go to the bank and buy foreign exchange, and does not have to walk around the country and waste hundreds or thousands of days, or write thousands of letters, in order to obtain foreign exchange, which in the end it fails to achieve anyway'.

Everyone in Yugoslavia now recognizes that the present system is inefficient and many would agree that it is inequitable. The official policy is, as it has been for many years, that the dinar should be fully convertible, i.e. that there should be a single free market price for dinars in terms of foreign exchange for use in current transactions. But there are two major obstacles to reaching this objective. The first arises from the nature of the self-management system itself. Because of the lack of facilities for encouraging new entry, competitive pressure on Yugoslav prices depends primarily on foreign competition. This means that, when the dinar is devalued, domestic prices quickly rise in the corresponding proportion, thus eliminating any price incentive to shift towards exports. Domestic prices could, of course, be held down by price controls; but experience has proved that price controls, except in the case of true monopoly, create other equally serious distortions.

The second obstacle arises from the special character of Yugoslavia and probably would not occur in more homogeneous countries. The system of retention ratios receives strong support from the local patriotism of the republics and provinces, more especially from the two republics—Slovenia and Croatia—which have the most favourable balance of payments. It was, indeed, the right of each republic to retain 'its own' foreign exchange receipts which was a central demand of the Croat nationalists in the late 1960s. When in 1981 a high-level working group, consisting among others of five members of the Federal Executive Committee (Council of Ministers) and the Governor of the National Bank, recommended the establishment of a unified foreign exchange market, to be operated through the National Bank, its report encountered strong opposition from Slovenia, where it was said that it was unconstitutional to compel enterprises to part with the foreign exchange which they had earned.[38] Whether this is true or not, the remarkable thing is that such an argument could be seriously discussed. Yugoslavia is probably the only country in the world where it could happen.

But the 'federal' argument for keeping the present system would wither away if the dinar were to be established at a realistic level, and people believed that that position would be held in the future. The only remaining method of achieving that objective seems to be the painful one of combining a sharp devaluation with a strong deflation of domestic demand, so as to push enterprises into sales on the export market. Measures announced in late 1982 for the year 1983 contain the latter ingredient, but it remains to be seen whether they will be fully implemented and whether they will be accompanied by an appropriate exchange policy.[39]

[38] Report in *Ekonomska politika*, 22 June, 1981, pp. 20–3.
[39] The remarkably tough proposals for 1983 include a reduction in total home demand of 10 per cent, with investment falling by 20 per cent, public expenditure by 10–12 per cent, and

3. HOUSING POLICY

This section is not intended to give a complete review of Yugoslav housing policy but rather to concentrate on problems of resource allocation in this area. Nevertheless, it will be useful to start with a short description of the factual background to housing policy.

The total stock of dwellings—both houses and flats, but excluding holiday homes, accommodation on business premises, and workers' barracks—increased from 3.5 million in 1951 to an estimated 6.3 million in 1980, of which dwellings in towns increased from 890,000 to 2.8 million while dwellings in rural areas increased from 2.6 million to 3.5 million.[40] In 1978, when the estimated total number of dwellings was 6.1 million, of which 2.7 million were in urban areas, the number of socially owned dwellings was 1.3 million (22 per cent of the total) and the number of privately owned dwellings nearly 4.8 million.[41] Most of the socially owned dwellings are in urban areas.

In the period 1971–80 nearly 1.4 million new dwellings were completed, of which 507,000 were in the social sector and 891,000 in the private sector.[42] Private dwellings are, on the average, larger than social sector dwellings but, because private owners often do much of the work themselves, and also make sure that money is not wasted, private dwellings cost less than social sector dwellings.[43] For dwellings completed in 1979 the cost per square metre was 6,231 dinars in the private sector and 11,356 in the social sector.[44] The average time taken to build a new social sector dwelling is normally about two years and for a private dwelling it is now nearly three years.[45] In 1978, the cost of a two-room social sector flat of 59.7 square metres was estimated to be 8.4 times average annual net personal income per worker in the social sector.[46] In 1982 it was reported that the current figure was 12 times average earnings.[47] As mentioned earlier, if a gross rent of 8 per cent of the capital cost were charged, this would absorb the entire personal income of one earner. The main reasons given for the extraordinarily high cost of housing in Yugoslavia, especially of social sector housing, are: the inclusion in the price of the dwelling of the cost of planning, road services, and connection with public utilities (nearly one-quarter of the total cost in 1978); shortages of materials, leading to high prices and delays in delivery; bad organization at all levels; and the building of costly tower blocks.

personal consumption by 6–7 per cent. This would make room for a 15–20 per cent rise in exports to convertible currency countries and a 13 per cent fall in imports from the same source. See *Ekonomska politika*, 15 November 1982, p. 5.

   [40] YB81, 119 – 17 and 119 – 18.
   [41] YB79, 119 – 17 and 119 – 18; *Yugoslav Survey*, February 1980, p. 49.
   [42] YB81, 102 – 23.
   [43] The average private dwelling completed in 1980 had an area of 76.3 square metres; the average social sector dwelling had an area of 60.9 square metres (YB81, 119 – 15).
   [44] YB81, 119 – 12 and 119 – 15.
   [45] YB81, 119 – 15 and 119 – 16.
   [46] *Yugoslav Survey*, February 1980, p. 45.
   [47] *Borba*, 16 July 1982.

Social sector houses are built mainly out of funds raised from social sector enterprises. The contribution rate is determined locally and varies between 6 and 8 per cent of gross personal income. The total amount collected in this way in 1978 was 37.5 billion dinars, which compares with total expenditure on new social sector housing in that year of 47.9 billion dinars.[48] Most of the balance was raised from bank credits. The funds set aside by enterprises are partly paid over to local communities of interest for housing, but mainly used by the enterprises to build dwellings for their own employees. They can build and rent directly, or build and sell to their employees, or lend an employee the deposit for building himself a dwelling. Dwellings and housing finance in the hands of enterprises are often used to attract workers with scarce skills, especially managers and technicians. But the use of housing money for this purpose causes discontent among other workers who have been waiting a long time for the allocation of an enterprise-owned flat.[49]

The average rent charged for a social sector flat is absurdly small. In 1974 it was less than one per cent of the cost of the dwelling.[50] In 1980 it was even less.[51] The average monthly rent of a social sector dwelling in 1980 was 467 dinars, equivalent to 4.6 per cent of the net income of a four-person worker's family.[52] The amount of rent collected is not even sufficient to cover depreciation and maintenance, and social sector housing, built at great expense, is allowed to deteriorate into 'a state of neglect and dilapidation'.[53] The only alternative is to provide even greater subsidies, on top of those already implicit in the provision of housing at such low rents. In New Belgrade a tower block with thirty floors has four lifts, and their maintenance is made possible only by a special subsidy from the local community of interest for housing equivalent to 53 per cent of the rent payable by the tenants.[54]

While the people who are fortunate enough to live in social sector dwellings are heavily subsidized, there is a long waiting list of people without a home of their own or with unsatisfactory housing. In 1978 the number on waiting lists was 522,100, equivalent to 13.4 per cent of workers in the social sector.[55] Many of these people live in crowded conditions with

---

[48] *Yugoslav Survey*, February 1980, p. 40.

[49] If the levy on gross personal income is 6 per cent, bank credit adds another 3 per cent, and a flat costs 12 times annual average net personal income (equivalent to 9 times annual average gross personal income), one in a hundred of the work-force can expect to receive a new flat in the course of a year. If the levy is 8 per cent, the chance increases to 1.3 per cent.

[50] *Yugoslav Survey*, August 1975, p. 102.

[51] Average rent per square metre in that year was 7.66 dinars per month (YB81, 112 – 9); the cost of social sector dwellings completed in the year was 52.1 billion dinars (YB81, 119 – 12); and the total area of social sector dwellings completed in the year was 2,969 thousand square metres (YB81, 119 – 15). This gives an annual rent of 0.52 per cent of the cost.

[52] Rent as above. Family income from YB81, 108 – 8.

[53] *Yugoslav Survey*, February 1980, p. 49.

[54] *Ekonomska politika*, 1 March 1982, p. 17.

[55] *Yugoslav Survey*, February 1980, p. 46.

their relatives. Others become sub-tenants, paying as much as 12 times the normal rent and up to half their income, especially in the large cities.[56] The resulting distribution of benefits is highly inequitable. Some people with social sector dwellings rent them to sub-tenants and make a large profit on the arrangement, while others, often young people, are forced to pay exorbitant rents.[57] In the words of *Ekonomska politika* (17 May 1982, pp. 20–2): 'In our society, getting a flat is the greatest privilege compared with those who fail to achieve this. It creates the greatest social and economic difference among workers.' Moreover, the people who get social sector flats are, on the average, those with higher incomes, as shown by a Zagreb survey (ibid.). Tenants of good flats in central locations often pay little more rent than others, thus adding to the privileges of a small minority.[58]

From what has been said above, which is based on frank criticisms expressed by the Yugoslavs themselves, it is obvious that Yugoslav housing policy is in a state of confusion. The main sources of inefficiency within the social sector are the wasteful use of capital, and inequities in the distribution of benefits. The latter aspect may be regarded by some people as falling outside the topic of allocation of resources. But, since the windfall benefits arising from existing housing policy are at best randomly distributed and at worst the result of personal or political influence, they are contrary to the approved principle of distribution of income, which is meant to be based on 'work and the results of work'. In that sense, therefore, they are also an example of the misallocation of resources.

The first step towards a more efficient use of resources would be to raise rents at least to the level where they provide sufficient funds for proper maintenance of the existing stock of social sector housing. In the case of some of the older buildings, as suggested in an article in *Vjesnik* (6 May 1982), it might be even better to offer to sell them to their tenants (presumably at a sufficiently low price to make the offer attractive). In all countries, owner-occupiers take more care of their dwellings than tenants, and are prepared to spend more on their maintenance than they would wish to pay for this purpose in rent. They are also more efficient in their use of such resources. Indeed, the more that the Yugoslav authorities shift available funds towards the encouragement of private housing or housing co-operatives, the more economically such funds are likely to be employed.[59]

---

[56] *Ekonomska politika*, 9 March 1981, p. 23 and 17 May 1982, p.22.

[57] *Borba* (13 November 1982) reports the case of a worker in Rijeka who was given a flat in 1977. Since he already had a social sector flat in Pula, he sub-let the Rijeka flat for a 'fat rent'. Later, he wanted to raise the rent further and the tenant and his family were 'thrown out on the street'. This kind of thing, says the paper, is happening everywhere.

[58] *Ekonomska politika*, 13 September 1982, pp. 18–20.

[59] A social compact of December 1977 included provision for the encouragement of private purchases of social sector houses and flats but, at least up to early 1980, it had little effect (*Yugoslav Survey*, February 1980, p. 44). The same article (ibid.) alleges that housing co-operatives are discriminated against in the allocation of sites, licences to build and credits, and through special taxation.

Secondly, the cost of new building needs to be reduced by faster official decision-making, encouragement of greater competition in the construction industry and, above all, by reducing the excessive pressure of demand on the industry.[60] This means reducing the demand for both housing and non-housing construction. The present output of dwellings (of about 140,000 a year) would be enough to eliminate excess demand for social sector housing within three or four years, if it were concentrated in the towns. The trouble is that a large proportion of these dwellings are holiday homes and weekend houses, which are second (or third) houses for people who already have a social sector flat.[61] Much of the finance for this form of investment comes from the savings of people working temporarily abroad, who might be willing to put their money instead into the foundation of small businesses, if they had confidence that the growth of such enterprises would not be frustrated. The construction component of business investment would be smaller than in housing, and the long-term employment and output effects of investment in businesses instead of houses would be very valuable. This is a problem which will be discussed further in Chapter 13.

4. EFFECTS OF SELF-MANAGEMENT ON ALLOCATIVE EFFICIENCY

An attempt will be made in this section to identify the misallocations of resources which are due to the existence of a self-management system, distinguishing so far as possible between the effects of the system as such and the effects of the Yugoslav environment.

The mobility of resources between firms, industries, and regions would be restricted by any kind of labour-management system in which the workers received part or all of the product of capital or other resources. The degree of restriction on mobility would be smaller in a Mondragon-type co-operative system than in a Yugoslav-type co-operative system, because in the former case much of the product of capital is distributed to individual members' capital accounts. In the Yugoslav system, however, there are substantial obstacles to labour mobility, to the mobility of enterprise savings and, consequently, to the mobility of enterprise know-how. These obstacles are further increased by the Yugoslav decentralized political system, which has the effect of restricting mobility of bank credit and creating a general bias towards autarky.

A Mondragon-type co-operative does not have a significant bias towards capital-intensive investment, but a Yugoslav-type co-operative, in which labour earnings incorporate part of the product of capital, does have such a

[60] The last measure has already been achieved in 1981, and will continue for at least another year or two, as part of the 'stabilization measures' required to check inflation and to strengthen the balance of payments. But, in the longer term, unless the capital-using bias of the Yugoslav system is curbed, excess demand for construction is likely to re-emerge, and Yugoslavia will become again, as a popular saying has it, 'the largest building site in Europe'.

[61] It is estimated that there are 332,000 weekend cottages and holiday homes, and that 5.5 per cent of households own one. At the same time, 90,000 families live in barracks, and 460,000 are sub-tenants (*Borba*, 12 December 1982).

bias. There is, also, a further difference. Members of a Mondragon-type co-operative can expect some assistance in times of difficulty from the *Caja Laboral Popular*; but the amount of such assistance will be limited, since it can only be given at the expense of the members of other co-operatives. In Yugoslavia, on the other hand, assistance to enterprises in difficulty comes mainly from the government, which is regarded by most people as having some kind of inexhaustible resources, or the ability to conjure resources from nowhere by expansion of bank credits. This 'socialization of risks' reduces the sense of responsibility of Yugoslav workers for the investment decisions of their enterprise; and this tendency is further accentuated by the high degree of political interference in Yugoslav enterprise decisions, which is partly the result of political decentralization but mainly the result of the one-party system.

These special Yugoslav characteristics are also responsible for the deplorable muddle in the allocation of foreign exchange. This is an area where the contradiction between self-management and a one-party state is especially acute. It is raised to an even higher level by the federalization of Yugoslavia. But clearly none of this would be necessary in a more unitary state with a democratic multi-party system and an agreed policy of 'self-management *laissez-faire*'. There remains, however, a crucial question whether a society in which self-management was accepted as the dominant, or even universal, form of industrial organization would ever come into existence, or continue to exist, without a one-party state. If not, self-management *laissez-faire* would be an unattainable ideal.

Finally, the problems of Yugoslav housing policy are entirely political in origin and in no obvious way created by the existence of a self-management system. The irresponsible attitude towards the management of capital, the obstruction of private business investment as an alternative to investment in private housing, and the lack of political courage in tackling the problem of low rents all stem either from ideological considerations or from the political weakness of a one-party regime.

CHAPTER 11

ORGANIZATIONAL EFFICIENCY

It is sometimes claimed that self-managed enterprises will be more efficient than either capitalist or state socialist enterprises.[1] The argument rests on the assumption that the very nature of a self-managed enterprise gives workers a motive to work efficiently and well. But organizational efficiency depends on other factors besides inner motivation. These include the system of incentives and the system of management.

This chapter is divided into two sections. In the first, we shall start by considering the motivation argument. This will be followed by an examination of the Yugoslav system of monetary incentives. The section will be completed with an assessment of the influence of other institutional arrangements on the level of efficiency of workers in Yugoslav self-managed enterprises. The second section will be concerned with the efficiency of Yugoslav managers. The topics to be covered include their recruitment, responsibilities, and powers, and their attitudes to their work. The section concludes with some comments on the importance of good management and the difficulty of reconciling it with self-management.

1. THE EFFICIENCY OF WORKERS UNDER SELF-MANAGEMENT

The motivation argument

The argument that workers in self-managed enterprises have a stronger motive for working efficiently than under capitalism or state socialism arises from the belief that there are some types of changes in worker-efficiency which cannot be measured by supervisors. If work output is easily measured or payment is made on a piecework basis, there is no obvious reason why workers in self-managed enterprises should work better than those in capitalist or state socialist enterprises. After this, the argument divides into two parts. In the first part, it is pointed out that a single self-employed person can accurately estimate the effects on his income of variations in his work effort and efficiency, and will adjust his efforts accordingly. He will work hard and well if the marginal return from better work more than compensates for the marginal effort, and vice versa. No output is lost simply because of unsatisfactory organizational arrange-

[1] See, for example, Vanek (1970, Chapter 12) and Horvat (1982, Chapter 6).

ments. It is then argued that, since a co-operative is a partnership of self-employed people, the same result should apply.

But, as soon as a partnership grows beyond a fairly small size, certainly beyond about twenty members, the marginal return to the individual member from increasing his work effort becomes insignificantly small. For example, in a twenty-member co-operative with equal division of income a worker who increases the enterprise income by £100 by an unmeasurable increase in his efficiency obtains a reward of only £5 (or less if taxes or social security contributions are levied on the extra income). The practical effects of this motivation, therefore, are likely to be extremely small or negligible in enterprises of the size typical in Yugoslavia.[2]

The second part of the argument is that there can be, in appropriate circumstances, a 'social' motive for work. This motive is clearly important in wartime, or in peacetime emergencies, when large numbers of people respond willingly to the call for sacrifice. This kind of social solidarity can achieve remarkable results, and one of the most pleasing things about it is that most people enjoy making efforts and sacrifices in the common cause. From an economist's point of view, if this kind of voluntary effort could be enlisted to raise productive efficiency, it would have everything to be said for it. By some kind of institutional change, presumed to be costless, output per unit of input would be increased, as if by magic. It would be a clear refutation of the maxim that 'there is no such thing as a free lunch'. Appeals for mass solidarity and sacrifice have played some part in the early post-revolutionary stages of economic development in communist countries. But, after at most one or two decades, they lose their effect. The argument is, however, that in a self-managed enterprise this social motive will continue to play an important role.

There may well be some truth in this argument, provided that one makes explicit the implicit assumption that, in the move from a capitalist to a self-management system, *other things remain equal*. Experience teaches that in the long run voluntary efforts of solidarity are vulnerable to the 'free rider' phenomenon, i.e. some people keep working hard while others take it easy but continue to enjoy the benefits of the collective effort. Once this begins to happen, *and nothing is done to stop it*, collective morale begins to crumble, and eventually cynicism takes over. The ultimate outcome may even turn out to be worse than if no collective effort had been made in the first place.

Thus, to be effective for more than a short period, solidarity needs to be accompanied by a system of discipline. The free rider has to be punished. For a while, in wartime, solidarity can be combined with tough discipline

---

[2] In 1973, before the movement to divide enterprises into basic organizations had gathered full momentum, the number of enterprises ('work organizations') in the productive sector employing less than 30 workers was 21 per cent of the total, and in industry only 8 per cent. In 1979, after the re-organization, the corresponding proportions were 18 per cent and 6 per cent (YB75, 107 – 9 and YB81, 113 – 1). The percentage of workers in organizations employing less than 30 workers was, of course, much smaller: in 1979, about 1.4 per cent and 0.4 per cent respectively.

without destroying the sense of voluntary sacrifice for the common good. But in peacetime this is more difficult. In any case, appeals to solidarity which are not accompanied by a strong system of discipline for slackers will almost certainly fail. Tyson (1979) has suggested that control of the free rider problem in a co-operative may be achieved by an implicit threat to the free rider that, if he persists in working badly, everyone else will retaliate by doing the same. But this threat is surely an empty one; one cannot think of any example of its application. It is surely a misreading of the psychology of free riders to believe that they would reform their behaviour simply because other people threatened to follow their example.[3]

The free rider problem is probably less acute in a Mondragon-type co-operative, which consists of carefully selected and ideologically committed workers, who also make their personal contributions to the capital fund of the co-operative. The majority of members in such a co-operative is more likely to take a strong stand on questions of discipline; there is a real risk to a persistent free rider that he will be excluded from membership.[4] In Yugoslavia, however, where all workers except those working on small farms or in artisan activities are obligatorily incorporated into self-managed organizations, there is no personal or ideological selection of members. Partly for this reason, but partly also because workers are in any case reluctant to discipline their fellow-workers, there are elaborate rules about disciplinary procedure. Managers have been deprived of their disciplinary powers, and even of the right to offer merit awards or promotions to workers whom they consider to deserve encouragement. A manager may bring a proposal for disciplinary action to the elected committee, but he has no guarantee that it will be accepted. If he fails, it discourages him from attempting to apply disciplinary measures in future. He will tend to wash his hands of the matter and throw the responsibility for poor discipline back on to the workers, where it legally belongs. The consequence is, as we shall see later, that Yugoslav organizations are full of free riders.

The pay system

In the absence of an effective disciplinary system to support a social motive for efficient work, the main work incentive in Yugoslavia is the same as it is in other countries, namely, monetary payment for work done. The Yugoslav pay system, however, is unsatisfactory in a number of ways.

---

[3] As Michael Conte pointed out, in commenting on Tyson's article, Tyson is implicitly assuming that workers are able to monitor each other's performance, although the management are unable to do so. There may be some kinds of work for which this is true, although surely not for all.

[4] Thomas and Logan (1982, 35) report that a strike in 1974 in the large Ulgor co-operative in Mondragon was followed by the dismissal of 17 workers by the supervisory board. After an 'acrimonious' discussion at an extraordinary general meeting of the work-force, this decision was endorsed by a 60 per cent majority. Despite the occurrence of a considerable number of strikes in Yugoslav enterprises, there is no known example where workers have been dismissed for striking.

The standard formula used to define the right to personal income in the social sector is that income should be determined by 'work and the results of work'. According to Horvat (1976, 184) the second part of this phrase was added on the suggestion of Raškovic and others 'that the principle of distribution according to work be replaced by a more appropriate principle of distribution "according to the results of work".' Unfortunately, however, the Yugoslavs compromised by including both criteria.[5] Since distribution according to work presumably means trying to measure the input of work effort, while distribution according to the results of work means trying to measure the product of labour, the two criteria can easily give different answers.[6] It may be argued that, since the amount of work done is influenced by the supply side of the labour market and the results of work determine the amount of labour demanded, the formula may be interpreted as saying that labour income should be determined by the supply and demand for labour. But, for ideological reasons, it is difficult for Yugoslav economists to put the matter in precisely that way. As a consequence non-economists, including the workers themselves, have no clear conception about how their incomes should be determined. Not only is there confusion between work and the results of work, but there is no clear statement in Yugoslavia about the meaning of the latter phrase.[7] Since 'bourgeois' economics is ultimately suspect, the concept of the marginal product, although accepted by many Yugoslav economists, receives no official recognition. Instead, official thinking is dominated by Marxist concept of the average product of labour, and any attempt to show the illogical and practically undesirable effects of its use would be frowned on.[8]

Consider, for example, two enterprises A and B, each of which produces approximately the same product, with similar technology and a similar skill-composition of its labour force. Enterprise A has a large amount of capital equipment per worker and a good management. Enterprise B has less equipment per worker, or less modern equipment, and a poor management. Income produced per worker in A is twice as great as in B. Does it follow that workers in A should be paid twice as much as in B?

The Yugoslavs have never been able to find a precise anwer to this question. To judge by the frequent comments of economists and politicians on income differences between workers of similar skill doing similar jobs in different enterprises, they start from the assumption that such incomes should be equal. But they would no doubt agree that workers of equal skill

[5] Stojanović (1982, 35) has pointed out that the poor regions favour payment according to work, while the richer regions favour payment according to the results of work. The official doctrine gives equal support to both sides.

[6] Most Yugoslav economists are aware that the official formula is full of contradictions.

[7] An article in *Borba* (27 July 1982) points out that, while the principle of payment according to the results of work is constantly repeated, the trade unions do not know what it means. Hence they are constantly asking that someone should establish 'criteria' for income payments.

[8] For a useful summary of Marxist views on the distribution of income under socialism, as well as Soviet practice, see Chilosi (1978).

may not all be equally effficient or hard-working. So some allowance would need to be made for such differences. It is also official doctrine that workers in enterprises which are better managed deserve to receive more pay. For, under the self-management system, the workers are theoretically responsible for major business decisions; and, if these decisions turn out to be right, the workers should benefit from them. Thus we have the following factors which justify differences in pay: (1) skill, (2) efficiency and intensity of work, and (3) quality of self-management decisions.[9] Implicitly, we are left with a long list of factors which do not justify differences in pay. These include natural resources, stock of capital (but see below on this), 'know-how', market power, 'speculation' (but efficiency in buying and selling should surely count), arbitrary interventions by the administrative superstructure (price control, foreign exchange retention quotas, allocations of credit), and pure luck.[10]

As regards the stock of capital, there is an official doctrine that workers who have contributed to enterprise saving deserve to receive a benefit from so doing. This stems from the Marxist view that capital is really saved-up labour (*minuli rad*). But there is no clear statement about how much benefit should be received. Are workers allowed to receive interest or profit on their saved-up labour? To agree to such a proposition would be to open up a major ideological debate. Alternatively, if workers are allowed only to receive back the value of their saved-up labour, i.e. the capital component, this runs contrary to the rule that once enterprise income has been accumulated it must be kept intact. The problem of what to do about *minuli rad* is still unresolved.[11]

It is clear from the list of factors which can legitimately influence

[9] Article 116 of the Associated Labour Act lists the following criteria for determining the total sum available for payment of personal incomes: 'the level of productivity of [the workers'] own labour', 'the success achieved in the management of and doing business with resources', 'the application of scientific achievements in production and the organization of work', and 'adjustment of activities of the basic organizations to market conditions and/or the socially-agreed division of labour'. Article 126 gives the following criteria for determining the individual worker's income: 'the results of his labour', 'the contribution he has personally made with his current labour', and 'the management of and doing business with social resources'. Article 129 states that 'a worker's labour contribution shall be determined in accordance with the quantity and quality of work, account being taken in particular of the extent and complexity of work, the quality of the results achieved, efficiency in the utilization of the instruments of labour, economics in labour, utilization of working time, responsibility in work and conditions in which he works'.

[10] Article 111 of the Associated Labour Act requires that 'the part of income of a basic organization which is the result of work performed under exceptionally favourable natural conditions, which is the result of exceptionally favourable circumstances on the market or the result of other exceptionally favourable circumstances in income earning' must be separately determined. Article 124 requires that such income shall be reinvested in the enterprise or, if provided by law, in other enterprises in the commune, republic or province. No method is suggested for ensuring that these funds do not simply replace funds which would otherwise be reinvested.

[11] Although *minuli rad* was given some legal basis in the 1974 Constitution, attempts to frame a draft law on the subject, which have been going on for several years, have not so far been successful.

personal income, together with the other list of factors which are not supposed to influence personal income, that the correct determination of the level of personal income is an impossible task. How, for example, is one to distinguish between the effects of good management and the effects of market power, or 'speculation'? How is one to assess the impact of administrative decisions? And, even if these effects could be excluded, how is one to determine what part of total income is due to natural resources, the stock of capital, and the contribution of labour? If the answer to all these questions is that workers of equal skill should receive the same income in all enterprises, and that all surpluses or deficits after subtracting this amount should have no effect on the level of personal income, then the whole object of self-management as an economic system is lost. The incentives to work better or more efficiently, and to take better management decisions, disappear. If, on the other hand, one starts from the other end and tries to estimate and subtract the effects of each of the illegitimate factors, one would certainly find oneself in a thicket of problems to which there are no objective answers. An attempt to impose arbitrary answers would arouse fierce disputes, and again undermine the incentive basis of the self-management system.

In the absence of a satisfactory theoretical basis for determining the level of personal income, Yugoslav enterprises pay out as much income as they can, given the market, political, and administrative constraints to which they are subject. The result is that personal income per worker varies widely between enterprises apparently doing similar work.[12] At the same time, there is considerable pressure to compress differentials within enterprises.[13] From an incentive point of view, therefore, Yugoslavia has the worst of both worlds: too many people enjoy rents arising from enterprise advantages to which they have not contributed, and too few are paid differentials within their enterprises which would encourage harder, better, or more efficient work. This leads to feelings of injustice, cynicism, and alienation—quite the opposite of the attitudes which a self-management system is supposed to generate.

Many ambitious and hard-headed young people in Yugoslavia seem to have accepted the following guidelines. First, make sure of the best qualifications available to you. Second, join the Party. Thirdly, use family and other connections in order to get a job in a well-paying and dynamic enterprise. Finally, do not work too hard, but reserve your energies for political and semi-political activities which bring you into contact with influential people. Fortunately, not everyone is as clever and unscrupulous as this. At the bottom of the social structure there are large numbers of

[12] The Slovenian economist Franc Černe recently quoted a range of 2.4 to 1 for similar work in Slovenia (*Ekonomska politika*, 15 November 1982, p. 25). The range in other republics may well be greater.

[13] Another economist, Dragoje Žarković, from Vojvodina, said at the same discussion: 'There is an increasing tendency to equalize individual incomes within working collectives' and 'Creative and productive work in this country is relatively more and more poorly rewarded' (ibid., p. 23).

semi-skilled workers, often of recent peasant origin, who are paid on a piecework basis. These workers carry a disproportionate share of the load. Without their efforts, the economic performance of the country would be much reduced. At the other end of the scale, there are some able and hard-working managers and technicians, who are motivated mainly by a desire to do a good job. In many ways, as we shall see, the system seems to be designed to discourage good managers and reduce their effectiveness. But, fortunately, the system does not always follow the lines suggested in political rhetoric, and many good managers are allowed to get on with their jobs.

Three specific problems of the Yugoslav pay system are so far unresolved. The first is what to do about enterprises which make losses. A loss occurs if the enterprise's annual accounts show that its income has been insufficient to pay the personal incomes already advanced, or the statutorily guaranteed amounts for periods for which no advances have already been made.[14] The enterprise can draw on its own reserves to cover a loss, and it may also receive a contribution from collective reserves. It also has an obligation to 'eliminate' the causes of the difficulties, for which purpose the local commune will intervene to make recommendations and to offer help, possibly by reducing taxes and contributions, possibly by arranging additional bank credits. If in spite of this the problems continue, 'the competent organ of the socio-political community shall institute proceedings for the [enterprise's] liquidation'.[15] In practice, however, this rarely happens, especially in the case of larger enterprises. Economists, and even politicians, constantly deplore the effect of this laxity in applying the law on the sense of responsibility of workers and managers. As mentioned earlier, the Commission on Problems of Economic Stabilization has expressed opposition to 'the prejudice or dogma that no organization should be allowed to fail'.[16] The problem is, however, that there has already been so much administrative intervention in the affairs of enterprises that the workers in an enterprise which is bankrupted would have a good case for blaming the government rather than themselves.

The second problem is the lack of proper pay discrimination within enterprises between good and bad workers. Self-management combines with one-party rule to create a strong pressure in favour of egalitarianism. The President of the Zagreb City Conference of the Socialist Alliance said recently: 'When our workers go abroad they are all good and disciplined workers. Clearly, there is something wrong here in the organization of work, in the sense of duty and responsibility. The trouble is too much egalitarianism' (*Borba*, 28 July 1982). The Commission on Problems of Economic Stabilization also points to the bad influence of another aspect of egalitarianism, namely, absolute job-security for those already in jobs.[17]

[14] Associated Labour Act, Article 154.
[15] Associated Labour Act, Article 160.
[16] Report on the 'basic prerequisites' of stabilization, *Borba*, special supplement, 27 April 1982, p. 23.
[17] Ibid., p. 30.

The third problem is how to measure changes in the productivity of labour over time. This is a crucial issue for determining changes in relative incomes in different enterprises or industries, and also for deciding how much of current increases in personal incomes is justifiable on grounds of an increase in productivity and how much is the result of inflation. The chief obstacle to clarity in discussing these problems in Yugoslavia is that there is no explicit recognition of the fact that the income at the disposal of enterprises is influenced by changes in both the volume of output (strictly, of real net value added) and the price of output. Relative prices are often implicitly assumed to be constant, so that real income per worker in each enterprise should be solely related to real product per worker. But what matters in a market economy is not only how much is produced but also the price at which the output can be sold (and the prices at which inputs can be bought). In a fully competitive economy the proper measure of the income available for distribution to the work-force is net value added in current prices, after deducting interest on capital. In that case, the debate about whether workers are receiving incomes proportional to 'work and the results of work' becomes redundant. The competitive market ensures that this will always be true. But there is no guarantee that workers' incomes in different enterprises will move in proportion to changes in their productivity. Any attempt in a self-managed economy to force relative incomes to move in line with relative productivity leads to absurd results. Yet the standard complaint by the Yugoslav authorities is that enterprises are not keeping their income payments in line with changes in *their own* productivity.

In general, the Yugoslav pay system is not well designed to give maximum incentives for worker efficiency. Differences between enterprises appear to the workers to be arbitrary and unfair; enterprises which make losses are kept going at the expense of more successful enterprises; idlers are paid as much as good workers; good management and creative work is not sufficiently rewarded; and there are innumerable interventions from outside which prevent enterprises from selling on a free market and using the income produced in ways of their own choosing. Much of the trouble stems from the nature of a self-management system; but the situation is made worse by the inability of a one-party regime to refrain from constant intervention in enterprise affairs.

The only logical way to ensure that workers in a market economy are paid in accordance with the results of their work is to maintain a convincing threat of competitive new entry and a competitive labour market. It would not be impossible for a self-managed system to meet the first condition, but it would require a radical rethinking of Yugoslav doctrine to meet the second.

The efficiency effects of other institutions

One of the institutional arrangements of Yugoslav life which arouses the surprise of a foreign visitor is the hours of work. The standard hours are 42 a week, usually arranged in the form of five days of eight hours, plus one

Saturday in four. But for most workers these hours run from 6 a.m. to 2 p.m. or from 7 a.m. to 3 p.m. Many workers travel long distances to work; some have to take children to crèches on the way. A great many must leave home at 5 a.m., without having a proper breakfast. After a few hours of work they have a half-hour break during which many factories provide a hot meal. Others, however, give their workers meal coupons for use in outside cafes or restaurants (some of which are alleged to be disposed of for cash). Thus the working day is not really eight hours but $7^1/_2$, probably less when the practical difficulties of serving a hot meal to a large number of people in a half-hour break are taken into account. By about mid-day most workers are getting tired and hungry, and productivity declines. The main meal of the day is taken after work, at 3 or 4 p.m.

This arrangement of the working day, which already existed before the First World War, seems to be designed to depress productivity. It encourages lateness, absenteeism, and real or reported sickness. The early start, frequently on an empty stomach, together with the low price of alcohol, encourages workers to take a few drinks to keep themselves going. A successful director of a large enterprise in Sarajevo has expressed strong opposition to starting work so early, and recommended starting instead at 9 a.m. 'like the rest of the world'.[18] But the great majority of workers are opposed to any change.[19] A major reason for this attitude is that many workers have two jobs. The present arrangement of hours in social sector jobs is ideal for making room for second jobs. But the effect on productivity in the main job is very unsatisfactory. Worker-peasants, for example, who constitute about 30 per cent of workers in social sector employment, often travel each day from their farms, leave home earlier than other workers and, in effect, do two jobs. Their productivity in their social sector jobs is estimated to be 8–14 per cent less than that of other workers.[20] For many other workers, also, the concentration of social sector hours in the early part of the day, together with almost absolute job security in social sector employment, must encourage a tendency to devote their thoughts to ways in which they can develop their secondary activities.

The Yugoslav arrangement of hours of work is in no way necessary for a self-management system. But the self-management system itself is an obstacle to the full use of working time. According to Schrenk (1981, 72) it was estimated some years ago that 'in one of the most successful enterprises of the country the loss of worktime for self-management and related matters was in excess of 10% of the number of total working hours'.[21] Zukin (1975, 211) gives an example of the disruption of work in a Belgrade liberal arts college when the secretaries in the administration departed for a meeting. Everyone who wanted to see the secretaries had to

[18] Paper by E. Blum, in Broekmeyer (1970, 184).
[19] When votes are taken, about 80 per cent vote in favour of retaining the existing system.
[20] See Stipetić (1981, 281).
[21] An ILO report (1981, 79) refers to a study of a Rijeka ship-building yard in which, on the average, 26.8 working days were spent in a year on self-management business. This is apart from meetings held outside official hours.

wait for two hours. Then it was announced that the meeting would continue indefinitely and 'office hours for the day are cancelled'. Similarly, a shop in a seaside resort, which is normally open from 6 a.m. to 6 p.m., had a notice at noon to say that it was shut because of a meeting until 2.30 p.m.[22] In the early days of self-management, meetings of the workers' council used to take place after hours. But by that time the workers were tired and hungry. Participation was poor and attendance fell. Now such meetings are held in working hours. In addition, there are general meetings of the whole staff, meetings of various committees, and meetings of the trade union, the youth organization, and the Party. Party meetings are sometimes held in working hours, but the practice seems to vary.[23]

Self-management, at least in Yugoslav conditions, leads to a considerable slackening of work discipline. Management has been deprived of disciplinary powers, which are under the control of an elected disciplinary committee.[24] According to Schrenk (1981, 50) frequently quoted examples of disciplinary problems include drinking during working hours, brawls, unpunctuality, and refusal to carry out assigned work. Dismissals are rare: in one enterprise employing 1,400 workers they averaged 3–4 a year. The complicated procedure for bringing up disciplinary matters and the reluctance of elected committees to impose severe penalties leads to a general condition of slackness among the hourly paid workers.[25] This is reflected in the high rate of absence on grounds of sickness. According to *Ekonomska politika* (2 November 1981, p. 7) at harvest time many workers report sick in order to go and work in the fields, thus supplementing their incomes. The paper alleges that Yugoslavia is 'the most sick nation in the world'. In addition, workers often arrive late, leave early, and take time off during the day for shopping and other purposes.[26]

---

[22] An ironic article in *Borba* (18 April 1982) describes how the writer has found a solution to the problem of too many meetings. It may be summarized as follows. 'There are only 24 hours in the day, but every day I have to attend 25 meetings lasting 2 hours each. So the day is too short. One suggestion is to go only for a few minutes to each meeting. But, if the meeting-places are not close together, that does not solve the problem. So I am forming a co-operative with four other people. We shall divide the meetings between us and specialize. In this way we can reduce the number of meetings which we each attend to 5 a day.'

[23] According to *Borba* (30 December 1982) a ship-building yard in Split, employing 6,000 workers, decided in the summer of 1982 that in future all meetings except mass meetings and 'production meetings' should be held after hours. Some workers argued that, in that case, people attending such meetings should be paid overtime, but the majority rejected that proposal. It remains to be seen what the effect will be on attendance at meetings.

[24] Schrenk (1981, 5) reports that operational management has not only no control over hiring and firing, but also no power 'to mete out discretionary rewards and penalties, including disciplinary measures'.

[25] An elected delegate has little incentive to impose strict discipline on his fellow-workers. The benefit to himself of excluding an inefficient worker is small. In return, he is likely to incur hostility from a large number of others. He is only temporarily a member of the disciplinary committee and will later have to resume his normal position as an ordinary worker. Management and discipline are not his permanent job, nor is he paid to fill that role.

[26] The director of a large enterprise in Slavonski Brod was reported by *Borba* (4 December 1982) as saying: 'We have created the possibility of such "free" attitudes to work and work

In the autumn of 1982, when there was a shortage of petrol and other goods in the shops, it was reported (*Ekonomska politika*, 13 September 1982, p. 6) that the trade unions had appealed to the workers not to leave work in order to queue up for these items. *Borba* (9 February 1982) reported on the situation in a bus company in Montenegro which constantly runs at a loss. Among the 280 workers there is much indiscipline and vandalism. Drivers often refuse to drive. Conductors fail to come to work. Much of the equipment in the workshop has been stolen. This is obviously 'self-management' at its worst.

Total time lost in Yugoslav enterprises is officially recognized to be excessive. Annual holidays are from 3 to 6 weeks; public holidays add another $1^1/_2$ weeks; sickness adds about 3 weeks; self-management and other meetings perhaps 5 weeks; the break for meals also perhaps 5 weeks (say three-quarters of an hour a day); and absenteeism and lateness perhaps 3 weeks. This comes to about 40 per cent of standard working hours and fits with the estimate in *Borba* (22 July 1982) that on the average workers do not work more than 5 hours a day. A peasant delegate from Montenegro to the Twelfth Congress of the League of Communists went even further when he said: 'Now we know that in factories people work only four or five hours a day' (*Borba*, 14 July 1982).[27]

It is not surprising that there are many complaints about the effects on output of inadequate discipline. The President of the Presidency of the Socialist Republic of Montenegro, in an interview with *Vjesnik* (31 October 1981), said:

It is necessary to say that we have at present a large amount of absence from work. But one part of organizations works well. If it were not so, we would not have what we do have. It is a bad thing that some people work while others do not work. Because of that lack of consistency one person exploits another, whether it be within the productive sector or in society as a whole.

The President of the Council of the Croatian Federation of Trade Unions is reported as having said (*Vjesnik*, 14 October 1981) that slackers are able to hide behind existing rules, and that disciplinary proceedings are dragged out. It is necessary to reduce the room for manœuvre, and this requires some changes in the law. The strengthening of work discipline is of decisive importance for economic stabilization. A resolution of the Federal Conference of the Socialist Alliance (*Borba*, 5 August 1982) stated bluntly: 'It is necessary to make a sharp distinction between work and slacking, between workers and slackers. By a quick removal of slackers room is

obligations that it is normal for many workers to arrive late, go out on private business, leave early, read newspapers during working hours (sometimes even novels), leave their workbenches and refuse any job which is not in their job description.'

[27] The report on 'basic prerequisites' for stabilization by the Commission on Problems of Economic Stabilization contains an estimate that 30 per cent of workers in the social sector are not fully occupied (*Borba*, special supplement, 27 April 1982, p. 29). It is not clear whether this is in addition to time lost. According to *Ekonomska politika* (22 November 1982, p. 23) 10–20 per cent of workers in the social sector are 'clearly economically and technologically redundant'.

created for new productive employment'. *Ekonomska politika* (10 May 1982, p. 18) makes the same point, and adds: 'Every day one can hear and read about cases where outside pressure prevents the management of enterprises from getting rid of slackers.'

2. THE EFFICIENCY OF MANAGEMENT

Recruitment

The system of appointment of directors of enterprises was described in Chapter 7. The selection committee consists of an equal number of representatives of the workers' council, the local commune, and the trade union organization in the enterprise, and the post must be advertised for open competition. In theory, the committee draws up a short list of recommended candidates (by a two-thirds majority) and the workers' council makes the final choice. In practice, however, the selection committee usually recommends only one candidate, indeed in at least 80 per cent of cases only one person applies for the job.[28] The power of appointment rests quite firmly in the hands of the local political establishment, who directly control the commune and the trade unions and indirectly the workers' council itself. To make sure that no mistakes are made, enterprises in the Belgrade area were in 1981 obliged to agree to a social compact giving a final veto on appointments to the co-ordinating committee of the local commune.[29] This is simply a formalization of a rule to which Professor Županov referred, namely, that final approval of apointments of directors is given by the president of the local commune and the head of the commune Party organization.[30] According to Eames (1980, 176) 90 per cent of advertisements for managers (at all levels) specify that they must have necessary 'moral-political qualities'. These are defined in an official document as follows. On the moral side a candidate must be honest, sincere, indulgent, unselfish, and humane, have respect for other ideas and attitudes, and an exemplary private life. On the political side he must have a commitment to the revolutionary course of the Party, he must support the Constitution and especially the principle of brotherhood and unity, he must be conscious of personal and social standards of behaviour, and he must have played an active role in the collective. The political conditions are sufficient to ensure that most managers are Party members. In 1965 in Zagreb 98.5 per cent of directors were Party members and 60.5 per cent of all managers down to and including foremen (Eames 1980, 178).

Apart from political qualities, managers usually have technical or other qualifications. In 1975, according to Eames (1980, 164–6) 68 per cent of managers had degrees in economics, law, or engineering and a further 18

[28] Eames (1980, 204). According to *Borba* (1 September 1982) 'It has become the practice that a suitable candidate is first found, that he is placed in the intended job, and only after that is the job advertised.'

[29] *Ekonomska politika*, 13 July 1981, p. 5.

[30] Granick (1975, 364).

per cent had other qualifications, mostly in economics. But 'there are no business schools, as such, and no professional institutes'. There are some studies of 'organizational sciences', but there is no institution offering 'an applied training in business administration'. There is, indeed, considerable hostility to the idea of courses in business studies. *Ekonomska politika* (3 August 1981, p. 15) reports that a proposal to set up a business school, to which managers would be sent for nine months' training at the expense of their enterprises, was greeted with hostility and the objection that it was 'contrary to the principle of self-management'.

In spite of these selection biases, it is obvious that Yugoslavia has quite a large number of good managers. But the quality of management, which is the key to efficient organization, could be much improved if some of the existing ideological prejudices and confusions were eliminated.

Responsibilities and powers

A director is obliged to make proposals on business policy and its implementation to the workers' council and, through them, to the workers generally. Once the self-management bodies have taken their decisions, the director (or the business board) is obliged to carry out those decisions.[31] But he is also responsible to the local commune 'for the legality of work and for the fulfilment of the statutorily-established obligations of the basic organization'.[32] In fact, his obligations to the local commune go much further than this, because the commune has a predominant say in his appointment, re-appointment and removal, and on the provision of credits and other facilities to the enterprise. The director 'is subject to recall at any time—for negligence, incompetence, legal misconduct, or the failure to maintain cordial relations with other bodies. Proceedings for dismissal can be initiated either by the workers' council, the assembly of the commune, or the trade union.'[33] In practice, the decisive role in any such move is played by the Party, both inside and outside the enterprise.[34]

While the responsibilities of managers are heavy, their powers to carry out their responsibilities are much restricted. Under the law, the director (or his board) have 'the right and duty to issue orders to individual workers or group of workers concerning the performance of individual affairs or tasks, in conformity with the self-management enactment'.[35] But the

[31] Associated Labour Act, Article 513.
[32] Ibid., Article 518.
[33] Schrenk and others (1979, 57).
[34] *Borba* (5 August 1982) reports the case of a firm making food products which has made losses for many years. Discipline is bad, mass meetings are not held according to schedule, and the president of the workers' council has not attended council meetings for four months. The basic organization of the Party in the firm is now demanding the replacement of three top managers. According to another report (*Borba*, 31 July 1982) the 2,200 workers in a wood-processing firm went on strike in support of the demand that 20 top managers, including the general director, should be replaced. This proposal was first discussed at an 'action conference' of the representatives of the Party and trade unions.
[35] Associated Labour Act, Article 515.

director and his managerial staff have very little power to enforce such orders. He has 'the right to suggest disciplinary measures, but not to hire and fire workers, take disciplinary action, determine the internal distribution of income, or make appointments to management positions at the middle and lower levels'.[36] As a result, managers have to spend much time and effort in persuading workers to accept their proposals. This increases both their workload and their sense of frustration. One top-level manager (a member of the Party) told Eames (1980, 296) that he would not be standing for re-election because 'the job is impossible under the present conditions of "responsibility without authority" '. Although 'the system is very "humane". . . too much time is needed for explanations'.

Rusinow (1978, 19) quotes the comments of a pre-war Party member, who had recently insisted on retiring early from his post of director of an enterprise.

Our system of self-management, instead of meaning self-management of and for the enterprise and society as a whole, means to most people self-management of one's self—working only when and as hard as one wants, but with assurance that one's job will go on and one's pay will continue to increase. I needed help when there was something to be done, but no one was there, and then I met them taking the promenade on main street, and they said: 'Why were you in the office, and not here with us?' This kind of work ethic and other things, including stealing in the usual sense, of which there is also a lot, are forms of stealing under socialism, which is worse than stealing under capitalism.

Apart from the pressures on managers from within the enterprise, and from the local commune and socio-political organizations, in the past ten years directors have had to contend with increasing administrative controls. In an interview with *Ekonomska politika* (26 July 1982, pp. 19–21) the general director of a large enterprise in Novi Sad said that his firm is no longer working for the market but for 'some individual or forum'. The result is that the basic organizations turn to these forums, ask them for papers, and are asked for papers in return.

We shall prove that we have fulfilled the conditions of the announced priorities, and they will prove that we have not. In that kind of mutual exchange of communications there will be multiplied the need for paper, and for officials to write and file these papers, and it leads to the position where in this country more than half the total work force is occupied with writing papers.

Attitudes of managers to their job

There are persistent reports that many managers are deeply discontented with their jobs, that they would not recommend their children to take such a job, and that there are difficulties in recruiting suitable people. Eames (1980, 279–80) quotes the results of a sample survey of managers which showed that 75 per cent 'categorically insisted that a crisis existed'. The main reasons given for this opinion were: the high level of responsibility

---

[36] Schrenk and others (1979, 56).

and low level of authority; inadequate training for the job; inadequate rewards and lack of social and other recognition for successful work; job insecurity; inadequately defined role of managers in a self-management system; general attacks on the management profession based on a few bad examples; enterprise successes attributed to the workers, failures to the managers; difficult personal relations with workers; and personal harassment. Eames (pp. 280–1) also quotes another survey which showed that 62 per cent of managers would not recommend their children to take up that type of work. Granick (1975, 355) reports that surveys show that people are reluctant to take the job of general director, and Hunnius (1975, vol. II, 69) makes the same point: 'Pressures on the director to maintain economic efficiency and at the same time adhere to national guidelines, combined with his responsibility to the self-management bodies have made it increasingly more difficult to attract qualified people to the position.' *Ekonomska politika* (13 August 1981, p. 5) has remarked that there is an 'atmosphere of general "unpopularity" of the profession of director'.

In these circumstances it is natural that some people point to the need to give managers higher pay. Granick (1975, 355) was of the opinion that the difficulty of recruiting good general directors in Yugoslavia was the result of low pay differentials, which in turn was a consequence of the self-management system. He pointed out that, while engineers and technicians can earn substantial extra income by 'moonlighting', directors have no time to take on other work. Eames (1980, 209) also says that differentials are fairly narrow and that this creates a good deal of discontent among managers. As a consequence, there is a tendency for managers to move out of industry into research institutes and similar organizations. Katušič (1970, 94) previously stated that, as a result of egalitarian pressures by the less skilled workers in industrial enterprises, technicians and experts look for jobs in research and other institutes and agencies, or go abroad. The Third Congress of Self-Managers of Yugoslavia met the point in a rather half-hearted way, when they resolved that 'In this connection it is necessary also to take into consideration the position of the organizer of production and business operations and to set the corresponding scales and criteria for determining their share in the generation of income.'[37]

The importance of management

Yugoslav enterprises vary widely in their degree of business success. Some enterprises have had consistently good results and, as a result, have expanded rapidly. Others regularly produce losses. Examples of the former type, as reported in the press, include a firm at Ohrid in Macedonia, employing 3,000 workers, which makes electric transformers, many of which are exported; a firm at Trstenik in Serbia which produces pneumatic and hydromatic gear for brake systems, whose employment nearly doubled between 1976 and 1980, reaching almost 10,000 in the latter

[37] *Yugoslav Survey*, August 1981, p. 12.

year; and a smaller firm in Sarajevo, which produces Bosnian pastry, whose employment rose in ten years from 40 to nearly 200 while its output rose from 360 tons to 2,500 tons. Yugoslav construction enterprises have been extremely successful in obtaining foreign construction contracts in face of strong competition. The value of foreign projects completed in 1977 was $1.25 billion, equivalent to about one-sixth of all Yugoslav construction work. In 1976 these enterprises were operating in thirty-six countries, most of which were developing countries, but work has also been done in the Soviet Union and eastern Europe and in the Netherlands and West Germany. The projects include roads, harbours, dams and irrigation systems, hydroelectric and steam power stations, airports, road bridges, and major building complexes, including an entire university in Libya. In 1982 a Belgrade construction enterprise concluded a contract to build 35,000 flats in Algeria over the following six years.[38] It is inconceivable that any of these success stories would have occurred without first-rate management. Equally, the many examples of failure must be due at least in part to bad management.

The quality of management is the major determinant of success or failure of any economy. Leading Yugoslav thinkers have recognized that a negative attitude towards management is one of the great weaknesses of the Yugoslav system. Professor Županov (1978, 86–8), for example, has written about the egalitarian biases in Yugoslavia, which are hostile to entrepreneurship, professionalism, management, innovation, and creativity. Rewards for inventions are small and grudgingly given. 'While Yugoslav inventors have received rewards and respect from colleagues abroad, they have sometimes been treated like criminals at home.' Under modern conditions the most important resource is 'labour as creative potential in areas of organization and management, science, education, and the level of civilization of the population in general. Intellectual equalization nonetheless inhibits the utilization of precisely these new, most productive resources.' Professor Bajt (1980, 248), in reviewing a book by Vanek, wrote:

The weakest point, both in L-M practice and in Vanek's theory, is entrepreneurship . . . In Vanek's theory there exist but two factors of production, capital and labour. Schumpeter is apparently missing from Vanek's dramatis personae . . .Whereas capital is the limiting factor in under-developed non-socialist countries, and new technology in developed capitalist countries, entrepreneurship appears to be the real problem in socialist countries.

And further (pp. 250–1).

The real problem in the L-M economy is how to incorporate efficient management into L-M decision making. The Yugoslav 1965 economic reform was designed with

---

[38] Examples of successful domestic enterprises are taken from *Borba* (1 February and 6 August 1982) and *Ekonomska politika* (15 December 1980). A general article about Yugoslav foreign construction operations is in *Yugoslav Survey*, August 1978. The Algerian contract was reported in *Ekonomska politika* (23 August 1982).

this purpose in mind. However, because of an uninvited co-traveller, the growing political power of managers, it did not take long before it was switched off its track.

These two comments, and especially the second one, raise a crucial question for those who advocate the self-management system: Is self-management compatible with efficient management in the usual sense, and hence with efficient work by the whole body of workers? It is a question which has always been thrown at those who have recommended producers' co-operatives as an alternative economic system to capitalism. The record of Yugoslav economic growth has been very impressive. But there remains a doubt whether the self-management system, at least in the form which it has taken in Yugoslavia, can give the people of that country the standard of living which they want in the long run.

CHAPTER 12

INFLATION

As was shown in Chapter 8, during the past twenty years Yugoslavia has experienced rapid and accelerating inflation. In the first section of this chapter we shall consider whether there are theoretical reasons for expecting a self-managed economy to have an inflationary bias; in the second section we shall examine Yugoslav experience in trying to control inflation; and in the third section we shall draw some conclusions about policies appropriate for this purpose in a self-managed system.

1. THE CAUSES OF INFLATION IN A SELF-MANAGED ECONOMY

Chapter 3 contains an outline of a theoretical model of a co-operative—or labour-managed—economy. For the purpose of that model it was assumed that, while there is complete freedom of entry, there are imperfections in product markets, the capital market, and the availability of private technology. In a closed economy in which all product markets are imperfect, and so long as demand conditions are not such as to push enterprises beyond their normal full capacity, the model predicts that prices will be fixed at, or slightly below, the 'entry price', and that they will not vary with the state of demand. The entry price of a product is that price which will be sufficient to induce the formation of a new co-operative to produce the product.[1] This price will be just enough to cover the unit costs of a new co-operative, which has initially only a limited amount of capital and technical knowledge, and a limited expected market for its product. At that price, larger and more experienced co-operatives will normally be able to earn a higher income per worker. Hence, smaller co-operatives will constantly strive to expand their scale of production in order to obtain the benefit of that higher income.

Since the entry price is the cost per unit of the given product to a potential new co-operative, that price will be affected by changes in each component of the potential new co-operative's cost structure. This means that the price will rise if the money costs of labour, capital, or material inputs increase, but will tend to fall as productivity improves through the application of better public technology. If we take a macroeconomic view

[1] This will usually be approximately the same as the price which will attract the entry of existing co-operatives into the same market.

of the economy, the cost of materials can be omitted, and the influences on the general price level are reduced to changes in the money costs of labour and capital and improvements in technology. In the short term, e.g. from one year to the next, changes in technology may be assumed to be predetermined, and if the rate of interest is held fairly constant, the dominant influence on the general price level will be changes in the cost of labour.

But what is the cost of labour in a co-operative economy? In such an economy there are no wages and no wage contracts. Instead, the cost of labour to a new co-operative is the amount of income per worker the expectation of which will be sufficient to attract a group of workers to establish a new co-operative. If the potential new members are unemployed, it might be thought that the minimum expected income would be that which would compensate them for working rather than not working. But, in practice, workers are usually unwilling to accept an expected income below the average income of workers in existing co-operatives of similar size. Since, for reasons explained in Chapter 3, proportional income differentials between workers in co-operatives of different sizes are likely to be rather stable, the supply price of labour to new co-operatives will tend to move in proportion to changes in the average level of labour incomes in the whole economy.

It is apparent that, with this set of relations, the general level of prices in a closed co-operative economy is potentially highly unstable. For, if the general price level depends on the average level of nominal incomes, and nominal incomes depend on the general price level, any change in one of these variables will set off a spiral of changes in the same direction. If, as is normally the case, the spiral of changes in incomes and prices has an upward bias, the only general market (i.e. non-administrative) pressures which would slow down the rate of inflation would be (1) improvements in technology, (2) a fall in the rate of interest, or (3) a tight control on the money supply. Of these, only the last is a short-term policy variable. If the money supply is kept under tight control when nominal incomes and prices are rising, the rate of interest will rise rather than fall, and the cost effect of changes in that variable will tend to encourage rather than to dampen inflation. Unless demand is at such a level as to cause a substantial number of enterprises to operate beyond their normal capacity, a tight money supply will not directly affect the price level. Instead, its effect will be to reduce aggregate demand, mainly through a reduction in investment demand, and thus to increase the level of unemployment. Since a moderate increase in unemployment is unlikely to have much effect on workers' expectations, there will not be an appreciable fall in the cost of labour to new co-operatives. However, if the shortage of money becomes acute, more and more existing co-operatives will be pushed into bankruptcy and, if this process continues far enough, there will eventually be a downward revision of money incomes and prices. But, before that point is reached, there is likely to be a political crisis, especially in a one-party communist country.

We must now introduce modifications into our model to bring it closer to the situation in Yugoslavia. The first modification arises from the fact that in Yugoslavia there is very little pressure of competitive new entry, and scarcely any new enterprises are being established. Moreover, the division of the Yugoslav market into semi-autarkic areas has gone so far that there is little competitive pressure from the threat of entry of existing enterprises into new product markets. Thus, if Yugoslavia were a closed economy, the level of prices would be difficult to predict on the basis of our theory.

The other modification is that Yugoslavia is not a closed economy but has a substantial foreign trade. One effect of this foreign trade is that Yugoslav domestic prices, especially of tradable goods and services, are strongly influenced by the level of world prices, converted at the current rate of exchange into dinars. Indeed, in the absence of significant domestic competition, or potential competition, from new entry, the main influence on the general level of Yugoslav prices of tradable goods and services is the level of world prices in dinars (or 'dinar world prices'). Moreover, dinar world prices for tradables have two further influences on Yugoslav domestic prices. The first is that a rise in dinar world prices of imports directly or indirectly raises the costs of enterprises in all sectors, irrespective of whether they are immediate producers of tradables or non-tradables, and these costs feed into prices as the enterprises try to maintain their existing income differentials. The second is that the rise in workers' income in the tradable sector increases the pressure for similar rises in incomes in the non-tradable sector. This pressure may be resisted by strongly enforced price controls in the latter sector, but it is not usually possible to maintain discriminatory price controls of this sort for very long, since they lead eventually to acute shortages of essential services.

Here we may notice an important difference between the situation in Yugoslavia and in developed capitalist countries. While world prices in terms of domestic currency have an influence on the level of domestic prices in capitalist countries, they are not the only influence. In capitalist countries, labour costs, which usually represent a much larger component of total costs than imports, are to some extent independently determined by the results of wage-bargaining. It is true that, in the long run, an increase in the domestic cost of imports feeds through into domestic prices, and so encourages demands for higher wages, demands which are more easily met if there is a parallel increase in the domestic prices received for exports. But there are time-lags in this process of adjustment, and there is a certain independent component which comes from the level of unemployment, and possibly from other factors. Thus, a devaluation in a developed capitalist country does not usually lead to an immediate upward adjustment of all domestic prices in proportion to the devaluation. But in Yugoslavia, where there is no 'wage drag' to hold prices back, there is a tendency for all prices to adjust rather quickly to changes in dinar world prices.[2]

[2] If laws and social compacts about prices were strictly enforced, there would be a slower adjustment, but only at the expense of a large crop of bankruptcies.

The consequence of this relationship is that the control of inflation in Yugoslavia is more difficult than in developed capitalist countries. Consider, for example, the effects in Yugoslavia of a persistent deficit in the current balance of payments. If the supply of foreign credits becomes inadequate to cover the deficit, there eventually comes a point where steps must be taken to reduce the deficit. Since the Yugoslav government does not wish to use physical controls on imports as its main instrument, and indeed cannot do so without seriously damaging domestic industries, it is obliged to devalue the dinar in the hope of stimulating exports (as well as reducing certain types of imports). But if a devaluation leads very quickly to a rise in dinar prices of domestic products, including products which are exported or which compete with imports, the price effect of the devaluation on the foreign balance will be quite short-lived. The first industries to adjust their prices to the new level will be those engaged in the production of tradable goods and services; but this will soon feed through into all other industries. During this lagged process of adjustment the lagging industries, or their workers, will suffer a temporary loss of relative income, while the industries which adjust most quickly will make temporary windfall profits. In order to redress the balance, it may happen that the lagging industries subsequently raise their prices in greater proportion than the rise in dinar world prices and thus perpetuate the cost–price spiral within the country.

In any case, a Yugoslav devaluation seems to have only a small terms-of-trade effect on the balance of payments and, if this were the only effect of devaluation, it would seem to be a very unsatisfactory instrument for correcting a foreign deficit. Indeed, under Yugoslav conditions, there are only two instruments which may be considered to be satisfactory for this purpose.[3] The first, short-term, instrument is a deflation of demand (whether by monetary, fiscal, or administrative methods). While this has little or no direct effect on prices in the social sector, it will encourage exports and discourage imports by reducing the quantitative level of domestic demand, while at the same time reducing prices in the private agricultural sector. It is this instrument which the Yugoslav government has eventually been forced—reluctantly—to use whenever the foreign deficit has become really critical. The second instrument, or rather policy, is more fundamental but also more long-term in its application. This is the policy of turning the attention of appropriate industries towards the export market. It is not only a matter of providing suitable monetary incentives for exports, although these are undoubtedly important. It is also a matter of the general attitude of managers and of the political superstructure towards exports, and of creating an understanding of the types of product in which Yugoslavia is most likely to be competitive and of the business methods which are necessary in order to create a sound long-term export market. On the whole, the bias of Yugoslav policy has been against exports. While they are accepted as being necessary, they have not hitherto

---

[3] In practice, much reliance is usually placed also on quantitative import restrictions.

been given the priority treatment which the planning process tends to give to infrastructure or so-called import-competing industries.

The relevance of these remarks to the question of inflation in Yugoslavia is that, since the major source of inflation in Yugoslavia is the rise in dinar world prices, part of which is the result of a persistent decline in the value of the dinar (either openly through devaluation or in a concealed form through a fall in its internal black market value), the ultimate remedy for Yugoslav inflation is a strengthening of the foreign balance and hence of the value of the dinar. If, as we have said, devaluation in itself does not solve the problem of the foreign deficit, and the only short-term remedy is a deflation of demand, it may well be asked why the Yugoslav government has so persistently resorted to devaluation. The principal answer probably is that the government is very reluctant to deflate demand and tries to avoid this by using devaluation instead, in the vain hope that deflation can somehow be shown to be unnecessary. The second, more sophisticated, answer might be that it is politically more easy to impose deflation after devaluation rather than beforehand. For deflation without devaluation implies an actual reduction in normal demand, while deflation after devaluation requires only a braking of the growth in nominal demand. This kind of make-believe is often the essence of successful political leadership (not only, of course, in Yugoslavia).

Apart from deflation, the Yugoslav government has also made use of two other instruments in the attempt to control inflation. The first is price control, and the second is incomes policy. We shall examine the results of applying these two instruments in more detail in the next section.

2. YUGOSLAV ATTEMPTS TO CONTROL INFLATION

Price controls[4]

In the period 1945–52 almost all prices were fixed by the central planners. Price ratios were arbitrary, discriminating against private farmers and yielding substantial surpluses for the social sector. But after the introduction of self-management it was gradually realized that the system could not operate efficiently without a liberalization of market prices. There were attempts to move in this direction in the early 1950s, but price controls were soon strengthened again. From 1958 to 1965 the major form of price control was compulsory prior registration with the Federal Price Office. The criteria for an authorized price increase were (1) the supply and demand position, (2) social considerations of the importance of the product for final consumers and as an intermediate good of wide use, (3) degree of monopoly of the supplier. If a registered price increase was not rejected within a prescribed period it could be implemented. The areas of price control were farm products, raw materials, the main manufacturing components, serially produced equipment, major consumer goods, power, and transport. The proportion of the value of industrial output covered by

---

[4] The first few paragraphs of this section are mainly based on Marsenić (1977).

price controls rose from 32 per cent in 1958 to 67 per cent in 1962. One of the effects of these controls was to cause large redistributions of income from the tightly controlled industries, such as agriculture, raw and processed materials, power, and transport, to the industries subject to little or no control. Some, but not all, of the losses imposed on the controlled industries was offset by grants from government investment funds.

In the early 1960s a new attempt was made to relax price controls as part of the movement towards economic reform. Since the 1965 Reform was designed to give enterprises the right to dispose more freely of their income, and especially to take their own saving and investment decisions, 'these decisions could be economically valid only if prices offered a reliable parameter for evaluating expenditures and results' (Marsenić 1977, 99). Although the ultimate aim was to free most prices, the Reform required a major readjustment of prices and this could only be done within the framework of price control. The intention was that in future the principal criterion for determination of domestic prices should be the corresponding dinar world price, increased in the case of imported goods by the tariff and reduced in the case of exported goods by the export subsidy. Some non-traded goods were also to be valued at 'world' prices, while others were to be valued at average domestic cost of production (including an allowance for enterprise saving). When the Reform began in July 1965, 67 per cent of industrial products were fixed according to world prices, 12 per cent by cost of production, and 21 per cent were uncontrolled. On the average, agricultural prices rose by 33 per cent and industrial prices by 14 per cent (of which raw materials and components rose by 23 per cent and finished goods by 8 per cent).

In the first year or two after the Reform most prices were kept firmly under control. In 1967 an attempt was made to throw the responsibility for price determination on to enterprises through a system of self-management agreements between the enterprises with an interest in the good in question, whether as buyers or as sellers. The intention was that in future government should not be involved in detailed price control but should influence the general level of prices through macroeconomic policy measures, such as fiscal, monetary, and exchange rate policies. But this system did not work, and price controls were maintained.

A further attempt to reduce the role of government in price control was made in the constitutional amendments of 1971. From 1972 onwards prices were to be regulated through social compacts between governments, enterprises, and trade associations. Most price control was in future to be exercised at the level of the republics, provinces, and communes, and only a few groups of products were to be controlled at federal level. The main criterion for price control was 'world prices', but regard was also to be given to 'development policy'. In principle, if prices were fixed below their proper level according to these criteria, governments would be required to compensate the enterprises affected. But, since the criteria themselves—especially the second one—are extremely vague, the likelihood of getting actual compensation was rather small. In fact, there seem to be no examples of compensation being paid explicitly for this reason, although many enterprises are given government assistance when they are in difficulties.

The 1972 system worked no better than the 1967 system, because both systems relied on the mysterious process of achieving voluntary consensus between parties with opposing interests. Self-management agreements were sometimes made 'horizontally' instead of 'vertically', in other words, groups of suppliers made a price agreement among themselves. The outcome in such cases was not social price control but monopoly. Even when genuine self-management agreements were made between buyers and sellers they omitted to specify 'the quantity and quality of goods supplied under such agreement and its binding character' (Marsenić 1977, 109).

Since 1972, the formal structure of the system has remained essentially unchanged, although it has been institutionalized by the establishment of 'self-management communities of interest' for prices. But the content of the system has deviated more and more from its original intention. Since the achievement of voluntary consensus on prices between buyers and sellers is an unattainable ideal, government representatives at the communities of interest have become the real arbiters. Increasingly, it has become clear that 'self-managed' prices are 'political' prices.[5]

It is not surprising that price control has in fact become a government responsibility. But the elaborate pretence that decisions are made by voluntary 'self-management' agreements can only encourage cynicism and disbelief in the whole self-management idea. Moreover, when government decisions are disguised as social compacts and self-management agreements there is less likelihood that they will be based on explicit and consistent criteria.

The typical Yugoslav feature of devolving as much responsibility as possible to republican, provincial, and even communal, agencies only adds to the confusion. Under a social compact made in late 1980 federal price responsibility was limited to petroleum and its products, iron ore and iron and steel, non-ferrous ores, metals and products, coal products, transport equipment, and tobacco. The communes continue to be responsible for the prices of local services, rents, and retail prices of basic foods. All the rest is either completely or partially the responsibility of the republics and

---

[5] 'The whole area of prices is such that prices are too much under the influence of subjective (political) factors, and too little under the pressure of objective (economic) factors' (Vojnić 1979, 93). Also, 'Present prices—we call them "political prices"—are not objective signals of real supply and demand' (ibid., 95). Oskar Fodor, general director of a large enterprise in Novi Sad, was recently reported as having said that prices 'are not determined on the market . . . but arbitrarily in closed local communities' (*Ekonomska politika*, 26 July 1982, pp. 19–21). A leading director of a steel enterprise in Macedonia remarked in another interview, 'As regards prices I think that basic industries have the least responsibility for rapid inflation, because the prices of these industries have always been, and are even now, under the control of organs of the federal government' (*Ekonomska politika*, 23–9 November 1981, p. 24).

provinces.[6] This division of responsibilities creates inconsistencies and economic distortions, and it strengthens existing autarkic tendencies. The general director of an important Croatian enterprise said in an interview with *Vjesnik* (7 June 1981) 'On the one hand we have a market, on the other we do not allow it to function . . . We were discussing here the law on prices. What do we have concretely in practice? Each republic can set a higher price for "its" producer or for "their" products, and in that way "cover" both its own lower level of technology and its inferior quality'. The previously quoted director of the Macedonian steel enterprise also pointed out in his interview that 'steel prices are controlled by the federal government while the prices of electricity and coal are controlled by the republics and provinces. The republics and provinces more easily give their approval for increases in the prices of electricity and coal but it is more difficult to get the federal government to agree to higher prices for steel and steel products' (*Ekonomska politika*, 23–9 November 1981, p. 24).

There are constant complaints that the present system of price control is irrational and unjust. Here are a few examples. In late 1980 the Federal Price Office rejected the demand of the leather industry that the price of raw leather, last fixed in 1977, should be raised from 27 to 48 dinars per kg. At the time, the current market price for raw leather from private farmers was already 60 dinars per kg. (*Ekonomska politika*, 29 December 1980, p. 7). Railway prices are constantly held back in comparison with other prices. In mid–1981 it was said that the price per ton for road transport was 4–5 times as high as on the railways (*Ekonomska politika*, 22 June 1981, p. 15). During 1981 the prices of railway services were allowed to rise by 9 per cent when the general rate of inflation was 40 per cent. In the same year the losses of the railways amounted to 2.3 billion dinars (*Ekonomska politika*, 8 March 1982, p. 13). The same squeeze is applied to the electricity industry (*Ekonomska politika*, 1 March 1982, pp. 11–12). In 1982 the Yugoslav airline JAT was said to have lost 350 million dinars on domestic flights as a result of price controls (*Ekonomska politika*, 23 August 1982, p. 14).

In 1981 it was reported that during the previous year the world price of silver rose from 4,000 dinars to 36,000 dinars per kg., while the domestic price was kept at about 4,000 dinars. For lead, the domestic price in 1981 was 22,000 dinars per kg. although the current world price for exports was 40,000 dinars. In fact, domestic transactions were being carried out at world prices under various fictional self-management agreements. The only trouble was that these transactions attract the attention of the price inspectors (*Ekonomska politika*, 20 July 1981, p. 6). In the same issue of the journal (p. 7) it was reported that the vice-president of the giant firm RMK Zenica had said:

For five whole months we have been making agreements with the consumers of our products. Much time was spent by highly qualified personnel from our own staff

---

[6] For the federal, republican, and provincial responsibilities see *Ekonomska politika*, 15 December 1980, p. 32. For the communal responsibilities see Govedarica (1972, 28).

and those of our consumers, because we worked on thirty self-management agreements for establishing the new levels of prices. We sent all these agreements to the Federal Community for Prices, but they were not accepted for discussion because we had not sent our price lists as well. Other people get what they want without self-management agreements by simply sending over the prices of a few products for approval.

An example of the time-consuming arguments about price increases is the case of electricity prices in 1981. In Serbia, the generating organization wanted a 47 per cent increase, while the distribution organization wanted 63 per cent. At a meeting of the self-management community of interest for electricity it was finally agreed, after long discussions, that the price to final consumers should rise by 31 per cent. But some delegates to the assembly of the community considered that electricity prices were already too high and that the increase should be postponed until a new social compact had been agreed for energy prices in Serbia. They pointed out that a major reason for high electricity prices was that personal incomes in that industry were much higher than average—in 1980 10,834 dinars per month compared with an average for the whole economy of 7,166 dinars. On the other hand, it was argued that electricity prices in Serbia were lower than elsewhere, and that in any case the industry was making heavy losses. Unless they received higher prices, both the producers and distributors of electricity would be unable to reach the savings target set for them in the plan (*Ekonomska politika*, 2 March 1981). Similar arguments go on in other countries, for example, in respect of the prices of nationalized industries in Britain. But in Yugoslavia they are going on all the time for almost every industry, and at nine different levels (six republics, two autonomous provinces, and the federation).

Not surprisingly, official price controls are widely evaded. Speaking in December 1980 at a session of the Council of the Economic Chamber of Yugoslavia, the vice-president said that there are 'massive' adjustments of prices above their officially permitted levels. A special system of double pricing had been created, which was more and more difficult to control. The methods of evasion included raising the price under the guise of pooling labour and resources, and announcing better quality or new products. Hence the official statistics of prices were 'completely different' from the true prices (*Ekonomska politika*, 22 December 1980, p. 6). In 1982 *Borba* (12 July 1982) wrote that controlled prices are widely ignored by all kinds of firms from the largest to the smallest. 'There are only a few who have not broken the price regulations.' Prices are surcharged with all sorts of 'extras', and 'to increase the irony, all of this is covered by various self-management agreements'. When prices cannot be raised, the quality of goods and services is reduced. Many firms give no guarantee of quality. For example, cement has been found to be of inferior quality, and in Serbia inspectors have found bags of cement which were 50 per cent below their correct weight. Many other products have been classified by the inspectors as unsaleable.

Reporting a meeting of the Presidency of the Council of the Yugoslav

Federation of Trade Unions, *Borba* (10 April 1982) wrote that there are 'massive' cases of 'new products' being launched in order to evade price control. An example of this practice was given in *Ekonomska politika* (17 November 1980, p. 7) when it reported that forestry enterprises had informed the coal mines that they had no more pit props but could supply poles at a higher price. Another method of squeezing the customer reported by the same journal (29 December 1980, p. 15) is for firms supplying raw materials, which are often subject to price control, to demand that their customers make part-payment in the form of low-interest credits. For example, the sole producer of rayon made an agreement with its customers that they would pay 15,000 dinars per ton of rayon thread in the form of a ten-year loan at 4 per cent. A similar loan from the bank would have cost 9 per cent. Meanwhile, as reported in *Ekonomska politika* (1 June 1981, p. 7), the unfortunate price inspectors in Croatia, confronted by a rising tide of price violations, pointed out that 'it was especially difficult to supervise the application of price regulations, primarily because of the untimely, incomplete and unclear normative regulation of the conditions and method of formation of prices'.

All these efforts to evade price controls absorb a vast amount of managerial time: 'it is quite normal for many basic and other organization of associated labour to direct more of their efforts to increasing the prices of their products than to improving the quality of their productive activity' (Vojnić 1979, 105). In a 1981 survey of seventy-two Yugoslav general directors and presidents of management boards of major enterprises the opinion was expressed that the main struggle of enterprises was not to raise productivity but to raise prices, and to obtain certificates, decisions and so forth. Some enterprises are impoverished and others enriched by 'overnight' decisions. The directors were in favour of allowing firms to follow their own price policies, subject to market conditions. They believed that this would actually reduce the rate of inflation, since greater market influence would stimulate productivity (*Ekonomska politika*, 12 January 1981, pp. 16–19). In the words of Stevan Doronjski, then President of the League of Communists of Yugoslavia, in a report to the Central Committee in September 1980, organizations of associated labour 'resort in practice to the increase in prices as to an almost exclusive way of solving the difficulties in business operations and as the most suitable and easiest way of increasing income'. There is an 'increasingly frequent practice that even within the organizations of associated labour solutions to the economic position are sought in charging higher prices to one another' (*Socialist Thought and Practice*, 1980, No. 12, p. 11).

Thus, price controls are not only irrational and unjust but encourage disrespect for social compacts, self-management agreements, and the law. Moreover, in the outcome they have been ineffective as a means of restraining inflation and of diverting supplies to the export market. According to the annual Economic Resolution for 1982 prices of industrial products were to rise by 22 per cent and of agricultural products by $21^1/_4$ per cent (what precision!). By the beginning of May 1982, prices of industrial products had already risen by 25 per cent (over the level reached twelve months earlier) and farm prices by about 40 per cent. After a steady downward slide, the dollar value of the dinar was reduced by 20 per cent in October. At that time it was announced that only those products which are based solely or primarily on imported raw materials would be allowed to raise their prices. But this position will be untenable for more than a short period, especially in the absence of a strong centralized system of controls.

Incomes policy

Most Yugoslav economists and many politicians believe that in the long run price controls do more harm than good. But something must be done to slow down inflation, the deterioration of the balance of payments and growing international indebtedness; and one suggested remedy is an incomes policy. For example, an article in *Ekonomska politika* (2 November 1981), after pointing out the weaknesses of administrative measures, argued for a 'realistic' exchange rate, and finally concluded that 'a serious programme requires both devaluation and an incomes policy'. The OECD annual economic surveys of Yugoslavia also usually give at least partial support to the idea of an incomes policy. The authors are aware that there are special difficulties in introducing such a policy in Yugoslavia, but they seem to think that, if there were sufficient political will, these difficulties could be overcome.

In a capitalist economy with a labour market and free entry, firms operating under conditions of imperfect competition usually fix their prices on the basis of labour and material costs plus a mark-up. Irrespective of the reasons for that behaviour, the outcome is that, if labour and material costs were kept stable, the prices of these firms would follow suit. In a country where most enterprises are operating under these conditions an incomes policy, if it could be maintained successfully for more than a short period, would be a powerful instrument for controlling inflation. It could be used in conjunction with a moderate reduction in final demand and a moderately tight monetary policy to achieve the desired end, without incurring the damaging costs of a recession and mounting unemployment.

But there is no evidence that Yugoslav social sector prices are determined in this fashion. The reason is that there is no wage system. The cost of labour to a new entrant is the level of income received by workers in similar existing enterprises, and this level, in nominal value, is not fixed by any contract. The only market constraint on Yugoslav prices is the dinar world price. If an incomes policy could be imposed, it would not reduce enterprise prices but merely increase enterprise saving. If investment were being held back by other methods, this would have a deflationary effect, but no direct effect on the price level.

While the advantages of an incomes policy in Yugoslav conditions are doubtful, the difficulties in the way of designing an acceptable incomes policy, and of enforcing it, are formidable. It must be remembered, first, that there are already wide inter-enterprise differences in workers' incomes.

Although some of these might be reduced if there were less administrative intervention over prices, others might become even wider. In any case, any proposal to freeze existing differentials would arouse strong opposition from groups of workers who currently believed themselves to be paid too little. They would be able to appeal to the doctrine of self-management as their justification and, in view of the sacrosanct nature of that doctrine, it would be impossible for the Party leaders to find a good counter-argument without undermining the whole ideological basis of the system.

Secondly, it is impossible to envisage methods of enforcement of an incomes policy in conditions where there are no wage contracts and no employers with an interest in supporting the policy. Previous so-called incomes policies in Yugoslavia have been designed to put pressure on richer enterprises to pay out a smaller proportion of their total net income per worker and to save more. This is partly to prevent excessive personal income differences and partly to encourage enterprise saving. But such incomes policies have been directed solely to the control of *relative* income differences, not the absolute level of money incomes. Since social compacts about income distribution require enterprises to have regard to the average level of personal incomes in their own industry, they place no constraint on changes in that average. Even these agreements are unenforceable, because no one has the effective power to stop an enterprise from paying its workers what they themselves decide.[7] During the last few years a great effort has been made to restrain the growth of nominal personal incomes. This policy has been successful, at least temporarily, in the 'non-productive' sector, where governments can exercise direct pressure on communities of interest and, of course, can impose an incomes policy on their own employees. But productive enterprises usually slip through the net. For example, in 1981, when the aggregate enterprise wage and salary bill rose by 38 per cent, enterprise expenditure on food and housing benefits (which were not covered by current restrictions) rose by more than 50 per cent (OECD 1982, 20). Even if this gap in the policy could be closed, some new method of evasion would almost certainly open up, all the more so because the determination and enforcement of incomes policy in Yugoslavia, as with so much else, is ultimately a matter for each republic and province.

Demand deflation

The main instruments of demand deflation are fiscal policy and monetary policy. Supplementary instruments may include consumer credit restrictions, investment licensing and so forth. But these are not reliable instruments for a stable long-term policy.

As a result of the extreme federalization of government in Yugoslavia, especially in the area of economic policy, it is almost impossible to use

---

[7] In addition, as OECD (1980, 37) rightly points out, an enterprise which is determining its level of personal incomes does not know at that time what is the average level of personal incomes in its own industry.

fiscal policy as a method of demand control.[8] Since 1971 the federal government has been deprived of any significant independent source of budget revenue other than customs duties, which cannot be arbitrarily raised so long as Yugoslavia remains a member of GATT. The major sources of federal revenue are a 50 per cent share in revenue from sales taxes, and contributions from the republics and provinces. Since sales taxes are imposed at all levels of government—the federation, the republics and provinces, and the communes—changes in rates of sales tax cannot be made without general consent, at least between the federation and the republics and provinces. The same applies to the contributions of the republics and provinces, which are laboriously negotiated each year.

On the expenditure side of the federal budget about two-thirds goes towards defence and veterans' benefits, and much of the remainder is committed to subsidies for the less developed regions. Hence very little federal expenditure can appropriately be reduced as part of a deflationary policy. Unless the present constitutional arrangements are greatly modified, giving the federal government independent authority, subject to parliament, to impose new taxes (for example on incomes, which are at present completely reserved for the republics, provinces, and communes) or to raise sales taxes, there will be little scope for fiscal policy in Yugoslavia.

So the Yugoslav government has been driven into relying mainly on monetary policy as a method of restricting aggregate demand. In 1980, for example, when it was recognized that the problem of foreign indebtedness had become critical, M1 (the narrowly defined measure of money) was allowed to increase by only 23 per cent while nominal social product rose by over 33 per cent. In 1981 the corresponding figures were 27 per cent and 43 per cent.[9] On a wider definition (M3) the money supply rose more rapidly (by almost as much as social product in 1980, but by only 31 per cent in 1981). One of the difficulties in controlling M3 in Yugoslavia is the existence of a large volume of foreign exchange deposits, mainly held by households. When the dinar is devalued, these deposits automatically rise in value and increase the size of M3. In 1980, the value of foreign exchange deposits more than doubled, and they are continuing to grow by leaps and bounds as the value of the dinar continues to fall. Fortunately for monetary policy, however, foreign exchange deposits are carefully hoarded and, while the windfall increase in their value reduces the pressure of monetary restriction on consumer spending, these deposits are unlikely to become a source of finance for enterprise investment, at least in the social sector.

As the figures just cited show, monetary policy in Yugoslavia—as in capitalist countries—produces its intended effects only with a considerable lag. The risk is that it will subsequently cause an 'overshoot'. But this risk is

[8] The Yugoslav fiscal system is described in an article with that title in *Yugoslav Survey*, November 1977, on which the remarks in this and the following two paragraphs are based.
[9] OECD (1982, Table 9).

less in Yugoslavia, where the pent-up demand for investment is so great (partly because of an insufficient degree of responsibility for its results) that any relaxation of bank lending would quickly lead to an expansion of investment expenditure.

3. CONCLUSIONS

The problem of controlling inflation in a self-managed economy is considerably greater than in a capitalist economy, even if the self-managed economy maintains strong competitive pressure on enterprises by ensuring actual or potential free entry. In Yugoslavia, where there is little or no competitive new entry, even this sanction is absent.

The disadvantage of a self-managed economy in comparison with capitalism is that, in the absence of a labour market, prices are not based on costs of labour and materials, but either on materials alone, or on world market prices for the final product. In either case, the tendency is for prices to adjust quickly to changes in world prices in terms of domestic currency, without any 'wage drag'. This both reduces the benefits of devaluation as a corrective for a foreign deficit and deprives incomes policy of any power to restrain inflation.

The only remaining short-term instruments for the control of inflation are fiscal policy and monetary policy. These can be used to deflate domestic demand and hence to shift supplies into the export market, thus strengthening the foreign balance and the world value of the domestic currency. This is a painful remedy, and it is made even more painful in Yugoslavia by the impossibility—for constitutional-political reasons—of operating an effective fiscal policy.

Despite all these problems, however, the one reassuring element is that, if a self-management system once succeeds in bringing inflation under control, and is not upset by new increases in world prices, there is less reason to expect an internally-generated inflationary process to begin than under capitalism. For under self-management there is no confrontation between workers and employers, and the trade unions do not try to show their mettle each year by winning nominal wage increases. But, in order to reach this state of bliss, a self-mangement system would need to find a way of restraining aggregate demand, especially investment demand, and this would mean ensuring that workers and managers took a responsible attitude to investment decisions. This would probably be easy enough in a Mondragon-type co-operative system, where the members have an equity interest in their enterprise, but it is difficult to see how it can be achieved under Yugoslav conditions.

There is one longer-term policy change which would be highly beneficial in Yugoslavia, both for strengthening the balance of payments and for controlling inflation. That would be to make a decisive shift in attitudes, both in enterprises and in government, towards the role of exports. To achieve a genuine export-orientation of the economy, however, it would be necessary to review a whole range of policies. These include investment priorities, managerial training, a more flexible attitude to joint ventures with foreign businesses, and perhaps even greater freedom for domestic private enterprise. This last point will be considered further in the following chapter.

CHAPTER 13

THE PRIVATE SECTOR

Since 1945 Yugoslavia has been officially a 'socialist' country. At the beginning the word expressed an aspiration, not a fact. As in Russia, the Yugoslav communists won power with the help of the peasants, who constituted at that time four-fifths of the population. Had the peasants been given freedom of choice, they would not have voted for socialism, as they proved when the communists tried to force them to join collective farms. But, once they had allowed the communists to take power, the peasants were helpless. From that moment onwards they were mere sheep to be shepherded. Because Yugoslavia was now in the hands of a one-party Marxist socialist regime, all constitutions, laws, and policies were fundamentally hostile to the peasantry and to all other forms of private enterprise.[1] The peasants were tolerated, but they were not to be encouraged. Indeed, especially in the first two decades, they were constantly hampered and discriminated against. As time passed, the proportion of peasants in the total work-force gradually declined, and for a number of reasons the Party began to feel the need to give more scope to small entrepreneurs. The first section of this chapter summarizes available information about the size and composition of the private sector. The second section describes the restrictive policies which have been applied to the private sector. And the third section considers some suggestions which have been made for relaxing these restrictions in the future.

1. THE SIZE AND COMPOSITION OF THE PRIVATE SECTOR

In 1953, after eight years of communist rule, three out of four workers were in the private sector, all but about 50,000 of them being self-employed or family workers, and nearly all of them peasant farmers. The contribution of the private sector to the gross material product in that year was between 35 and 40 per cent. As Table 13.1 shows, both these measures of the size of the private sector have declined over the years. It was not, however, until about 1970 that more than half of the active work-force was employed in the social sector; and in 1980 there was still more than a third

[1] For a short period, in 1945–6, there was an agrarian reform, which benefited some peasant families, mainly by distributing land in Vojvodina expropriated from the German settlers in that province.

TABLE 13.1

The Size of the Private Sector

Year	Percentage in private sector	
	Active work-force	Gross material product at market prices
1953	74.8	36.9[a]
1958	65.1	31.6
1960	60.1	24.3
1965	53.1	21.5
1970	49.7	18.4
1975	41.2	15.3
1980	34.1	12.2

Sources: Work-force: Social, YB81, 102 – 5.
Private, Vinski (1981, Table 1).

GMP: YB60, 2 – 64; YB64, 105 – 2; YB66, 105 – 6; YB68, 105 – 2; YB72, 105 – 8; YB77, 106 – 15; YB81, 107 – 8.

[a] At 1960 prices.

of the active work-force in the private sector. By the latter year the share of gross material product generated in the private sector had fallen to about one-eighth.

In 1980, out of an estimated 3.5 million workers engaged in the private sector, 2.94 million were in agriculture or fishing, 200,000 in road transport, 68,000 in catering and tourism, and nearly 300,000 in construction and artisan work. As Table 13.2 shows, private sector workers accounted for 94 per cent of all workers in agriculture and fishing, one-third of those engaged in transport and communications, one-quarter of those engaged in catering and tourism, and more than a quarter of those engaged in construction and artisan work. Their contribution to gross material product at factor cost was nearly 72 per cent in agriculture and

TABLE 13.2

Industrial Composition of the Private Sector in 1980

Industry	Active work-force		GMP at factor cost	
	Total number (000)	Per cent in private sector	Total value (din. bill.)	Per cent from private sector
Agriculture and fishing	3,132	93.9	186.2	71.5
Transport and communications	600	33.5	120.1	6.6
Catering and tourism	269	25.3	43.0	12.8
Construction	} 1,082	27.1	166.5	10.6
Artisan work			55.5	41.3

Sources: Work-force: YB81, 105 – 3 and Vinski (1981, Table 1).

GMP: YB81, 107 – 8. GMP at market prices minus turnover tax.

fishing, and over 40 per cent in artisan work, but a much smaller proportion in the other three industries.

These figures, however, do not give a complete picture of the importance of the private sector to the Yugoslav economy. In the first place, as mentioned in Chapter 11, a large number of social sector workers are engaged in 'moonlight' activities, either on their family farms or in other occupations, such as construction (of their own or other people's houses) and services (such as repairs to cars and other household durables, and various intellectual and professional services). Granick (1975, 355) quotes an estimate that 'moonlight' income amounts to as much as 30 per cent of employee income.[2] It is not clear whether this includes the value of work done on family farms, although it would be unusual to describe such work as 'moonlighting'. Accordingly, in the estimates presented in Table 13.3 the value of pure 'moonlight' income has been given as a range running from 15 per cent to 30 per cent of total social sector net personal income.

A second addition to private sector income is the value of remittances sent by household members or relatives currently working abroad. In 1979 this amounted to nearly 66 billion dinars, an additon of more than 60 per cent to net personal income from registered private sector work. Thirdly, there is a substantial income from interest on household bank deposits, which in 1979 was of the order of 20 billion dinars.

TABLE 13.3
Components of Private Sector Income, 1979

Line		din. bill.
1.	Net personal income from registered productive activities	108.6
2.	Income from 'moonlighting'	64.0–128.1
3.	Remittances from abroad	65.9
4.	Interest on bank deposits	20.0
5.	Total of above	258.6–322.6
6.	Line 5 as per cent of Line 5 plus net personal income from the social sector	37.7–43.0

Sources: Line 1 YB81, 107 – 7.

Line 2 15 per cent and 30 per cent of total net personal income of the social sector (YB81, 107 – 7 and 125 – 1).

Line 3 YB81, 106 – 6.

Line 4 Approximate estimate on the assumption of 7 per cent interest on the average balance of interest-bearing deposits at end 1978 and 1979 (YB81, 111 – 1).

Line 6 Net personal income from social sector: YB81, 107 – 7 and 125 – 1.

[2] In an article in *Yugoslav Survey* (February 1980, p. 116) it is stated in regard to the period 1973–7 that 'It is estimated that about 30 per cent of services and repairs were performed illegally.' This, of course, is a different percentage from the one quoted by Granick.

When these four sources of private sector income are aggregated and compared with total household net income from work or property (not including rental income from private flats or houses) it appears that in 1979 private sector sources amounted to from 38 to 43 per cent of the total. This implies that a very large number of Yugoslav households, probably a majority, are deriving a significant proportion of their total income from private sector sources.

Private agriculture is by far the largest component of the private sector. In 1977 private farmers produced 76 per cent of agricultural gross value added, 60 per cent of wheat, 84 per cent of maize, 97 per cent of tobacco, 98 per cent of potatoes, 99 per cent of beans, 96 per cent of plums and 81 per cent of wine grapes. They owned 84 per cent of the arable land, 97 per cent of cows, 79 per cent of sheep and 92 per cent of pigs. They produced 83 per cent of the beef, 97 per cent of the mutton and lamb, 80 per cent of pork and 64 per cent of poultry meat (*Yugoslav Survey*, November 1979, p. 71).

Although private farmers own all but about 15 per cent of arable land, the quality of the land taken into the social sector is, on the average, better, since it is concentrated in the rich lowland areas, especially in the fertile plain of the Vojvodina. For many years private farmers were starved of capital and supplies, which were directed almost exclusively into the social sector. Since the 1965 Reform there has been some improvement in this respect, but even now social sector farms have far more capital per worker than private farms.[3] Indeed, socialized agriculture has approximately the same amount of fixed assets per worker as industry and mining, despite the fact that investment in socialized agriculture has had a low effectiveness. 'On many socialist farming estates major resources have been invested in projects which do not or will not produce the necessary economic effect.' Some investments have to be written off, while irrigation works are not in full use even ten years after completion. In Yugoslavia a tractor on a socialist farm is written off after 6.6 years whereas in the United States they last for 14 years.[4]

During the period 1953 to 1980 the number of persons actively engaged on private farms fell from over 5 million to less than 3 million. But the total area of arable land in private hands fell only slightly, and the number of farm holdings remained almost constant at about 2.6 million. The average size of holding fell slightly from just over 4 hectares of arable land to just under 4 hectares. In 1969, at the last farm census, more than half the holdings were of less than 3 hectares of arable land, and one million were of less than 2 hectares.[5] But the number of plots was much larger, and their average size was correspondingly smaller. In 1969 there were, on the average, 6.5 separate plots per holding and the average size of plot was less

---

[3] According to Stipetić (1975, 64), 'A worker in socialized agriculture is estimated to have from five to six times a higher value of basic assets [i.e. fixed capital] than the private farmer.'

[4] Ibid., pp. 69–71.

[5] Ibid., pp. 53–5.

than 0.6 hectare. Only 12 per cent of farms were in one undivided plot and 20 per cent had 10 or more plots.[6]

As a result of persistent migration from the farms—either to the towns or to work abroad—the age structure of the farm population has changed. From 1948 to 1971 the proportion of active males in farming aged less than 35 fell from 48.5 per cent to 33.4 per cent, while among active females the proportion fell from 69 per cent in 1953 to 42 per cent in 1971. 'An ever-increasing number of farms are being managed by elderly people with no heirs or young labour.'[7] Many of these elderly people are illiterate and unable to understand or employ modern agricultural techniques; and, when they have no heirs willing to take over the farm, they fail to make new investments, and the property gradually runs down.[8] A great deal of land has been left derelict. According to *Ekonomska politika* (9 February 1981, p. 21) about one million hectares of arable land is uncultivated, or 10 per cent of the total.

Among the younger people who have stayed on the farms an increasing proportion have taken jobs in factories and other nearby occupations, and commute each day, or several times a week, to their non-farm place of work. As a consequence, the proportion of private farm households in which at least one person is employed outside agriculture has risen from 19 per cent in 1949 to 48 per cent in 1976.[9] Peasant households now receive nearly half their total income from non-farm sources, and in the case of farms of under 2 hectares the proportion is as much as two-thirds (YB81, 114–49).

Despite all the handicaps of an ageing workforce, restricted size of holding, scattered plots, low capitalization, and difficulty in obtaining adequate supplies of fuel, parts for machines, fertilizers and so forth, the output from private agriculture has continued to grow. Gross value added at constant prices approximately doubled from 1952–3 to 1979–80 (YB81, 102–17) and output per worker increased in the same period almost three-and-a-half times. But private agriculture is moving towards a critical point as the farm population shrinks further and more farms are abandoned. Unless there is a reform of the law restricting ownership to 10 hectares of arable land, farm output will begin to stagnate and eventually to decline.

Almost all that is known about other enterprises in the private sector is summarized in Table 13.2. There is no doubt that, under the surface, there is a huge potential of small enterprise which is at present frustrated. An example was given in *Ekonomska politika* (17 November 1980, p. 6). At that time certain coal mines had a surplus of coal, because power stations

[6] Stipetić (1981, Table 23). Strangely enough, even social sector farms are often quite small. In 1972, out of 1,172 social sector farms 870 were of less than 100 hectares and 707 of them less than 50 hectares (Stipetić 1975, 122).

[7] Stipetić (1975, 23).

[8] Ibid., p. 24.

[9] Stipetić (1981, 279). Out of more than 5.3 million workers in the social sector in 1978 almost 30 per cent were estimated to be living in farm households (ibid.).

which they were intended to supply were not yet completed. But there were consumers in the towns who were short of coal. The republican and provincial governments asked for permission to import nearly a million tons of coal to meet these needs. But in the meantime private truck operators went to one of the opencast mines, where there was a surplus, loaded up, and transported the coal directly to the consumers.

2. RESTRICTIVE POLICIES

Hostility to the private sector is embedded in the 1974 Constitution. In the introductory part on 'Basic Principles' (Section IV) we find: 'In the Socialist Federal Republic of Yugoslavia all power shall be vested in the working class in alliance with all working people in towns and villages.' The 'working people' means the self-employed, mainly the peasants. What this clause says is that these people are the 'allies', i.e. that they have an inferior status. To continue: 'In order to create a society of free producers, the working class and all working people shall develop socialist self-management democracy as a special form of the dictatorship of the proletariat.' The 'working people' are given no choice: this is their destiny whether they like it or not. And, to make the position quite clear, they are obliged to accept the 'dictatorship of the proletariat', which means the dictatorship of the Party.

The creation of socialist self-management democracy is to be achieved through 'the revolutionary abolition of and constitutional ban on any form of socio-economic and political relations and organization based on class exploitation and property monopoly, or on any kind of political action aimed at the establishment of such relations'. What does this mean for the mass of self-employed in the private sector? In practice, it means that the Party must be allowed to maintain its property monopoly in the social sector and that the 'working people' shall be exploited by that sector in order to squeeze out of them the maximum of surplus for the benefit of the social sector.

It is a standard Marxist dogma that the 'petty-bourgeoisie' are a most dangerous element who, in Lenin's words 'give birth to capitalism every day and every hour'. On another occasion he wrote: 'It is a thousand times easier to vanquish the centralized big bourgeoisie than to "vanquish" the millions upon millions of petty proprietors' (*Selected Works*, 535). In accordance with this doctrine, Yugoslav artisans and peasants have been severely restricted in the amount of resources which they may employ. Peasant households are allowed (Constitution, Article 80) to own a maximum of 10 hectares of arable land (except in mountain areas), and the self-employed generally are prohibited from employing more than a few non-family workers (usually 5). In practice, the great majority of peasant households have much less than 10 hectares, and the average number of employees per private sector non-farm business is less than one.[10] By way

---

[10] Official data are given only for artisan work where, according to Schrenk and others (1979, 264), the average number of non-family workers per workshop in 1974 was 0.4. 'Thus

of exception, the 1974 Constitution allowed the establishment of 'contractual organizations of associated labour', in which a private entrepreneur is allowed to pool his labour and resources with a group of workers (who pool only their labour). Under the terms of the contract the entrepreneur is entitled to be the manager for a limited period (so long as his investment has not been repaid to him), but the workers have normal self-management rights. Not surprisingly, this arrangement has not proved to be very popular, and up to the end of 1982 only 104 contractual organizations had been established, employing 2,500 workers.[11]

In addition to businesses, individuals are allowed to own flats and houses, up to a maximum of three per person, and this is the principal form of private investment.[12] The Constitution (Article 194) gives a 'guaranteed' right to inheritance, but subject to limits to be determined by statute. Property may be expropriated (Article 82) 'against equitable compensation', which may however be restricted 'if so required by the general interest determined in conformity with statute'. The compensation must be sufficient to prevent a 'serious deterioration of the living and working conditions which the owner of expropriated real property had before on account of the use of this real property'.

Although these Constitutional rights are important, so far as they go, the real conditions facing the self-employed in the private sector are determined by individual statutes and, above all, by administrative practices. From time to time, also, they are subjected to intimidation by propaganda, in the press or in political speeches, to which they have no right to reply. These are the restrictions which really bite, and which ensure that the private sector is kept permanently in a subordinate and insecure position.[13]

Many examples of official discrimination against the private sector are given in the press, and even in official reports. The report on 'basic prerequisites' by the Commission on Problems of Economic Stabilization (*Borba*, special supplement, 27 April 1982, p. 25) contains the following passage:

In many areas agriculture is developed for the purpose of supplying the local population and not for the purpose of a long-term increase in income, trade is quite often regarded as a speculative activity, the capacity of service industries is unsatisfactory, and the failure to satisfy demands is so great and the quality of work in these activities is such that the growing needs of the population are met in part by

the private handicrafts sector consists principally of owner-operators. The same is likely to be true in catering, tourism and transport.'

[11] *Ekonomska politika*, 22 November 1982, p. 24.

[12] A person who has a social sector flat in one town or district may not own a private house or flat in the same area. But this does not prevent other members of his household from owning property in that area, nor does it prevent him from owning up to three houses or flats elsewhere.

[13] Rusinow (1977, 121) describes how, after Tito's hard-line speech at Split in 1962, a campaign was mounted against private craftsmen, 'who were so hard-pressed that they closed their shops by the thousands, ultimately bringing about a grudging retreat by authorities who could no longer find anyone to repair their own TV sets, cars and plumbing.'

the work of social sector employees who carry on part-time work outside their organizations, as private operators.

They also pointed out that agriculture has been given unfavourable treatment with the intention of keeping down the living costs of the population. But this has damaged agriculture's long-term development, and hence the standard of living. *Ekonomska politika* (22 February 1982, p. 17) reports that the main problem facing small private enterprises is raising loans. The banks do not normally lend to them but, when they do, they charge them 10–12 per cent compared with 9 per cent for social sector enterprises. Small firms also have difficulty in obtaining foreign exchange. Petrin (1978, 356) says that the number of artisans fluctuates widely because of 'tight money credits available to artisans, heavy taxation and high rents'.

Another report in *Ekonomska politika* (12 January 1981, p. 15) remarks that there are many obstacles to starting a new private business. For example, in order to start a bakery it is necessary to obtain forty-eight documents. The procedure in the commune administration takes a long time and much effort, and there are heavy taxes to pay and high rents for accommodation. Returning migrant workers who came originally from agriculture are not encouraged to invest their savings in farming because of the limit on the size of land holding, price policy, and the inferior social and economic status of farmers. 'Without a change in conditions it is doubtful whether it is realistic to see farming as an attractive form of employment either for returning migrants or for the unemployed'.

The establishment of a 'contractual' organization is even more difficult. According to *Ekonomska politika* (16 February 1981, p. 15) a migrant worker who returned with 8 million dinars of savings had already spent more than six months trying to establish a locksmith's shop in Kragujevac. He found that not one of the sixty-five documents needed for establishing a contractual organization was available. Other obstacles include the obligation to register with the court registrar, the obligation to conclude large numbers of self-management agreements, the difficulty of finding premises, or a piece of land on which to build, and the difficulty of obtaining credit from the bank.

Private enterprises often encounter organized hostility from the social sector. *Borba* (14 July 1982) reports that private sawmills in Slovenia, of which there are 252 registered and many more unregistered, are allowed to work only for the needs of the local population. The owners recently asked for permission to supply local social sector enterprises, but this request was unanimously rejected by all delegates to the three chambers of the Slovenian assembly except the few delegates representing artisans. The main reason given was that social sector sawmills are working at only 60 per cent of capacity. Another argument was that private sawmills would be using timber which would otherwise be available to social sector sawmills. Timber is a 'social property' and private firms should not be allowed to use it. If they do, this will give rise to capitalism. The private sawmills also asked for permission to raise the limit of employment from seven to ten.

But speakers in the discussion said that this would open the door to capitalism, and the request was turned down. The communes, the paper says, regard artisans as a source of budget revenue. In some Slovenian communes they contribute as much as 30 per cent of the total revenue.

In another issue *Borba* (23 April 1982) reported that in Herzegovina social sector catering enterprises are resentful of the growth of private enterprises (presumably restaurants). It is said that private enterprises are given 'favours' under existing laws and that this should stop. No new private enterprise should be established without first consulting local social sector enterprises, and thereafter private enterprises should be subject to strict controls.

The most astonishing example of local disregard for the property rights of private farmers was reported by *Borba* (1 February 1982) from an area near Niš in South Moravia. A group of communes made a plan to plant tobacco on pastures belonging to local peasants and on some 'sandbanks'. Without consulting the peasants, tractors were sent to plough up their land. The peasants, however, objected, and the ploughing was stopped.

3. A NEW ATTITUDE TO THE PRIVATE SECTOR?

Many Yugoslavs, including people in high positions in the Party, know that present policies towards the private sector are stupid and damaging to the interests of the country. For some years there has been talk about relaxing restrictions, reducing the bureaucratic obstacles to the formation of new small private enterprises, allowing them equal access to the banks, eliminating punitive taxation, providing suitable premises for rent, and so forth. Some republics have even passed laws or arranged social compacts along these lines. But nothing much ever comes of these gestures. For the fact is that a real change in attitude to the private sector requires a change in ideology. So long as Yugoslavs are indoctrinated with the works of Marx, Engels, and Lenin they will be filled with prejudice and hatred against the 'petty-bourgeois', the 'kulaks', and the 'speculators'. And the peasants and other self-employed are well aware of this. They are tolerated, but their future is uncertain. At any moment, the regime may turn and rend them. In these conditions, even if the limits on land holding and employment were raised quite substantially, for example to 20 hectares and 20 employees, it is doubtful whether there would be a large response. It is not worth the while of a small entrepreneur to make the sacrifices necessary to establish a flourishing new business unless he has a reasonable expectation of being allowed to maintain it and expand it over a period of 20–30 years.

Intelligent and honest people recognize that the ultimate need is for a change in ideology. Yugoslavia must become an explicitly 'mixed' economy, in which self-management and private enterprise are allowed to co-exist and compete. But, in the meantime, the argument proceeds at a more detailed and pragmatic level. The country faces increasingly serious economic problems, of which the most acute are those of the balance of payments and employment. In both these areas, it is now officially recognized that the private sector could play a valuable role. For example, a more efficient use of Yugoslavia's rich natural resources could make a large contribution to the balance of payments, both by raising exports of farm products and by reducing imports.[14] Small industrial enterprises could also make a contribution to exports. Although very few 'contractual' organizations have been established, of the 21 existing in Serbia proper in early 1981, many were reported to be engaged in the export trade (*Ekonomska politika*, 16 February 1981, p. 15).

As regards employment, a genuine relaxation of restrictions on private sector service enterprises could lead to a great expansion of job opportunities. This would, of course, meet resistance from the 'moonlight' bridgade, who now enjoy two incomes while the unemployed have none. The opposition would no doubt be couched in political terms, as opposition to 'capitalism', 'exploitation', 'tax-evasion' and so on. But its real basis would be the determination of one section, at present in a privileged position, to hold on to its privileges. So long as the social sector is protected from competition, the only method which the Yugoslav authorities can think of for reducing unemployment is to put pressure on social sector enterprises to take on more unwanted labour. This is becoming more and more difficult and, if the Party pushes too hard in this direction, they will arouse serious opposition, which will become politically dangerous. Already, in many enterprises, there is so much overmanning that the workers can save their energies for 'moonlighting', which is anyway the only way in which they can expect to raise their incomes. A policy of stuffing more and more unemployed workers into existing social sector enterprises and thereby increasing the volume of 'moonlighting' is the *reductio ad absurdum* of present thinking.

An article in *Yugoslav Survey* (August 1980, p. 34) draws attention to 'the inability of the socialized sector of the economy more successfully to organize the development of various services, which is a characteristic feature of all socialist countries'.

The need to create new jobs in tertiary and quartary activities is indisputable, but available investment funds for the purpose are not too big. The problem here is not so much resources as initiative, organization, know-how or talent which, engaged in appropriate measure, can ensure provision of better and more diversified services required by the economy and society, which is entering a stage of maturity. Development in this direction is hindered by many circumstances, such as lack of interest in small-scale projects on the part of competent authorities, non-existence of a mechanism which would set in motion these activities, high levies on services, destimulating measures for the redistribution of gross national product etc.

These views have found an official echo in one of the reports of the

---

[14] Domestic production of hides is only enough to meet half the needs of the leather and leather products industries (*Ekonomska politika*, 26 April 1982, p. 16). This is an absurdity in a country with Yugoslavia's potential for stock-raising. In 1980 a million tons of wheat were imported from the United States and 200,000 tons of oilseeds (YB81, 121 – 15).

Commission on Problems of Economic Stabilization, on 'Problems of Employment and the Directions of Action for their Solution', 21 July 1980, published as a special supplement to *Borba*. The Commission resolved that:

It is necessary energetically to stimulate the development of all kinds of small enterprises, in both the social and the private sectors, by economic measures, especially by fiscal policy, in order to complement large enterprises and also directly to satisfy the needs of the population for services. Parallel with that it is necessary to change the social climate, which does not favour the strengthening of small enterprises . . . . Those people who wish to use personal labour and private capital to engage in production or in the supply of services ought not to be subjected to administrative obstacles and delays, unrealistic taxes and hostile political attitudes.

In particular, the self-employed should be given, 'not only in words but in deeds, the same conditions of health and social insurance as others, and equality in the political sphere'.

These are brave words, and they show how far enlightened opinion has moved. The crucial test, however, is whether the Party itself, from top to bottom, can be made to face reality and to accept new ideas.

CHAPTER 14

CONCLUSIONS

In the course of this book we have become deeply involved in describing the Yugoslav system and in analysing its operation and effects. It is important, however, to remind the reader that our main purpose is to understand the 'laws of motion' of a labour-managed economy as such, without regard to the special conditions ruling in Yugoslavia. Such a task can be approached in two ways. The first is to construct an *a priori* theoretical model of a labour-managed economy, and to derive conclusions about its behaviour as logical deductions from the model's assumptions. The second is to study the behaviour of an existing labour-managed economy and to attempt to construct an appropriate model or models to explain it. Both methods can, of course, be used in parallel; and it is usually in this way that the most fruitful scientific results are obtained. In this book an attempt has been made to combine these two methods. Existing theoretical models of a labour-managed economy have been considered, and an alternative model has been proposed which is believed to be more appropriate to modern conditions. In addition, a major effort has been made to sift through the experience of the only existing (at least nominally) labour-managed economy, that of Yugoslavia, with a view to testing the theoretical model, as well as throwing light on aspects of the real operation of a labour-managed system which are not normally taken into consideration by economists.

THE THEORETICAL APPROACH

A theoretical model of a labour-managed economy requires assumptions about the legal and political environment and the motives of the worker-managers. Models of this sort have been constructed by Ward, Domar, Vanek, Meade and others. But such models inevitably rest on only a few major assumptions, which may or may not be appropriate. The standard models assume a *laissez-faire* market environment, with perfect competition in all markets and perfect mobility of technical knowledge. Worker-managers, i.e. the members of the labour co-operatives, are assumed to have the objective of maximizing their (immediate) income per member. On these assumptions some interesting conclusions have been derived. They suggest that the short-run elasticity of supply from a labour co-operative will be smaller than from capitalist firms, but that the long-run equilibrium position will be the same as under perfectly competitive capitalism. The models stress the great importance for optimal resource allocation in a labour-managed economy of ensuring free entry of new enterprises. But this is true also for capitalism.

The assumption of perfect competition in all markets is strong and unrealistic. Vanek (1970) has recognized this and he has modified his basic model in a number of ways to try to take account of more realistic situations. For example, if there is no unique optimal size of firm, or there are obstacles to firms reaching that size, labour income will include rents arising from differential costs of production in different firms. This will generate an imperfect labour market and corresponding misallocations of resources. If, further, co-operatives plough back income without attributing the sums to individual capital accounts, inter-enterprise differentials in labour income will widen further. For this reason, Vanek recommends that all gross investment by co-operatives should be financed out of loans paying the market rate of interest.

But these modifications to the perfect competition model do not go far enough. The real truth is that perfect competition has never existed in the capital market, nor ever could do, and that technical knowledge has never been a free good. Moreover, in the modern world competition in most product markets is imperfect, in the sense that products and their suppliers are differentiated, so that new entrants cannot immediately sell as much as they would like to do at a 'going' price. For these reasons in most industries new entrants—with no previous experience of business operation and no accumulated profits from such activity—cannot start up at the optimal scale. The same situation exists also in many services and in agriculture in developed countries. Consequently, in all these cases the pressure from new entrants, or the threat of new entry, is not sufficient to eliminate the long-run equilibrium profits of larger enterprises enjoying economies of scale.

Under capitalism differential profits, or rents, accrue mainly to the owners of the equity capital, although the workers in the more profitable enterprises usually obtain a share of the profits, partly because it pays to give them the incentive to work well and partly through the exercise of trade union power (which tends to be greater in larger enterprises). In a labour-managed economy, however, these rents are treated entirely as the 'labour' income of the workers; and this has a number of undesirable consequences. The first is that there will be considerable, and growing, differences in worker income between enterprises, even when comparative skills and other relevant considerations are taken into account. This is politically disturbing in a socialist economy—or indeed in any modern economy; it leads to immobility of labour between enterprises, and hence to a misallocation of labour resources; and it encourages corruption in the filling of job vacancies.[1] The second effect is that, since the cost of labour

---

[1] All of these phenomena are very much in evidence in Yugoslavia.

in the more profitable enterprises is higher than in the less profitable, the more profitable enterprises will have a bias towards capital-intensive investment decisions. This bias would not occur to the same extent under capitalism, since workers in capitalist enterprises do not receive 'the full proceeds of their labour'.

Thirdly, since higher incomes per worker in the more successful enterprises are to a large extent the result of special technical 'know-how', or experience, and since the transfer of such technical knowledge to other labour-managed co-operatives cannot be paid for through the return of the resulting profits to those who make the transfer, the transfer of technology is much inhibited. The transfer of technology becomes an act of charity, or 'solidarity', instead of being motivated by a search for its most profitable use. Socially organized charity sounds like a noble aim, but it often proves to be politically difficult, or even corrupting, when pushed too far.

These are the most important implications of our model of a labour-managed economy. In addition, the model shows that these undesirable effects would not be eliminated, although they would be somewhat reduced, if all investment by labour co-operatives were to be financed out of interest-bearing loans, since the rents arising from private technology and economies of scale would still be attributed to labour. The model also suggests that the elasticity of short-run supply from labour co-operatives would not be very different from the corresponding elasticity of capitalist enterprises operating under conditions of imperfect competition. This point, which has occupied such a prominent place in Western theoretical literature, is shown to be rather trivial.

Finally, this model, or indeed any realistic model of a labour-managed economy, draws attention to a difference in the response of such an economy to changes in world prices of tradable goods and services (expressed in terms of domestic currency). In a capitalist economy, where there is a labour market and—as an 'imperfection'—wage contracts run for a year or more, a rise in domestic prices for tradable goods (for example, through devaluation) will have a stimulating effect on exports and a restrictive effect on imports so long as labour contracts do not fully adjust to the new price levels. But in a labour-managed economy there are no wage contracts and hence there is no 'wage drag'. An incomes policy is more difficult to establish in a labour-managed economy than under capitalism, and in any case has little or no relevance to changes in product prices, which are dominated by world price changes. The control of externally induced inflation is, therefore, likely to be more difficult under labour management than under capitalism, and may require an even greater restriction of domestic demand with a view to strengthening the exchange rate. As against this, a labour-managed system which is in equilibrium in its balance of payments does not have to contend with the internal pressure towards inflation which arises in modern capitalism through the leap-frogging demands of trade unions. Since in a labour-managed economy all net income belongs to the workers, there is no motive for trade union wage demands, and trade unions are an anachronism.[2]

THE YUGOSLAV ENVIRONMENT

If an economist were free to choose a country in which to carry out the experiment of installing a labour-management system, with a view to drawing general conclusions about the effects of such a system, he would be unlikely to choose Yugoslavia. For Yugoslavia is, by any standards, a very unusual country. It was created in 1918 by the amalgamation of Serbia and Montenegro with the predominantly Slav parts of Austria-Hungary in the vicinity of, or to the south of, the Drava: Slovenia, Croatia, Bosnia and Herzegovina, and Vojvodina. The peoples of these countries or regions had never previously been under one ruler. Those of the north-west— Slovenia and Croatia—were predominantly Catholic and economically more advanced than those of the south and east. The people of Bosnia and Herzegovina were partly Croats and partly Serbs by the criterion of language, but they were divided in religion into Catholics, Orthodox, and Muslim. The majority of the people of Serbia were Serbs, speaking a slightly different language from the Croats, and Orthodox in religion. But Serbia also included a substantial population of Macedonians and Albanians in the south. Montenegro was a small, mountainous, and rather isolated country populated by Serbs, with a minority of Albanians. Vojvodina was a melting pot of many nationalities, including Serbs, Croats, Hungarians, Germans, Slovaks, and Romanians.

The problem of forming a united country out of these disparate elements, who were in addition at widely different levels of economic development, would have been enormous under any regime. But it was rendered more difficult by the nature of the regime which was in fact established: the Serbian King ruled, with a parliament consisting mainly of Serbs, and a Serbian military, civil, and police apparatus. The principal objectors to this arrangement were the Croats, who were the largest minority and the most conscious of the sacrifice made by linking themselves with the more backward peoples of the south and east. Throughout the inter-war period the Croats struggled for greater autonomy and a federal system. As the Second World War approached they seemed to be on the verge of success, only to encounter a reaction among the Serbs. These problems were still unresolved when, in April 1941, Yugoslavia was brutally invaded by the Axis powers.

It is unnecessary to repeat the story of the growth of guerrilla activity in Yugoslavia and its increasing dominance by the communist partisans, led by Tito. It is important, however, to stress that a major reason for communist success was the party's advocacy of 'brotherhood and unity'

[2] Trade unions are artificially kept alive in Yugoslavia, mainly as a means of keeping the workers under the ideological and organizational control of the Party. If the Party did not impose its own trade unions, there would always be the possibility that independent trade unions would come into existence, primarily as a vehicle for political opposition, as in Poland.

among the Yugoslav peoples in the common struggle against the occupiers. Emphasis on the need for federalism and respect for the rights of most nationalities (with the total exception of Germans and some reservations about the Albanians) laid the basis for a series of post-war federal constitutions which increasingly gave real powers to the six republics and the two autonomous provinces.

The outcome has been that Yugoslavia is the most genuinely federalized country in the world (not excluding Switzerland). The federal government now has very limited power, except in relation to defence and customs duties. Its budget is carefully scrutinized by the parliamentary representatives of the republics and provinces, who also have to give their unanimous approval for any major change in economic policy. Each republic and province has its own national bank (although not its own currency), its own economic plan (only partially integrated with the federal plan), and—in effect— its own balance of payments.

But decentralization goes even further than this. When Yugoslavia first adopted 'self-management' as its objective, the Party, which had previously held total power over the economy, as well as over every other aspect of life, under a Stalinist-type system, recognized the dangers to their own position of giving real decision-making authority to the workers in their enterprises. The method of maintaining Party control under the new arrangements was to devolve much economic power to local governments (the communes), giving the communal authorities the right to supervise all important enterprise decisions. Thus the Party's political apparatus, which had complete dominance in the communes, as elsewhere, could still maintain effective control. Since those early days the communes have lost some of their power to the republican and provincial governments (and the corresponding levels of the Party apparatus), but the local commune officials are still very much in evidence, and many communes are run almost as if they were independent republics.[3] Yugoslavia is not only federalized but 'Balkanized'.

But this is not the only peculiar feature of the Yugoslav environment. It must never be forgotten that Yugoslavia is ruled by a Marxist-Leninist party, with complete monopoly of political power, and absolute dominance in the media, education, the youth movement, the trade unions, the army, the police, and every other organization except the Church. The great paradox of Yugoslavia is that such a Party ever agreed to introduce worker 'self-management' which, if taken to its logical conclusion, would deprive the Party of its power. There are probably two explanations: the first was the need to provide a new ideology in face of Stalin's threat to Yugoslav independence; but secondly, at a deeper level, this choice was influenced

---

[3] 'The commune is so much involved in economic affairs that without its approval it is not possible to appoint a director, to build a new factory, or to pool labour and resources . . . We constantly build factories, often without justification, on the orders of the commune, because only in that way can the commune solve its local problems—from employment to the building of flats, hospitals, schools and roads' (*Borba*, 30 October 1982).

by the Yugoslav tradition of local loyalties and the Party's wartime commitment to 'brotherhood and unity'.

Thus Yugoslavia is a country which is trying simultaneously to ride two horses, which often pull in different directions: self-management, and the Party monopoly of power in the name of the proletariat. A logical reconciliation of the objectives of self-management and the dictatorship of the proletariat would be to say that worker self-management is indeed the dictatorship of the proletariat. But that would eliminate any role for the Party. There was an effort to move in this direction in the 1950s, when the Party was supposed to relinquish its stranglehold on administration and to become an organization of philosophers and ideologists—a sort of communist priesthood separated from temporal power. But, for obvious reasons, this never happened, and in the 1970s there was a backlash. In the meantime, in the 1960s, the upsurge of national feelings in the republics and provinces had used the doctrine of self-management as a means to secure genuine federalization. The reassertion of Party control in the 1970s was, therefore, obliged to work within the new constitutional framework, which had led to a federalization of the Party itself. In a sense, Yugoslavia is now a federation of one-party states, subject to the restriction that the eight parties are still held together by the threat of a revival of the never-abandoned rule of 'democratic centralism', and the risk that too much disagreement between the parties would weaken Party control over the population and provide opportunities for foreign intervention.

In spite of ubiquitous Party intervention, either directly or indirectly through the government apparatus or the Party-controlled 'socio-political organizations', such as the trade unions and the Socialist Alliance, Yugoslavia still retains some of the crucial characteristics of a labour-managed economy. There is no central planning and enterprises operate in a market environment. Despite abundant, and increasing, administrative interventions, on such matters as prices, foreign exchange and credit allocations, investment and employment decisions, and the selection of managers, in the final analysis the enterprise has to try to make a living by producing for the market. In many respects, Yugoslav social sector enterprises face the same problems as British nationalized enterprises: a combination of market and political pressures which can easily lead to a decline in morale and efficiency. But the Yugoslav workers do have important nominal rights—to elect their workers' councils, to approve all major business decisions, and to endorse the selection of their top managers—and much time and effort is devoted to the operation of self-management institutions. As a result, many Yugoslav workers probably feel a greater degree of loyalty towards their enterprises than is characteristic of workers in British nationalized industries.[4]

[4] But the proportion is apparently not high. In a survey made among workers in Slovenia 60 per cent of those interviewed said that they did not feel that the basic organization in which they worked was 'theirs', and that it was all the same to them if they worked in some other organization (*Ekonomska politika*, 13 December 1982, p. 24).

My conclusion is that, in spite of all qualifications, the Yugoslav system is essentially a market economy, and that the basic motivation of the workers in social sector enterprises is to use their self-management rights, so far as they are allowed to do so, to take decisions which will raise their own income prospects. Yugoslavia is by no means a *laissez-faire* market system. But very few market economies are, or ever have been, so. The market is a potent force and, even when it is smothered by a mass of regulations and interventions, it still continues to work, although in a distorted and weakened way. Yugoslav experience, therefore, yields much relevant and useful information about the underlying tendencies of a self-management market system which, when interpreted with care, can throw light on how such a system would behave in a different, less restrictive, environment.

THE INTERPRETATION OF YUGOSLAV EXPERIENCE

The record of Yugoslav economic achievements over the past thirty years is mixed. In some respects it has been a story of great success; but there have also been a number of weaknesses and failures. It will be convenient to divide our subsequent discussion into two parts, in the first of which we shall attempt to account for the successes, and in the second for the failures.

Reasons for success

From 1950 to 1979, with only temporary lapses, Yugoslavia enjoyed very rapid rates of growth of real national product, industrial production, labour productivity in industry and agriculture, employment in industry and in the social sector generally, and real personal income and consumption per head. Since 1979 all these rates of growth have fallen, in some cases—such as personal income and consumption—quite sharply. Indeed, between 1979 and 1982 real personal income per worker in the social sector is estimated to have declined by a total of about 15 per cent.

The major explanation for the rapid growth of output and productivity in the social sector from 1950 to 1979 was the high investment ratio. Investment in industry was given top priority in the early post-war years, and the government kept control over total investment and its allocation for a long time after the introduction of 'self-management'. After the relaxation of government control in 1965, enterprises continued to invest heavily, partly out of reinvested income but increasingly out of bank loans. A high investment ratio was encouraged in this later period by the maintenance of low real interest rates, by the urge of local politicians to establish 'political factories', and by the fact that workers and managers had only a limited sense of responsibility for the use of 'social' capital, in which they had no equity stake. Consequently, aggregate investment was always tending to grow too fast, and from time to time it was necessary to rein it in by deflationary measures.

The second major reason for the rapid growth of social product was the strength of 'animal spirits' released by the victory over the occupying armies and by the manifest opportunities for rapid economic development of a country which, like others in southern Europe, was more than ready for the introduction of modern technology. In the early post-war years these energies found expression in voluntary labour on reconstruction projects and in long hours of poorly paid work. After the introduction of self-management more attention was paid to modernization and improvement of product quality, with a closer regard for market demand. Released from their Stalinist strait-jackets, managers began to introduce new technology and new products, and to take more account of costs. The results gave clear proof that decentralization of decision-making and a market economy can produce results superior to those produced by a command economy. Unfortunately, however, the bias of a self-managed system towards capital-intensive reinvestment within existing enterprises, combined with a generally irresponsible attitude towards investment, for both political and economic reasons, led to a concentration of too much investment in selected industries and enterprises. The depressing effect of this policy on the absorption of labour was offset for many years by political and social pressure on enterprises to take on more staff than required by their technology. The economic reform of 1965 led to a sudden reduction of this overmanning, and growing unemployment and emigration. These adverse trends were slowed down in the 1970s, but only by renewed political pressure for overmanning. This is one reason for the sharp fall in growth rates of output and productivity in recent years, despite the maintenance of a high (although somewhat lower) investment ratio.

Another factor, of course, which has had a depressing effect on the Yugoslav economy in recent years has been the rise in petroleum prices and the ensuing world economic recession. Like many other countries, Yugoslavia tried to ride out the balance-of-payments effects of the rise in petroleum prices and to continue to give major emphasis to growth of output through high investment. The result was a dramatic rise in foreign indebtedness and in the rate of inflation, which eventually provoked sharp deflationary measures and a fall in living standards which might, with better foresight and a more rational economic policy, have been largely avoided.

Reasons for failure

The main weaknesses of the Yugoslav system—apart from its drift into its present crisis—have been growing unemployment (and emigration), a weak balance of payments, accelerating inflation, and a failure to reduce regional income disparities. Many of these weaknesses spring from the self-management system as such—at least in the form adopted in Yugoslavia—but they have been exaggerated by inherent characteristics of a Marxist regime, especially the monopoly of power by a single Party and the ideological biases of Marxist dogma.

The central problem of any self-management system is the efficient allocation of resources. Since self-management implies that enterprise surpluses (or rents) are distributed to existing members, or ploughed back for the benefit of future members, to be divided between them in proportion to their labour input, the apparent cost of labour in most enterprises is higher than the true cost, and there is a bias towards capital-intensive investment decisions. In addition, retained enterprise income, existing labour, and accumulated technical knowledge will only with great difficulty—and largely for political or charitable reasons—move from one enterprise to another even when their marginal productivity in the second enterprise would be higher. For both these reasons a self-management system tends to be less successful in absorbing unemployed labour, as well as in shifting resources of all kinds towards regions with abundant labour supplies, than a system in which both capital and labour move more freely towards the use in which their marginal productivity is highest.

These undesirable effects could be reduced if, firstly, enterprise savings were allocated to members' capital accounts, i.e. if such savings were treated as loans from the members, and, secondly, if a major effort were made to encourage the formation of new self-managed enterprises. But in Yugoslavia political ideology has so far stood in the way of the first policy, despite the fact that Yugoslav enterprises borrow heavily from banks, which are largely passing on the savings of private households. And, since the time of the economic reform, the second policy has been blocked by, on the one hand, distrust of the economic efficiency of new enterprises created by governments and, on the other, an unwillingness to allow other agencies, including groups of citizens, to take the initiative in this area. The result has been that new investments are more and more concentrated in the hands of existing enterprises, where they mainly favour existing members and the developed regions, which have the largest flows of enterprise savings. The adverse effects on inter-regional mobility of capital have been partly offset by a major programme of inter-regional aid. But, because these funds are offered on very favourable terms and are channelled through regional governments, they have been used to an excessive degree for capital-intensive and 'political' projects, and they have not created either as much new employment or as much extra output as they would have done if allocated by an agency which aimed to maximize the rate of return.

In recent years the Yugoslav authorities have recognized the weaknesses of their regional aid programme and have tried to overcome them by encouraging direct inter-enterprise investment between richer and poorer regions (so-called 'pooling of labour and resources'). Enterprises in the richer regions have been given substantial incentives to follow this path by allowing them to offset such investments against part of their compulsory contribution to economic aid funds; but this programme has so far had little success, presumably because the investing enterprises still expect little or no return on their funds, while being expected to incur substantial additional costs in training the staff of the recipient enterprises. Moreover, very few Yugoslav enterprises would be willing to transfer technology to enterprises in other regions for the manufacture of similar products, nor would they be allowed to do so by their local political authorities. This is one of the symptoms of the increasing tendency towards local and regional autarky in Yugoslavia, which is partly the result of self-management as such, but mainly the result of the special political situation in Yugoslavia created by traditional nationalism and the desire of the Party to keep control over the policies of self-managed enterprises through a decentralized system of political power.

A further symptom of autarky has been the tendency for the share of inter-regional (and even inter-communal) trade to decline. Communes encourage their enterprises to favour local supplies of materials and components, and local retailers and wholesalers often discriminate against 'foreign' products which are competitive with locally produced goods. In the autumn of 1982, when the Yugoslav balance of payments was officially recognized to be in a critical state, many communes began to ration commodities in short supply, to make sure that available supplies would not be bought up by outsiders. This dangerous tendency—which leading Yugoslav politicians openly deplore—is the consequence of granting major economic powers to local political authorities and of the emphasis on the importance of local 'planning'. Social planning almost inevitably has an autarkic bias, and the results can be seen in Yugoslavia both at national and local levels.

The chronic weakness of the Yugoslav balance of payments is not attributable to self-management as such, but to the Marxist biases towards planning and heavy industry, and towards import-substitution rather than export-promotion. Yugoslavia has made considerable efforts to rid itself of this ideological heritage and to force its enterprises to compete in the world market. But, since it is impossible for a Marxist Party to maintain a consistent attitude towards the market, the government has shown a recurrent tendency to slip back into using restrictions on imports and arbitrary methods of stimulating exports. Despite the long-avowed aim of making the dinar convertible, the will to face the consequences of convertibility is still lacking, and the methods of allocating foreign exchange are increasingly irrational and distortive. The current debt crisis, and the consequential efforts to overcome it, will provide a severe test of the viability of the Yugoslav compromise between the market and Party control. There are strong forces pulling in both directions, and the issue merges with the underlying conflict between centralizers and federalists at the political level. Whatever the outcome, however, it will not prove anything about the efficiency of a self-management system as such.

The acceleration of inflation in Yugoslavia, especially since 1979, and the apparent inability of the authorities to bring it under control, appear to be attributable mainly to the lack of 'wage drag' in a self-management system, the difficulty of establishing an incomes policy in such an environment, and the doubtful effectiveness of incomes policy in restraining price increases in an economy in which the whole of enterprise net income (at least nominally) belongs to the workers. The consequence is that a self-managed economy is especially sensitive to external changes in prices and its balance of payments. For Yugoslavia, the steep increases in petroleum prices in the 1970s were a disaster, since they injected rapid inflation into the system and, in the absence of effective countervailing measures, created large deficits in the balance of payments. In an effort to avoid restricting investment demand, and with inadequate instruments—and perhaps too little political courage—to restrict consumption demand, the government was obliged eventually, especially after 1979, to allow the exchange value of the dinar to fall, and this fed back very quickly into further internal inflation. It is now being forced to maintain severe deflationary policies on both consumption and investment demand, in the hope of bringing equilibrium into a balance of payments which has been much weakened by the accumulation of foreign debts during the second half of the 1970s.

While a large part of these difficulties arise from the inherent lack of resistance of a self-management system to unfavourable external events, some part is also attributable to the political weakness of a one-party, but not completely totalitarian, state. A totalitarian regime can suppress all open criticism, and even the facts, and can force the population to accept greater sacrifices than regimes which allow some freedom of discussion and comment. Multi-party parliamentary regimes are also capable of taking strong action in some circumstances, since the government can claim to have a mandate from the electorate. But the weakest type of government is probably one which, while refusing to allow alternative parties and a free electoral choice, gives the population some opportunities to be informed and to criticize, as a self-management system must necessarily do, and as the Yugoslav federal system also inevitably allows. The conclusion seems to be, therefore, that, while externally induced inflation is more difficult to resist in a self-managed system than under capitalism, effective counteracting measures are more likely to be taken in a fully democratic regime, in which the government can demonstrate that it has the support of the majority of the electorate.

Some of the major obstacles to a satisfactory policy of regional development in Yugoslavia have been mentioned above. Self-management as such, especially in its Yugoslav form, tends to put a brake on the mobility of capital and technology from more developed to less developed regions. But the problem is increased by a number of political factors. First, there is the influence of Marxist ideology and rhetoric, which encourages the idea that workers in the social sector in all regions are entitled to approximately equal incomes. The result is that the less efficient workers (and the politicians) in the backward regions insist on having at least as capital-intensive and technologically advanced enterprises as those in the more developed areas. And, when the workers in the backward regions fail to produce equivalent results with that equipment, they nevertheless expect to be paid as much, or very nearly as much, as workers in the more advanced regions. While the levels of personal income per worker in the backward regions are lower than in the more advanced regions, the differences are smaller than the differences in output per worker (see Table 8.16 above). Hence enterprise savings per worker in the backward regions are smaller than in the advanced regions and the enterprises are correspondingly restricted in their growth potential. Secondly, the Party policy of giving priority to heavy industries, especially in the early years, has had a particularly adverse effect on the development of the backward regions, partly because some of them have important mineral resources and partly because they lived in the illusion that the building of, for example, a steel works or an oil refinery was the essential key to local industrial development. If at an earlier stage incomes had been somewhat lower (and the gap between incomes in the social and private sectors less exaggerated), and more emphasis had been placed on the development of labour-intensive industries, especially those directed to the export market, the present levels of productivity in the economically backward republics and Kosovo would be more satisfactory, and their contributions to the Yugoslav balance of payments more positive (or, rather, less negative).

Misguided economic policies have been further complicated by political factors, especially in Montenegro and Kosovo. Because of their important contribution to the resistance struggle, and also because of their close alliance with their fellow Serbs in Serbia, the Montenegrins have always claimed, and usually received, exceptionally favourable treatment in the allocation of investment funds. Much of this investment has gone into large capital-intensive projects, many of which are economically unsuitable and badly located. Montenegrin enterprises are particularly unproductive, especially when account is taken of their large volume of capital per man; and a high proportion of them make losses. There are also many scandalous examples of enterprises in which workers show poor discipline, and of fraud and other illegal activities. One cannot escape the impression that many Montenegrins believe that Yugoslavia owes them a living.

A different political situation, but one which produces very similar results, exists in Kosovo. Here the overwhelming majority of the population are Albanians (in the census of 1981 1.23 million out of a total of 1.58 million) among whom there is a long-standing feeling that they have been oppressed by the Serbs. The Yugoslav government has tried to overcome this hostility by heavy injections of funds for the finance of investment and of the social services. But the government has refused to make any concession to the demand that Kosovo, like Macedonia or Montenegro, should become a full republic (which would give it the nominal right to secede). The demonstrations which occurred in 1981 were severely repressed, and people are still being sent to prison for distributing leaflets or writing up slogans.[5] The state of political alienation in Kosovo is at least partly responsible for the tendency in that region for people to break the law and to refuse to pay taxes, rents, and other legal

---

[5] Four schoolboys were sent to prison for 15 days in October 1982 for writing 'Kosovo-republic' on the surface of the road on their way home from school (*Borba*, 26 October 1982).

obligations.[6] The result is that industrial productivity is low and that Kosovo is a considerable economic burden to the rest of the country. Since the Albanian population has a much higher birth rate than the local Serbs and Montenegrins, who are also slowly but steadily moving out of the province, it will not be long before 90 per cent of the population is Albanian (or at least non-Serb). The only long-term remedy for the vicious circle of economic backwardness and political alienation is a consistent application of the Yugoslav principles of self-management and equality of nationalities, i.e. the granting of republican rights to Kosovo. Unfortunately, this is at present anathema to the Serbs, who regard Kosovo as their ancient homeland.

In both these regions local political factors are mainly responsible for the unsatisfactory results of Yugoslav regional aid programmes. While self-management as such does put a brake on inter-regional transfers of technology, this need not be a great handicap in a country like Yugoslavia which is reasonably open to the outside world. In the more enterprising republics of Bosnia-Herzegovina and Macedonia, both of which are classified as less developed, there are many successful enterprises which have been started with the help of Western technology.

A GENERAL ASSESSMENT

In comparison with a command economy of the Soviet type a self-management system is an enormous step forward. Decentralization of decision-making through the market gives enterprise managers, and to a smaller extent the workers, an opportunity to show initiative and enterprise, and hence to raise productivity. The market system is also the foundation stone of freedom and the rule of law and, even in the absence of full political democracy, it gives men more scope for genuine civilization and the development of the human personality than any totalitarian regime can do. This is the strong point in the argument for replacing Soviet socialism by self-management socialism.

Whether self-management reduces intra-enterprise alienation is more difficult to say. In the Yugoslav environment, in which the outside political authorities have never really surrendered their power to the workers, there is much evidence of poor discipline, bad work, cynicism, and—increasingly—of 'economic crime'. Most Yugoslav workers in socialist 'self-managed' enterprises have the same 'them and us' attitude as that which prevails in other economic systems. There are exceptions to this rule in Yugoslavia, as there are in other countries. Everything depends on the quality of management and its ability to command the respect and allegiance of the workers. Examples of good management and high morale seem to occur as often under private enterprise as under self-management. On a naïve view,

---

[6] Stane Dolanc, Federal Minister for Internal Affairs, said on television: 'For a long time there has been a kind of anarchy in Kosovo. It has been normal, for example, for people not to pay taxes, rents, water and electricity charges, and television licences, as well as to drive without a licence and to fail to register a car, and so on' (*Borba*, 30 September 1982).

self-management solves the problem of alienation and should, therefore, boost morale. But the essential conditions for good morale are good management, strong but fair discipline, and a substantial effort to keep the workers informed and consulted. There is a risk that self-management will reduce the quality of business management, especially in a political system like that of Yugoslavia in which the dominant ideology is anti-management. There is an even greater risk that self-management will loosen discipline and encourage 'free riders', and so undermine morale.

From a purely economic point of view, self-management gives a capital-intensive bias to investment decisions by established enterprises, and hinders the mobility of resources between enterprises and hence between regions. These defects could to some extent be overcome if there were an active policy for promoting new enterprises with independent finance and technology, for example, through special consulting agencies as in Mondragon, or through international joint ventures. These problems are more serious in Yugoslavia, where all initial and ploughed-back capital is 'social' and belongs, in effect, to existing and future cohorts of workers employed in the enterprise. They are less serious, but not entirely absent, under the Mondragon system of individual member capital accounts. Moreover, the Mondragon system, in which membership of the co-operative is voluntary and requires the payment of a capital contribution, is likely to be more conducive to good management and good discipline.

Unfortunately, most of the paths to reform of the Yugoslav self-management system are blocked by the ruling ideology. The 'social' ownership of capital, with its accompanying capital-intensive bias and encouragement of irresponsible investment decisions, anti-manager propaganda, and the refusal to treat the training of managers as a serious task requiring specialized courses and institutions, and the constant intervention of the political authorities in enterprise affairs, with a consequential obligation to 'socialize risks', thus depriving the workers of both the power and the incentive to take responsibility for enterprise decisions—all of these phenomena arise directly from the nature of the ruling ideology and the determination of the Party to retain its monopoly of power. Despite genuine efforts to promote the idea of self-management, and to establish corresponding rules and institutions, loyalty to the principles of self-management has always taken second place to loyalty to this more fundamental ideology.

This raises a major dilemma for anyone who is so favourably inclined towards self-management that he wishes to see the system made compulsory (if not over the whole economy, at least over large parts of it). For, unless there were, by some miracle, a general consensus to make such a change in social institutions, the imposition of a self-management system would probably be the work of a one-party Marxist regime, as in Yugoslavia. But, at least in the long run, such a regime is fundamentally incompatible with self-management, since it does not really trust the workers to make their own decisions, and it does not trust the market to be the dominant equilibrating force in the economy. If, therefore, one starts from a democratic capitalist market position, the potential gains from self-management, if the system were imposed, would be more than offset by the losses on the political side. This suggests that the wisest policy in such countries is to encourage the establishment of voluntary producers' co-operatives as an element, perhaps a growing element, in a mixed economy. The example of Mondragon shows that this is not a utopian dream.

For those who start from a Soviet-type command economy, however, the introduction of self-management, even without any fundamental reduction in the monopoly power of the Party, offers a great step forward in economic efficiency, the encouragement of initiative and enterprise, the liberalization of some aspects of political life and the increasing application of the rule of law. One cannot completely exclude the possibility that self-management would eventually lead to a withering away of the state and the Party, as the Yugoslavs officially predicted in the early days. In any case, self-management is the only hope for the people now governed by the Russian system. It is not surprising, therefore, that all movements for liberalization in the Soviet empire have tried to move in this direction. Although it is easy to find weaknesses and unsolved problems in a self-management system, especially in the complex political and 'national' environment of Yugoslavia, these arguments should not be used to discourage workers in these countries from making 'self-management' one of their principal demands.

REFERENCES

Adizes, I. (1971), *Industrial Democracy: Yugoslav Style*, The Free Press.
Arrow, K. J. (1964), 'The role of securities in the optimal allocation of risk-bearing', *Review of Economic Studies*, vol. 31.

Babić, M. (1980), 'Some aspects of plan coordination in Yugoslavia', *Economic Analysis and Workers' Management*, vol. 14.
Bajt, A. (1980), Review of Jaroslav Vanek, *The Labor-Managed Economy: Essays* in *Journal of Comparative Economics*, vol. 4.
Bass, R. and Marbury, E. (eds.) (1959), *The Soviet-Yugoslav Controversy, 1948–1958: A Documentary Record*, Prospect Books.
Bazler-Madžar, M. and others (1981), *Sistem samoupravnog društvenog planiranja*, Institut ekonomskih nauka, Belgrade.
Blagojević, S. (1980), 'The system and level of investment, 1974–1978', *Yugoslav Survey*, vol. 21, November.
Bonin, J. P. (1983), 'Innovation in a labor-managed firm: a membership perspective', *Journal of Industrial Economics*, vol. 31.
Broekmeyer, M. J. (ed.) (1970), *Yugoslav Workers' Self-Management*, D. Reidel Publishing Company.
Brus, W. (1975), *Socialist Ownership and Political Systems*, Routledge and Kegan Paul.

Carter, A. (1982), *Democratic Reform in Yugoslavia: The Changing Role of the Party*, Frances Pinter (Publishers), London.
Chilosi, A. (1978), 'Socialist and communist income distribution in Marxian and Soviet Marxist thought', *Il Politico*, vol. 43.
Comisso, E. T. (1979), *Workers' Control under Plan and Market*, Yale University Press.
Comisso, E. T. (1980) 'Yugoslavia in the 1970's: self-management and bargaining', *Journal of Comparative Economics*, vol. 4.
The Constitution of the Socialist Federal Republic of Yugoslavia (1974), Belgrade.
Constitutional System of Yugoslavia (1980), Jugoslovenska stvarnost, Belgrade.
Crosland, C. A. R. (1956), *The Future of Socialism*, Jonathan Cape.

Debreu, G. (1959), *Theory of Value*, Wiley.
Denitch, D. D. (1976), *The Legitimation of a Revolution: The Yugoslav Case*, Yale University Press.
Dirlam, J. B. and Plummer, J. L. (1973), *An Introduction to the Yugoslav Economy*, Charles E. Merrill Publishing Company.
Djilas, M. (1969), *The Unperfect Society*, Methuen.
Djilas, M. (1980), *Tito*, Harcourt Brace Jovanovitch.

Domar, E. (1966), 'The Soviet collective farm as a producer cooperative', *American Economic Review*, vol. 56.

Drulović, M. (1978), *Self-Management on Trial*, Spokesman Books.

Društveno planiranje i proširena reprodukcija, Informator, Zagreb 1980.

Eames, A. H. (1980), *The Yugoslav System of Self-Management*, Ph.D. thesis submitted to the University of Bradford.

Estrin S. (1981), 'Income dispersion in a self-managed economy', *Economica*, vol. 48.

Federal Statistical Office (1974), *Anketa o prihodima, rashodima i potrŏsnji domaćinstava 1973, prvi rezultati*, Statistical Bulletin No. 833.

Federal Statistical Office (1979), *Anketa o prihodima, rashodima i potrošnji domaćinstava 1978, prvi rezultati*, Statistical Bulletin No. 1125.

Flora, P. and Heidenheimer, A. J. (1981), *The Development of Welfare States in Europe and America*, Transaction Books.

Furubotn, E. G. and Pejovich, S. (1970), 'Property rights and the behaviour of the firm in a socialist state: the example of Yugoslavia', *Zeitschrift für Nationalökonomie*, vol. 30.

Govedarica, S. (1972), 'Price system and policy', *Yugoslav Survey*, August.

Granick D. (1975), *Enterprise Guidance in Eastern Europe*, Princeton University Press.

Hoffman, G. W. and Neal, F. W. (1962), *Yugoslavia and the New Communism*, Twentieth Century Fund.

Horvat, B. (1967), 'Prilog zasnivanja teorije jugoslavenskog preduzeća', *Ekonomska analiza*, vol. 1.

Horvat, B. (1976), *The Yugoslav Economic System*, M. E. Sharpe, Inc.

Horvat, B. (1982), *The Political Economy of Socialism*, Martin Robertson.

Hunnius, G. (1975), 'Workers' self-management in Yugoslavia', in Horvat, B. and others (eds.) *Self-Governing Socialism*, International Arts and Sciences Press, Inc.

International Labour Organisation (1981), *Workers' Participation in Decisions within Undertakings*, Geneva.

Jain, S. (1975), *Size Distribution of Income*, The World Bank, Washington, D. C.

Jerovšek, J. and Možina, S. (1978), 'Efficiency and democracy in self-managing enterprises' in Obradović and Dunn (1978).

Johnson, A. R. (1972), *The Transformation of Communist Ideology: The Yugoslav Case, 1945–1953*, M.I.T. Press.

Jurić, D. (1979), 'Associated labour and socialist self-management', *Yugoslav Survey*, vol. 20, May.

Kalogjera, D. (1981), 'Samoupravno odlučivanje u organizacijama udruženog rada', *Ekonomski pregled*, no. 3–4.

Katušić M. (1970), 'Economic efficiency and workers' self-management' in Broekmeyer (1970).

Kolakowski, L. (1978), *Main Currents of Marxism*, 3 vols., Oxford University Press.

Kravis, I. B., Heston, A. and Summers, R. (1982), *World Product and Income: International Comparisons of Real Gross Product*, Johns Hopkins University Press for the World Bank.

Lendvai, P. (1969), *Eagles in Cobwebs*, Macdonald, London.
Lenin, V. I., *Selected Works*, Lawrence and Wishart, 1968.
Lydall, H. F. (1968), *The Structure of Earnings*, Oxford University Press.
Lydall, H. F. (1978), 'Some problems in making international comparisons of inequality', in J. R. Moroney (ed.) *Income Inequality*, Lexington Books, 1978.
Lydall, H. F. (1979), *A Theory of Income Distribution*, Oxford University Press.

Maddison, A. (1979), 'Long run dynamics of productivity growth', *Banca Nazionale del Lavoro Quarterly Review*, No. 128, March.
Madžar, L. (1979), 'The role and effectiveness of social and self-management agreements', *Economic Analysis and Workers' Management*, vol. 13.
Marković M. (1982), *Democratic Socialism: Theory and Practice*, The Harvester Press.
Marsenić, D. (1977), 'Primary distribution in the Yugoslav economic system', *Socialist Thought and Practice*, June.
Marx, K. and Engels, F., *Selected Works*, Lawrence and Wishart, 1968.
Mates, N. (1981), 'Fiskalno opterećenje raspodjela i činioci formiranja dohotka', *Ekonomski pregled*, nos. 5–6.
Maximoff, G. P. (ed.) (1953), *The Political Philosophy of Bakunin*, The Free Press of Glencoe.
Meade, J. E. (1972), 'The theory of labour-managed firms and of profit sharing', *Economic Journal*, vol. 82.
Meade, J. (1980), 'Labour co-operatives, participation, and value-added sharing', in A. Clayre (ed.) *The Political Economy of Co-operation and Participation*, Oxford University Press.
Michal, J. M. (1978), 'Size-distribution of household incomes and earnings in developed socialist countries' in W. Krelle and A. F. Shorrocks (eds.) *Personal Income Distribution*, North-Holland.
Milenkovitch, D. (1971), *Plan and Market in Yugoslav Economic Thought*, Yale University Press.
Moore, J. H. (1980), *Growth with Self-Management: Yugoslav Industrialization 1952–1975*, Hoover Institution Press.

Neuberger, E. and James, E. (1973), 'The Yugoslav self-managed enterprise: a systemic approach' in M. Bornstein (ed.) *Plan and Market*, Yale University Press.
Nikić, G. (1979), *Karaksteristike formiranja i upotrebe raspoloživih sredstava stanovništva u Jugoslaviji*, Ekonomski institut, Zagreb.

Obradović, J. and Dunn, W. N. (eds.) (1978), *Workers' Self-Management and Organizational Power in Yugoslavia*, University of Pittsburgh.
OECD (1965), *Wages and Labour Mobility*, Paris.
OECD (1978), *Economic Survey of Yugoslavia*, Paris.
OECD (1980), *Economic Survey of Yugoslavia*, Paris.
OECD (1981), *Economic Survey of Yugoslavia*, Paris.
OECD (1982a), *Economic Survey of Yugoslavia*, Paris.
OECD (1982b), *National Accounts, Vol. I, Main Aggregates 1951–1980*, Paris.

OECD (1982c), *National Accounts, Vol. III, Detailed Tables 1963–1980*, Paris.
OECD (1983), *Economic Survey of Yugoslavia*, Paris.

Petrin, T. (1978), 'The potential of small-scale industry for employment in Yugoslavia', *Economic Analysis and Workers' Management*, vol. 12.
Phelps Brown, E. H. (1973), 'Levels and movements of industrial productivity and real wages internationally compared, 1860–1970', *Economic Journal*, vol. 83.
Pollard, S. and Crossley, D. W. (1968), *The Wealth of Britain, 1085–1966*, Batsford.
Popov, S. (1972), 'Intersectoral relations of personal incomes', *Yugoslav Survey*, vol. 13, May.
Puljić, A. (1980), 'Utjecaj technološkog napretka na rast društvenog proizvoda industrije', *Economic Analysis and Workers' Management*, vol. 14.

Radević, M. M. (1981). 'The trade union in the self-management society', *Socialist Thought and Practice*, April.
Robinson, J. (1967), 'The Soviet collective farm as a producer co-operative', *American Economic Review*, vol. 57.
Royal Commission on the Distribution of Income and Wealth (1977), *Third Report on the Standing Reference, Report No. 5*, HMSO, London.
Rus, V. (1978), 'Enterprise power structure' in Obradović and Dunn (1978).
Rus, V. (1979), 'Limited effects of workers' participation and political counter-power' in T. R. Burns and others (eds.) *Work and Power*, Sage.
Rusinow, D. (1977) *The Yugoslav Experiment 1948–1974*, C. Hurst and Company for the Royal Institute of International Affairs.
Rusinow, D. I. (1978), *Notes from a Yugoslav Party Congress*, American Universities Field Service Report No. 41.
Rusinow, D. I. (1980), *After Tito . . .*, American Universities Field Service Report No. 34.

Sacks, S. R. (1973), *Entry of New Competitors in Yugoslav Market Socialism*, Institute of International Studies, University of California, Berkeley, Research Series No. 19.
Sacks, S. R. (1979), 'Vertical integration and decentralization in Yugoslav enterprises', *Economic Analysis and Workers' Management*, vol. 13.
Sapir, A. (1980), 'Economic growth and factor substitution: What happened to the Yugoslav miracle?', *Economic Journal*, vol. 90, June.
Saunders, C. and Marsden, D. (1981), *Pay Inequalities in the European Community*, Butterworths.
Schrenk, M. (1981), *Managerial Structures and Practices in Manufacturing Enterprises: A Yugoslav Case Study*, World Bank Staff Working Paper No. 455.
Schrenk, M. and others (1979), *Yugoslavia*, The Johns Hopkins University Press.
Sen, A. K. (1966), 'Labour allocation in a co-operative enterprise', *Review of Economic Studies*, vol. 33.
Seton-Watson, H. (1945), *Eastern Europe between the Wars, 1918–1941*, Cambridge University Press.
Seton-Watson, H. (1950), *The East European Revolution*, Methuen.
Shoup, P. (1968), *Communism and the Yugoslav National Question*, Columbia University Press.
Singleton, F. (1976), *Twentieth-Century Yugoslavia*, Macmillan.
Sirc, L. (1979), *The Yugoslav Economy under Self-Management*, Macmillan.

Stipetić, V. (1975), *Yugoslavia's Agriculture 1945–1975*, Belgrade.
Stipetić, V. (1981), 'Ekonomski factori transfera poljoprivrednog stanovništva u nepoljoprivredne djelatnosti, iskustvo Jugoslavije od 1945. do 1978. godine', in *Suvremeni ekonomski problemi—knjiga 6*, Yugoslav Academy for Science and Art, Zagreb.
Stojanović, R. (ed.) (1982), *The Functioning of the Yugoslav Economy*, M. E. Sharpe Inc. and Spokesman Books.

Thomas, H. (1973), *Personal Income Distribution in Yugoslavia: A Human Capital Approach to the Analysis of Personal Income Differences in the Industry of a Labor-Managed Economy*, Ph.D thesis, Cornell University.
Thomas, H. and Logan, C. (1982), *Mondragon: An Economic Analysis*, George Allen and Unwin.
Toš P. (1980), 'The socio-economic position of the workers in associated labour', *Socialist Thought and Practice*, July-August.
Tyson, L. D'A. (1979), 'Incentives, income sharing, and institutional innovation in the Yugoslav self-managed firm', *Journal of Comparative Economics*, vol. 3.
Tyson, L. D'A. and Eichler, G. (1981), 'Continuity and change in the Yugoslav economy in the 1970's and 1980's', in *East European Economic Assessment, Part 1—Country Studies 1980*, a compendium of papers submitted to the Joint Economic Committee of the US Congress, February 27, 1981, US Government Printing Office, Washington, DC.

UNCTAD (1980), *Handbook of International Trade and Development Statistics*, United Nations, New York.

Vanek, J. (1970), *The General Theory of Labor-Managed Market Economies*, Cornell University Press.
Vejnović, M. (1978), 'Influence structure in a self-managing enterprise' in Obradović and Dunn (1978).
Vinski, I. (1981), 'Dugoročno kretanje zaposlenosti u privatnom sektoru privrede Jugoslavije', *Ekonomski pregled*, Nos. 3–4.
Vojnić, D., (ed.) (1979), *Aktuelni problemi privrednih kretanja i ekonomske politike Jugoslavije*, Informator, Zagreb.
Vušković, B. (1981), 'The growth and fluctuation of the LCY membership', *Socialist Thought and Practice*, August.

Ward, B. M. (1958), 'The firm in Illyria: market syndicalism', *American Economic Review*, vol. 48.
Wilson, D. (1979), *Tito's Yugoslavia*, Cambridge University Press.
World Bank (1975), *Yugoslavia: Development with Decentralization*, The Johns Hopkins University Press.

Zukin, S. (1975), *Beyond Marx and Tito*, Cambridge University Press.
Županov, J. (1978), 'Egalitarianism and industrialism', in Obradović and Dunn (1978).
Zvonarević, M. (1978), 'Social power, information, and motivation', in Obradović and Dunn (1978).

INDEX